SO-AKF-795

117°

49°

Kootenai R.

Priest L.
BOUNDARY
BONNER

Oreille R.

L. Pend
Oreille

48°

KOOTENAI
Coeur
d'Alene
L. Coeur
d'Alene

Wallace
St. Joe R.
BENEWAH
SHOSHONE
LATAH
Moscow
CLEARWATER
Lewiston
Clearwater R.
LEWIS
NEZ
PERCE

Lochsa R.

IDAHO
Selway R.

Salmon R.

Imnaha R.

0   100
Miles

ADAMS
VALLEY
LEMHI
Lemhi R.
45°

WASHINGTON

CLARK   FREMONT

PAYETTE
GEM
BOISE
Payette R.
CANYON
Boise
Arrowrock
Res.
Boise R.
CAMAS   BLAINE
ADA
Anderson
Ranch
Res.
ELMORE
GOODING
LINCOLN

CUSTER
xBorah Pk.
Big Lost R.
x
Castle Peak
BUTTE
xHyndman Pk.
JEFFERSON   TETON
MADISON
Idaho Falls
BONNEVILLE
BINGHAM   Palisades
Blackfoot   Res.
Grays L.

Snake R.
Bruneau R.
JEROME
MINIDOKA
Twin Falls
OWYHEE
TWIN
FALLS
CASSIA

Pocatello
CARIBOU
POWER   BANNOCK
Bear R.
BEAR
LAKE
ONEIDA   Bear
FRANKLIN   L.

42°

111

117°

The Pacific Northwest

DATE DUE

The Pacific
Northwest

An Interpretive History

7291

*

CARLOS A. SCHWANTES

*

UNIVERSITY OF NEBRASKA PRESS
LINCOLN AND LONDON

The paper in this book meets the minimum
requirements of American National Standard for
Information Sciences – Permanence of Paper for
Printed Library Materials, ANSI Z39.48–1984.

Typeset in Linotron Galliard by
Keystone Typesetting, Inc.
Printed by Thomson-Shore Inc.

The preparation of this book was funded by the
John Calhoun Smith Memorial Fund of the
University of Idaho and sponsored by the Institute
for Pacific Northwest Studies

Library of Congress Cataloging-in-Publication Data
Schwantes, Carlos A., 1945–
The Pacific Northwest.
Bibliography: p.
Includes index.
1. Northwest, Pacific – History. I. Title.
F851.S34   1989   979.5   88-20782
ISBN 0-8032-4169-0
ISBN 0-8032-9166-3 (pbk.)

Maps and charts supervised by Allan Jokisaari,
University of Idaho Cart-O-Graphics Lab.

Dedicated

to

ROBERT E. BURKE

There was a time not long ago
when the Pacific Northwest might have
qualified as one of the country's best
kept secrets. Life in this far corner
of the United States was an unpublicized
pleasure that residents jealously guarded
and people elsewhere usually associated with
endless rain. But the weather may be one
of the few things that has stayed the same.
Change is coming to the coastal states of
Washington, Oregon and neighboring Idaho,
and it is not entirely welcome.

WILLIAM V. THOMAS
in *American Regionalism:
Our Economic, Cultural and
Political Makeup* (1980)

Contents

Contents

Contents

Illustrations

xvii

MAPS AND FIGURES

Preface

This book presents a short interpretive history of the Pacific Northwest. It seeks main themes, paints with broad strokes, and engages in what one of my colleagues calls responsible reductionism. Capsule biographies of representative figures introduce each of the five parts and are intended to capture a sense of the past.

Some readers may wonder whether the hinterland theme introduced in chapter 1 is appropriate to describe the Pacific Northwest. For geographers a hinterland is an area that lies behind a seaport or seaboard and supplies the bulk of its exports. *Hinterland* as used in this book has a broader though still legitimate meaning: it describes a region that until the Second World War was remote from the continent's main centers of economic and political power and until recent times was often tributary to more developed cities and regions.

Readers may also question why I did not spend more time on one topic or another or why I profiled Tom McCall, for instance, instead of some other figure to introduce the modern Pacific Northwest. The choice of what material to emphasize represents an author's value judgment, tempered by suggestions from colleagues and by the availability of previously published histories.

Alas, for the Pacific Northwest, much still remains to be written about events after the Second World War and, indeed, about many other aspects of the region's history. A number of these gaps result from what can be labeled the heroic nature – heroic men approach to Pacific Northwest history. Its persistent theme is that, because nature assumed heroic proportions in the far Northwest, heroic men were needed to tame or subdue it. A classic photographic image is that of loggers reposing full-length in an undercut they have just made in a giant Douglas fir or cedar. Perhaps because such images are so common, both popular and scholarly histories tend to emphasize the "heroic" accomplishments of outstanding men—or sometimes a group of men—but only occasionally those of women.

Typically, the women who find their way into the region's history texts are those who individually or collectively fit the heroic image—pioneer women of the Oregon Trail or Rosie the Riveter and her sisters in the region's war industries. Individual women who may fit the heroic mold include Sacagawea and the Oregon suffragist Abigail Scott Duniway.

Numerous other classes of Northwest women—like farmers' and miners' wives—generally have not made it into prominent regional histories. Even now a great deal remains to be written about them. Their important contributions to the household economy have typically been eclipsed by the image of their men driving thirty-mule-powered combines over the rolling wheat fields of eastern Washington or blasting for silver ore far below the surface of Idaho's panhandle.[1]

The heroic nature–heroic men approach has also had the effect of stunting research and writing on the region in the twentieth century, particularly after 1920. In the minds of many people, Pacific Northwest history after the First World War is pale and unappealing compared with the heroic phase that centers on subduing wild and unpredictable nature. Whether conscious of that tendency or not, scholars and publishers tend to reinforce it by their choice of subjects to present to the public—and the public in turn by what it buys. I can only hope that this brief interpretive account will encourage readers to write a good deal more about slighted or ignored aspects of Pacific Northwest history.

For their suggestions and other forms of help, I am indebted to a fine group of historians, anthropologists, librarians, and archivists: William R. Swagerty, Roderick Sprague, Terry Abraham, and Barry Rigby, my colleagues at the University of Idaho; Mary Reed of the Latah County Historical Society; Lewis Saum and Vernon Carstensen of the University of Washington; Alfred Runte, Seattle historian; Lawrence Dodd of Whitman College; Richard M. Brown and Keith Richard of the University of Oregon; David H. Stratton,

---

1. A new book that promises to stimulate further work in this area is Karen J. Blair, ed., *Women in Pacific Northwest History: An Anthology* (Seattle: University of Washington Press, 1988).

George Frykman, and Lawrence Stark of Washington State University; Merle Wells, Judith Austin, Larry Jones, and Elizabeth Jacox of the Idaho State Historical Society; Edward Nolan and Doug Olson of the Eastern Washington State Historical Society; Paul Spitzer, historian of the Boeing Company; Nancy Gale Compau of the Spokane Public Library; Laurie Filson of Oregon State University; Susan Seyl of the Oregon Historical Society; Richard Engeman and Carla Rickerson of the University of Washington's Pacific Northwest Collection; Elaine Miller of the Washington State Historical Society; and Carolyn Marr of the Museum of History and Industry, Seattle. I am indebted also to the many students who took my Pacific Northwest history classes and helped to shape my thinking about this region.

For the time they spent reading the entire manuscript, I owe special thanks to Robert E. Burke, University of Washington; G. Thomas Edwards, Whitman College; William G. Robbins, Oregon State University; and Siegfried Rolland, University of Idaho. In fact, by encouraging me to move to the University of Idaho, Sig became the godfather of the entire project. Also present at the creation were the National Endowment for the Humanities and Walter Nugent of the University of Notre Dame. It was in Walt's 1984 NEH-sponsored Seminar for College Teachers that I found the courage to undertake this work.

To W. Kent Hackmann, chairman of the Department of History at the University of Idaho; Galen O. Rowe, dean of the College of Letters and Science; and Arthur R. Gittins, former dean of the Graduate School, I am grateful for the support they gave to the research and writing. Of course, I alone am responsible for any errors of fact or judgment in the chapters that follow.

CHAPTER I

A Sense of Place:
The Pacific Northwest as an
American Hinterland

*

Our region is a familiar place, where we know, to some extent, the lay of the land, the traits of the people and their resources, needs, and problems.
—V. B. Stanbery quoted in Howard W. Odum and Harry Estill Moore, *American Regionalism* (1938)

*

In the far northwestern corner of the United States lie Oregon, Washington, and Idaho, three states commonly labeled the Pacific Northwest. That is a simple definition of the geographical scope of this book, but it represents only one of several ways to draw the regional boundaries. Some scholars classify Oregon and Washington within the Far West or Pacific states and Idaho within the mountain states, or they separate the lush, green Douglas-fir country of Oregon and Washington west of the Cascade mountains from the high, often arid country of the interior. Some include western Montana and even British Columbia and Alaska within the boundaries of the Pacific Northwest.

Idaho presents the greatest challenge to easy classification. While most Oregon and Washington residents consciously locate themselves within the Pacific Northwest, those of Idaho cannot agree. Some Idahoans perceive their state as oriented toward Oregon, Washington, and the Pacific rim; others consider it part of an intermountain West that includes Montana and Utah. It has often been said that Idaho is the only American state with three capitals: Boise, Salt Lake City, and Spokane. Despite such disagreements, the three Pacific Northwest states have enough in common to form a distinct region.

A region is defined by discontinuities that mark its borders and by the geographical, political, economic, social, and cultural bonds that give it a sense of internal unity or community. The Pacific Northwest is shaped like a parallelogram, with the Canadian border, the Pacific Ocean, the Klamath (Siskiyou) Mountains and Great Basin desert, and the Rocky Mountains defining its four sides. At its maximum reach the Pacific Northwest extends 480 miles north to south and 680 miles east to west.

Several unifying forces operate within this 250,000-square-mile region: networks of transportation and communication, patterns of trade and commerce, and a special sense of place derived from history and geography. These unifying forces lessen internal divisions caused by mountain ranges, distance, state boundaries, and differing economic activities and political and religious cultures.

An understanding of the main currents of Pacific Northwest history begins with an appreciation of the region's geographic setting, one of the most diverse natural landscapes in North America. It continues with an awareness that, for the better part of its recorded history, life in the Pacific Northwest revolved around supplying the world with raw materials—furs and skins, logs and lumber, wheat and a variety of agricultural commodities, fish and other seafoods, precious and base metals.

Yet, no matter how valuable its natural resources were to succeeding generations of entrepreneurs, the Pacific Northwest remained geographically remote from the continent's centers of economic and political power. That remoteness, combined with its historic role as supplier of raw materials, defined the Pacific Northwest as a colonial hinterland. Even in the closing years of the twentieth century, northwesterners must still grapple with the economic and social consequences of their hinterland status.

ENVIRONMENT AND REGIONAL CHARACTER

What special qualities define the Pacific Northwest? What makes the Pacific Northwesterners' sense of place distinct from the Californians', the southerners', or the New Englanders'? One simple and obvious answer is the environment, the region's spectacular natural setting—the stunning juxtaposition of mountains and water that characterizes its coastline and the Columbia River gorge; the vastness of its interior, a land of sagebrush plains and empty spaces. Residents occasionally refer to the region as "God's Country," and the opening stanza of "America the Beautiful" could well be describing its mountain peaks and amber waves of grain.

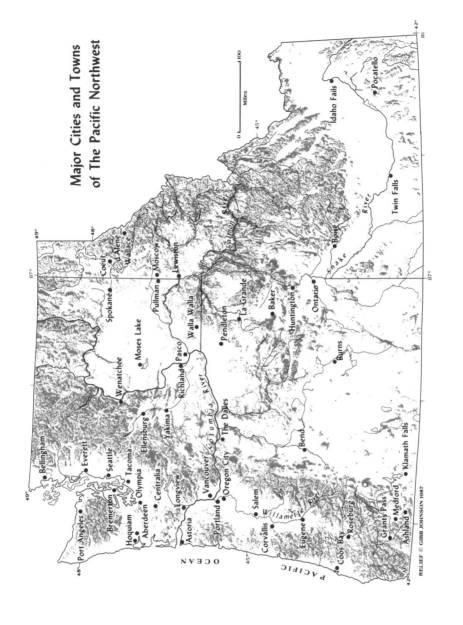

Major Cities and Towns
of The Pacific Northwest

RELIEF © GIBB JOHNSON 1987

Fundamental to a Pacific Northwesterner's sense of place is the awareness that much of the region remains uninhabited or only lightly populated.
A person trapped in rush-hour traffic on one of Seattle's floating bridges
may not believe that claim, yet the population of the entire Pacific Northwest was only 7.5 million in 1980—approximately that of greater Los
Angeles. But residents of the region are spread out over an area the size of
the six New England states and New York, Pennsylvania, Delaware, Mary-
land, Virginia, and North Carolina. Oregon alone encompasses more area
than the United Kingdom of Great Britain and Northern Ireland.

To describe the Pacific Northwest as lightly populated is technically
correct but very misleading. The region's residents tend to gather like bees
into a few urban hives. More than half of Washington's population lives in a
handful of counties that border the east side of Puget Sound and embrace
the cities of Seattle, Tacoma, Olympia, Everett, Bellingham, and Bellevue.
A second population center is Spokane on the state's eastern edge.

Two-thirds of Oregon's population is concentrated in the Willamette
Valley, which extends one hundred miles from Portland south to Eugene. Of
Oregon's eight cities with populations of thirty thousand or more, only
Medford lies outside the Willamette Valley. Idaho has always been more
rural than the other two states, yet two separate urban complexes centering
on Boise and Pocatello contain half its population. Idaho has only three
cities of thirty thousand or more, and all are situated on the Snake River
plain in the southern part of the state. Washington, with thirteen cities of
thirty thousand or more, is the most urbanized of the three states. The
percentage of population living in urban areas—communities with twenty-
five hundred or more residents—varies from 73.6 in Washington to 67.9 in
Oregon and 54.0 in Idaho. The national average in 1980 was 73.7 percent.

Because of the tendency of Pacific Northwesterners to cluster in a few
urban areas, the population density of King County, Washington—site of
the region's most populous city, Seattle, with half a million residents—is
597 people per square mile. Yet some counties in eastern Washington have
fewer than 6 people per square mile. Counties in eastern Oregon and central
Idaho are even more lightly populated.

This settlement pattern means that even urban residents of the Pacific
Northwest experience a strong sense of their natural setting. The composite
city stretching from Everett to Olympia—sometimes referred to as Pugetopolis—is ninety miles long but narrow enough to afford boaters and fishermen easy access to the open waters of Puget Sound in one direction and

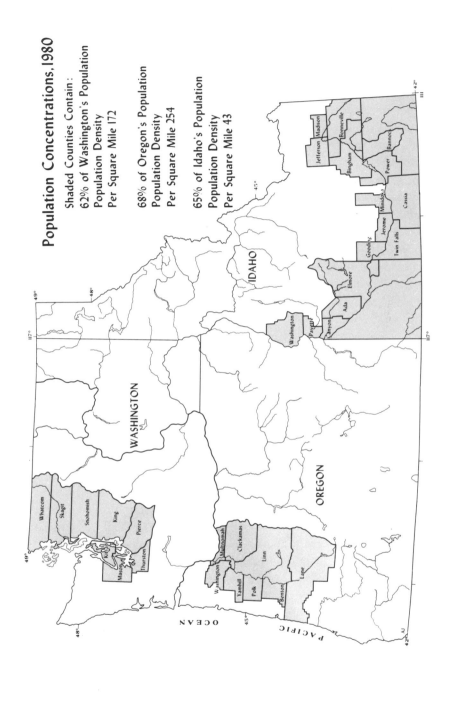

Population Concentrations, 1980

Shaded Counties Contain:
62% of Washington's Population
Population Density
Per Square Mile 172

68% of Oregon's Population
Population Density
Per Square Mile 254

65% of Idaho's Population
Population Density
Per Square Mile 43

backpackers, skiers, and hunters convenient escape to the Cascade mountains in the other. From the shores of Puget Sound to the ski slopes at Snoqualmie Pass is little more than an hour's drive, about the same time it takes Portlanders to reach Timberline Lodge on Mount Hood.

It is even easier to maintain visual contact with the region's spectacular natural setting. On a clear spring day after a winter of leaden skies and intermittent drizzle, many a resident of Seattle or Portland draws fresh inspiration from the sight of Mount Rainier or Mount Hood standing majestically on the horizon. A person can travel the length of Puget Sound or the Willamette Valley and never lose sight of the Cascades or the Coast Ranges.

Except for the Snake River plain, Idaho is one vast sea of mountains and foothills dotted with a few modest islands of farmland such as the Camas Prairie and the Palouse in the northern panhandle. One wit suggested that if its vertical surfaces could be rolled flat Idaho would become the largest state in the union. But Idaho without its mountains is inconceivable. The rugged, nearly inaccessible terrain of much of the state—especially the Bitterroot and Sawtooth ranges—is one reason why Idaho possesses more congressionally designated wilderness land (approximately four million acres) than any state outside Alaska. Some Idahoans are convinced that their license plates should bear the legend Wilderness State instead of advertising Famous Potatoes.

The landforms of the Pacific Northwest are not matters just of geology and real estate but also of aesthetics and culture. The most repetitive theme in the region's literature is the interaction of people and their natural environment; much of the region's history is played out against a backdrop of dramatic landforms. Not surprisingly, Pacific Northwesterners commonly translated their sense of place into a belief that natural environment determined the types of people who settled Oregon, Washington, and Idaho. Rugged mountains and gargantuan trees called forth strong-willed, self-reliant individuals to match them, or so northwesterners have often claimed.

Even if this romantic notion was impossible to prove, it remained central to the thinking of generations of settlers and helps to explain why so many newcomers defined progress as taming nature through exploitation of the region's abundant natural resources. Perceptions of abundance still shape public discussions of how best to treat the region's land, timber, and water resources.

6

THE MOUNTAINS' SHADOW: PACIFIC NORTHWEST GEOGRAPHY

In a sense, the entire Pacific Northwest can be described as lying in the mountains' shadow. Few areas are situated so that mountains are not readily visible, and even those anomalous places experience the influence of mountain ranges on regional weather patterns, vegetation, and economic activities.

At many points along the Pacific coast of Oregon and Washington, mountains touch the sea. The Coast Ranges extend from northern California to the Olympic Peninsula of Washington and average about fifty miles in width. For most of the distance their peaks seldom top three thousand feet, and in southwestern Washington they flatten into a series of low rises called the Willapa Hills. Farther north, the land again rises dramatically to form the Olympic Mountains, topped by Mount Olympus at eighty-two hundred feet above sea level.

Lying between the coastal mountains and the Cascade Range is an alluvial plain about 350 miles long and 50 miles wide that forms the Puget Sound–Willamette lowlands. Separating the northern from the southern portion of the plain are gentle hills located about halfway between Olympia and Vancouver, Washington. The Puget Sound–Willamette lowlands constitute the heart of the Pacific Northwest. In this area are located two state capitals and a greater concentration of cities, colleges and universities, television and radio stations, corporate headquarters, banks, and manufacturing establishments than anywhere else in the region. Despite its essentially urban character, this alluvial plain also supports a thriving and diverse agricultural industry.

The Cascade mountains extend from northern California into southern British Columbia and vary in width from more than one hundred miles at the Canadian border to less than fifty miles at the California border. Numerous lava flows surmounted by large and small volcanic peaks characterize the range. The most famous of these volcanos is Mount Saint Helens, which erupted violently in 1980 but since then has been relatively quiet. The Cascades also include several dormant volcanos, some of which have erupted within the past two centuries. Other well-known Cascade peaks are Lassen and Shasta in California, Hood in Oregon, and Rainier, Adams, and Baker in Washington. Rainier at 14,410 feet is the highest mountain in the Pacific Northwest and is topped in the forty-eight contiguous states only by Mount Elbert (14,433 feet) in the Colorado Rockies and Mount

MOUNT SAINT HELENS

Mount Saint Helens once was the loveliest of Cascade peaks. At 8:32 on the morning of May 18, 1980, it stunned the nation and the world when it blasted away its crown with a force five hundred times greater than the atomic bomb dropped on Hiroshima in 1945. Speeding at two hundred miles per hour, a whirlwind of heat, ash, and debris denuded two hundred square miles of heavily forested land within a fifteen-mile arc to the north. All told, the blast killed sixty people, an estimated fifteen hundred elk, five thousand black-tailed deer, two hundred black bears, and literally hundreds of thousands of birds and fish.

A dense boiling cloud rose from the crater and deposited several inches of ash in eastern Washington and northern Idaho and left its traces even on the East Coast, giving rise to a wry comment: "Don't come to Washington this year; Washington will come to you." On that Sunday in May and for several days following, the predominant mood in the Pacific Northwest was one of apprehension and fear. Some residents wondered whether this eruption was a prelude to something worse. Perhaps Mount Baker would erupt next. Perhaps the ash was poisonous or radioactive. Yet, after clean-up crews reopened streets and highways in eastern Washington, life re-

turned to normal. Nonetheless, the Pacific Northwest Regional Commission published a pamphlet called "Exploding the Myth: The Pacific Northwest Remains Beautiful" to counteract any erroneous impressions in other parts of the United States.

Mount Saint Helens was not the only Cascade volcano to erupt in the twentieth century. In 1914–17, Mount Lassen vented steam, ash, and lava. During the nineteenth century, several peaks including Hood, Saint Helens, and Rainier, put on eruptive displays, though none was as violent as the May 1980 blast or the even more spectacular one half a dozen millennia earlier when Oregon's Mount Mazama exploded with a force forty-two times greater than that of the Saint Helens eruption. When filled with water from rain and melting snow, a caldera nearly two thousand feet deep and six miles wide formed the natural wonder of Crater Lake, famed for its breathtaking color of indigo blue.

Mount Saint Helens and its immediate vicinity became a national volcanic monument in 1983. Nature is now at work healing the scars caused by the eruption. The event reminds Pacific Northwesterners what it means to live in the mountains' shadow, especially when some of those mountains turn out to be dormant rather than extinct volcanos.

Whitney (14,494 feet) in California's Sierra Nevada. But Mount Rainier appears far more spectacular than the other two because it rises abruptly from the coastal plain and towers high above lesser peaks. Its massive slopes support twenty-seven named glaciers, the single largest mountain glacier system in the lower forty-eight states and the source of several Northwest

1. Steam and ash billow from Mount Saint Helens,
May 18, 1980. Courtesy Forest Service Collection, National Agricultural Library: 530800.

rivers. The Cascade Range includes three national parks and the Mount
Saint Helens National Volcanic Monument.

At the eastern edge of the Pacific Northwest stand the Rocky Mountains,
an uplifted area that includes numerous ranges like the Bitterroots, which
form the Idaho-Montana border. Local chains like the Wallowas of northeastern Oregon or the rugged Klamath Mountains that straddle the Oregon-
California border add variety to the region's landscape.

The common impression that the Pacific Northwest is a land of ever-
greens, ocean mist, and snowcapped peaks contrasts with reality: much of
the region's surface is treeless and arid. First-time visitors to the dry areas

9

are often surprised witnesses to the ways mountains and elevation influence rainfall. Most of the world's arid regions result from a planetwide system of air currents, but those of the Pacific Northwest result from mountain rain shadows.

The Cascades, the Rockies, and other ranges influence weather as part of a complex process that begins over the Pacific Ocean. As prevailing northwesterly winds sweep across its surface during the winter months, they become laden with moisture later lost crossing the land. The marine air enables much of the region to enjoy relatively mild winters. Portland, Oregon, for example, experiences far less snow and subzero weather than Saint Paul, Minnesota, or Portland, Maine, cities that lie farther south. During the winter months, much of the region is covered with marine air and layers of clouds that restrict the total hours of sunshine. Northern Idaho, for instance, though located more than three hundred miles from the ocean, receives only about 50 percent of the maximum sunshine available in winter because of the marine climate.

As moist air from the Pacific rises to cross the coastal mountains, atmospheric pressure decreases, the air cools, and like a squeezed sponge the clouds release some of their moisture in the form of rain or snow. The rain forest of the Olympic Peninsula ranks as one of the wettest locations on earth. An annual rainfall of 120–140 inches is common in places, and some years it can top 180 inches, or the equivalent of two billion gallons of water for each square mile of forest. The result is a veritable evergreen jungle.

In the Puget Sound–Willamette lowlands, the average annual rainfall is about the same as that in New York City or New Orleans (thirty to fifty inches), but because the precipitation so often occurs as drizzle, the winter rain seems interminable and the weather dreary. In Portland and Seattle it rains an average of 150 days each year.

Wet winters and relatively dry summers characterize much of the Pacific Northwest, just the reverse of the weather pattern of the Great Plains and Rocky Mountains. People in Portland and Seattle must water their lawns during the summer, and August is a time of forest-fire danger. The relationship between temperature on land and sea explains this phenomenon: during winter the land is cooler than the sea; during summer the reverse is true. Summertime air increases in temperature as it moves from sea to land and thus is able to retain more of the moisture it collected from the Pacific.

Regardless of the season, when clouds from the Pacific Ocean sweep up the face of the Cascades, they reach higher, cooler elevations than in the Coast Ranges. Snowfall on some peaks during the winter months may total three hundred inches and on occasion may exceed one thousand inches annually. Paradise Inn, located at the fifty-four hundred–foot level on the south slope of Mount Rainier, recorded a total of 93.5 feet of snow during the winter of 1971–72.

The clouds lose much of their remaining moisture by the time they pass two dozen miles beyond the summit of the Cascades. Farther down the eastern slope the land becomes noticeably drier, and the moisture-loving Douglas firs and tangled undergrowth that thrive on the west side give way to ponderosa pines and eventually to grasses and sagebrush that survive where annual rainfall averages ten inches or less.

The lowest precipitation occurs in the central and eastern portions of both Washington and Oregon and in southern Idaho—a highly varied landscape of hills, eroded slopes, rugged mountains, flat plains, and sandy deserts, all underlain with basalt, a volcanic rock. Precipitation increases gradually as one travels across eastern Washington to the Idaho panhandle, from an annual average of six inches along the Columbia River in central Washington to twenty-one inches at Pullman, 140 miles east and 1,300 feet higher.

Famed for its fertile soil, the Palouse country that surrounds Pullman and overlaps a portion of the Washington-Idaho border is one of the most productive wheat-growing regions in the United States, yet immediately northwest of the Palouse lie the channeled scablands, a series of dry canyons called coulees, where the soil is thin and the country suitable mainly for grazing cattle. From the Palouse to the Rockies, annual precipitation increases until it almost equals that in parts of the Puget Sound–Willamette lowlands, enabling stands of western white pine, red cedar, and Douglas fir to thrive in the Idaho panhandle. Commercial forests account for 65 percent of the total land area of northern Idaho and 70 percent of Oregon and Washington west of the Cascades, but only 30 percent of those two states east of the Cascades.

Much of the annual precipitation eventually returns to the Pacific Ocean to repeat the cycle, but not before it generates electric power and irrigates arid lands. If water from rain or snow does not evaporate or sink into the soil, it reaches the Columbia River and reenters the Pacific near Astoria, Oregon. Primary exceptions to this pattern are local rivers and streams that drain into Puget Sound or directly into the ocean.

On a map of the Pacific Northwest, the Columbia River and its tributaries resemble a giant gnarled oak tree resting on its side. Its topmost branches reach into southern British Columbia, western Montana, and northeastern Wyoming. From its source in the Canadian Rockies, the Columbia River extends a distance of 1,270 miles to the Pacific Ocean and drains 258,000 square miles, an area larger than France, Belgium, and the Netherlands combined.

Joining the Columbia just north of the Canadian border is the Pend Oreille River, which drains far northern Idaho and western Montana. The Columbia's largest tributary, the Snake River, joins it near Pasco, where the growing river twists south and then abruptly west. Originating a thousand miles east in Yellowstone Park, the Snake is itself one of the major rivers of the United States. After cutting through the plains of southern Idaho, where a portion of its water irrigates six million acres of farmland, the Snake plunges into Hells Canyon, the deepest gorge in North America. Thirty miles long and in places 7,700 feet deep, one-third of a mile deeper than Grand Canyon, Hells Canyon compresses the river into a maelstrom of white water that terrorized explorers and completely blocked river communication between northern and southern Idaho. The Deschutes and John Day rivers enter the Columbia east of the Cascades after draining the sparsely populated land of central Oregon. A hundred miles from the sea, the Willamette River, having served Portland, Salem, and Eugene, joins the Columbia's massive trunk.

The Columbia River flows through four mountain ranges, pours more water into the ocean than any other river in North America except for the Saint Lawrence, Mississippi, and Mackenzie, and exceeds every river on the continent in the generation of hydroelectric power. In fact, its waters contain an estimated 40 percent of the nation's total hydroelectric potential. Except for a fifty-mile stretch bordering the Hanford Nuclear Reservation in central Washington, the Columbia has been engineered into a chain of lakes formed by dams. Through a series of locks, towboats and barges can climb the Columbia and Snake rivers to Idaho's only seaport, Lewiston, about four hundred miles inland and seven hundred feet above sea level.

The Columbia River served as a highway of trade and commerce and knitted together the Pacific Northwest even before the coming of Euro-Americans. For Indian people as well as for newcomers, the Columbia counteracted the divisive influence of mountains, especially the Cascade Range, a wall breached only by the Columbia and one other river, the Klamath, in southern Oregon.

There can be little doubt that the Cascades once hindered easy communication and transportation in Oregon and Washington, and that the mountains bordering the Salmon River divided Idaho—and still do during

12

2. Hells Canyon of the Snake River. Courtesy
Forest Service Collection, National Agricultural
Library: 417430.

the season when snowdrifts and avalanches block the passes and grades. Today, in the legislatures of all three states, opinions frequently divide along these mountain barriers.

Even so, the divisive quality of the region's mountain ranges has probably been overstated. The sight of Mount Rainier or Mount Hood inspires people regardless of whether they live east or west of the Cascades. The Cascade Range forms a backdrop for residents of Seattle and of Ellensburg on the opposite side and is equally a part of a sense of place in both communities. Central Idaho's rugged Salmon River country affords the same recreational opportunities to hunters, fishermen, and backpackers whether they live in Lewiston to the north or Boise to the south, lending credibility to Idaho's promotion of itself as the Great Getaway.

Mountains contribute to the irregularity of natural and manmade landscapes in the Pacific Northwest. Unlike the prairie states, where rectangular fields of corn and soybeans extend to the horizon, the far Northwest gives the appearance of being rugged and unfinished. Except for state and

13

international boundaries and city streets, straight lines are uncommon features of the landscape. The region's coastline is irregular and its land is uplifted into jagged peaks and sinuous hills that give the Palouse country in July and August the appearance of a swelling ocean of wheat. To become accustomed to the Pacific Northwest climate and landscape—to become accustomed to life in the mountains' shadow—is crucial to developing a sense of place.

AN AMERICAN HINTERLAND

Patches of clear-cut forest land and abandoned sawmills and, in certain places, closed mines and fish canneries were increasingly common features of the Pacific Northwest landscape in the 1970s and 1980s. A sense of place, it seems, must also come to terms with economic activity, or lack thereof.

The region's role as supplier of raw materials gave economic life in the Pacific Northwest its special contours. Even before contact with European and American traders in the late eighteenth century, Native Americans had established among themselves elaborate trade networks based on the use of natural resources like fish and roots. Beginning in the 1780s with the trade in furs and skins, Pacific Northwest commodities played important supporting roles in the metropolitan-dominated economic systems of Europe and North America, although the region itself remained a colonial hinterland.

Even in the mid-1980s—despite the existence of urban centers such as Portland and Seattle and the great aircraft-manufacturing plants of Boeing—the Pacific Northwest remains a hinterland, at least much of that portion lying outside the Puget Sound and Willamette Valley metropolitan areas. Along with other regions of the United States, it experienced a severe economic slump in the early part of the 1980s, but its overall economy, unlike that of some other regions, did not fully recover by middecade.

The problem was the Pacific Northwest's continued dependence on national and international markets for its raw materials or semifinished products like aluminum. The mining industry centered in northern Idaho remained depressed because of low silver prices. Mountains of wheat formerly destined for Asia went unsold because of new foreign competition.

The forest products industry, once the backbone of the Northwest economy, reeled from a series of disasters ranging from high interest rates that discouraged the construction of new houses to a slumping Canadian dollar that encouraged American builders to import less expensive lumber from north of the border. Because the Pacific Northwest was remote from the major markets of North America, distance translated into higher freight rates than those paid by competing mills in the South. Not even the most efficient sawmill in the Pacific Northwest could withstand those disadvantages for long. In one case, a Louisiana-Pacific mill newly built in Idaho in 1983 shut down within a year.

Employment in the forest products industry in Oregon and Washington dropped from fifty thousand to thirty-five thousand between 1978 and 1983. During the same period, employment in the Idaho timber industry dropped 26 percent, representing a loss of more than five thousand jobs. Many millworkers saw their jobs exported to Asia in the form of raw logs that were converted into plywood or finished lumber in Japan and reexported to the United States.

The hinterland status of the Northwest made the region economically vulnerable to forces beyond its control. The problems of extractive industry in the 1980s, therefore, are simply a variation on an old theme. For the past century the region has ridden an economic roller coaster that has alternated between boom-and-bust. No one has yet found a way to get off.

By the late twentieth century it had become obvious that there were actually two Pacific Northwests, economically speaking: the relatively prosperous high-technology, manufacturing, and exporting businesses centering on Seattle and Portland, and the traditional extractive industries of the less populated areas. Troubles in the latter sector inevitably affected the entire region in the form of diminished tax revenues and underfunding of state services and institutions. Other imponderables such as freight rates and the cheap electricity needed to lure new businesses and industries or to keep the existing ones competitive in distant national and international markets further clouded the region's economic future.

Hinterland status also shaped the Pacific Northwest past. Certain features of the region's early history bear more resemblance to the natural resources frontier of Canada than to the commercial and agricultural settlements of the eastern United States. The Pacific Northwest was integrated into the fur trade centering on Montreal and the Saint Lawrence Valley and later the Hudson's Bay region before it developed close economic and social ties with the United States. The reorientation of the region did not occur until after American missionaries arrived in the late 1830s and a substantial number of settlers from the Ohio and Mississippi valleys came the following decade.

When Oregon achieved territorial status in the late 1840s, two generations had passed since the opening battles of the Revolutionary War, thirty states had entered the Union, eleven men had served as president of the United States, Harvard College was already two hundred years old, and the population of New York City was rapidly approaching seven hundred thousand. In the late 1840s about ten thousand non-Indian people lived in the entire Oregon Territory, which included not only the future states of Oregon, Washington, and Idaho, but also western Montana and a portion of western Wyoming. The territory's most populous non-Indian community was Oregon City, with fewer than a thousand residents. Nearby Portland had even fewer residents, and the future cities of Seattle, Tacoma, Spokane, and Boise did not exist.

The northwestern corner of the United States, in short, was both geographically remote from the East Coast and chronologically distant from the mainstream of American history. But rather than be merely a backwater of American history, the Pacific Northwest followed a separate watercourse toward regional development. The following chapters chart its main features.

Part One
Isolation and Empire

Profile: The Third Voyage of Captain James Cook

The fur of these animals, as mentioned in the Russian accounts, is certainly softer and finer than that of any others we know of; and therefore the discovery of this part of the continent of North America, where so valuable an article of commerce may be met with, cannot be a matter of indifference.—James Cook and James King, *A Voyage to the Pacific Ocean* (1784).

Geographical isolation fundamentally shaped the course of Pacific Northwest history. Far longer than most temperate areas of the world the Northwest remained beyond the reach of Europe and the rest of North America. The region's geographical isolation in turn contributed to a pronounced time lag in its historical development. The frontier seemed to linger longer, and social and economic changes that evolved over a period of decades elsewhere often were telescoped into a much briefer period of time in the Northwest or skipped entirely.

The year 1776 offers a good promontory from which to observe the region's chronological isolation. In Philadelphia, thirteen American colonies formally declared their independence from Great Britain on July 4 and set forth on an uncharted political course. Only eight days later the distinguished explorer Captain James Cook sailed from Plymouth, England, on his third great voyage of discovery. That venture, which had important consequences for the Pacific Northwest, neatly coincided with the course of the American Revolution: the expedition's two ships—but not Cook—returned home in 1780, four years and three months after setting sail.

James Cook was the most famous navigator of his day. The son of a Scottish farm laborer who had settled in Yorkshire, he was apprenticed as a youth to a grocer and a dry goods merchant. At the age of eighteen he was apprenticed to the owner of a fleet of coal-carrying ships, and a career at sea followed. Cook became a military man and student of science, a careful and conscientious captain in the Royal Navy, an explorer of new lands for the British Empire, and a dispeller of geographical myths.

In his day Cook was recognized foremost for his efforts to improve the health and save the lives of men at sea. He promoted the use of sauerkraut and lemon and orange syrups to cure scurvy—a disease characterized by lethargy and anemia, bleeding gums, loosened teeth, stiffness of the joints, and slow healing of wounds. This medical advance made lengthy voyages practicable. Upon returning from his second voyage, Cook was elected a Fellow of the prestigious Royal Society and received its highest award for his work of preserving the health of his crew on long voyages.

A tall and unpretentious man, he was forty-seven years old at the start of his third voyage. Having been around the world twice—once in each direction—he intended to retire when he completed his second voyage in 1775. But the lure of solving one of the world's most tantalizing geographical mysteries and the opportunity to collect a handsome financial reward for doing so caused Cook to set forth once again, leaving at home his thirty-eight-year-old wife, Elizabeth, eight months pregnant.

Cook's mission, as stated in sealed instructions from the British Admiralty, was to find the fabled Northwest Passage. That quest was so important in the eyes of the English-speaking world that Benjamin Franklin, confident that the explorer would soon be sailing through the long-sought waterway, issued an order prohibiting the fledgling American navy from interfering with "that most celebrated navigator and discoverer, Captain Cook." Although Americans were in the midst of war with Britain, they should treat Cook and his crewmen "with all civility and kindness, affording them as common friends to mankind."

The nation that discovered the Northwest Passage would achieve a short-cut through North America to the markets of Asia. In other words, that nation stood to gain immense riches and power. The belief that such a passage really existed rested on a combination of hope, myth, and geographical possibility. Since the time of Columbus, explorers from several European nations had sought in vain for an entrance from the Atlantic. The British Parliament offered the discoverer a £20,000 prize in 1745—perhaps $500,000 in today's money—and extended the offer to include ships of the

3. Captain James Cook (1728–79). Courtesy Museum
of History and Industry, Seattle: 11863.

Royal Navy in 1775. Cook was to seek the Pacific entrance to the passage, a
quest that would take him to the last of the world's temperate coastline to
be brought into close association with Europe.

Cook was no stranger to the Pacific. During two previous voyages of
discovery, he had visited the exotic lands of the South Pacific, even to the
Antarctic Circle. On his third voyage he sailed first to the Cape of Good
Hope, then west to Australia, New Zealand, and islands he had previously

visited in the South Pacific. He even had the good fortune to discover a new group of islands that he named after his patron, the Earl of Sandwich. Today they bear a familiar name: the Hawaiian Islands.

Nearly two years after leaving England, Cook reached the Pacific Northwest coast in early March 1778. A reception of hail, sleet, fog, and howling winds prompted him to name the first landmark Cape Foulweather, a promontory that juts into the ocean a few miles north of present Newport, Oregon. His was not the first expedition to reach these shores, but European contact before Cook had been sporadic, the work of discovery and exploration haphazard, and any national claims to the area exceedingly vague.

Two hundred years earlier, in 1579, a fellow Englishman, Francis Drake, had sailed northward along the Pacific coast perhaps as far as Oregon or even British Columbia. He described the area as one of "most vile, thicke, and stinking fogges," named it Nova Albion, claimed it for England, and left. His territorial claim was ambiguous, because even today there is no agreement about how far north he sailed. After Drake, the Pacific Northwest remained largely unknown to the European world, and Russian and Spanish expeditions along the coast in the mid-1700s did but little to change that. Moving northward from Mexico, the Spanish knew more than any other Europeans about the Pacific coast, but they endeavored to keep their records secret. Their discoveries, as far as the rest of Europe was concerned, were scarcely discoveries at all.

Cook's expedition was methodical in a way no previous voyage to North Pacific waters had been. The admiralty instructed him to reach the west coast of North America at about forty-five degrees north latitude to avoid provoking an international incident with the Spanish, who, with expeditions launched from their base in Mexico, had established imperial claims to the lands south of that line. From that point, Cook was to proceed north but not explore the coast in detail until he reached sixty-five degrees. If he found the Northwest Passage he was to sail east through it. In addition, he was to remain alert for a north*east* passage navigable across the top of Russia.

Cook's instructions also made clear the scientific nature of his third voyage. He was to make a careful record of the natural resources of the region and to take possession of unclaimed lands for the king of England—unclaimed, that is, by nations such as Russia and Spain, because the presence of native peoples was of little consequence in European eyes.

As his two ships, *Resolution* and *Discovery,* sailed north through troublesome and dangerous waters, Cook remained well offshore and thus missed discovering both the mouth of the Columbia River and the Strait of Juan de Fuca, the gateway to Puget Sound. But he did enter Nootka Sound, an exceptionally fine anchorage on the west coast of Vancouver Island, which he mistook for the North American mainland. There he made contact with the native peoples of the coast. Juan Pérez, a Spaniard, was the first European to visit the area when his expedition anchored just outside the entrance to Nootka Sound in August 1774 to barter pieces of metal, iridescent shells, and beads for sea otter robes.

During the month Cook's expedition remained at Nootka to repair its ships, officers compiled detailed accounts of Northwest Coast Indian life. Crew members exchanged trinkets with the Indians for the luxuriant pelts of the sea otter, some of which they used for shipboard bedding. The sea otter pelts acquired in almost casual fashion later proved a surprisingly valuable treasure.

The *Resolution* and *Discovery* continued north along the coast of Alaska and the Aleutian chain and entered the Arctic Ocean in May. By midsummer the expedition had advanced beyond seventy degrees north latitude when an impenetrable wall of ice blocked its way and threatened to crush the ships against the shore. Forced to retreat, the explorers turned south to spend the winter in Hawaii, reaching the islands late in 1778.

The Hawaiians were friendly and accommodating hosts, but they had a passion for anything they could pry loose from Cook's ships, especially iron goods, even down to the long nails that fastened a protective sheathing to the ship's hull. Finally, when Cook could tolerate the stealing no longer, he and an armed guard went ashore at Kealakekua Bay on February 14, 1779, in an attempt to recover a stolen boat or secure a hostage. The Hawaiians became enraged when they heard that another party of crewmen had killed a chief. They hurled stones at the English, who responded by firing into the crowd. When Cook's men paused to reload their weapons, the Hawaiians rushed forward with knives and clubs, killing five expedition members including Cook.

The survivors sailed north once again, but the Arctic ice defeated their quest for the Northwest Passage. As they headed for home along the China coast, they made the fortuitous discovery that sea otter pelts from Nootka Sound were worth a fortune in Canton. The crew men came close to mutiny because of their desire to return for more pelts, but their officers prevailed and the two ships sailed for England.

Captain Cook's third voyage failed to locate the Northwest Passage—a route that indeed existed, as the Norwegian explorer Roald Amundsen proved in 1906, but it was so ice choked as to have little practical value. Cook's expedition nonetheless added new lands to the British Empire and new knowledge about the North Pacific Coast. Publication of the expedition's official records in 1784 gave the Pacific Northwest for the first time a clearly defined place in European imperial and commercial systems. But even before that date, news about the expedition had set in motion a commercial rush to exploit the fur resources of the Northwest Coast. In short, Cook's ships initiated the region's role as a resource-rich hinterland open to exploitation by more developed parts of the world.

Cook's third voyage clearly illustrates the geographical and historical remoteness of the Pacific Northwest from Europe and the settlements on the eastern seaboard of America. For the English-speaking world, the Pacific Northwest remained a blank sheet of paper at a time when American history had already recorded the battles of Lexington and Concord and the Declaration of Independence.

Cook's third voyage served as a training school for mariners who would subsequently return to the Pacific Northwest, some as captains of fur-trading vessels and others as explorers. Best known among the explorers who sailed with Cook was George Vancouver, who during a voyage of discovery for the British government in the early 1790s explored and mapped many sites on Puget Sound—including the body of water itself, named for his lieutenant, Peter Puget. Another crewman of note was John Ledyard, an American, who in 1783 published an account of the voyage and encouraged fellow countrymen to pursue the North Pacific–China trade.

Most important, Cook's third voyage ended the previous pattern of sporadic and haphazard European contact with the Pacific Northwest and its native peoples. As an increasing number of fur traders from several nations cruised the coastal waters, it became obvious that a new era had dawned, one that was especially ominous for the Northwest's first inhabitants: the Indians.

CHAPTER 2

The First Pacific
Northwesterners

*

As has been said of Columbus on the eastern shore of the Americas, Cook in
the west "did not discover a new world; he established contact between two
worlds, both already old."—Robin Fisher quoted in *Captain James Cook
and His Times* (1979)

*

Captain James Cook's third expedition had its main encounter with native
peoples of the North Pacific at Nootka Sound. During a month's layover in
April 1778 to repair their ships, Cook and his officers prepared detailed
reports of the Nootkas' physical appearance, customs, material culture, and
trading preferences.

It was apparent to Europeans that the Nootka Indians physically resembled Asians or Polynesians. They were short and stocky, with round and full
faces and high cheekbones. Long black hair hung down over their shoulders.
"The women are nearly of the same size, colour, and form, with the men,
from whom it is not easy to distinguish them, as they possess no natural
delicacies sufficient to render their persons agreeable," penned one European revealing his cultural biases. This, however, did not keep the crewmen
from making wistful remarks about the sexual reticence of native women.
Some women eventually did spend their nights aboard ship with the men,
though probably not on the *Resolution* commanded by Cook. Being anxious
to avoid the spread of venereal disease from Europeans to native populations, he had forbidden such contacts. Those women were probably slaves.
Indian men likely had arranged their services in exchange for items of trade.

4. A Nootka village in 1778. Courtesy Historical
Photograph Collection, Washington State University
Libraries: 70–0072.

The Nootkas practiced elaborate ceremonial rituals. When Cook first entered the sound, the Indians paddled around his ships, throwing feathers and red ocher on the water. Although the ritual signified peaceful intentions, the uncomprehending Europeans might just as well have mistaken it for a sign of hostility. The Nootkas' subsequent encounters included singing, dancing, and displays of wealth. Europeans missed much of the significance of those rituals, interpreting them as simple buffoonery or silly tricks.

The main source of Nootka sustenance was the sea. From it the Indians skimmed an abundance of fish and other marine life. Cured kelp stems made strong fishing lines, and the plant's hollow bulbs served as convenient containers for whale oil. The Nootkas were quite proficient in the use of oceangoing canoes, but unlike the Vikings or Polynesians, they were not really deep-sea navigators. They sailed along the coast and disliked getting beyond the sight of land.

Europeans observed that the Nootkas lived in extended wooden buildings—longhouses some twenty to forty feet wide and fifty to one hundred feet long. Overlapping red-cedar planks attached to a permanent frame were easily removed and transported to another homesite. The Nootkas had three homes: one facing the sea for the summer fishing season, another in a sheltered cove for the winter, and a third upriver at the site of the salmon run.

From all indications, the Nootkas were eager to trade sea otter pelts for metal objects. Cook noted that they were already familiar with iron and wanted metal blades of any sort. He learned too that they could be sharp traders. On one occasion they deceived his men by selling them containers of oil partly filled with water.

Despite the fact that each culture found aspects of the other that were strange, there is no indication that the Nootkas regarded Europeans as superior to or more powerful than themselves. At that time neither group dominated the other; their trading relations were for the most part friendly. Cook's third voyage thus represented a harbinger of more extensive contacts to come, not an end for the Indian way of life.

What Cook and his officers observed of the Nootkas was in varying degrees true of the physical appearance and culture of other Northwest Coast Indian groups. The Nootkas were only one group that anthropologists classify within the Northwest Coast cultural area. Within the Pacific Northwest, scholars identify two other great cultural areas: Plateau and Great Basin. Each of those included a variety of subgroups commonly called tribes (although some were only extended families) that shared traits and styles of life, though not necessarily a common language. In all, there were about 125 different tribes speaking more than fifty languages. The boundaries of the three cultural areas are indistinct, and today are the subject of scholarly disagreement, as are other aspects of Indian culture.

Much of the complexity of Indian life was lost on Euro-Americans, who tended to lump together disparate families and villages under tribal designations. On the eve of white contact, the Nez Percés of the Plateau cultural area, for instance, numbered approximately four thousand people scattered among 130 bands and villages, some associating more closely with neighboring peoples than with other Nez Percé Indians. Euro-Americans also misspelled and invented Indian names, an obvious case being Nez Percé, a French derivation. The name Kalapuyan, applied to the Indians of Oregon's Willamette Valley, was spelled more than thirty ways. Those differences incorporated into treaties between Indians and whites led to years of confusion. Euro-Americans also had difficulty grasping the fact that many Indian cultures had no set territorial boundaries. Tribes had concepts of territory, but their idea of the "ownership" of village, hunting, and berry-picking sites was very different from that of Euro-Americans. In traditional times, land was sacred to the natives, something never to be actually owned, although human occupants might serve as its guardians or custodians. Herein too lay the seeds of misunderstanding and conflict when Indians signed treaties with whites.

INDIANS OF THE COAST

Indians of the Northwest Coast cultural area occupied a narrow fringe of North America extending from southern Alaska to northern California. Mild climate, heavy rainfall, lush forests, an abundance of food and leisure time, a rich and varied material culture, and homesites on sheltered bays and harbors characterized their habitat. Physically isolated by mountain ranges from other native peoples, their orientation was toward the sea and the protected coves where their villages were located.

In their isolation they developed a common dependence upon marine resources, canoe navigation, and a material culture that emphasized woodworking. They were among the finest woodworkers in the world. Despite their common characteristics, Indians of the Coast cultural area were divided one from another by the rugged land and the barriers posed by language and locally oriented forms of society and government. Their primary social and political unit was the extended family, represented in certain tribes beginning in the nineteenth century by free-standing totem poles—essentially family crests.

Among the Indians of the North Pacific Coast, moving south from the panhandle of present-day Alaska, were the Tlingits (who consisted of fourteen subdivisions), the Haidas of the Queen Charlotte Islands, the Tsimshians, Kwakiutls, Bella Coolas, and the Nootkas, all of British Columbia, and the Coast Salish people, who inhabited the land from southern British Columbia to the Oregon coast south of the Columbia River. Among the Coast Salish were the Makahs, Quinaults, and Puyallups. Stretching south from Coos Bay, Oregon, were independent Athapascan-speaking villages and bands like the Tolowas and Chetcos. In the midst of several broad language groupings lived enclaves of linguistically diverse peoples like the Penutian-speaking Chinooks of the lower Columbia River.

The Coast peoples were hunters and gatherers. They did not cultivate crops, and their only domesticated animal was a special breed of woolly dog kept in pens and sheared twice a year for fibers. They were almost totally and directly dependent upon naturally occurring products for their sustenance. Anthropologists have often considered cultures of that type primitive by comparison with those based on agriculture, yet therein lies an anomaly. The environment yielded such a surplus of natural resources that Coast Indians had no trouble feeding themselves and finding enough leisure time to improve and elaborate their material culture and to conduct a lively trade. At the same time they developed a highly stratified and class-

5. The Makahs, who lived on the northernmost tip of
the Olympic Peninsula, were famed for their skill as
whalers. Courtesy University of Washington Libraries:
A. Curtis 19229.

conscious social structure atypical of other North American maritime
hunting and gathering groups.

The economy and life-style of Coast Indians centered on the resources of
the sea. Hunting marine mammals was economically important and it
enhanced the prestige of the participants. Most spectacular of all were the
whale hunts of the Nootkas and the Makahs, the latter inhabiting the
Olympic Peninsula. Land mammals were more difficult to exploit, and
therefore Coast peoples practiced hunting only to a limited extent.

But life in the Coast culture area was hardly idyllic. Warfare aimed at
driving out or exterminating another lineage or family was an established
practice in the northern portion of the region. Peoples to the south carried
on feuds, much more limited in violence and extent. After a successful
attack, the northern warriors sometimes beheaded their victims, brought
the heads home, and impaled them atop tall poles in front of their villages.
Only the Tlingits practiced scalping.

Several groups practiced slavery, though more for symbolic than for economic reasons. Slaves were primarily war captives and retained no rights. Tlingit chiefs, for example, were reported to have crushed slaves to death beneath enormous posts set up at a house-building ceremony. On the arrival of a visiting chief, the Kwakiutls sometimes killed slaves on the beach in order to use their bodies as rollers for the visitor's canoe. Such conspicuous displays of wealth enhanced the group's prestige.

Ceremonies of various types were a significant part of daily life, especially during the winter months. Summer was a time for work; the rainy, blustery days of winter were reserved for ceremonial performances. Indians did not separate material objects from things of the spirit. Consequently, food gathering, especially of salmon, a dietary staple of Coast peoples, involved some of their most important religious ceremonies. It was believed that salmon represented a race of supernatural beings who dwelled in a great house beneath the sea. When a salmon died, its spirit returned to its place of origin, and thus it behooved humans not to offend the salmon people by the careless disposal of their bones. If the bones were properly returned to the water, the being resumed a humanlike form without discomfort and could repeat the trip next season. All Northwest Coast peoples had long lists of taboos and prohibitions designed to maintain good relations with the salmon people. Although it may have been inadvertent, in that way they displayed a superlative ecological wisdom.

The Kwakiutls, Nootkas, and others also practiced a world-renewal ceremonial cycle. Performances were spectacular, with sensational stage effects unsurpassed among Indians of North America. Many of their masks had movable parts; tunnels, and trap doors, allowed actors "miraculously" to appear and disappear; lines of hollow kelp stems concealed under the floor enabled performers to project their voices from unexpected places.

Anthropologists have studied the potlatch more than any other ceremony. In its many variations and elaborations, the potlatch was a feature of Indian culture from southern Alaska to the Oregon coast. The elaborate, competitive potlatch that prevailed among the northern peoples received the most comment. In this classic encounter, two powerful rivals might give away and destroy valuable trade goods and money during the course of the contest. Ostensibly the occasion might be a young person's coming-of-age, a marriage, or a funeral, but the destruction of property also signified that a person was so powerful and rich that material goods were of no consequence to him. The potlatch served to unite people, because each member of the host's lineage or extended family was expected to contribute to the extent of his or her ability.

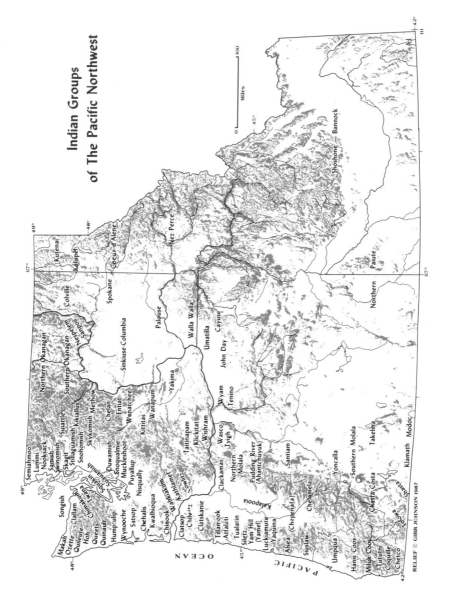

Indian Groups
of The Pacific Northwest

RELIEF © GIBB JOHNSON 1987

The oratory, elaborate form, and disposal or destruction of enormous accumulations of wealth scandalized foreign observers and sparked controversy among anthropologists. Some scholars viewed the potlatch as a way to redistribute the wealth. Others thought that it addressed the great religious issues of life renewal or was part of a class struggle by traditional chiefs to maintain their hereditary power. Canadian missionaries promoted legislation in 1884 that made giving or assisting in a potlatch dance a misdemeanor punishable by up to six months in prison. That law remained on the books until 1951.

The word *potlatch* comes from the Chinook jargon, a trade language that enabled Indians of the Northwest Coast to overcome communication difficulties. The Chinookan peoples—the Clatsops, Cathlamets, Skilloots, and others whose homeland lay along the lower Columbia River—occupied a strategic position as middlemen in the trade between Indians to the north and south and between those of the Coast and the Plateau cultural areas. They traded slaves captured in California to the Nootkas for canoes and other products. Through Chinookan traders, prized shells from the west coast of Vancouver Island reached Indians of the interior.

Often classified with Indians of the Northwest Coast cultural area are those who inhabited Oregon's inland valleys: Kalapuyans and Molalas of the Willamette Valley and various independent groups that whites popularly referred to as Rogue River Indians. Those peoples, far more than the natives living along the coast proper, added nuts, roots, and game to their diet.

INDIANS OF THE PLATEAU

Like the Indians of the Coast, those of the Plateau cultural area are grouped by anthropologists into numerous tribes, bands, and families. As distinct entities, they divided roughly according to river valleys and watersheds and occupied an area extending from the Cascades to the Rockies and from central Idaho to central British Columbia. Living along the upper reaches of the Columbia were the Kalispels (whom French-speaking trappers called Pend d'Oreilles), Kutenais, Coeur d'Alenes, Flatheads, Colvilles, Sanpoils, Okinagans, and Spokanes. In the Columbia basin country lived the Yakimas, Klikitats, Umatillas, Walla Wallas, Palooses, and Nez Percés (known in their own Sahaptian tongue as Ne-Mee-Poo, "the people"). The Klamaths and Modocs lived in south-central Oregon. As a rule, the tribes living in the northern portion of the region spoke Salish languages and dialects and those in the central and south spoke various Sahaptian tongues.

THE CHINOOK JARGON

The first Pacific northwesterners spoke a bewildering variety of languages and dialects that were as mutually unintelligible as English and Japanese. In western Washington the prevailing tongue was Coast Salish. Chinookan dialects were spoken in Oregon from the mouth of the Columbia to Tillamook Bay and east to the Cascades, but the Tillamooks belonged to the Coast Salish–speaking people. The interior tribes spoke languages derived from the Algonquin language stock and the Salish, Sahaptian, and Numic families.

The Chinook jargon facilitated communication among Indians as well as with Euro Americans. A simply structured hybrid language of approximately three hundred words of Indian, English, and French origin, augmented by signs, the Chinook jargon proved remarkably adept at embracing additional words to describe new trade goods. But it was poorly suited to Euro-American attempts to explain complex matters like land holding and religion. One unhappy result was a series of treaties negotiated between whites and Indians, the language and meaning of which are still a matter of legal dispute.

Here are some examples of Chinook jargon:

Boston	American
Hiack	Make haste, hurry
Cultus	Worthless
Memelose	Dead
Muckamuck	Food, to eat
Potlatch	Give or gift
Skookum	Strong
Tillicum	Man
Kleutchman	Woman
Tyee	Chief
Too-tooche'	Breasts, milk
Too-tooche' gleece	Butter
Gleece	Grease
Pire	Fire
Gleece-pire	Candle

The Plateau Indians' economy was based on hunting and gathering. Their diet was rich in salmon, which made annual runs up all the major rivers of the interior. Depending upon the season, the Plateau people engaged in various types of food-gathering and -preserving activities. They dried fish and ground a nutritious fish meal for later use and for trade. They dug several kinds of roots, such as wild turnip and the starchy bulb of the camas—second in importance only to fish in their diet. They also harvested berries in season and hunted deer and other game. Some natives even hunted bison, which appear to have lived on the Columbia plateau in limited numbers until the 1770s and in southern Idaho until the mid-1800s.

Plateau Indians had home territories, but they traveled more often and over longer distances than did Coast Indians because of the dispersed nature of their food supply. Most Plateau people had a casual attitude toward community property, although the Nez Percé and Coeur d'Alene peoples fiercely protected their territory. They regarded intruders on their hunting and gathering grounds as trespassers.

Before the coming of the horse and extensive contact with tipi-dwelling Plains Indians, Plateau Indians spent their winters in protected valleys housed in circular earthen-roofed structures built partly underground. During the summer they moved to cooler elevations and lived in rough pole lodges covered with mats of tule or cattail. Plateau peoples were ideally situated to borrow and give freely through contact with their neighbors, especially after they acquired horses in the early 1700s. Before the horse, they had traveled entirely by foot or water.

The horse had an impact on Indian society and culture not unlike that of the automobile on twentieth-century America. The Nez Percés used horses to make regular trips to the Great Plains to hunt bison and exchange trade goods. Through contact with natives there they adopted such innovations as skin tipis, buckskin clothing, and feathered headdresses for festive occasions. Their diet also changed after the coming of the horse; fish, which had constituted approximately 80 percent of the Nez Percé diet, increasingly gave way to buffalo, elk, deer, and antelope.

The Nez Percés first obtained horses from the Shoshoni Indians of the Great Basin around 1730; the latter had acquired them from the Comanches of the southern plains, who in turn got them from Spaniards who had introduced horses in the New World. Large horse herds flourished on the rich natural grasses of the plateau, and the natives of the region became adept horsemen. Although Plateau Indians did not place the same value on acquisitiveness and material possessions as their contemporaries on the coast, they considered a man with many horses to be rich. Some Oregon headmen had as many as five thousand horses apiece.

When Euro-American fur traders and explorers reached the Plateau cultural area in the early years of the nineteenth century, the Indians lived in small semipermanent fishing settlements along major streams and tributaries. Each settlement was usually an autonomous unit with its own leaders, most of whom had gained their standing through democratic methods of selection rather than heredity. On occasion, villages or bands (groups of villages associated voluntarily by common bonds) came together to trade, fish, hunt, gather roots in a communal harvest, socialize, or wage limited warfare against a common enemy. Because whites only poorly understood that decentralized arrangement, they eventually forced the notion of a single tribal chief upon the Indians. Prior to Euro-American intrusion, the Nez Percés had a permanent governing council, a political organization that could speak for all of them, but they had no head chief empowered to sign away their lands in treaties.

Great intertribal meetings that took place at the Dalles of the Columbia River occupied an important place in the lives of Plateau Indians. In the spring, before the salmon reached them, the Nez Percés often journeyed down the Snake and Columbia rivers to the rapids at Celilo Falls and the Dalles. That was the home territory of the Wishrams, Wascos, and other peoples and the most important point of contact between Coast and Plateau cultures. Here was the cosmopolitan center of Northwest Indian life, site of great month-long trade fairs analogous to those held in medieval Europe, a time for trading, dancing, ceremonial displays, games, gambling, and even marriages. The Wishrams and Wascos sometimes hosted several thousand visitors who came to trade dried salmon meal, bison robes, and slaves from the interior for canoes, marine shells and shell beads, and fish oil from the coast. Those trade goods have been found as far away as Alaska, southern California, and Missouri.

INDIANS OF THE GREAT BASIN

Few regions of the present United States were more inhospitable to human habitation than the lands of the Great Basin, the high desert country of southern Idaho, eastern Oregon, Nevada, and Utah. The Shoshoni-Bannock peoples dwelled in Idaho, and to the west and south lived the Northern Paiutes. Collectively they were known as the Snake Indians, a name apparently derived from claims that they frightened Plains natives with sticks having snakes painted on them.

Given the meager resources available in the Great Basin environment, the Shoshoni-Bannocks were well-off, utilizing salmon, game, birds, and edible plants of the Boise and Salmon river drainage systems in their diet. They possessed numerous horses and occasionally visited the Great Plains to hunt and trade.

The Northern Paiutes were not so fortunate, at least by Euro-American standards. Theirs was an arid land where even in the best of times small scattered bands lacking permanent villages and complex social organization spent their time traveling by foot from one oasis to another in a never-ending search for water, firewood, and food. Although individual bands occasionally cooperated with one another, there was no tribal unity. Usually only a few families remained together for any length of time, for there simply was not enough food for large groups.

The Northern Paiutes did not practice agriculture, although they developed rudimentary forms of irrigation so as to increase the yield of natural vegetation. They subsisted on what the environment offered—roots, seeds, berries, nuts, mice, grasshoppers, and lizards. They developed a nutritious flour compounded from seeds and roasted pine nuts and crafted woven baskets to store and transport their food. The jackrabbit, the equivalent of the bison to desert people, supplied food and the clothing worn by Northern Paiutes. Because they used digging sticks to unearth roots, Euro-Americans referred to them contemptuously as Digger Indians.

Trigger-happy whites seemed unusually quick to make war with that peaceful people, often in the casual way sportsmen shot bison on the Great Plains. Although the Northern Paiutes represented the best human adaptation to extremes of heat and cold and the desiccation of a desert environment, they remained the least favored materially of North America's native peoples.

THEIR NUMBERS BECAME THINNED

Two speculative questions should be asked about the first inhabitants of the Pacific Northwest: where did they originate and what was their population at the beginning of sustained European contact? Once it was believed that the Coast culture was essentially an extension of that of Asia. Anthropologists now argue that it was derived from that of ancient Eskimos and spread through the interior to the coast. Although no definitive answer is yet possible, it has been documented that Indian civilization on Washington's northwestern coast has existed continuously since at least 3,000 B.C., and some scholars estimate that human habitation of the Pacific Northwest dates back twelve thousand years.

Equally speculative are the estimates of Northwest Indian population before the coming of Euro-Americans. There may have been a hundred thousand natives or two or three times that number. It does make a difference, because unless some idea of the original Indian population is known, it is impossible to assess the Euro-American impact on the first Pacific Northwesterners. This much is certain: the advent of an ongoing relationship with Euro-Americans brought about a significant reduction in the Indian population.

That Euro-Americans ultimately prevailed over Indians was less a matter of warfare than of disease. It was neither the guns of the whites nor their whiskey that really decimated the Indian population, but their germs. Violent clashes between Euro-Americans and Indians have attracted the attention of historians, but far more deadly than bullets were the invisible killers—smallpox, malaria, measles, and influenza—germs to which Indians had no natural immunity. As a result of epidemics of both identifiable and unknown origin, the biologically vulnerable Indian population declined rapidly after the 1780s.

In some cases, disease spread from Euro-Americans to nearby tribes and then to distant people who had never seen a white person. A smallpox epidemic struck the Nez Percés in 1781–82 when white traders unintentionally introduced the disease into eastern tribes, and it spread across the plains to devastate the Nez Percés and other residents of the plateau. Disease wiped out whole villages of the Chinooks of the lower Columbia River and the Kalapuyans of the Willamatte Valley between 1829 and 1833. Over a three-year period the Chinook population declined to one-tenth its former size. How different the subsequent history of the Pacific Northwest might have been had there been twice as many Indians living in the region at the time of European contact, or had the Indians not been so susceptible to European diseases, or had the Europeans contracted a deadly plague from the Indians. By the time missionaries and settlers came to the Pacific Northwest in the 1830s, disease already had reduced the region's Indian population to a fragment of its former size.

One can speculate that this demographic disaster had a devastating impact on Indian morale and spiritual life. The Black Death that ravaged Europe in the mid-1300s wiped out about one-third of its population and contributed to profound changes of all types. The far greater death rate among Native Americans weakened social structures and traditions, demoralized survivors, and thus opened the way for new forms of religion that might offer solace and future protection from such calamities.

CHAPTER 3

The North Pacific
Maritime Frontier

*

Nothing can be more iniquitous than the rule which Civilized Governments have established, of taking Possession of the Countries of every People, who may be more rude and barbarous than themselves.—Alexander Walker in *An Account of a Voyage to the North West Coast of America in 1785 and 1786* (1982)

*

Almost every place-name on a map of the Pacific Northwest has a story behind it. Some of the stories are biographical; some are capsule histories. Names like Snoqualmie Pass and Moses Lake; the counties of Snohomish, Skagit, Yakima, Walla Walla, Tillamook, Clackamas, Nez Perce, and Shoshone; and the communities of Spokane, Yakima, Coos Bay, Klamath Falls, and Pocatello recall the first Pacific Northwesterners. Another set of names, those of Puget Sound, Vancouver Island, Mounts Rainier and Saint Helens, the Strait of Juan de Fuca, the San Juan Islands, and the Columbia River, remind of still another aspect of Pacific Northwest history: the era of the North Pacific maritime frontier.

During the span of a generation or two—from the 1740s to the 1790s—seafarers from Europe and the United States dispelled the fog of geographic ignorance that had previously shielded the North Pacific Coast from outsiders. This was the world's last temperate zone coastline to yield its secrets to Euro-Americans. By the end of the 1790s, explorers had effectively consigned a practicable Northwest Passage to the dustbin of theoretical geography. At the same time, those voyages provided cartographers with detailed information on the coasts of Oregon and Washington, the lower Columbia River, the Strait of Juan de Fuca, and Puget Sound. During those same years, seaborne traders from several nations developed a profitable commerce in the region's furs and skins.

Motivating explorers and traders from Russia, Spain, Great Britain, France, and the United States were the three C's of empire: *curiosity, conquest,* and *commerce.* Rarely were those three forces separate from one another. Curiosity is perhaps too weak a term to describe the intense intellectual passion of the Age of Enlightenment. Yet Europeans and Americans of the 1700s were curious about the world as never before, relentlessly pushing back boundaries of ignorance whether they ran through the heavens, under a microscope, or along the shores of the Pacific Ocean.

THE EMPIRE BUILDERS

Spain was the preeminent power in the Pacific basin for nearly three centuries after 1493. In that year Pope Alexander VI issued a proclamation giving all New World lands not held by a Christian ruler to Spain and Portugal and treating the Pacific Ocean as if it were a Spanish lake. Spain concentrated its attention on the Pacific coast south from Mexico and on equatorial trade routes linking its American empire and the Philippines. Interlopers like the Englishman Francis Drake had penetrated its waters and plundered Spanish ships, but their activities scarcely posed any immediate territorial threat to Spain.

From time to time, Spain dispatched exploratory voyages along the west coast of North America, and on occasion her mariners were blown off course and shipwrecked, according to the tales of Northwest Coast Indians. But Spain showed little interest in a region that seemed so pitifully lacking in either economic resources or good harbors. Only Russian exploration in the mid-1700s aroused Spain from her imperial lethargy. When Russian explorers and traders started probing south through the seas off Siberia and Alaska, reaping a great harvest in furs and skins along the way, Spain finally cast a concerned look northward.

In the search for furs, the Russians had established a modest presence in the far eastern reaches of Asia as early as 1639, but sustained Russian interest in the waters off North America began only in the latter years of the reign of Czar Peter the Great. Because no one had yet discovered whether Asia and North America might be joined together at some northern latitude, Peter dispatched an expedition from the Russian capital at Saint

Petersburg in 1719 to learn more about the relationship between the two continents. Four years later, after an overland crossing of more than ten thousand miles, the explorers returned without a conclusive answer. Peter did not give up, and on his deathbed, he planned another expedition.

His widow and successor, Catherine I, shared his interest; within weeks after ascending the throne in 1725, she dispatched an expedition commanded by Vitus Bering, a Danish captain in the Russian navy. Bering returned five years later and reported that the two continents were not joined. Catherine soon sent Bering on a second and far more elaborate and ambitious assignment. The main body of this five hundred–person expedition—soldiers, surveyors, interpreters, painters, and secretaries in addition to a large library of scientific books—departed in 1733 and made its way slowly across Siberia to the Pacific. After constructing two ships, the Russians explored along the coast of Alaska in 1741. Misfortune overtook Bering, marooning him on a cold, forbidding island where he and many crewmen perished.

Aleksei Chirikov, commander of the expedition's other ship, fared better. The survivors straggled back to Saint Petersburg, the last of them arriving in 1749, sixteen years after they first set out. Although many lives were lost, Bering's expedition established that it was possible to travel from Asia to North America by water and that the North Pacific region was rich in furs. A profitable commerce might be developed.

During the next fifty years other Russians followed Bering and Chirikov, expanding the trade in sea otter and other furs. Outstanding among them was Grigori Shelekhov who established the first permanent Russian settlement in North America in 1784 at Three Saints Bay on Kodiak Island. That was, in fact, the first permanent settlement of Euro-Americans anywhere on the North Pacific. Shelekhov envisioned a string of posts extending hundreds of miles south along the coast, each settlement a mark of Russian possession. Of even greater importance was Aleksander Baranov, a businessman who headed the monopolistic Russian-American Company, founded in 1799, and made it a major economic force in the North Pacific. His headquarters at New Archangel (Sitka) was one of the first nonnative communities in the region. Under Baranov, the Russian company established a presence as far south as Fort Ross (short for Russia) near Cape Mendocino north of San Francisco.

Although much of the Russians' activity was shrouded in secrecy, including the extent of their fur trade, their expansion into the North Pacific did not go unnoticed in other capitals of Europe. First to challenge the

Russians was Spain. Spain undertook land and sea expeditions northward from Mexico into California in 1769 and 1770 and established permanent settlements there. Juan Pérez led an expedition in 1774 that sailed slightly north of the Queen Charlotte Islands before scurvy forced it to turn back.

On the return voyage, the Spanish anchored in the vicinity of Nootka Sound, which Pérez called San Lorenzo. Twenty-one canoes carrying nearly 150 Nootka villagers made contact with the Spanish and exchanged gifts. Some bolder Indians boarded the *Santiago* and took silver spoons that Cook's expedition noted four years later. The Spanish studied the natural setting and its inhabitants, but Pérez failed to make any charts or take formal possession of the region.

The following year a Spanish expedition under the command of Juan Francisco de la Bodega y Quadra sailed north along the Pacific coast and reached fifty-eight degrees north before scurvy forced it to retreat. An associate, Bruno de Hezeta (or Heceta), sighted the entrance to the Columbia River on his return voyage, but because he hesitated to cross the Columbia's treacherous bar, credit for the discovery goes to the American Robert Gray who in 1792 sailed a short distance upriver.

In 1776, the year James Cook began his third voyage, the Spanish founded San Francisco, the settlement destined to become the most important on America's West Coast. Another major Spanish expedition followed in 1779 under the command of Ignacio de Arteaga. It probed as far north as 59°52', where Mount Saint Elias loomed in the distance. At this point, which Bering sighted from a different direction in 1741, the empires of Russia and Spain made tentative contact. Arteaga's ships continued slightly farther north before turning south, adding on paper a large area to the far-flung Spanish empire.

But as Russians pushed south and Spaniards north, the British under James Cook wedged themselves in between the two expanding empires at Nootka, creating the potential for a major international clash. The British intrusion intensified interest in profiting from the region's furs, or "soft gold" as some have labeled it. That development was the first of many extractive endeavors that have dominated the Pacific Northwest economy.

THE MARITIME FUR TRADE

Cook's men understood that the Russians had turned a profit in furs, but they did not realize the full economic potential of the trade until they reached Canton, where they sold twenty worse-for-wear animal skins for an exorbitant price even in today's money. And the Chinese besieged Cook's men for still more.

The object of their attention was the lustrous pelt of the sea otter, a rich jet-black glossy fur with shimmery silvery undertones. One of Cook's contemporaries remarked that "excepting a beautiful woman and a lovely infant" the pelts were among the most attractive natural objects. Sea otters occasionally weighed eight pounds and attained a length of nearly four feet, making them a much larger creature than the smaller land otter. They fed in relatively shallow water, searching the bottom for abalone and occasionally preying on squid, octopus, and sea urchins. Their breeding grounds covered a six thousand–mile arc from Japan's northernmost islands through the Aleutian Islands southward along the Northwest Coast to California. Almost wholly aquatic, sea otters came ashore only in severe storms. The bonds between parents and offspring were so strong that trappers seized the young to lure the adults to their death.

After Cook's expedition discovered this new source of fortune, the first trader to reach the Northwest Coast was James Hanna, who sailed from the port of Macao on the China coast in 1785. At Nootka Sound he traded iron bars for furs and skins, which he sold a year later in Canton for twenty thousand Spanish dollars, a handsome profit. Hanna hastened back to Nootka only to find that two other ships had taken nearly all the furs the natives had to offer. Hanna was forced to search farther north along the coast. Such were hazards of the trade.

During the remainder of the 1780s, Nootka was a busy place as European and American trading ships made ports of call. In a typical transaction, the Indians exchanged sea otter pelts for such trade goods as sheets of copper, heavy blue cloth, or muskets, powder, and shot. In China, Euro-Americans traded the pelts for tea, porcelain, silk, and similar items that commanded high prices in Europe or on the Atlantic seaboard.

Even as Nootka Sound became the most important anchorage for fur traders on the North Pacific Coast, imperial claims to the region remained unresolved. Although Juan Pérez had anchored off Nootka's entrance, the secretive Spaniards published no account of his activities. Cook, during his month there, made no effort to take formal possession of the area because he heard vague reports of Spanish visitors and assumed that they had already claimed it for their king.

The matter of conflicting imperial claims finally led to an international incident in 1789 known as the Nootka Sound controversy. In that year the Russians were a well-established presence in the North Pacific; Spain laid claim to Nootka and the entire western coast of North America; Great Britain challenged that notion; and the United States, seeking new markets to replace those lost by the separation from Great Britain, showed increased interest in the Pacific fur trade. A French scientific expedition under Jean de Galaup, Count La Pérouse, also had explored the area between 1786 and 1788, but that effort ended disastrously with only one man surviving. The tragedy, coupled with the outbreak of the French revolution a short time later, discouraged follow-up voyages. In short, despite their vastness, the North Pacific waters had become too small to accommodate the territorial and economic ambitions of rival nations.

In mid-1789 a Spanish expedition took formal possession of Nootka and erected a post. When an English ship commanded by Captain James Colnett arrived a short time later and constructed a trading post, Spaniards seized the vessel, arrested Colnett and his crew, and sent them to Mexico as prisoners. The rival empires stood at the brink of war.

Despite Nootka's remoteness, the conflict between Britain and Spain nearly engulfed the infant United States. The administration of President George Washington debated the possibility that British troops might try to conquer Spanish Louisiana by marching across America's sparsely populated Ohio country from bases in Canada. The crisis at Nootka thus sparked the first cabinet-level foreign policy debate in the United States under the new Constitution of 1787.

How European nations established claims to these lands lay at the heart of the controversy. For three centuries Spain, backed by the Pope's 1493 edict, had done so through a symbolic act of taking possession. The ritual consisted of going ashore, planting a cross with an appropriate inscription, reciting a religious litany, and burying a bottle containing a written version of the act of possession beneath a pile of stones at the foot of the cross. With the Malaspina expedition of 1789–94, Spain adopted a new practice of establishing sovereignty through a limited act of possession, mapping the claim, and publishing the results of any new discoveries. Indeed, because the English had published a record of Cook's third voyage, they were thus able to establish a more convincing claim to Nootka than the Spanish. Native peoples, incidentally, initially counted for little in this Eurocentric notion of sovereignty. Even when whites negotiated treaties with the Indians, the concept of transferring title to the land remained alien to the Indian view of the world.

England and Spain averted war over Nootka when they signed a convention limiting Spain's dominions to discoveries secured by treaties and immemorial possession and compensating the English for damages done them at Nootka. The actual limits to Spanish claims were not set, however, and Spain maintained a presence at Nootka for five more years until a second Nootka convention resolved the controversy. Distracted by affairs in Europe and unable to discredit the territorial claims of its rival, Spain yielded Nootka to the English. The decline of the Spanish empire accelerated during the next two decades. Having lost interest in the Pacific Northwest, Spain ceded to the United States all claims to the region north of the forty-second parallel by signing the Adams-Onís Treaty of 1819.

An agreement with the United States in 1824 and with Britain in 1825 extinguished Russian claims to the lands south of 54°40' (today the southernmost tip of the Alaska panhandle). That left Americans and Britons in joint possession of the Oregon country. As for Nootka Sound, the decline of the maritime fur trade left it isolated. Today it remains one of North America's backwaters, reachable only by boat or plane.

EXPLORATION

As seafarers exploited the natural resources of North Pacific waters in the 1780s and 1790s, they continued to explore its islands, bays, and inlets. Voyages of discovery up the Strait of Juan de Fuca provide a vivid illustration of the process of knowledge accumulation. It is ironic that the man who gave his name to that body of water did so by a simple feat: telling what most authorities regard as a big lie.

A Greek named Apostolos Valerianos, commonly called Juan de Fuca, claimed to have made a voyage for Spain in 1592 that took him north from Mexico along the Pacific Coast to a point between forty-seven and forty-eight degrees latitude. In a region he described as being rich in gold, silver, and pearls, he discovered the Strait of Anian, the Spanish designation for the fabled Northwest Passage. For twenty days he sailed through the strait, he said, reached the North Atlantic, and then backtracked to Mexico. By the early 1600s the curious tale had found its way into histories and maps of the North Pacific.

On his northern voyage, James Cook looked in vain for de Fuca's fabled strait and acidly commented, "We saw nothing like it, nor is there the least possibility that ever any such thing existed." In the fog he missed seeing the body of water that separates Vancouver Island and the Olympic Peninsula, a twenty-mile-wide strait opening remarkably near where de Fuca claimed to have crossed the continent.

THE MALASPINA EXPEDITION

To the three C's of empire might be added a fourth: competition. When Alejandro Malaspina, a Spanish naval officer, sought imperial approval for a round-the-world scientific expedition, he cited the exploits of Cook and La Pérouse and urged Spain to do as Britain and France had. Receiving all necessary official assistance, the Malaspina expedition departed Spain for the New World in 1789 and after two years reached the waters off Alaska's Yakutat Bay. The Spaniards remained among the Tlingits for nine days, compiling extensive written and visual records and collecting artifacts. The expedition continued its scientific activities for two weeks at Nootka and then cruised south along the coasts of Washington and Oregon, delineating various headlands with some exactness.

Ethnographic records were vital to the scientific part of the expedition, but the Spaniards also made hydrographic and oceanic charts to aid commercial navigation in these remote waters, and they assessed the political intent of other nations in the North Pacific. The discovery of the fabled Strait of Anian, which persistent Spaniards believed might yet be found, and the strengthening of Spain's pretensions to exclusive sovereignty in the Pacific Northwest and the entire Pacific Ocean were two added objects of the Malaspina expedition. In that regard the mission failed, but it provided the world with a wealth of North Pacific Coast artifacts and observations of native life-styles.

An Englishman, Captain Charles Barkley, made the first indisputable European discovery of the Strait of Juan de Fuca in 1787. He made no attempt to penetrate its hundred-mile length, but a year later John Meares sent in a company of explorers who he later claimed took possession of its shores for Great Britain.

Further British and Spanish explorations followed, until in 1792 Captain George Vancouver sailed through the strait and around the island that today bears his name. For two months, his men explored the great inland sea that Vancouver called Puget Sound. To the principal bays, inlets, and other physical features, he assigned names that in many cases still identify them: Admiralty Inlet, Dungeness, Port Orchard, Port Discovery, Possession Sound, Restoration Point, Deception Pass, Bellingham Bay, Whidbey and Vashon islands, and the Gulf of Georgia. Vancouver also named Mounts Baker and Rainier. Hood Canal and Mount Rainier were named after two of Vancouver's friends in the British admiralty who never sailed in Pacific waters.

The last of the great eighteenth-century discoveries along the Pacific Coast of Oregon and Washington was made by an American, Captain

Robert Gray, whose ship, the *Columbia*, the first United States vessel to circumnavigate the globe, became an object of great national pride when she sailed into Boston harbor in 1790. A swarm of American fur traders and whalers followed Gray's lead, making the long voyage from New England ports, rounding Cape Horn, and fanning out into all parts of the Pacific.

Gray was a trader who came late to the North Pacific. Like all latecomers to any frontier, he found the field of opportunity considerably narrowed. Undiscouraged, he returned to the North Pacific in 1791 to trade for pelts. In the process, Gray discovered the harbor on the coast of Washington that bears his name and, in May 1792, the majestic river he named for his ship: Columbia's River, a spelling soon modified to a more familiar form. Although Gray's men explored only thirty or thirty-five miles upstream, they laid the foundation for a United States claim to the area.

There would be no more surprise discoveries of major consequence on the North Pacific Coast after the 1790s, but the unknown lands of the interior were another matter. No Euro-Americans knew what lay east of the Cascade mountains, nor did they know the course of the Columbia River. Here were more curiosities, more possibilities for commerce, and more lands to claim. In 1793, even as Vancouver undertook to dispel the last wisps of mystery surrounding de Fuca's Northwest Passage, Alexander Mackenzie and a party of fur traders from the opposite side of North America crossed the Continental Divide and approached the very waters Vancouver was mapping.

The peak years of the maritime fur trade lasted from the 1790s until the War of 1812, and during that time Americans had edged out the British. Overtrapping took such a toll on profits that, by the first decade of the nineteenth century, the future clearly belonged to fur empires spanning the continent by land. Other Pacific Northwest place-names—Lewiston, Clarkston, Sacajawea Park, Astoria, and Boise—recall that era.

CHAPTER 4

Continental Dreams and Fur Empires

*

The progress of discovery contributes not a little to the enlightenment of mankind; for mercantile interest stimulates curiosity and adventure, and combines with them to enlarge the circle of knowledge.—Alexander Ross, *Adventures of the First Settlers on the Oregon or Columbia River, 1810–1813* (1849)

*

Pacific Northwesterners honor the names of Lewis and Clark above all others. Cities and counties, rivers and peaks, streets and schools, all testify to the importance of the two explorers who have long symbolized the westering impulse in American life.

THE CORPS OF DISCOVERY

The overland expedition led by Meriwether Lewis and William Clark reached the Oregon coast in late 1805, twenty-seven years after James Cook. Though the two ventures differed in obvious ways, they had certain common features: both were military expeditions; both sketched in details on the map of North America; and both spurred the commerce in furs. Publication of official and unofficial records of each expedition stimulated the curiosity and commercial ambition of those who followed.

Like Cook, Lewis and Clark sought the Northwest Passage. Their quest was for an easy portage through the mountains that separated the head of navigation on the Missouri River and that of a river draining into the

47

HONORING LEWIS AND CLARK

Lewiston, Idaho	Clark Fork River (in Montana and northern Idaho)
Clarkston, Washington	
Lewis County, Idaho*	Lewis and Clark State Recreation Area, Washington
Lewis County, Washington	
Clark County, Washington	Lewis and Clark Trail State Recreation Area (Washington)
Lewis-Clark State College (in Lewiston, Idaho)	
	Lewis and Clark State Park, (Oregon)
Lewis and Clark College (in Portland, Oregon	
	Lewis and Clark Exposition (Portland, 1905)
Fort Lewis, Washington	

*But not Clark County, Idaho, named for Sam Clark, a pioneer settler.

Pacific. Such a passage did not exist, but until Lewis and Clark proved that, the dream fired the imagination of Thomas Jefferson. As early as 1786, when he dined frequently in Paris with John Ledyard, a Connecticut adventurer who visited the Pacific Northwest as a member of Cook's third voyage, Jefferson enthusiastically embraced the idea of exploring the West. Only months after becoming president, he commenced laying the groundwork for a great overland odyssey.

In January 1803, a short time before the United States completed purchase of the sprawling Louisiana Territory and doubled the nation's size, Jefferson sent Congress a secret message requesting an appropriation of $2,500 to finance an expedition up the Missouri River and thence to the Pacific Ocean. The president spoke of the need to extend the external commerce of the United States and to learn more about the unknown lands of North America. Curiosity and commerce were thus inextricably part of the Lewis and Clark expedition, and not mere idle curiosity, but carefully planned scientific reconnaissance. Jefferson, it must be noted, had no explicit territorial ambitions in the far Northwest, although the expedition's accomplishments would bolster future United States claims to the area.

The Corps of Discovery commenced its historic journey from its winter camp near Saint Louis on May 14, 1804. Jefferson selected his private secretary, Captain Meriwether Lewis, to command the expedition. With the president's approval Lewis invited his old friend William Clark to be co-leader. Although Clark was commissioned only a second lieutenant be-

6. Meriwether Lewis (1774–1809). Courtesy Library
of Congress.

cause of bureaucratic myopia within the War Department, Lewis kept that
fact secret and treated him as a captain, in every respect his equal.

Lewis was thirty years old in 1804 and had for most of his life been a
soldier. Clark was thirty-four years old and a soldier, but unlike Lewis, he
had seen considerable Indian fighting. The two captains complemented one

49

7. William Clark (1770–1838). Courtesy Library
of Congress.

another well: Lewis, the better educated, functioned as businessman and
scientific specialist; Clark served as engineer, geographer, and master of
frontier lore. Lewis usually left daily management of the boats to Clark,
who was also more diplomatic in dealing with Indians.

In addition to Lewis and Clark, the corps included twenty-seven young
unmarried soldiers, a mixed-blood hunter named George Drouillard, and

Clark's black slave, York. A few other soldiers accompanied the expedition partway up the Missouri and then returned with its first records and scientific specimens.

The corps ascended the lower Missouri River in a fifty-five-foot keelboat and two pirogues or large dugout canoes. Traveling about fifteen miles each day, they reached the villages of the Mandan and Hidatsa Indians about fifty miles north of present Bismarck, North Dakota, in late October. There they spent the winter. Accompanying Lewis and Clark when they resumed their progress in early April 1805 were an interpreter named Toussaint Charbonneau; his young Shoshoni woman, Sacagawea; and her baby, Baptiste, affectionately nicknamed Pomp by Clark. Sacagawea did not become the expedition's guide, as some have erroneously claimed, but she proved an important aid to its progress. When the explorers reached the land of her Shoshoni people in east-central Idaho, she helped the party to secure pack horses for the arduous climb ahead. The presence of Sacagawea and her infant, who accompanied the corps to the Pacific and back, reassured Indians along the way that this was not a war party.

The "portage" over the Rockies through present Idaho—the last American state to be visited by Euro-Americans—proved unexpectedly long and disappointingly difficult. In the company of their Shoshoni guide, Old Toby, the explorers struggled across the Bitterroot Mountains through heavy snow and endured near starvation in late September. Surviving that ordeal, they entrusted their horses to friendly Nez Percés and continued down the Clearwater, Snake, and Columbia rivers in five canoes. When the corps reached the long-sought Pacific on November 7, Clark rejoiced in his journal, "Ocean in view! Oh! the joy." A few days later the men erected a small stockade on the southern bank of the Columbia and named it Fort Clatsop in honor of the nearest Indian tribe.

After enduring an exceedingly damp and disagreeable winter (only twelve days were free of rain), the Lewis and Clark expedition headed for home on March 23, 1806. Retracing their way upriver and over the Bitterroot Range, the explorers reached the mouth of Lolo Creek in midsummer. There the corps divided temporarily into two parties. Lewis took nine men across country to the falls of the Missouri, while Clark and the others explored a more roundabout passage along the Yellowstone River. The two captains and their troops were reunited on August 12 below the confluence of the Missouri and Yellowstone rivers in eastern Montana. Six weeks later, on September 23, 1806, they reached Saint Louis, where they were greeted with great rejoicing.

During the twenty-eight-month odyssey, the expedition traveled more

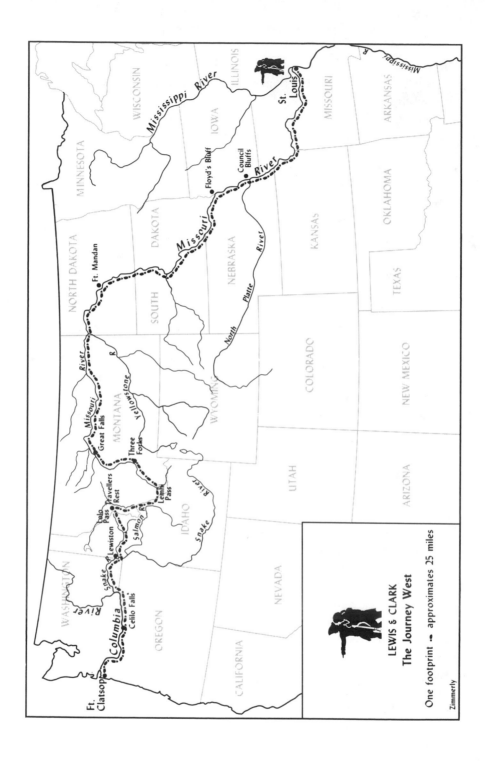

LEWIS & CLARK
The Journey West

One footprint ▬ approximates 25 miles

Zimmerly

than four thousand miles, and, remarkably, only one man lost his life. Sergeant Charles Floyd died of "biliose chorlick"—probably a ruptured appendix—on the journey up the Missouri River. The only violent encounter occurred when Indians attempted to steal the explorers' horses in the Blackfeet country of north-central Montana. In the ensuing scuffle one Indian was stabbed to death and another shot through the abdomen.

Lewis and Clark accomplished much more than simply adding a noteworthy chapter to the history of exploration. Most obviously, they revealed that the far Northwest was rich with beaver and other fur-bearing animals. Their journal entries, drawings, maps, and artifacts added greatly to knowledge about terrain, native peoples, and the flora and fauna of the West. They bolstered America's claim to a part of the world that was remote but hardly ignored. From a global perspective, the Lewis and Clark expedition represented only one more act in an ongoing imperial and commercial drama, but it was one that more than any other captivated the interest of scholars and fired the imagination of ordinary American citizens.

THE NOR'WESTERS

The fur trade, so entwined with the early history of the Pacific Northwest, was the first large-scale corporate enterprise in North America. Great profits were to be made selling the warm, beautiful, and fashionable furs. During Europe's Middle Ages, only the nobility and clergy had the right to wear furs such as ermine and sable, but in the eighteenth century a rising middle class also sought such luxuries. Growing demand and the discovery of fur-bearing animals in the New World coincided with a declining supply from Russia and Scandinavia. Thus, the whims of fashion made it worthwhile for trappers to "risk their skins for a skin," as it was popularly phrased. The most significant of the various furs and skins during the continental phase of the trade was beaver. Fashion-conscious gentlemen favored its slick fur for their tall, broad-brimmed stovepipe hats.

Oldest and most prominent of the fur companies in North America was the Hudson's Bay Company chartered by King Charles II in 1670, but beginning in the 1780s it faced a vigorous young rival in the newly formed North West Company of Montreal. The new firm's corporate motto was Perseverance, an apt description of the force that drove Nor'westers steadily westward to the Pacific when the Hudson's Bay monopoly blocked them from North America's choicest hunting and trapping grounds. A generation of Nor'westers—some explorers, some canny businessmen, some expert

53

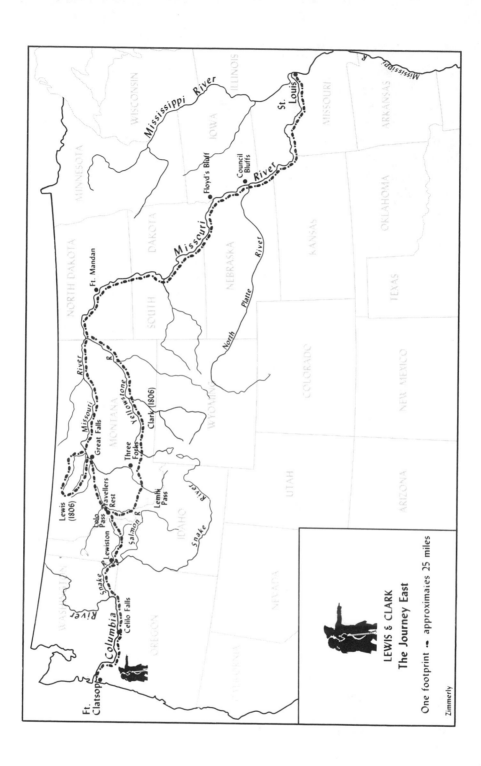

LEWIS & CLARK
The Journey East

One footprint ⚫ approximates 25 miles

Zimmerly

managers, and some combining all three qualities—boldly probed the continent's western passes and rivers to establish the first permanent European outposts among the native peoples of the Pacific Northwest.

On their journey to the Pacific, Lewis and Clark may have carried with them a book written by a Nor'wester, Alexander Mackenzie. Lewis was certainly familiar with it. Titled *Voyages from Montreal . . . to the Frozen and Pacific Oceans, in the Years 1789 and 1793* and published in 1801, the book influenced Jefferson's thinking with its powerful declaration of British intent to secure the fur commerce of the Columbia River. Aware that rival agents of Great Britain, France, and Spain had already penetrated the western wilderness, the president of the American republic responded with the Lewis and Clark expedition.

For fifteen years prior to Lewis and Clark, Mackenzie had spearheaded efforts to expand the North West Company's fur-trading network. In 1789 he led a party of Nor'westers down the great Canadian river later named for him, but to his disappointment he discovered that it emptied into the frozen Arctic Ocean, not the Pacific. That failure dampened the enthusiasm of the North West Company for Mackenzie's explorations, but he succeeded in becoming the first Euro-American to cross the breadth of North America, reaching the Pacific Ocean near present Bella Coola, British Columbia, in 1793. Though the route proved commercially futile, Mackenzie continued to nurture his dream of British territorial sovereignty and economic power extending from sea to sea. For those feats of exploration he was later knighted.

Jefferson hoped that Lewis and Clark would find ways to redirect the fur trade of the Northwest south into the United States, but well before that happened, preliminary reports from the expedition further stimulated exploratory and trade activity by the North West Company on the Pacific slope. In 1805–1806, even before Lewis and Clark returned to Saint Louis, Simon Fraser, a twenty-nine-year-old Nor'wester, conducted an extensive exploration of the region that became British Columbia. In the area then called New Caledonia, he established two of the North West Company's first three trading posts west of the Continental Divide. Fraser also in 1808 traced the wild currents of a river mistakenly thought to be the Columbia. That river now bears his name. The realization that the difficult and dangerous Fraser River was useless as a highway for furs, together with information from the Lewis and Clark expedition, caused the North West Company to shift its attention southward.

David Thompson, a trader, surveyor, map maker, and gifted explorer for the North West Company, responded to Lewis and Clark in 1807 with the first of several journeys that led him through a labyrinth of mountains and valleys that comprised the upper reaches of the Columbia River system in British Columbia, Idaho, and Montana. His travels culminated in 1811 with a descent of the Columbia to its mouth, where he was disappointed to find that American rivals had already established a crude fort. Thompson is remembered for his explorations and for the several important fur posts he established, including Kullyspell House in northern Idaho (1809) and Spokane House (1810), located northwest of the present city of Spokane.

ASTOR AND THE AMERICANS

American fur traders first entered the Rocky Mountains as Lewis and Clark returned to Saint Louis. When Private John Colter was released from the expedition near the Mandan villages, he immediately headed west to search the Teton Valley of Idaho and the upper Yellowstone country for beaver. Also released was George Drouillard. Both men eventually ended up as employees of the wily merchant and trader Manuel Lisa, a Spaniard who lived in Saint Louis. Excited by information gathered by Lewis and Clark, Lisa dispatched parties of traders up the Missouri from his Saint Louis base.

Andrew Henry, Lisa's partner in the Missouri Fur Company, and a group of men entered Idaho and in 1810 built a temporary winter post called Fort Henry on a fork of the Snake River near present Saint Anthony. Of still greater significance for future American involvement in the Pacific Northwest was John Jacob Astor, a businessman whose interest in the region was stimulated by news of Lewis and Clark and the North West Company explorers.

A stout, arrogant immigrant who came to the United States from Germany in 1784, Astor had been involved in the fur trade of the upper Great Lakes. But after learning about the "soft gold" farther west, he organized the American Fur Company in 1808 to exploit fur-bearing animals on a grand scale. Two years later he created a subsidiary, the Pacific Fur Company, to tap the riches of the Oregon country, a move that was in defiance of British claims to the area. In that enterprise, Astor put up the money, and a group of Canadians and Americans served as partners and managed operations in the field.

Establishment of Astor's base of operations at the mouth of the Columbia River was accomplished by a two-pronged thrust: one by land, the other by sea. Loaded with thirty-three young Scots and Canadians, trade goods, and materials to erect a fortified post, the *Tonquin* sailed from New York City in September 1810 and made its way around Cape Horn to the Columbia River. The eight-month, twenty-two thousand–mile voyage was an ill-starred affair, filled with bickering and feuding between the irascible Captain Jonathan Thorn on one side and his crew and passengers on the other. Even as they prepared to enter the Columbia, Thorn's stubbornness cost eight crewmen their lives when he ordered them out in small boats to seek a passable channel through the treacherous waters of the bar. The ship battled its way to a protected cove on the south bank of the river where in late March 1811 passengers and supplies were unloaded and Fort Astoria took shape.

Astor hoped to use the *Tonquin* to transport furs to China, but that was not to be. What actually happened to the *Tonquin* after it left Astoria to trade with the Indians of Nootka Sound will never be known, but according to the natives, the tyrannical Captain Thorn so antagonized them that they rushed aboard the vessel, overwhelmed and slew the entire crew except for one man. The wounded sailor made his way to the hold where he touched off 4.5 tons of powder, blowing himself, the Indians, and the *Tonquin* to bits.

The leader of Astor's overland expedition was Wilson Price Hunt, a twenty-seven-year-old Saint Louis fur merchant woefully inexperienced for an undertaking of this magnitude. Assisting him was Donald Mackenzie, formerly with the North West Company. The Hunt party departed Saint Louis in October 1810, a month after the *Tonquin* sailed from New York. Assigned to reconnoiter an overland route and to seek sites for a string of trading posts extending from the Missouri to the Columbia, members of the expedition—consisting of a small group of company officials and about fifty employees—fared little better than did the Astorians who went by sea.

Plagued by blunders, Indians, and scheming rivals, the Hunt party meandered needlessly and endured great hunger, thirst, sickness, and death crossing rugged and barren expanses of wilderness. An advance guard reached the log palisades of Fort Astoria in January 1812, and others straggled in during the next several days and weeks. Along the Columbia River in eastern Oregon, Astorians later located two lost partners, Ramsay Crooks and John Day, whom the Indians had stripped naked and left stranded without even flint. Day apparently went insane before he died a year later. Hunt's overlanders found no practical route between the Missouri and the Columbia, but their arrival reinforced the modest American presence in the Pacific Northwest.

8. Fort Astoria was established in 1811 by the men of
John Jacob Astor's Pacific Fur Company. Courtesy
Washington State Historical Society, Tacoma.

The Astorians fanned out from the mouth of the Columbia in several directions to explore and exploit the fur resources of the Northwest. They built Fort Okanogan (the first American structure in the future state of Washington) and Fort Spokane, next door to the North West Company's Spokane House. A seven-man party led by Robert Stuart returned overland from Fort Astoria to New York in mid-1812. By traveling slightly south of the route followed by Hunt, the Stuart party discovered South Pass, an easy crossing through the Rockies and a key part of the future Oregon Trail. But for competitive reasons, they did not immediately make this information known.

British and American fur traders engaged in a lively competition in the Oregon country that ended prematurely with the outbreak of the War of 1812. News of the conflict reached Astoria early in 1813, and after months of indecision, the Americans sold out under duress to their British competitors at a substantial loss. But the Pacific Fur Company had not made a profit, and the men of Astoria probably would have been driven out shortly anyway, because in December 1813 the commander of a British warship occupied the post and renamed it Fort George.

The brief presence of the Astorians in the Pacific Northwest proved highly significant. The Treaty of Ghent (1814) settled the war by restoring all territory taken during the conflict, including that lost by the Astorians. Americans thus reasserted their claims to the region, even as Spain pulled back to the present Oregon-California border in 1819 and Russia to north of the 54°40' line in 1825. That left Great Britain and the United States alone to settle the future of the Oregon country. But what they agreed to do with their imperial claims was nothing. Conventions in 1818 and 1827 failed to produce agreement. Thus the Pacific Northwest remained "free and open" to residents of both nations until 1846, when Great Britain and the United States divided the Oregon country along the 49th parallel, the present international boundary.

THE HUDSON'S BAY COMPANY

During the years after the War of 1812, it appeared that the major Euro-American presence in the Oregon country would be that of the North West Company. Astor declined to reenter the contest for the region's furs and pulled his operations back to the upper Missouri and Rocky Mountains country. Here he carefully nurtured his fortune, which after subsequent investments in New York real estate made him the richest man in America.

Plagued by dwindling revenues, the North West Company entered several hitherto unexploited areas of the Pacific Northwest in search of furs. It erected Fort Nez Percés (later named Fort Walla Walla) at the confluence of the Columbia and Walla Walla rivers in 1818 and from there dispatched trapping parties into the Snake River country. The Snake brigades became an annual event, and Donald Mackenzie, formerly of Hunt's overland party of Astorians, led the parties from 1818 to 1821. Departing from customary practices, the Snake brigades sought no trade with the Indians but instead lived off the land and trapped for themselves.

In another of their business practices, however, the Nor'westers continued an arrangement initiated by Astorians: furs from the company's Columbia Department moved westward to the Pacific Coast instead of overland to the East. By arrangement with American shipowners, the "soft gold" traveled from Fort George to markets in China. This mutually beneficial arrangement was a response to the East India Company's trading monopoly, which froze other British but not American traders out of China. It lasted until the company's charter was modified in the early 1830s.

For the company that had done so much to open the interior of Oregon, the year 1821 proved fateful: the North West Company of Montreal was forcibly absorbed by its old rival, the Hudson's Bay Company—a firm of such ancient lineage that some claimed that its initials meant "Here Before Christ." The rising incidence of violence between employees of the rival outfits in the Great Lakes and Hudson's Bay region was chiefly responsible for the merger. To halt the brawling, kidnapping, hijacking, dueling, and other forms of mayhem, the British colonial secretary forced union with the Hudson's Bay Company upon the younger rival. The enlarged Hudson's Bay Company (the "Honourable Company") thus acquired the operations, organizational structures, and personnel of the North West Company. The resulting empire stretched from the Atlantic to the Pacific and north to the Arctic, encompassed millions of square miles, thousands of employees, and hundreds of establishments.

The size and complexity of this new domain prompted Hudson's Bay Company leaders to reassess their operations, particularly whether they should continue the fur trade in the Oregon country. Prior to acquisition of the North West Company, the older outfit had shown little interest in this distant land. Overland communication was long, difficult, and costly; moreover, to evaluate its economic potential, Hudson's Bay directors had little more than dismal ledger accounts and rumors. The beaver pelts of the North Pacific, for example, were not as luxuriant as those taken in the colder Hudson's Bay region, and the trade consequently did not turn as great a profit. Some directors suggested abandoning the far Northwest, but a majority considered such a step premature.

George Simpson, a thirty-four-year-old Scotsman recently named governor of the Northern Department of Rupert's Land, to which the Columbia Department was subordinate, undertook a quick field inspection in 1824. His recommendations on how to streamline operations and nurture trade in the Pacific Northwest had a far-reaching influence.

Simpson ordered the regional headquarters moved from Fort George to a new site a hundred miles upstream. There on the north bank of the Columbia River rose Fort Vancouver, the site of today's Vancouver, Washington. Because it was strategically located and offered better agricultural possibilities than Fort George (which was abandoned in 1828), Fort Vancouver was likely to remain on British soil should the jointly occupied Oregon country be divided along the Columbia River. Simpson's reorganization included a stepped-up effort to bar American rivals from the Snake River country, to improve administration, and to add new trading posts and shift or alter operations at others.

To carry out his plans, Simpson appointed Dr. John McLoughlin as chief factor for the Columbia District. A man of dominant and vivid personality,

60

9. Dr. John McLoughlin (1784–1857), "the Father of
Oregon," photographed late in life. Courtesy Oregon
Historical Society: 251.

the thirty-nine-year-old McLoughlin (pronounced McLocklin) left a lasting
imprint on Pacific Northwest history. He was born in Quebec in 1784 and at
the age of fourteen was apprenticed to a physician. After four years he

earned a license to practice medicine and surgery. Young Dr. McLoughlin entered the service of the North West Company, first as an assistant to the regular physician and later as a trader east of the Rockies.

Little is known of McLoughlin's personal life: he was of mixed Irish, Scottish, and French-Canadian ancestry and became a Roman Catholic late in life. He married the half-Swiss, half-Indian widow of a fur trader, who bore him four children in addition to the four she brought to the marriage from her first husband. McLoughlin was a man of striking appearance, standing six feet, four inches tall, raw boned, well proportioned, and strong. His eyes were piercing; a flowing mane of prematurely white hair hung down over his massive shoulders. Local Indians called him the White Headed Eagle. McLoughlin ruled the sprawling Columbia Department from 1824 until 1846. Given the tenuous nature of British and American authority in that region, this single Hudson's Bay Company official wielded extraordinary power.

Between 1823 and 1832, officers of the Hudson's Bay Company ranged over a huge portion of the Pacific Northwest in search of both furs and knowledge of the country. Peter Skene Ogden, a burly, ruthless veteran of the old North West Company, traveled from the Columbia River to the Great Salt Lake, through the Klamath and Shasta regions, and in 1827–28 through the Great Basin south to California. George Simpson put Ogden in charge of the Snake brigades in 1824 and ordered him to trap the area ruthlessly in order to create a "fur desert" that would keep Americans away from the more valuable Columbia River lands. In the vast and dangerous Snake country, company employees risked encounters with American competitors and hostile Indians. Here, too, were the torments of nature—driving sleet, deep snow, bitter winds, and barren landscape, conditions that prompted Ogden to exclaim: "What cursed Country is this." For five years Ogden led the Snake brigades.

The Hudson's Bay Company maintained an extraordinary presence in a remote frontier region. Fort Vancouver constituted a small, almost self-sufficient European community that included a hospital; thirty to fifty small houses where employees (*engagés*) lived with their Indian wives; storehouses for furs, trading goods, and grain; and workshops where blacksmithing, carpentry, barrel making, and other activities were carried on. A sawmill provided lumber for repairs and the construction of buildings and equipment. The company also operated a shipyard, gristmill, dairy, orchard, and farm of several hundred acres where employees planted crops and raised herds of cattle and other domestic animals. Ships from distant ports called

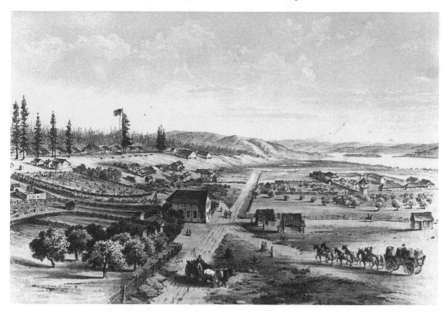

10. In this picture by Gustavus Sohon, the old fur-trading post of Fort Vancouver is located on the low land to
the right, and army's new post is on the bluff to the
left. Courtesy Historical Photograph Collection, Washington State University Libraries: 78–889.

at Fort Vancouver bringing news, books, and periodicals to stock the post's
library.

An unusually cosmopolitan population collected around Fort Vancouver: Delaware and Iroquois Indians from the East, local Chinooks, Hawaiians, mixed-blood Métis from the prairies, French Canadians, and Scots-
men, and presiding over them all was the imperious John McLoughlin,
harsh, brooding, and given to occasional temperamental outbursts. More
than profit and loss were involved in a Hudson's Bay post: each enclave was
a visible link in a truly imperial system joining London with the vast
hinterland of the Pacific Northwest.

In its effort to reinforce British territorial claims in the Oregon country,
the Hudson's Bay Company formed a subsidiary in 1839, the Puget Sound
Agricultural Company, to carry on commercial farming at Fort Nisqually
south of present-day Tacoma. Fort Nisqually and Cowlitz Farm, sixty miles
farther south, raised 4,530 sheep and 1,000 cattle in 1841 and substantial
crops of wheat, oats, barley, peas, and potatoes. Fort Colville, about halfway
up the Columbia River, specialized in grain production. All that was lacking

to make the Hudson's Bay Company farms a long-term success was settlers who were willing to remain subject to the paternalism of the company.

COMPANY MEN AND MOUNTAIN MEN

For nearly fifteen years after Astor's West Coast adventure, few Americans entered the Oregon country, although they maintained a modest presence in the Rocky Mountains country on the region's eastern fringe. A Missouri businessman, General William Henry Ashley, dispatched his first expedition of fur traders up the Missouri River in 1822 and thereby launched a new phase of American activity in the mountain West. Ashley's men were not employees like those of the Hudson's Bay Company but free agents, people like Jedediah Smith, Jim Bridger, and others whose explorations opened up vast areas of the West. The twenty-four-year-old Smith, with the aid of friendly Crow Indians, rediscovered South Pass through the Rocky Mountains in 1824 and two years later led an exploring expedition across the Mojave Desert into California. His was the first American party to travel overland through the Southwest.

Ashley popularized the "rendezvous system" in 1825, a scheme that replaced the permanent trading post and thereby saved money. This arrangement dominated the Rocky Mountains fur trade during its heyday—small bands or brigades of trappers worked the beaver streams, then gathered at prearranged meeting places each summer to trade pelts for goods sent west by packtrain. These colorful rendezvous were usually held on the Green River but also met at various times at Pierre's Hole and Bear Lake in southeastern Idaho. The last major rendezvous occurred in 1840.

The rendezvous system spawned a group of individuals unattached to any company—"mountain men," as they loved to call themselves. No group of westerners has ever been more thoroughly romanticized. Mountain men have often been portrayed as knights-errant clearing the way for American civilization in the West. Their familiarity with the land certainly furthered knowledge of western geography. Their extreme individualism contrasted with the corporate paternalism of the Hudson's Bay Company.

During the years the Hudson's Bay Company dominated the Oregon country, United States citizens retained free access to the region under the conventions negotiated with Britain. Although few Americans actually went to the Northwest until the 1830s, one who did was Captain Benjamin L. E. Bonneville, who ostensibly took a leave of absence from the United States Army in 1831 and posed as a fur trader for three years to reconnoiter

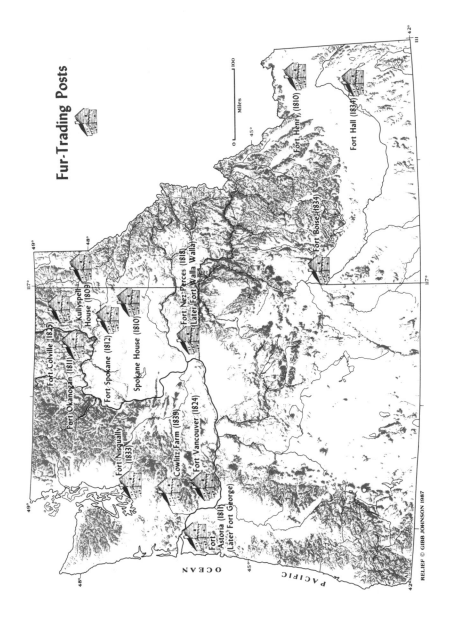

Fur-Trading Posts

Fort Colville (1835)
Fort Okanogan (1811)
Kullyspell House (1809)
Fort Spokane (1812)
Spokane House (1810)
Fort Henry (1810)
Fort Boise (1834)
Fort Hall (1834)
Fort Nez Percés (1818)
(Later Fort Walla Walla)
Fort Nisqually (1833)
Cowlitz Farm (1839)
Fort Vancouver (1824)
Fort Astoria (1811)
(Later Fort George)

PACIFIC OCEAN

0   Miles   100

RELIEF © GIBB JOHNSON 1987

the region. Bonneville demonstrated the feasibility of taking loaded wagons across South Pass and gained information that later proved valuable in shaping American policy toward the Oregon country.

None of the handful of American fur traders who entered the region during this time was particularly successful. For five years beginning in 1832, a wealthy Boston ice merchant, Nathaniel Wyeth, attempted to revive the old dream of John Jacob Astor by establishing a fur-trading venture on the lower Columbia River. Despite repeated failures, he expanded his economic horizon in 1834 to include the Rocky Mountains country. To dispose of goods he had been unable to sell at the annual fur rendezvous, he built Fort Hall near present-day Pocatello, Idaho. The Hudson's Bay Company responded with the erection of old Fort Boise. When Wyeth's fortunes continued to sag, he returned to Boston in 1836 and sold Fort Hall to the Hudson's Bay Company.

Despite his hard luck, Wyeth stirred further interest in the Pacific Northwest by bringing the first American missionaries and scientists to the region. In that way he helped usher in the next phase of Pacific Northwest history, one in which souls and homesites were as important as the search for profits or national glory.

The fur trade era in the Pacific Northwest lasted about sixty years—from the 1780s until the late 1840s. At that time, changing fashions, overtrapping, and pioneer settlement opened a new chapter in the region's history. In little more than half a century, explorers from several nations had described the region's main geographic features so well that subsequent scientific and topographic exploration only refined and classified existing knowledge. Although the fur traders had revealed to the world the treasures of nature in the Pacific Northwest, their contribution to settlement of the region was at best indirect. They knew only too well that population growth and commerce in furs were incompatible.

The fur trade era inaugurated the role of the Pacific Northwest as a colony whose natural resources were ripe for outsiders to exploit. The first Pacific Northwesterners typically used only those resources that were part of their diet or material culture. As a consequence, their impact on the environment was minimal. But the cultural practices of the Euro-Americans prevailed, and in subsequent decades their attitudes justified ruthless exploitation of the region's mineral and timber wealth. Hence, the era of the fur trade revealed economic attitudes and patterns that were to be replicated in the future and with far greater impact upon the region's natural environment.

Part Two
The Pioneers' Northwest

Profile: The Whitman Massacre

They are an exceedingly proud, haughty and insolent people. . . . We feed them far more than any of our associates do their people, yet they will not be satisfied. Notwithstanding all this there are many redeeming qualities in them, else we should have been discouraged long ago. We are more and more encouraged the longer we stay.—Narcissa Whitman, describing mission life among the Cayuse, to her mother, Clarissa Prentiss, May 2, 1840

Narcissa Prentiss was an idealist. Had she lived a century and a half later she might have joined the Peace Corps or done volunteer service in Appalachia or an inner-city clinic. In the 1830s she was willing to leave her family and comfortable home in upstate New York to become a Christian missionary among Indians living beyond the Rocky Mountains. Only one thing blocked her way: she was single, and the American Board of Commissioners for Foreign Missions rarely sent an unmarried female on an errand into the wilderness.

Her marriage to Marcus Whitman in February 1836 removed that impediment. Narcissa and Marcus actually knew little about each other when they exchanged their vows, but strengthening the bond of romantic love was their shared desire for mission service. The bride was an attractive woman, twenty-seven years old, endowed with a fine singing voice and strong religious convictions. The groom was thirty-three years old, a devout Presbyterian and handsome physician possessed by a desire to become a medical missionary. Like Narcissa, he had offered himself to the American

11. No likenesses of Marcus Whitman (1802–47) and Narcissa Whitman (1808–47) have ever been positively identified. Nonetheless, these sketches made by the Canadian artist Paul Kane during a trip to the Pacific Northwest in 1846–47 are believed to be of the Whitmans. Courtesy Royal Ontario Museum, Toronto, Canada.

Board and been turned down, in his case because of a history of illness. But that proved only a temporary setback, because the board reversed itself, and Whitman journeyed west in 1835 as an assistant to Samuel Parker, an autocratic, egotistical minister. The pair traveled with the annual fur trade caravan to the Green River valley in western Wyoming, site of that year's annual rendezvous and an excellent place to learn about Indians who lived farther west.

Fur traders, a hard-boiled lot by any standard, did not welcome the men of God and subjected them to derision and name-calling. Whitman nonetheless won their respect when he contained a cholera outbreak and removed a three-inch iron arrowhead that had lodged for months in Jim Bridger's back. Thus began a friendship that continued until Whitman's death twelve years later. At the rendezvous, the Nez Percés and Flatheads appeared genuinely happy to have Christian missionaries in their midst. Parker traveled ahead to select suitable sites for their work, while Whitman returned home to raise money and recruits—and to marry Narcissa Prentiss, to whom he had hastily proposed before his western trip.

April 1836 found the newlyweds hurrying west across the Great Plains to overtake the annual fur caravan. Three Nez Percés, two hired men, William H. Gray, and Henry and Eliza Spalding accompanied the Whitmans. The American Board had selected Gray to serve as mechanic and carpenter and Spalding as a minister. Marcus may not have been acquainted with the thirty-three-year-old Presbyterian cleric before that spring, but Narcissa knew him well. Born out of wedlock, Spalding had endured an unhappy childhood and matured into an embittered, suspicious, and quick-tempered man. At Franklin Academy in New York, he fell in love with a fellow student, Narcissa Prentiss, or at least he thought she would make a suitably religious wife. Spalding apparently proposed to her, but in vain; he then turned to Eliza Hart. Spalding's past created tensions between the Whitmans and Spaldings during the long journey to Oregon and subsequently disrupted their missionary labors.

The sojourners celebrated the Fourth of July crossing the Continental Divide at South Pass and arrived at the Green River rendezvous two days later. From that point Hudson's Bay Company traders guided them to their destination. Just east of Fort Hall, a broken axle forced Spalding to convert his flimsy wagon into a two-wheeled cart. The contraption bumped over the Snake River plain as far as Fort Boise before the missionaries discarded it, much to the relief of Narcissa, who considered it an encumbrance. Yet, no wheeled vehicle had traveled that far west before, a fact that would not be lost on would-be emigrants back east.

The missionaries pressed ahead on horseback, crossing the Blue Mountains to reach Fort Walla Walla and finally Fort Vancouver, where on September 12, 1836, Chief Factor John McLoughlin received them with great courtesy. The journey had lasted 207 days and covered more than three thousand miles. Narcissa and Eliza became the first white women to cross North America from coast to coast. Despite the difficulties, no one suffered greatly; Narcissa, in fact, arrived at Fort Vancouver three months pregnant. What the Whitmans and Spaldings accomplished, other families were inspired to duplicate.

But what about Samuel Parker, who was to have prepared the way for Whitman and his recruits? He sailed for home before they arrived. In his midfifties and feeling his age, Parker gave up the venture and spent his time writing a descriptive book about Oregon. For their part, Marcus Whitman and Henry Spalding journeyed back up the Columbia to evaluate suitable mission sites, while their wives remained at Fort Vancouver. Life at the fort dazzled Narcissa, who called it "the New York of the Pacific Ocean" in one of her letters home.

Whitman located an especially fertile and attractive site for his mission station on the Walla Walla River, twenty-five miles upstream from the Columbia and near the tree-covered slopes of the Blue Mountains. As long as anyone could remember, the Cayuse Indians had built their lodges in the same area. They called the site Waiilatpu, meaning "Place of the Rye Grass."

Whitman's choice disappointed the Nez Percés, who had expected both missionaries to settle among them. They reminded Whitman that the Nez Percés did not have the same difficulty with whites as the Cayuses did, and they prophesied that the missionaries would soon see the differences. McLoughlin, too, warned Whitman that he would encounter trouble with the Cayuses.

A band of Nez Percé Indians escorted Whitman and Spalding another 110 miles inland to their principal village on Lapwai Creek, a short distance upstream from its junction with the Clearwater River, where Lewis and Clark had passed thirty-one years earlier. At Lapwai ("Butterfly Valley") the Spaldings built a house and school. Convinced that white encroachments would inevitably destroy the game hunted by the Nez Percés, Spalding sought to convert them to farming and for that purpose acquired seeds and simple tools. Spalding was responsible for the first irrigation project in Idaho and the first publishing venture in the Pacific Northwest. But fellow missionaries publicly criticized the Spaldings for devoting more time to educating the Nez Percés in matters of agriculture and home economics than in religion.

The Whitmans' first two years at Waiilatpu were pleasant enough. They worked with vigor to build their station and gain the confidence of the proud Cayuse people. Adding sparkle to their lives was the birth of a daughter, Alice Clarissa, the first child born of United States citizens in the

73

Pacific Northwest. Among their visitors during these early years were Hudson's Bay Company men, American mountain men, and the first trickle of settlers traveling overland to Oregon. With the help of able-bodied Hawaiians, Marcus sawed lumber from the Blue Mountains, milled grain, and slowly erected a complex of buildings. The Whitmans learned the Nez Percé language, which the Cayuses understood, and attempted to teach the Cayuses the rudiments of writing, agriculture, and Christianity. To round out his busy days, the doctor ministered to the physical needs of whites and Indians.

The Whitmans served as foster parents to a growing number of Indian and white children. The mountain men Joe Meek and Jim Bridger each enrolled a daughter in the mission school. Joining them were the seven Sager children, orphaned in 1844 when their parents became sick and died on the journey west.

Ministering to the Cayuses was always challenging and often frustrating. The common goal of Protestant missionaries was not only to Christianize Indians but also to "civilize" them. That meant destroying Indian culture. The Whitmans thus hoped to convert the Cayuses to farming, an activity wholly alien to their hunting and gathering way of life but one better suited to missionary education and conversion. Unlike the Spaldings, who hoped to postpone extensive contact between whites and Indians, the Whitmans were located on the main trail to Oregon and saw no hope for Indians unless they assimilated the ways of white settlers.

The cultures of the Cayuse people and the Whitmans conflicted in many ways. Cayuses viewed the manual labor of tending fields as beneath their dignity; they practiced polygamy and wondered why Whitman had only one wife; and they helped themselves to crops raised at the station. Marcus, though, regarded this as stealing and punished them for it. When mission personnel put emetics in melons to discourage the Cayuses from taking them, the Indians wondered about people who would poison the fruits of the earth.

On one occasion an angry Cayuse claimed that the land belonged to them and demanded to know what the Whitmans had paid for it. Marcus pointed out that the Cayuses had seemed eager to have missionaries settle in their midst; moreover, he resisted giving anything for the land because he feared that he would forever be paying tribute to the tribe. As tensions increased, there were occasional acts of Indian vandalism, like breaking windows at the mission house.

With mounting frustration and cultural misunderstanding came personal tragedy: little Alice Clarissa Whitman drowned in the Walla Walla River that flowed just a few feet beyond the door of her home. She was twenty-seven months old. The child's death weighed heavily on the once ebullient Narcissa: she became depressed, developed a growing dislike of the "filthy" Indians, and doubted her own fitness for frontier missionary service. Her health deteriorated, and when her husband was gone for nearly a year to plead the mission's case to the American Board, fear and loneliness nearly overcame her.

Because of reports of feuding among the Whitmans, Spaldings, and other American Board missionaries, and, even worse, because the missionaries had made few converts among the Indians, the American Board ordered Waiilatpu and Lapwai closed, the Whitmans transferred to Tshimakain (a mission established in 1838 just northwest of present Spokane), and the Spaldings to return east. When word of the decision reached Waiilatpu, the impetuous Marcus Whitman and an associate rode east during the fall and winter of 1842 to persuade the board to change its mind.

Crossing the Rocky Mountains during winter was a remarkable feat of endurance. That accomplishment coupled with his later "martyrdom" provided the basis for the legend that Marcus Whitman saved Oregon for the United States. One admirer even claimed that Whitman stopped at the White House where he persuaded President John Tyler to wrest Oregon from the grasping British. Whitman's trip was successful in that the American Board reversed itself and permitted the mission stations to remain open.

Culture conflict between whites and Cayuses worsened. When Marcus returned in 1843, the first large contingent of white immigrants to Oregon accompanied him. Numbering nearly nine hundred, they drove their wagons overland from Missouri as far as the Columbia River. The Indians, not without reason, believed that Whitman had gone east to gather reinforcements of American farmers and soldiers.

The Cayuses viewed the changes with apprehension, knowing well the fate of Indian people elsewhere. Nearly five thousand whites crossed the Blue Mountains on their way to the Willamette Valley in 1847. Although the main trail bypassed Waiilatpu after 1844, those who were sick and destitute turned their wagons north to the mission, bringing with them their alien culture and an epidemic of measles and dysentery. An estimated 50 percent of the Cayuses died in less than two months. With rising anger, they noted that white children treated by Dr. Whitman usually recovered, but not Indian children. On a cold, foggy day—November 29, 1847—

shortly after the last wagon departed, the Cayuses attacked the mission station at Waiilatpu.

Two of their leaders, Tiloukaikt and Tomahas, entered the compound, and while Tiloukaikt distracted Marcus by deliberately provoking him into an argument, Tomahas killed the unsuspecting missionary with tomahawk blows to the head. The Indians also killed Narcissa and eleven others and destroyed the mission buildings. A few whites escaped, but the rest were taken captive.

When word of the tragedy reached Fort Vancouver, an outraged Hudson's Bay Company dispatched Peter Skene Ogden and a party of sixteen men to ransom survivors and impress upon surrounding Indians the wisdom of remaining neutral should war break out between whites and the Cayuses. The negotiators exchanged blankets, shirts, tobacco, handkerchiefs, muskets, flints, and several hundred musket balls for forty-seven survivors. Meanwhile, friendly Nez Percés delivered the Spaldings and their party from Lapwai. The events of 1847 concluded a chapter in the history of Protestant missions.

Shortly after the dawn of a new year, when survivors were safely out of the Walla Walla Valley, the first "Indian war" in Pacific Northwest history erupted between the Cayuses and a volunteer force of five hundred riflemen from the Willamette Valley. After eluding their pursuers for two years, the Cayuses surrendered five tribesmen including Tiloukaikt and Tomahas to save the rest of their people from suffering and destruction. Taken west to Oregon City, they were given the formality of a trial and hanged in mid-1850.

Joseph Meek, the United States marshal, used his Indian hatchet to cut the rope and drop the five Cayuses to their death. The former mountain man never forgave the Cayuses when his daughter Helen sickened and died following the massacre. It was Meek who had carried news of the tragedy and petitions from Willamette Valley settlers to Washington, D.C., in 1848, a move that spurred Congress to create the territory of Oregon, the first territorial government west of the Rocky Mountains.

After the massacre, Spalding settled in the Willamette Valley where he became a farmer and Indian agent before returning to Lapwai as a teacher in 1863. He resumed his missionary work following reappointment by the American Board eight years later.

Until his death in 1874, Spalding carried in his mind the notion that rival Catholic missionaries had masterminded the Cayuse attack on the Protestant Whitmans. From the time he reached the safety of the Willamette

Valley, he thundered against the murderous conspiracy hatched by the Roman Catholic hierarchy and the Hudson's Bay Company, and he so fanned the flames of religious prejudice that Catholics feared that their churches and schools in the region would be burned. So insistent were Spalding's accusations that even some of his fellow Protestants thought he was insane. When Eliza Spalding died in 1851, he had carved on her headstone: "She always felt that the Jesuit Missionaries were the leading cause of the massacre."

Ironically, the first outsider to reach Waiilatpu after the massacre was a Catholic priest, J. B. A. Brouillet, who performed the burial service. Considering the bloody circumstances, it was the decent and honorable thing to do, but Spalding never forgave him.

The tragic story of the Whitmans eventually generated an enormous body of writing that has nearly overshadowed the rest of Pacific Northwest history, transformed Marcus and Narcissa from well-meaning missionaries into long-suffering and sacrificing saints, and for years sustained the legend that Marcus Whitman saved Oregon. Despite these excesses, the episode highlights several significant features of the region's pioneer era. It vividly illustrates the potential for conflict, cultural and otherwise, between white settlers and native peoples, and between missionaries of differing faiths and backgrounds.

The Whitman story reveals, too, an inevitable tension between the missionary ideal of saving Indian souls for the heavenly promised land and the day-to-day reality of providing sustenance to white newcomers and even fostering their settlement of the earthly promised land in Oregon. In the latter work, the Whitmans, Spaldings, and their associates were far more successful than in the former. During the eleven years preceding the massacre, only twenty-two natives had been accepted into the First Presbyterian Church of Oregon. During that same time the Whitman mission served as an important beacon guiding several thousand emigrant whites bound for fertile lands in the Willamette Valley.

Today Waiilatpu is the Whitman Mission National Historic Site, and Lapwai is part of the Nez Perce National Historical Park. Honoring the Whitman name are a liberal arts college in Walla Walla and Washington's leading wheat-producing county. The term Cayuse is seldom heard, however. Tribal descendents have been incorporated into the Confederated Tribes of the Umatilla comprising the Umatillas, Cayuses, and Walla Wallas who live on a small reservation east of Pendleton, Oregon.

CHAPTER 5

Bound for the Promised Land

*

It is a great undertaking to leave comfortable homes for greater advantages than our State possesses, in Oregon. There is a toilsome journey before them. Long and tiresome it will be. True there will be many circumstances that will render portions of it interesting; still it will be tiresome and at times must come among the emigrants feelings of anxiety for the end.
—*David Newsom: The Western Observer, 1805–1882* (from his comments for April 3, 1851)

*

A major stimulus to missionary activity in the Pacific Northwest was the practice of some Indian tribes of flattening their babies' foreheads. And therein lies a mystery. Why did the practice evoke a powerful response only in the 1830s? Euro-Americans had known about it for years. Lewis and Clark described forehead flattening among the Chinook people of the lower Columbia River in 1805–1806. What new set of circumstances aroused the missionary impulse among Euro-Americans thirty years later?

One factor was growing popular enthusiasm for the Oregon country. Hall Jackson Kelley, a well-educated New England schoolteacher, became obsessed with colonizing the remote region with white settlements, and by the 1820s he was the leading advocate of immigration. To his single-minded crusade he sacrificed home, family, and position. Kelley was initially little more than an armchair theorist because he knew of Oregon only through reading the journals of Lewis and Clark and talking to seamen and hunters. But that did not stop him from extolling its virtues in countless speeches, pamphlets, circulars, and petitions.

In a memorial to Congress in 1828, Kelley described Oregon as "the most valuable of all the unoccupied parts of the earth." The following year he organized the American Society for Encouraging the Settlement of the Oregon Territory, but his plan to lead a party of settlers to Oregon soon collapsed. Undiscouraged, Kelley remained an Oregon booster until the 1850s, but only once, in 1832, did he actually visit his promised land. After an adventure-filled overland trek that took him across Mexico and through California to Fort Vancouver, the Hudson's Bay Company gave him a reception that could best be described as frigid: he was mistaken for a horse thief wanted in California. The conviction that the Hudson's Bay Company persecuted him only heightened his interest in wresting the lands of the Pacific Northwest from Britain.

Nathaniel Wyeth, another New Englander and would-be fur entrepreneur who founded Fort Hall on the Snake River, led colonizing experiments in 1832 and 1834. His activities interested Americans in the continent's far corner by popularizing a route later christened the Oregon Trail and by taking the first American missionaries and scientists to the region. The Virginia congressman John Floyd spoke eloquently of Oregon though he had never been there. The same was true of Senators Thomas Hart Benton and Lewis F. Linn of Missouri, who kindled further interest in the region. Collectively, Oregon's boosters were responsible for a flood of books, newspapers, and lectures that portrayed the region as paradise on earth. There were skeptics, of course, but their words of caution were not compelling to most Americans.

Coinciding with the promotional enthusiasm—"Oregon fever"—was a quickening of the Protestant conscience as a result of the revivalism promoted by Charles G. Finney and other evangelists beginning in the mid-1820s. An incident that occurred in 1831 provided the specific impetus to missionary activity in the far Northwest: an Indian delegation consisting of three Nez Percés and one Flathead journeyed to Saint Louis seeking William Clark, superintendent of Indian affairs and a tribal hero since the days of the Lewis and Clark expedition. Conversing only in sign language, they requested the "book" and the "black robes" for their people. They may have meant the Holy Bible and the Jesuits, but it is equally possible that they wanted a portion of the white man's power that appeared to reside in his printing and religion.

Christianity was certainly not new to the Pacific Northwest. Roman Catholic voyageurs from Quebec pursued the fur trade among the region's Indians, and some married native women. In this way they transmitted elements of Christianity to the Indians. The Hudson's Bay Company in

1825 sent the sons of Spokane and Kutenai leaders to an Anglican mission school at the settlement of Red River in present Manitoba. Their return four years later encouraged other Indian fathers to send their sons away to pursue similar courses of study. Best known of the mission-educated young men was Spokan Garry, who, armed with a King James Bible and an Anglican Book of Common Prayer, ministered to the Indians of the plateau. Influenced by Flathead contacts, the Nez Percés were curious enough—or impressed enough by the possibility of tapping into a source of the whites' power—to send representatives to Saint Louis to learn more.

Word of their arrival spread from pulpit to pulpit, accompanied in the Methodist *Christian Advocate and Journal* by a drawing of one Indian's profile, his malformed forehead sloping back from his eyebrows to a peak above his ears. All of this electrified the Protestant world, which remained blissfully ignorant of the fact that the heads of the Indians who visited Saint Louis were shaped normally. When the call went forth for all good Protestants to help the poor, misguided, deformed Indians, the response was immediate.

THE MISSIONARY ERA

First to answer the prickings of conscience was Jason Lee, a young Methodist minister. Fortunately for Lee, Nathaniel Wyeth had returned to Boston with two Indians, one of whom was a Nez Percé with a congenitally malformed head. Wyeth did not disabuse Lee of his belief that the native was a genuine Flathead, and in fact Wyeth allowed Lee to display the two Indians at fund-raising meetings throughout the East.

Jason Lee, his nephew Daniel, and a few associates traveled overland to Oregon with Wyeth and his party in 1834. When they arrived at Fort Vancouver, the missionaries took John McLoughlin's advice to remain in the Willamette Valley instead of traveling to the remote and wild country of the Flatheads in western Montana, their original destination. With McLoughlin's help, Lee established his mission on the banks of the Willamette River about 20 miles north of present Salem. The site was near French Prairie, a small settlement of French Canadians, many with Indian wives, who had retired to agricultural pursuits after serving the Hudson's Bay Company.

The Indians of the Willamette Valley, including some Chinooks with deformed heads, were broken and dispirited as a result of the great malaria epidemic of 1829–33. Lewis and Clark had estimated their number at ten thousand, but disease had reduced them to a mere fragment by the 1830s.

Lee did his best for them—maintaining a mission school and conducting religious services—but he gave most of his attention to letters and trips to the East extolling the new promised land and further fanning the flames of Oregon fever. He returned from the East Coast in 1840 with a shipload of fifty-one New Englanders—called the Great Reinforcement—and used funds from church donations to help establish pioneer settlements at The Dalles and other locations. In that way Lee succeeded in creating a modest American counterpresence to the Hudson's Bay Company, which, ironically, had encouraged him in the first place. The Methodist's Mission Society in New York dismissed Lee in 1844 on the grounds that his efforts had grown too secular.

The second major Protestant venture in the Pacific Northwest commenced in 1836 when the American Board of Commissioners for Foreign Missions, an ecumenical coordinating body for Congregationalist, Presbyterian, and Dutch Reformed believers, sponsored the Whitman and Spalding party. The American Board operated a mission called Tsimakain among the Spokans. It was headed by Elkanah and Mary Walker and Cushing and Myra Eells, New England Congregationalists who lived there from 1839 to 1848. A fourth American Board mission operated from 1839 to 1841 among the Nez Percés at Kamiah, fifty miles up the Clearwater River from Lapwai.

Like Lee's activity in the Willamette Valley, the work of the Whitmans, Spaldings, Walkers, and Eellses was replete with irony. While seeking to help Indians develop what Euro-Americans regarded as a better way of life, the missions divided native peoples into Christian and non-Christian factions, and the coming of white settlers brought disease and ultimately disruption to the lives of Indians living near the missions.

The era of Roman Catholic missions in the Pacific Northwest dates from 1838 when two Franciscan priests from Canada, Francis Norbert Blanchet and Modeste Demers, responded to a call from French-Canadian employees of the Hudson's Bay Company who had retired to farms along the Willamette River. The Hudson's Bay Company supplied canoes and provisions to Blanchet and Demers during the long and difficult overland journey. The bishop of Quebec instructed them "to regain from barbarism and its disorders, the savage tribes scattered over that country" and to extend their help "to the poor Christians who have adopted the customs of the savages and live in license and forgetfulness of their duties."

Blanchet and Demers established the first Roman Catholic mission in the Pacific Northwest on the Cowlitz River north of Fort Vancouver, and

12. Tshimakain, the American Board mission in the Spokane country, was sketched by Karl Geyer, a German botanist who visited the post in the winter of 1843–44. Courtesy Historical Photograph Collection, Washington State University Libraries: 70–0401.

another on the Willamette not far from Jason Lee's post. Unlike the Protestants, the priests did not bring wives or families with them, nor did they have an interest in fostering settlement.

Roman Catholic missions continued with Pierre Jean De Smet, a Jesuit missionary from Belgium, who journeyed from Saint Louis to the Oregon country in 1840 with an American fur trading caravan. A year later he founded Saint Mary's Mission among the Flathead people. During the next six years, De Smet and his fellow Jesuits Anthony Ravalli, Nicholas Point, and others established several missions including the Sacred Heart Mission among the Coeur d'Alenes.

A man of charm and unusual endurance, De Smet became a skilled negotiator between Indians and whites as well as a tireless advocate of missionary activity. During his lifetime he supposedly traveled 180,000 miles, making sixteen trips to Europe to promote Indian missions.

These outposts of Christianity existed for varying lengths of time at more than thirty sites in the early Pacific Northwest. There were six Methodist mission sites, four American Board, some two dozen Roman Catholic, and one Mormon (Church of Jesus Christ of Latter-day Saints). The latter, named Fort Limhi (usually misspelled Lemhi) after a king in the Book of Mormon, was established in 1855 on a remote fork of the Salmon River by twenty-seven missionaries who journeyed north from Salt Lake City in response to a call from Brigham Young. The Salmon River mission was not a success and was abandoned three years later during a time of tension and violence between Mormons and Indians and the United States Army.

Catholics and Protestants have historically differed on many tenets of Christian faith, even as Protestant denominations and sects differed among themselves. The Methodists, for example, resented the intrusion of other Protestants into their Northwest domain, but Protestants were of like mind in believing that Roman Catholic popery represented the greatest of dangers. Members of one Catholic order, the Jesuits, appeared especially sinister to Protestants, who shuddered at tales of Jesuit plots and intrigue. A literature of horror arose to exploit that fear—much as happened during other eras when Americans developed exaggerated fears of organizations and beliefs that they did not understand.

13. The Coeur d'Alene or Cataldo Mission as it appeared in 1884. It is currently Idaho's oldest standing building. Courtesy Montana Historical Society: Photo by F. Jay Haynes, H-1392.

83

Catholics in turn were suspicious of Protestants, believing that, while they pretended to spread their faith, their true mission was to foster trade and commerce. Catholics feared that the Protestants' authoritarian approach toward Indians, particularly their lack of sensitivity to native cultures, fostered conflict between Euro-Americans and Indians. Protestants responded that Catholic accommodation to native traditions like polygamy and shamanism showed too great a willingness to compromise with sin in all its blackness. They feared, too, that Jesuits encouraged Indians to massacre Protestants. This conviction haunted the mind of Henry Spalding after the Whitman massacre, and Protestants frequently accused Jesuits of masterminding the subsequent Indian wars in the interior Northwest. Indians, not surprisingly, factionalized into Christians and traditionalists, Protestants and Catholics.

The heyday of the mission era lasted not even two decades (1834–48) and merged into the advent of pioneer settlers moving overland to Oregon. In the work of Christianizing Indians, the missionary record was at best mixed. The missionaries' ideals were lofty, their motivation generally sprang from the best of human qualities, but in too many cases the results of their effort reflected an inability to surmount cultural and religious biases. Despite such failings, the missionary era did much to shape the course of pioneer settlement that followed.

THE WAY WEST

The Oregon Trail resulted from the fortuitous discoveries of Robert Stuart's returning Astorians in 1812 and of the mountain man Jedediah Smith, who after 1824 publicized South Pass (in future Wyoming) as an easy crossing of the Rockies. Narcissa Whitman and Eliza Spalding's journey in 1836 provided a precedent for family travel over the trail. Their party proved that wheeled vehicles could go as far west as Fort Boise; others subsequently drove their wagons all the way to the Columbia River and beyond.

The Oregon Trail extended to the Willamette Valley from several jumping-off places along the Missouri River—the favorite prior to 1850 being Independence, Missouri, located on the river's great bend near present Kansas City. Council Bluffs, Iowa, became a favorite starting place after 1850. On a map the trail resembled a badly frayed rope, with strands originating in several locations and alternate routes unraveling at intervals. Winding across future Wyoming and Idaho, the Oregon Trail traversed some of the most inhospitable terrain in North America. Until the building

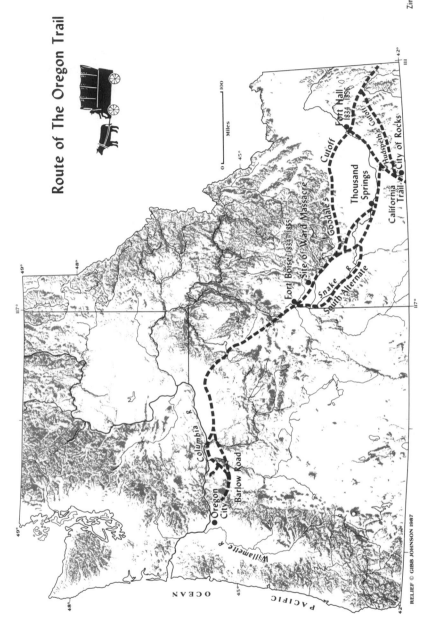

Route of The Oregon Trail

Miles

0   100

Fort Hall
1834-1856

Hudspeth Cutoff

California Trail

City of Rocks

Thousand
Springs

Cutoff

Goodale's

Site of Ward Massacre
1834-1855

Fort Boise 1834-1855

Snake
&
South Alternate

Columbia R.

Barlow Road

Oregon
City

Willamette R.

PACIFIC

OCEAN

Zimmerly

RELIEF © GIBB JOHNSON 1987

of Fort Hall in 1834, there was not so much as a cabin along the route, and even ten years later the situation had improved only slightly. The two thousand–mile trek to Oregon represented the longest overland journey that American settlers attempted.

The first family to move to Oregon for the expressed purpose of establishing a home arrived in 1840. The party used wagons as far west as Fort Hall. A larger group of twenty-four headed west from Independence in 1841. That same year the Bartleson-Bidwell company became the first party of emigrants to trace the overland route to California.

More than a hundred persons and eighteen wagons rolled west in 1842 under the guidance of Dr. Elijah White, a former Methodist missionary assigned as an Indian subagent for Oregon. The White party was the first to form a typical wagon train in which families predominated. That year thus marked the beginning of the familiar saga of covered wagon migration to Oregon. The White party also brought Marcus Whitman the news that the American Board planned to abandon the mission at Waiilatpu. After his famous winter ride east, Whitman returned to Oregon in 1843 with the largest party of emigrants to that time. That group was also the first to get its wagons intact to the Columbia River. Called the Great Migration, it consisted of nearly nine hundred emigrants in a hundred wagons accompanied by as many as seven hundred head of oxen and cattle.

The number of emigrants journeying overland to Oregon in 1844 reached nearly fifteen hundred, and the following year grew to twenty-five hundred. Those pioneers traveled not in one great caravan but in several smaller groups, departing at intervals sufficient to allow the native grasses along the route to replenish themselves. Migration became an annual event, with an estimated four thousand emigrants heading west along the trail in 1847. Between 1840 and 1860, some fifty-three thousand people completed the journey from jumping-off points along the Missouri River to Oregon.

The Oregon Trail remained the major highway to the Pacific Northwest until a railroad line paralleling its route through southern Idaho was completed in 1884. The trail also served for cattle and sheep drives east. Not all Oregon pioneers arrived by way of the trail, however. Some came by ship, enduring a six-month voyage from the East Coast around Cape Horn.

LIFE ON THE OREGON TRAIL

During the early years a typical overland journey required seven months. Starting in April, emigrants made their way west from the Missouri Valley

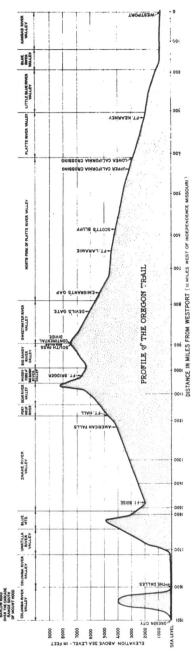

14. A profile of elevation on the Oregon Trail. Courtesy
University of Washington Libraries: UW Neg. 6356.

across the lush grasses of the Great Plains. At the Platte River, they traveled upstream until the river forked to become the North Platte and then the Sweetwater. Beyond South Pass they continued to the Green River, then west to the Hudson's Bay Company oasis at Fort Hall. From there Oregon-bound travelers crossed the Snake River plain to the Hudson Bay Company's Fort Boise, then on to the Grande Ronde Valley, the Blue Mountains, and the Whitman mission. Finally, they followed the south bank of the Columbia River to the Dalles. From that point they usually portaged downriver to the Willamette Valley, reaching their destination in October.

The emigrants timed their departure from the Missouri Valley so that livestock could feed off the lush grasslands of the Great Plains at their peak. Compared to what followed, the physical obstacles posed by the Great Plains proved relatively unimportant; the main dangers were thunderstorms, flooded rivers, and quicksand. A far more difficult obstacle was the Snake River plain. Immigrant parties reached there during the hottest part of summer, having already endured nearly thirteen hundred miles on the trail. Animals were tired and thirsty, but the cool waters of the Snake River lay far below the canyon's rim, so tantalizing and yet so impossible to reach. Moreover, the sharp-edged basalt lacerated the hooves of draft animals. No emigrant considered settling the semiarid, sagebrush-covered plains of southern Idaho until irrigation later transformed the land. Another obstacle was the Blue Mountains, where emigrants were forced to winch their wagons up and down steep slopes by means of ropes and pulleys.

A final difficulty lay at the very edge of the promised land. In the shadow of Mount Hood, where the Columbia River had cut a deep gorge through the Cascade mountains—and where today's motorist speeds along an interstate highway blasted from cliffs that crowd the water's edge—pioneers were obliged to take to the water in crude, poorly constructed rafts and barges to complete the eighty-mile trip from the Dalles to the Willamette Valley. For unskilled navigators, the raft journey through the Columbia's turbulent waters was exceedingly dangerous. Rafts often disintegrated in midstream or became engulfed in giant whirlpools. The loss of goods or life was always tragic, but especially so near the destination. In 1846 a welcomed but crude and expensive alternative to the river was Sam Barlow's toll road, which ran eighty-five miles from The Dalles along the southern slope of Mount Hood to Oregon City in the Willamette Valley. Travelers paid tolls of five dollars per wagon and one dollar for each head of livestock. For all who completed the great trek to Oregon, it was an experience they never forgot and quite unlike anything they had done before or would likely do again.

Emigrant trains represented temporary communities on the trail. Members organized themselves into semimilitary units and elected slates of officers. The earlier in the history of the trail the migration occurred, the more complex the organization might be.

Once they left Missouri or Iowa, emigrants were beyond the pale of law; hence, they usually adopted rules and regulations specifying punishments for crime. One code decreed that every man was to carry a Bible and other religious books with him, "as we hope not to degenerate into a state of barbarism." Harmony was the ideal, but tension and friction inevitably arose, sometimes necessitating reorganization or division of the train into several parties.

The chief expense of getting to Oregon was transportation—oxen, wagon, and gear—which cost close to $400. Wagons had to be constructed with great care to endure the rigors of the trail. Only well-seasoned hardwood could withstand great extremes of temperature and humidity. After packing the bare essentials into a four-by-ten-foot wagon, pioneers added their farm implements. Any leftover space might contain a few books, some extra clothing, or a little furniture. But the total must not weigh too much, because it was foolhardy to overburden and exhaust the team of six mules or four yoke of oxen upon which survival depended.

Men and women shared responsibilities on the trail. Men usually drove, although one traveler recalled meeting a train of eleven wagons in 1852 all driven by women. As a result of a cholera epidemic, not a single male had remained alive in the entire train. Overlanders averaged about fifteen miles a day. Sometimes they arranged their wagons in parallel fashion so as to travel relatively free of the dust of those ahead, or they might rotate their positions in line. At night, they arranged their wagons in a circle to form a temporary fort and corral for the animals.

Indian attack was an overlander's primary fear, yet in actuality it seldom occurred. The majority of early travelers saw few Indians and, in the 1850s and 1860s, could take some comfort from the forts that the War Department built along the trail. Only in the mid-1850s, when Indians began to worry about encroachments on their lands, did they become hostile and aggressive, especially in the region beyond South Pass. Even so, most immigrants got to Oregon with little or no difficulty with Indians. Statistics indicate that the most likely site for an Indian attack was on the Snake River plain. Here some bloody massacres were recorded, one of the worst being the massacre of the Alexander Ward party on the Boise River in 1854. Only two young boys survived out of a party of twenty overlanders. The last major conflict with Indians on the trail occurred in 1862.

Not all Indian attacks were what they were purported to be. White highwaymen masquerading as Indians occasionally preyed on overlanders. Thievery and not murder constituted the major threat posed by Indians. And counterbalancing this picture were numerous cases in which Indians provided Oregon-bound pioneers with information, food, equipment, horses, survival skills, and other forms of assistance.

As encounters with Indians suggest, the Oregon Trail experience changed over time. The trail itself evolved, so that the experience for travelers headed west in 1845 was not exactly the same as for those who followed a decade later. The way west was never easy, but as new cutoffs were discovered and developed, the average number of days required to make the journey decreased, from 169.1 during the years 1841–48 to 128.5 during the 1850s. In the early years, parties employed special guides. Later groups seldom required their services because the way to Oregon had become so well known. By the 1850s, as private trading posts and army forts sprang up alongside the trail, talk of leaving civilization behind to go west was no longer appropriate.

After 1848 the character of travel east of Fort Hall changed, too, with the addition of many gold seekers bound for California. Emigrants to California and Oregon followed the same route to Fort Hall. Beyond there, the California trail branched to the southwest. A common belief among Oregon pioneers was that the less respectable overlanders sought quick fortune in the goldfields of California, while conservative, orderly, family-oriented folk sought Oregon. That feeling was clearly captured in an Oregon anecdote about a fork in the trail where "a pile of gold-bearing quartz marked the road to California; the other road had a sign bearing the words 'To Oregon.' Those who could read took the trail to Oregon." Whether the anecdote is true or not, clearly the society that developed in the Willamette Valley after the 1840s was different from that in California. The agrarian, family-oriented values that the firstcomers brought with them to Oregon were communicated to potential settlers through letters and pamphlets, and those who were attracted by such things tended to reinforce the community's values.

Why did people undertake the long overland journey to Oregon? Their motives were varied, and no doubt many emigrants would have been hard pressed to explain their real reasons for moving west. Some hoped to improve their health; others relished the challenge and excitement of starting a new life out West or wanted simply to escape the virulent passions that surrounded the issues of race and slavery. Record-setting floods in Missouri, Iowa, and Illinois in 1836, 1844, and 1849 inundated and destroyed farms,

15. Fort Hall as it appeared ca. 1849. Courtesy Idaho
State Historical Society: 1254 C.

and the receding waters left sickness in their wake, causing desperate people to seek alternatives.

Standing out most clearly was the desire for economic improvement. In an agrarian society that measured wealth in terms of landholdings, the belief that Oregon contained an abundance of fertile land easily acquired under federal laws was compelling, especially after the panic of 1837 caused many midwestern farmers to sink hopelessly into debt. For whatever the reason, many of the Oregon-bound pioneers were impoverished farmers from the Mississippi Valley, and predominating in the 1840s migrations were Missourians.

PIONEER SETTLEMENT

For many an overlander, that first year in Oregon proved nearly as difficult as life on the trail. Very few of the early emigrants were rich, and many arrived in extreme poverty, having lost their belongings to the remorseless Columbia River. To survive the first winter, they purchased goods on credit from the Hudson's Bay Company or sought temporary employment in one of its many enterprises. People already in residence aided the newcomers, partly because of a genuine desire to assist and partly because they realized that good public order depended on their charity. As for shelter that first winter, newcomers lodged in the homes of relatives or friends or resorted to

16. Erecting a log cabin in rural Idaho. Courtesy Idaho
State Historical Society: 60–72.43.

bunking in local schools and meeting houses. For some pioneers, only a cold, damp campsite in the open was available.

Willamette Valley settlers hastened to lay the foundations for economic survival and growth. As early as 1846 their valley produced 160,000 bushels of wheat. In that grain the pioneers discovered a good "poor man's crop" that required little operating capital and usually returned a good profit from the first year. Indeed, wheat was the only major crop durable enough to be sold outside the West Coast before refrigerated railroad cars, in the late 1880s, made it possible to ship fruit to the East.

The discovery of gold in California in 1848 attracted some adventurers from the Willamette Valley to the diggings; at the same time, the new California market stimulated commercial agriculture in the Pacific Northwest. The price of wheat climbed from one dollar to six dollars a bushel, and a steady stream of ships sailed up the Columbia River to load wheat for California. Oregon in 1850 produced a total of 208,000 bushels of wheat, mostly in the Willamette Valley. Farmers were not the only ones to benefit from the region's first economic boom; operators of flour mills and sawmills, tradesmen, and professionals prospered as well.

Oregon City in 1844 became the first incorporated American municipality west of the Rocky Mountains. Located at the falls of the Willamette a few miles upriver from present-day Portland, Oregon City was the capital of

Oregon Territory from 1849 to 1852. It became Oregon's largest settlement by 1850, when its 933 residents accounted for almost one-tenth of the territory's population. Blessed with a growing population and abundant water power to run its two flour mills and five sawmills, Oregon City seemed to have prosperity assured. But Portland soon overshadowed it.

Portland was situated near the confluence of the Willamette and Columbia rivers and enjoyed a favorable location during an age when commerce moved by river and ocean. Its wharves formed the heart of an expanding commercial network that extended along waterways and trails far into the interior and up the Willamette Valley. The city's trade ultimately extended to San Francisco and the world beyond. In its first decade, Portland established itself as Oregon's center of commerce and population and the capital of the Northwest hinterland.

Portland's early control of the region's economic lifelines gave the growing city an advantage it maintained even after the arrival of railroads and the growth of population centers in Idaho's mining regions and on Puget Sound.

17. Front Street south of Morrison in Portland in 1852.
Courtesy Oregon Historical Society: 5490.

93

Only Seattle, which got off to a slow start in 1852, eventually surpassed Portland in population and in regional importance—although the latter assertion remains a matter of heated debate and the basis for an ongoing urban rivalry.

Even as emigrants perfected techniques of overland travel and planted communities in the Oregon country, a pressing need arose to clarify matters of law and government. Early land claimants in the Willamette Valley wanted to protect their property, and by the mid-1840s there was an equally pressing need to define the international boundary between British and American territory in the Pacific Northwest.

CHAPTER 6

Rearranging the Political Landscape, 1843-1868

Already we are sending numerous emigrants every year across the Rocky mountains; and we are sending them there without the protection of law, and without the restraints of civil government. We have left them, hitherto, to the unlimited control of their own passions. We must send them laws and a regular form of government.—Senator James Buchanan of Pennsylvania, Speech, March 12, 1844

Some of the most profound changes in Pacific Northwest history occurred during the 1840s. When the decade dawned, the Oregon country had no political boundaries and no effective government apart from the influence of Hudson's Bay Company officials and the American missionaries. Ten years later, an international boundary divided the country along the 49th parallel, and the Hudson's Bay Company had shifted its main operation to the British side of the border. Chief Factor John McLoughlin, long-time patriarch of the Oregon country, retired in early 1846 to land he owned near Oregon City, and three years later, the Hudson's Bay Company moved its departmental headquarters north to Fort Victoria on Vancouver Island.

Thousands of land-hungry settlers supplanted fur traders and missionaries as the most representative non-Indian group in the new Northwest. They brought permanent changes to the Willamette Valley and other areas when they laid out farms, towns, and a network of roads. They organized a government for themselves in 1843, and five years later pressured Congress into creating the Oregon Territory. Finally, the Whitman massacre of 1847

95

initiated a change that no one wanted, three decades of periodic warfare between Indians and whites; those conflicts, too, contributed to rearranging the region's political landscape.

GRASS-ROOTS GOVERNMENT

In 1818 and again in 1827, Great Britain and the United States agreed to occupy the Oregon country jointly. As a result of that unusual arrangement, British residents were subject to the authority of the Hudson's Bay Company, the agent officially responsible for enforcing British civil and criminal law in several remote parts of North America. In cases of criminal misconduct, the accused were transported to the nearest permanent British settlement for trial in a regular court. The company ruled effectively, for there was no legacy of western badmen and outlaws in its domain.

By contrast, the Americans in the Oregon country were beyond the limits of the United States government and its laws. Moreover, Congress, having more important concerns, seemed in no hurry to remedy that arrangement despite settlers' petitions urging establishment of a territory there to protect property and insure public morality. The alternative—submission to Hudson's Bay Company rule—was anathema to a people who often perceived the British enterprise as a grasping monopolistic octopus. The American settlers debated whether it would be better to form an independent government or wait until the United States acted.

For Americans, in other words, settlement preceded establishment of effective government. When only a handful of non-Indians lived in the Oregon country, government was of little consequence. But new circumstances arising in the early 1840s forced pioneers to fashion a government for themselves. Following a time-honored American tradition of compact writing and constitution making, early Oregonians simply took matters of law and order into their own hands.

The process of creating a government and laws took place over a period of several months and initially amounted to nothing more than a series of ad hoc responses to specific problems that confronted pioneers. First they faced a legal dilemma: Ewing Young, a trapper and cattleman who had amassed a substantial estate in the Willamette Valley, died without leaving a will or apparent heirs. To dispose of his property, a committee of settlers met at Champoeg on the banks of the Willamette River on three separate occasions in 1841. They appointed a missionary, Ira Babcock, as temporary judge to probate Young's estate using New York laws as a model.

The settlers took another halting step toward creation of a full-fledged government in February and March 1843 when they met to discuss wild animal attacks on their livestock. They established an executive committee to administer a rudimentary system of tax collection and disburse funds for a wolf bounty. The so-called wolf meetings are credited with setting the stage for the formal creation of a provisional government.

Approximately one hundred American and French-Canadian settlers met at Champoeg in May 1843 "to take into consideration the propriety for taking measures for civil and military protection of this colony." By a slender majority they voted to organize a provisional government. Most French Canadians dissented for fear that organization was but a step toward incorporation into American territory, and McLoughlin refused to recognize the new government's legitimacy, thus heightening anti-British, anti–Hudson's Bay Company sentiment in the American community.

The homespun government that Americans fashioned during the spring and summer of 1843 was a patchwork that embodied familiar traditions and materials readily at hand. Working from the one law book in their possession, *Organic Laws of the State of Iowa*, which in addition to Iowa laws contained a trilogy of hallowed documents—the Declaration of Independence, the Constitution, and the Northwest Ordinance of 1787—settlers framed a constitution that provided for an executive committee of three men and a system of voluntary taxation. The following summer, when a wave of newcomers made its influence felt, settlers revised the constitution to provide a single executive and compulsory taxation. They also prohibited alcoholic beverages and excluded black settlers. Despite its obvious shortcomings, Oregon's grass-roots government lasted until Congress approved a territorial government in 1848.

MANIFEST DESTINY: DIVIDING THE OREGON COUNTRY

Even as Oregon pioneers fashioned their provisional government, they weighed momentous changes of another sort. During the mid-1840s an expansionist mood termed Manifest Destiny gripped the United States as never before. An influential and growing number of citizens asserted that it was the nation's God-given destiny to expand to the limits of the continent. The Democratic party nominated James K. Polk as president in 1844 on an expansionist platform calling for the "re-annexation of Texas and the re-occupation of Oregon"—not just the Willamette Valley but the entire Oregon country, in defiance of British counterclaims. A year later American expansionists took up the cry, "Fifty-four Forty or Fight," a provocative reference to the northernmost boundary of the disputed territory. The Pacific Northwest soon occupied center stage in a complex diplomatic drama, the outcome of which was by no means certain.

For three decades—from the end of the War of 1812 to the conclusion of the Oregon Treaty in 1846—American opinion remained divided on the worth of the far Northwest. Counterbalancing the rhapsodies of Thomas Hart Benton, Hall Jackson Kelley, and other Oregon boosters were the assertions of skeptics and naysayers, like the New York newspaper that described the hinterland as fit only for a penal colony.

On several occasions during the era of joint occupation, United States and British negotiators considered ways to divide the Oregon country. But it was not until Polk became president that anything decisive happened. In his inaugural address in 1845, he declared that American title to Oregon was "clear and unquestionable." A few months later, however, Polk proposed to the British that Oregon be divided at the forty-ninth parallel, a location American negotiators had favored in earlier talks. When the British declined to accept that boundary, the president resumed his belligerent stance. He informed Congress that he was no longer willing to compromise and asserted that both national honor and interest were at stake in Oregon.

Only the most ardent expansionists seriously believed that the United States had a legitimate claim to the entire Oregon country. In the Willamette Valley and other lands south of the Columbia River, Americans predominated by virtue of occupation, but north of the Columbia, their presence was negligible. In that area lived hundreds of Hudson's Bay Company employees and their families, all British subjects, but only a handful of United States citizens. Still farther north—in the area between the forty-ninth parallel and the 54°40' line—there were no Americans. Thus, the focal point of the dispute was the territory north and west of the Columbia River, which forms the present state of Washington.

According to the historian Norman Graebner, the United States was unyielding in its claims to the Puget Sound country because the nation was actually battling for a commercial position on the Pacific coast. Unlike the Atlantic seaboard, the Pacific Coast from Baja California to the Strait of Juan de Fuca lacked good harbors. California was still part of Mexico, and a dangerous sandbar diminished the commercial value of the Columbia River mouth. Only Puget Sound, therefore, offered the United States a gateway to the Pacific and the ports of Asia. For reasons of commerce and the less tangible matters of national pride and destiny, the United States stubbornly

---

THE WILKES EXPEDITION

From 1838 to 1842 the United States Exploring Expedition, or Wilkes expedition, made a voyage of discovery around the world. The ships arrived off the coast of Oregon in 1841. Lieutenant Charles Wilkes and the expedition crew members named more than 250 landmarks in what is now Washington. From lower Puget Sound, survey groups and scientists explored and mapped the interior of the Oregon country.

While on a mission to explore the Columbia River, the *Peacock* ran afoul of the notorious bar at the mouth and sank. When Wilkes was able to report to Congress on his discoveries, the fate of the *Peacock* dramatized the importance of Puget Sound as the only truly valuable harbor in the region. "Mere description," recalled Wilkes, "can give little idea of the terrors of the bar of the Columbia"; on the other hand, he lauded the beauty and safety of Puget Sound waters. Because of its reconnaissance, the Wilkes expedition played an important role in the final determination of the international boundary.

---

maintained its claim to Puget Sound despite the modest number of its citizens north of the Columbia River.

Congressional debate on the boundary issue dragged on until the spring of 1846, when the United States invited Great Britain to reopen negotiations. At that time a cabinet crisis and other internal problems bedeviled the British. Moreover, it no longer seemed vital to retain the lower Columbia River in order to protect Hudson's Bay Company interests because in 1845 the company had announced plans to move its regional headquarters to Vancouver Island. As a result of those developments, the British government was in a far more conciliatory mood than earlier.

In the end, Polk got less than he publicly demanded but avoided serious trouble with Britain at a time when the United States was edging toward war with Mexico. The Senate ratified the treaty in June 1846: the agreement divided the Oregon country by extending the international boundary along the forty-ninth parallel from the crest of the Rocky Mountains to the middle of the Strait of Georgia. From there the line dipped south and west through the Strait of Juan de Fuca to leave southern Vancouver Island and Fort Victoria in British hands. The Hudson's Bay Company retained the right to navigate the Columbia River south of the forty-ninth parallel until 1860, and it was promised protection for its posts and lands in American territory.

Thomas Hart Benton no doubt spoke for many Oregon boosters when he predicted that the commercial advantages of the settlement "will be greater—far greater than any equal portion of the Atlantic States." Only the matter of a poorly defined water boundary south of Vancouver Island caused further trouble between the United States and Great Britain. The so-called Pig War, an incident of comic opera proportions, erupted in 1859 on tiny San Juan Island, one of several islands claimed by both countries. At issue was a pig belonging to an employee of the Hudson's Bay Company that had strayed into an American's potato patch and was shot. That unneighborly display touched off a noisy dispute between British and American residents and elicited some posturing by troops from both nations. Fortunately, common sense prevailed, and the fifty-six-square-mile island remained under joint military occupation until arbitration by the emperor of Germany finally fixed the international boundary in 1872. The settlement gave the United States title to the contested islands.

OREGON: FROM TERRITORY TO STATE

The formal settlement of the boundary issue had little immediate impact on Americans living in Oregon. Until the Whitman massacre of late 1847 dramatized their isolation, they continued to be treated as Uncle Sam's stepchildren. After the Whitman incident, the provisional government sent the former mountain man Joseph Meek to plead its case in the national capital. Arriving in Saint Louis in May 1848 after crossing half a continent in the dead of winter, he announced himself as "Envoy Extraordinary and Minister Plenipotentiary from the Republic of Oregon to the Court of the United States." Newspapers played up Meek's dramatic odyssey and helped publicize the cause he represented; some even suggested that, had the federal government done its duty in Oregon, the massacre might never have occurred.

Congress created the territory of Oregon the following August. President Polk named Meek—who also happened to be a relative of the president's wife—marshal and Joseph Lane of Indiana, a loyal Democrat and a hero of the Mexican war, governor of the new territory. Traveling by sea the pair arrived in Oregon on March 2, 1849, and with appropriate fanfare, Lane proclaimed the existence of a new territory the following day. A few months later, United States Army troops established bases alongside the Hudson's Bay Company posts at Fort Vancouver and Fort Nisqually, and United States mail service began.

Oregonians soon realized that territorial status was not all they hoped it would be. The proud framers of their own government and laws now found

18. Joseph Lane (1801–81), first governor of Oregon
Territory, 1849–50. Courtesy Oregon Historical
Society: 891.

themselves treated very much like colonials. That lowly status was hardly
unique to Oregonians: residents of all territories remained second-class
citizens for an indeterminate time prior to statehood. According to the
federal Constitution, Congress retained supreme power over all territories.
It could, for example, determine the length of territorial legislative sessions
and the number of legislators, and it might veto their enactments. Congress
could also alter territorial boundaries, a power that accounts for the existence of Idaho and the peculiar shape of its boundaries.

As in any colonial system, the potential for tyranny was great, but Uncle

Sam generally remained too indifferent to territorial affairs to guide them with a firm hand. He was, nonetheless, generous enough to pay most territorial expenses.

Federal power functioned most directly through officers appointed in Washington, D.C., and residing in each territory. Those officials included a governor, a secretary, three or more justices, and any lesser functionaries to administer local federal offices. An "organic act" modeled after the Northwest Ordinance of 1787 provided a general framework for territorial government. Over time, specific features of America's colonial system changed to permit a certain amount of improvisation by both the federal government and individual territories.

As a result of America's far-flung colonial system, outsiders could easily mismanage a territory; presidential appointees might be wholly insensitive to local needs and feelings. Inexperience, administrative difficulties, low pay, frontier discomforts, and changes of presidents contributed to a high rate of turnover among territorial officers. Richard D. Gholson, one of Washington's fourteen territorial governors, left so little impression that no portrait of him is known to exist. There were, of course, those who left quite a mark, including the first territorial governors of Oregon and Washington, Joseph Lane and Isaac Stevens.

Each territory selected a delegate to represent it in Congress. Although he lacked a vote and the other formal powers of a congressman, the delegate functioned as publicist, lobbyist, agent of the territory and its officers, and major dispenser of Uncle Sam's political plums. Lane, who resigned as Oregon's governor before Polk's Whig successor could replace him, was repeatedly elected the territory's delegate to Congress in the 1850s. He became a powerful figure in Oregon and in national Democratic party politics.

The decade of territorial government was for Oregon a time of political acrimony. Residents fought over where to locate the capital, Salem winning over Oregon City and Corvallis; and Democratic and Whig cliques battled over political appointments in venomous verbal duels that enlivened early-day journalism. Oregon voted three times—in 1854, 1855, and 1856—against statehood, only to vote overwhelmingly for it in 1857. Underlying much of the controversy and seemingly contradictory political behavior was the issue of race. Oregonians were responding to the great national issue of the day: slavery.

For nearly two decades, debate over slavery agitated politics in the Pacific Northwest despite the region's remoteness from slave states. The reason

THE DONATION LAND CLAIM ACT OF 1850

In rearranging the landscape of the new Northwest in a geographic as well as a political sense, few congressional enactments had greater impact than the Donation Land Claim Act of 1850. This measure recognized the generous claims established under Oregon's provisional government and set up a system for acquiring additional land. According to this early-day homestead act, each white male citizen eighteen years of age or older was entitled to 320 acres of land if single; if married, his wife could hold an additional 320 acres in her own right. A person had only to reside on the land and cultivate it for four years. In the eyes of congressional supporters, that was a way to reward immigrants who had helped the United States win a very generous boundary settlement.

The effects of the first large-scale disposition of land in the Pacific Northwest were far reaching. During the five years of its existence, more than seven thousand claimants ac-quired in excess of 2.5 million acres. By far the largest number of donation land claims was located in the Willamette Valley. Because claims were supposed to be square in shape—or if not square, then oblong—the act superimposed a recognizable pattern on the face of the land.

Likewise, it superimposed a racial and ethnic pattern on pioneer Oregon. The act stimulated white immigration and settlement, but its provisions excluded blacks and Hawaiians. Prior to 1850, Hawaiians had constituted a substantial portion of the region's work force, but most of them eventually returned to the islands. Moreover, the land was given away free to white settlers before Indian title to it was extinguished. Finally, because a white family could acquire a 640-acre tract of farmland—the size of many a Southern plantation—the Donation Land Claim Act contributed to a debate over slavery that increasingly agitated Oregon politics during the 1850s.

was that Oregon's first white settlers brought their cultural baggage with them, and for those moving from Missouri and other states of the Mississippi and Ohio valleys, that included a strong set of opinions about blacks and slavery.

Many of the pioneer settlers were antiblack but differed over whether slavery should be permitted in their territory. It was hardly an irrelevant question: the generous grants permitted under the Donation Land Claim Act together with a mild climate made the Willamette Valley well suited for slave labor, or so some residents claimed. A few Oregonians actually owned slaves despite their prohibition by the territorial organic act.

Other Oregonians feared that slavery would enable the rich to dominate the poor and thus re-create the caste system that many an immigrant farmer from Missouri or Kentucky had sought to escape. Oregon's majority party, the Democrats, included many advocates of slavery, most notably

Joseph Lane. The Supreme Court's *Dred Scott* decision in early 1857, which disallowed territorial but not state legislation regarding slavery, may have been the prime reason Oregonians switched their position on statehood between 1856 and 1857. The *Dred Scott* case strengthened the hand of those who argued that statehood was necessary to protect Oregon's special interests. The Oregon constitution of 1857, which Congress approved in 1859 after lengthy debate, declared against slavery, but by the same document Oregon became the first American state to exclude blacks other than by ordinary statutory law.

After a decade as a territory, Oregon became the thirty-third state on February 14, 1859. Residents of Washington and Idaho would wait another thirty years before following Oregon's lead, becoming the forty-second and forty-third states in 1889 and 1890.

WASHINGTON TERRITORY

The Oregon Territory encompassed an enormous geographical area—approximately 350,000 square miles—that was never truly unified. People in the scattered settlements north of the Columbia River, in what was then termed Northern Oregon, believed that Willamette Valley farmers dominated territorial affairs and neglected the interests of others. Settlers met at Cowlitz Prairie in August 1851 and at Monticello (now Longview) in November 1852 to petition Congress to grant them a separate territory. Congress approved legislation on May 2, 1853, creating a sprawling new territory named for the nation's first president. Few other American territories were launched with so small a population, less than four thousand non-Indian residents.

Washington's early legislature spent most of its time granting special acts or privileges, creating new counties, chartering railroads that were never built, authorizing construction of bridges and ferries, and chartering all kinds of social organizations—temperance, literary, and music associations and fraternal lodges. The legislature also granted divorces until the judiciary assumed that function in 1866.

Washington's first governor was Isaac I. Stevens, a young Massachusetts native and officer in the Corps of Engineers during the recent war with Mexico. Afflicted by a mild form of dwarfism that gave him a large head and short, stubby legs, Stevens seemed driven by a limitless supply of energy to surmount his physical difficulties and prove himself. At West Point he graduated at the head of his class in 1839. He combined the roles of gover-

19. Isaac Stevens (1818–62), Washington's first territorial governor, 1853–57. Courtesy Oregon Historical Society: 701.

nor, Indian agent, and chief of a national railroad survey project to further his dream of building an empire of white settlers in the Pacific Northwest.

Stevens concluded a series of heavy-handed treaty negotiations with the Indians of Washington (which then included western Montana and northern Idaho). Occasionally, he used the medium of the imprecise Chinook jargon to explain complex land transactions, and where necessary he appointed "chiefs" and "subchiefs" to sign for their people. To the impatient young governor, Washington's seventeen thousand Indians were children whose culture was of little value. In the end, Stevens forced the Indians to relinquish title to more than sixty-four million acres of land in exchange for the retention of fishing rights and for various federal allowances or annuities along with instructions and tools for farming, the latter even though much of the land was poorly suited for agriculture. Despite the haste of the negotiations, Congress ironically failed to ratify the Stevens treaties for several years.

Native Americans greatly resented the results of the treaty making, and warfare erupted on both sides of the Cascade Range. Some treaty provisions dealing with Indian fishing rights remained unaccepted by whites for more than a century. Meanwhile, Stevens won election in 1857 as Washington's delegate to Congress and, like his friend and fellow delegate, Joseph Lane of Oregon, plunged into national Democratic party affairs.

IDAHO TERRITORY

When Oregon became a state, an immense but sparsely settled eastern segment of the former territory was attached to Washington, thus creating a geographical monstrosity that stretched from the Olympic Peninsula to the Rocky Mountains and included Idaho and the far western portions of Montana and Wyoming. The great distance that separated its capital at Olympia, on the southern edge of Puget Sound, from several new mining settlements in the interior complicated the governing of Washington Territory.

E. D. Pierce sparked a mining rush to the Clearwater region in 1860 when he discovered gold on Nez Percé land. Within a year, Pierce City numbered four thousand people. From there, prospectors fanned out to scour the land for other promising sites. They discovered more of the precious yellow metal along the Salmon River and in the Boise basin in 1862. By the summer of 1863, there were nearly thirty-five thousand non-Indian residents in the interior regions, and for a brief time the population of Idaho City exceeded that of Portland.

The dusty frontier village of Walla Walla emerged as a major supply point for the mining camps. It soon grew to be the largest settlement in Washington Territory and a dangerous rival to Olympia, which feared that Walla Walla might displace it as capital. The discovery of gold in what is now Montana further complicated political life in the sprawling territory.

Olympia, in short, was only too glad to have Congress combine Washington's remote mining regions into a new territory, called Idaho (despite a last-minute attempt to name it Montana), on March 4, 1863. President Abraham Lincoln appointed William H. Wallace, former governor of Washington Territory, to serve as Idaho's first executive. But because Congress had hastily established Idaho just before adjourning, the territory received no federal money to run its government.

Except from the perspective of Olympia's boosters, Idaho's boundaries made little sense. At first they extended far beyond the eastern limits of the old Oregon country to encompass Idaho, Montana, and all but the southwestern corner of Wyoming, an area one-quarter larger than Texas. Within this vast territory lay a hodgepodge of mining regions so scattered that scarcely a trail connected them. Even after Idaho's boundaries contracted in 1864 and again in 1868 to their present contorted limits, the territory remained geographically and culturally divided, perhaps the most awkwardly constituted in United States history. Today only U.S. 95 connects northern and southern Idaho, and that highway was not paved until 1938. During the heyday of railroad passenger service (from the 1880s to the 1920s), it was impossible to travel from the panhandle to the capital at Boise without leaving Idaho and changing trains. In 1905 it took residents of far northern Idaho longer to reach Boise than it took them to reach the capitals of Washington or Montana. Of the continental states, only California and Texas extend a greater distance from north to south.

Another of Idaho's continuing divisions resulted from its peculiar pattern of settlement. Unlike neighboring states, except Nevada, it was settled largely by immigrants from other parts of the West, not from the East or Midwest, and many of them were Mormons moving north from Utah. This pattern meant that a restless mining camp population centering in the panhandle and Boise basin confronted pietistic Mormon agrarians who were colonizing the territory's southeastern quarter. Nowhere in the United States did the Mormon and non-Mormon populations divide as sharply as they did in Idaho, and therein lay the seeds of a future anti-Mormon crusade. The division between Union and pro-Confederate factions during and after the Civil War further complicated matters.

Idaho's first territorial capital was Lewiston, a supply center for mining camps to the east and south. Like Olympia, it was not centrally located; moreover, the population of the nearby Clearwater mining region had already peaked by 1863 and been overtaken by that of the Boise basin, where more than sixteen thousand of the territory's forty thousand people resided. When the second session of the territorial legislature met in Lewiston in December 1864, the shifting center of the mining boom together with boundary adjustments gave the Boise region more than 90 percent of Idaho's population. When legislators voted to relocate the capital to Boise, they embittered Lewiston and northern Idaho and further contributed to sectional division.

The territorial phase of government and politics lasted twenty-seven years and had few redeeming features. Idaho seemed forever to be tottering on the brink of insolvency or incompetency. At one point the published volumes of the territory's civil and criminal codes were impounded in San Francisco awaiting payment of a printing bill, and for the next three years Idaho's territorial courts were forced to rely on unsatisfactory newspaper copies of those laws. Governors were for the most part an odd lot of scheming or incompetent carpetbag politicians who seemed to serve the territory best by leaving it—or not arriving at all.

Caleb Lyon, a faithful Republican whom President Lincoln appointed the territory's second governor, had a reputation as a New York art and literature critic. Being something of a dandy, he never fit in with the rough-and-tumble miners of Idaho. When he became embroiled in the bitter conflict over moving the capital from Lewiston to Boise, the egotistical and ambitious Lyon quietly departed for the more promising environment of the national capital. For two months Idaho had no governor at all. The acting governor, the territorial secretary, Clinton Dewitt Smith, took eight months to reach Idaho and soon thereafter drank himself to death. Meanwhile, the Boise County treasurer embezzled $14,000 in revenues he had collected for the territory, nearly bankrupting it. The next de facto governor, Horace Gilson, was a thief who quietly looted the treasury of $41,000 before absconding to Hong Kong and Paris.

As for Caleb Lyon, after an eleven-month absence, he unexpectedly returned in 1865 to finish his term. When he left for good the following year, he was suspected of having stolen $46,000 in Indian funds that he was responsible for distributing as Idaho's superintendent of Indian affairs. Lyon claimed that he was trying to return the money to Washington and that, while en route on a sleeping car, a thief had stolen it from under his pillow. Some of Lyon's successors added additional chapters to this tale of incompetence.

THE CIVIL WAR ERA

From a national perspective, the crucial issues of the 1860s were the causes and consequences of the Civil War. The war remains the bloodiest conflict in American history, and although few of the sixty-four thousand residents of the Pacific Northwest participated directly, they became involved nonetheless. If nothing else, Civil War events gave residents much to think and

20. Caleb Lyon of Lyonsdale (1822–75), as Idaho's
eccentric territorial governor from 1864 to 1866 preferred to style himself. Courtesy Idaho State Historical
Society: E-544.

talk about. They suffered a fright when the Confederate raider *Shenandoah*
was rumored to be cruising off the coast.

The rapidly changing fortunes of Joseph Lane mirrored the passions and
disagreements that animated Civil War politics in the Pacific Northwest.
Though he was once immensely popular, Lane's unyielding proslavery, pro-
Southern stand alienated many Oregonians. In the 1860 election he ran for

vice-president with John C. Breckenridge on a Democratic ticket devoted to those principles. Their loss to Lincoln and the Republicans brought an end both to Lane's political career and to Democratic party dominance of Oregon. The region's first territorial governor returned to the Pacific Northwest an outcast; in several communities, residents hanged Lane in effigy. From that time until he died in 1881 on his homestead near Roseburg, Lane had no political influence.

While most Pacific Northwesterners remained loyal to the Union cause, Southern sympathizers talked openly of seceding to form a Pacific republic. The idea of an independent nation had been discussed for several years, but the Civil War made its advocates so bold that the legislatures of Oregon and Washington Territory passed resolutions repudiating such a creation.

In many ways, Idaho was as much Confederate as it was Union territory. Its remote location coupled with the appeal of mining camp bonanzas made it a haven for draft-dodging fortune seekers from both sides. Because those men might loathe military service yet loyally support their respective causes, their presence made for lively discussions and flag-waving demonstrations that led to an occasional mining camp brawl. Incidents were reported at several locations, not just mining camps, but conflict between Unionists and Secessionists seemed especially violent in the Boise basin. In the Idaho legislature also, a large contingent of pro-Confederate Democrats battled for their cause.

The United States Army had stationed units in the Pacific Northwest since the late 1840s, primarily to protect travelers on the Oregon Trail and to enforce treaties with the Indians. Civil War tensions between Republicans and pro-Southern Democrats prompted the federal government to establish a series of new army posts in the Pacific Northwest, notably Fort Boise (distinct from the old Hudson's Bay Company post of the same name on the Snake River) in 1863. In addition, the Union stationed troops at Fort Vancouver, Fort Steilacoom, Fort Walla Walla, and several lesser posts. When most of the regulars were called east, Pacific Northwest volunteers manned those posts.

Several soldiers who distinguished themselves on eastern battlefields were well known to Pacific Northwesterners. In the Union army were Major General Isaac Stevens, who fought to stop Stonewall Jackson's advance and died at Chantilly in northern Virginia in 1862, and Oregon's first Republican senator, Colonel Edward D. Baker, killed at the Battle of Ball's Bluff on the Potomac River in 1861. As a young captain, the Union general George B. McClellan had led a party surveying a road across the Cascades.

General Ulysses S. Grant served at Fort Vancouver in 1853, and General Philip Sheridan was there in 1855. General George Pickett, who served as a commander on San Juan Island, joined the Confederate army and was immortalized in "Pickett's Charge" at Gettysburg.

BOUNDARIES IN PERSPECTIVE

For Pacific Northwesterners the three decades from 1840 to 1870 were a time for establishing boundaries. Not just the obvious ones like those that separated American from British territory, or Oregon from Washington, or one person's farm or mining claim from another's, but boundaries of mind and spirit as well. Territorial and state laws, constitutions, and organic acts attempted to define the often imprecise boundaries between permissible and impermissible conduct. Even the outcome of the Civil War set more precise constitutional limits on state power than existed before.

The boundaries between personal success and failure were perhaps harder to draw, although frontier society was inclined to err on the side of generosity. Certainly if fashioning three territories and one state, platting cities and planting farms, raising crops and numerous children, laying out roads and putting down roots were tokens of success, then the pioneer generation of Pacific Northwesterners had reason to be proud of its successes.

But there was also that other boundary, the rigidly confining one that white settlers drew between themselves and others—the Indians, blacks, and Asians. Although whites might minimize its existence, that boundary appeared in their thinking, codes of law, and newly redrawn maps.

CHAPTER 7

Holes in the Social Fabric

*

Men come and go like the waves of the sea. A tear, a tomanawos [medicine man], a dirge, and they are gone from our longing eyes forever. Even the white man, whose God walked and talked with him as friend to friend, is not exempt from the common destiny. We may be brothers after all. We shall see.—Chief Seattle, 1854, as quoted in the Seattle *Sunday Star*, November 5, 1887

*

The social fabric that the Pacific Northwest's first Euro-American settlers wove together was for the most part sturdy and serviceable, embodying their vision of a good society. But as might be expected of any homespun effort, the result was not without its flaws. Most conspicuous were the several holes and a ragged fringe symbolizing treatment of those people that the dominant groups excluded or confined to the margin. Indians, blacks, Asians, Mormons, women, and others were at various times victims of blatantly discriminatory laws and activities. Complicating matters was the fact that on occasion the victim became victimizer, as when ancient quarrels between Indians led one group to cooperate with whites against another, or when Indians attacked and killed approximately fifty Chinese miners in southern Idaho in 1866. Yet, the discerning observer can also find instances of goodwill and social harmony and examples of individuals who successfully shaped their lives despite prejudice or legal impediment.

One of the most profound changes of the 1840s was a noticeable alteration of the region's racial composition. During the years of the fur trade, there had been much intermixing of Caucasian, Indian, and Polynesian peoples. Fur company personnel—Scots, French Canadians, and Iroquois Indians coming overland from the East—frequently were joined by Plains Cree and Plains Ojibwa (Chippewa) wives, or they married women from western tribes. The wife of John McLoughlin was of Swiss and Ojibwa ancestry; Peter Skene Ogden twice married Indian women.

Ships traveling through the Sandwich Islands often hired Hawaiians—known in the Pacific Northwest as Owyhees, Kanakas, or Sandwich Islanders—to work as laborers. John Jacob Astor's ship, the *Tonquin*, brought twenty-four Owyhees to the lower Columbia River, and subsequent ships increased their numbers in the Northwest. When Indians killed two Hawaiians accompanying a Hudson's Bay Company brigade near the present-day Oregon-Idaho border, Ogden named the nearby river Owyhee in their memory. Most Hawaiians who came to the Northwest were single men, yet some women arrived also. Missionaries occasionally employed Hawaiians as servants and laborers.

The racial blends in the old Oregon country included French-Indian, Scots-Indian, Owyhee-Indian, French-Owyhee, Iroquois–western Indian, and an occasional Negro-Indian, because blacks sometimes jumped ship or came overland. Although that was a unique population pool, beginning in the 1840s the great migration of people of northern and western European ancestry overwhelmed it and gave the region the predominant racial and cultural characteristics it retains to this day. The exceptions proved only temporary, as in 1870 when the census recorded that 25 percent of Idaho's population was Chinese, a figure never again equaled in a Northwest state by any racial minority. Various discriminatory taxes and land laws—including the Oregon Donation Land Claim Act of 1850, which excluded blacks and Hawaiians from its provisions—mirrored the pioneers' racial views. The Washington legislature in 1861 forbade intermarriage between whites and Indians, thus halting a long-standing practice. Oregon in 1866 prohibited intermarriage between whites and blacks, Chinese, Hawaiians, or anyone more than one-quarter black or more than one-half Indian. Idaho enacted similar legislation.

PHASES OF INDIAN-WHITE RELATIONS

Indian-white relations in the Pacific Northwest passed through four overlapping phases. The first, a time of generally peaceable contacts between equals, dated from early maritime exploration until the Whitman massacre of 1847. For the traders and trappers, Indians often provided a labor force and served as sources of supply in a complex economic system. Petty misunderstandings occasionally erupted, and some led to violence. Euro-American diseases also afflicted native society, but during that first phase, there was no sustained effort to drive out newcomers or dispossess Indians of their land.

The second phase, involving three decades of conflict, lasted from the Cayuse War of 1848 until 1879, when the United States Army routed a band of Shoshonis known as Sheepeaters. By that date most of the region's Native Americans were confined to reservations. During the third phase, Indians became a colonized and beleaguered people, confined to shrinking and increasingly undesirable land. Finally, the General Allotment Act (or Dawes Severalty Act) of 1887 encouraged them to become agrarians and assimilate into white society in defiance of a tradition of collective property relations.

Although the Dawes Act was intended as a reform measure, it diminished reservation lands across the United States by nearly two-thirds between 1887 and 1934 by periodically opening major portions of the natives' land base to white settlement. Each of the 638 remaining Coeur d'Alene Indians of northern Idaho, for example, received 160 acres under the Dawes Act. At the same time, however, the federal government opened three-fourths of their former reservation to white homesteaders. The state of Idaho purchased a scenic portion of Coeur d'Alene lands, which, as Lake Chatcolet, became the Pacific Northwest's first major state park.

There were also periodic land rushes: a pistol shot at high noon on November 18, 1895, opened the Nez Perce Reservation to white homesteaders, who scrambled to claim three thousand pieces of real estate. The tribe received a cash settlement of $1.6 million for the alienated land. Today the Nez Percés retain only a fraction of the 784,000 acres that their reservation comprised in 1863.

Indian people sometimes received token compensation for the loss of their land, and sometimes they received nothing but unfulfilled promises. Most whites viewed Indians as a broken people, a casualty of the onward rush of progress; as the author of one of the region's local histories phrased it in 1903, "When the indomitable Anglo-Saxon race began following the course of destiny to the westward the doom of the thriftless aboriginal peoples was sealed. . . . The day of a grander development for the vast, prodigious west, teeming with the crude elements of wealth production,

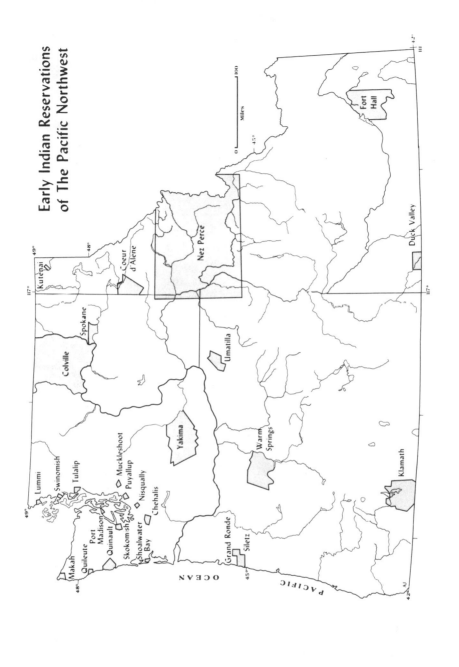

Early Indian Reservations
of The Pacific Northwest

had at last dawned. The night of savagery was over."[1] For Indians the night had only begun.

The fourth phase of Indian-white relations was a time of contradiction and of reluctant white recognition of Indian rights coupled with the Indians' growing pride in their own heritage. That phase began when Congress granted United State citizenship to Indian people in 1924, and it continued with the Indian Reorganization Act (known as the Indian New Deal) of 1934. The latter attempted to prevent further shrinkage of reservations and even to obtain some land for landless bands. And yet the fourth phase still saw Congress in 1954 terminate federal aid granted by treaty to the Klamaths and some Oregon coastal Indians and sell their remaining tribal land. Indians increasingly asserted their rights during the 1960s and 1970s, and the national government made some effort to turn federal programs on the reservations over to Indian control. At that time, courts recognized Indian fishing claims in cases that represented long-delayed responses to three crucial decades of Indian-white conflict and treaty making.

THREE DECADES OF INDIAN-WHITE CONFLICT

Two things above all else lay at the root of Indian-white violence between 1847 and 1879: land and precious metals. Whites were greedy for both, and too often that meant their crossing, digging up, or appropriating Indian lands. A contributing cause was the failure of two cultures to comprehend one another.

Nothing preoccupied the first generation of white settlers in the Pacific Northwest more than land—buying and selling, dividing and developing. Many newcomers of the 1840s and 1850s were family-oriented agrarians who, unlike the fur traders and trappers of years past, perceived nothing of an economic or social partner in the Indian. They believed that the nomadic natives, being scarcely more civilized than deer and other wild creatures, should yield the land to agriculturists who would settle and cultivate it. Violence was inevitable under those circumstances.

One result of the Pacific Northwest's first Indian war in 1848 was that Oregonians retained an enduring memory of the Whitman massacre and a spirit of bitterness that left neither sympathy for the fate of native peoples

---

1. *An Illustrated History of North Idaho* (Chicago, 1903), p. 44.

nor respect for Indian claims to the land. Between 1851 and 1868 the Indians of Oregon were forced onto ever-shrinking reservation lands.

Anson Dart, Oregon Territory's first superintendent of Indian affairs, initially considered relocating Indians living west of the Cascades onto remote and semiarid lands to the east, but people whose culture was rooted in the lush green country of the coast and Willamette Valley balked at the move, even as Indians living east of the Cascades feared the importation of diseases unfamiliar to them. But efforts to obtain reservation land west of the Cascades ran afoul of Oregon's Donation Land Law, which sanctioned homesteading without regard for the legal obligation to extinguish Indian title to the land. Dart finally located a few remote parcels not yet encumbered by white claims.

Serious trouble erupted in the Rogue River country in 1851 when gold seekers and agrarians entered the land occupied by native bands collectively known as the Rogue River Indians. The Table Rock Treaty of 1853 set aside a temporary reservation to quell the conflict. Although the treaty served as a model for subsequent ones, it failed in its immediate aim, because friction between Indian and gold seeker worsened and sparked a full-scale war in 1855.

In that year warfare also erupted in Washington Territory. Isaac I. Stevens, the brash young governor and Indian agent, intended to open the rest of his domain to white settlement by concentrating the natives on reservations and teaching them how to farm. Quite simply, the governor and many others never questioned the necessity of removing Indians from the path of white civilization, although he did hope that it could be accomplished peaceably through negotiation.

Stevens staged one treaty council after another in 1854 and 1855 from Puget Sound to the Rocky Mountains. He intimidated and cajoled Indian people into signing away most of their land in exchange for a variety of goods and promises. In the end it proved far easier to confine Indians of the coast to small reservations encompassing their traditional homes and fishing grounds than to pen up the seminomadic groups of the interior. Stevens met with tribal spokesmen of the Plateau peoples at a great council in May and June 1855 in the Walla Walla Valley, not far from the remains of the Whitman mission. The gathering, attended by approximately five thousand Nez Percés, Yakimas, Cayuses, Walla Wallas, Umatillas, and other Indians, was not altogether harmonious. But Stevens's policy prevailed, especially after he allotted the two largest and most powerful tribes, the Yakimas and

21. Governor Isaac Stevens at the 1855 council in the
Walla Walla Valley. Courtesy Eastern Washington State
Historical Society: L86–1264.

Nez Percés, sizable reservations encompassing much of their traditional hunting and gathering ground. The smaller tribes reluctantly acquiesced in that arrangement. In return for three reservations and several promises, Indian leaders signed away forty-five thousand square miles of land.

Four years passed before Stevens's treaties won Senate approval, but even before he concluded the one-sided negotiations, the discovery of gold on the upper Columbia River in 1855 brought whites trooping across Yakima lands. When the Indians rose in violent protest, Stevens declared martial law and temporarily closed the area to white settlement. Although General John E. Wool, commander of the United States Army in the Pacific Northwest, believed that the governors of Oregon and Washington had wronged the natives, it became his duty as a good soldier to subdue both the Rogue River and Yakima Indians. Oregon volunteers and United States Army regulars decisively crushed the Rogue River peoples in 1856 and exiled them to a new reservation in the Coast Ranges. Trouble with the Yakimas ended temporarily that same year with the defeat of Chief Kamiakin. In one of several hostile incidents that took place during the last half of the decade, Indians attacked the village of Seattle in early 1856.

East of the Cascades, Indian resentment burst forth in renewed conflict in 1858 when most tribes of the Columbia basin, with the conspicuous exception of the Nez Percés, united to resist white encroachments. In that struggle, Colonel Edward Steptoe and 156 army soldiers marched north from Fort Walla Walla into the land of the Spokanes. Near Rosalia, a combined force of Spokans, Yakimas, Coeur d'Alenes, and Palooses dealt the army a humiliating defeat. To avenge the army's honor, Colonel George Wright returned with nearly six hundred well-armed regulars. He proved a ruthless adversary, using new long-range rifles and slaughtering seven hundred Indian horses to demoralize his enemy. Wright then marched grimly through Indian country, preemptorily hanging a total of twenty-four chiefs and others considered guilty of fomenting what was then termed the Yakima War.

No more wars erupted in Washington (except in the portion that later became Idaho), and Indian-white conflict in Oregon remained confined to local incidents east of the Cascade mountains until the Modoc War flared up just south of the Oregon-California border in 1872. Once again the main cause was white land hunger, this time in a remote part of the region where settlers wanted a Modoc band removed and confined to a nearby reservation. In the ensuing struggle, a handful of Modocs, well camouflaged in a rugged area known as the Lava Beds, kept hundreds of soldiers at bay. The army suffered 120 casualties including the respected General Edward Canby, who was murdered under a flag of truce. During peace negotiations, the Modoc leader Keintpoos, called Captain Jack by whites, suddenly drew a pistol from beneath his coat and shot Canby in the face. The death of the Civil War hero and the highest-ranking officer ever killed in conflict with Indians stunned the nation and outraged the army, fueling its determination to subdue the Modocs.

The six-month struggle ended with an army victory and the surrender of Captain Jack, who along with three other Modocs was subsequently tried and hanged at Fort Klamath for murder. In a grotesque turn of events, their heads were shipped to the army medical museum in Washington, D.C. One hundred fifty-five Modoc prisoners of war, one-third of whom were children, were exiled to Indian Territory (Oklahoma).

Some of the most vicious fighting occurred in Idaho, where at the Battle of Bear River in 1863, California volunteers killed between two hundred and four hundred Indians (mostly Shoshonis, including some women and children). That ranks as one of the worst slaughters of Indians in the West. Far better known, despite fewer casualties, is the so-called Nez Percé War of 1877. Two decades earlier, the Nez Percés had acceded to one of Stevens's 1855 treaties confining them to a large reservation. In 1863, after trespassing whites discovered gold within its boundaries, some Indian leaders consented to a much-shrunken reservation bordering the Clearwater River east of Lewiston. About one-third of the Nez Percé (the "nontreaty" group) disavowed the agreement that cut their reservation from 7.7 million acres to one-tenth of that amount. They continued to make their homes elsewhere. White Bird's band of Nez Percés remained on the lower Salmon River south of the new reservation, and Chief Joseph's band lived west of the Snake River in Oregon's majestic Wallowa Valley.

Hin-mah-too-yah-lat-kekht ("Thunder Traveling to Loftier Mountain Heights"), young Chief Joseph, inherited his father's leadership role in 1871. Young Joseph insisted from the first that his four hundred people in the Wallowa Valley were not bound by the treaty of 1863 because his father had never signed it. The federal government initially agreed, and President Ulysses S. Grant ordered part of the valley set aside as a reservation in 1873. But after protests from land-hungry whites, the government changed its mind, and two years later it insisted that Joseph and his people move to the reservation on the Clearwater River. With the Wallowa Valley opened to white settlement at the same time, the nontreaty Nez Percés appeared to have little choice but to obey the government's ultimatum. In mid-May 1877, General Oliver O. Howard gave them thirty days to leave the valley, to cross Hells Canyon and the Snake River, dangerously swollen by spring runoff, and to settle on the reservation. The Indians began relocating when on June 13 and 14 three young warriors from White Bird's band, brooding upon an injustice by local whites, killed four settlers. War inevitably followed.

The events of mid-1877 cannot actually be described as warfare. Eight hundred Indian men, women, and children, including a herd of more than two thousand horses, made a desperate flight across the Bitterroot Mountains to the plains of Montana, where they hoped to find safety among their

22. Chief Joseph flanked by Alice Fletcher, general allotment agent on the Nez Perce Reservation from 1889
to 1892, and James Stewart. Courtesy Idaho State Historical Society: 3771.

friends the Crows. Failing that they planned to seek sanctuary in Canada.
Theirs was less a retreat than a flight to safety, a tragic odyssey in which
they were pursued by Howard and his soldiers. The commander of the
army's Department of the Columbia, Oliver O. Howard was a one-armed
Civil War hero, a friend of freed blacks, and a man known as the Christian or
praying general because he delivered sermons to the garrisons he inspected.

At the Battle of the Big Hole River, August 9 and 10, the Nez Percés lost
30 warriors and 40 men, women, and children. The army suffered 29 killed
and 40 wounded. The desperate Indians continued across Montana, winding through Yellowstone National Park (where their presence frightened
and scattered tourists), and continued on toward the international border.
On September 30 in the Bear Paw Mountains, troops led by Colonel Nelson
Miles intercepted them just forty miles from their goal. After the seventeen
hundred–mile odyssey, only 480 Nez Percés remained to surrender. The

captives were exiled to Oklahoma and not allowed to return to the Pacific Northwest until 1885. Because of continuing ill will in Idaho, Joseph and a band of 150 followers settled on the Colville Reservation in north-central Washington, where Joseph died in 1904 and was buried. The conflict cost the federal government $930,000 and the lives of 177 whites, mostly soldiers, and 151 Indians, and it drastically curtailed the freedom of the Nez Percé tribe. Joseph was more politician than military leader, but when whites glorified his military genius, it made his pursuers' difficulties seem more plausible.

Friction with settlers provoked an uprising of Bannocks in south-central Idaho in 1878. After several engagements, General Howard drove the fugitives back onto their reservation. A year later the last resisters, a few families of Sheepeaters, a Shoshoni band hiding out in the rugged Salmon River country, surrendered to Howard's persistent troops and were moved onto the Fort Hall Reservation. The government soon diminished the size of the reservation by three-fourths when it opened the best land to white settlement. The newcomers built a town, which they named for the prominent Shoshoni leader Pocatello. If nothing else, whites could always afford to be magnanimous in the naming of their settlements.

The United States government had placed most Indians of the Northwest on reservations by 1880. Ostensibly this arrangement had been accomplished through treaty making between sovereign and independent nations, but it was actually through disease, intimidation, corruption, and sheer force of numbers that whites established a clear boundary between themselves and Indians and left a gaping hole in the social fabric.

BLACKS AND ASIANS

Unlike the Indians who were driven onto reservations, blacks and Asians had no prior claim to the land. Racism, cultural biases, and a host of vague fears explain the discrimination they encountered, not white land hunger.

Probably the first black to reach the Pacific Northwest was one of Robert Gray's seamen killed by Indians near present-day Tillamook, Oregon. Blacks were among the pioneers who emigrated to Oregon in the 1840s. Some came as free persons and some as slaves. One notable black pioneer was George Bush, who fought with Andrew Jackson to defeat the British in the Battle of New Orleans (1815). When his home state of Missouri later passed a law barring free blacks from residence, the legislature made an exception for the popular Bush. In 1844 he financed a racially integrated

23. The acculturation of Pat Tyee. Before: photographed in traditional Shoshoni dress. After: photographed with his hair cut and in non-Indian garb to
"show he was a Christian." Courtesy Idaho State Historical Society: 78–97.15.

party of overlanders to Oregon, but because of the race prejudice he found at
the end of the trail, Bush moved north to land near present Olympia. There
he founded the community of Bush Prairie, where he lived a long life as its
first citizen.

Bush's chilly reception in the Willamette Valley stemmed from the fact
that Oregon's white pioneers of the 1840s brought with them the fears and
prejudices common in the border states from which many originated. Despite their distance from the South, Oregonians participated in an acri-
monious public debate over slavery and related issues for two decades. The
provisional government in 1844 required slaveholders to free their slaves
and all blacks to leave the territory within three years. Any black who
violated the law was to be whipped, a punishment to be repeated after six
months if he or she still refused to leave. The immediate cause of the
punitive measure was not a growing number of blacks in Oregon, because

the 1850 census records only 207 in the entire Oregon country. Many whites disliked blacks and simply wanted to create a new society free of the racial tensions they had experienced back in the border states. Whites also became alarmed when a black man who had married an Indian threatened to incite his wife's people to war.

The provisional government limited land ownership to free white males who could vote. The Donation Land Law excluded blacks from its largesse. The laws of Oregon Territory and later the state constitution included similar antiblack provisions. Although federal constitutional amendments after the Civil War overturned those provisions, the state of Oregon did not formally remove the antiblack clause from its constitution until 1926; it did not ratify the Fifteenth Amendment to the United States Constitution until 1959, eighty-nine years after that measure had granted blacks the right to vote. Even in the early days, however, Oregon seldom enforced its discriminatory provisions.

The black population of Oregon numbered 128 in 1860. It included farmers, miners, barbers, cooks, blacksmiths, and common laborers. Some blacks worked as domestics for white families, and a few were slaves. Blacks preferred to form subcommunities in urban areas rather than endure the greater hostility common in rural districts. But the city of Portland assigned black and mulatto children to a segregated school that opened in 1867. In the Northwest, the black population increased only gradually; as late as 1930, it accounted for just .3 percent of the total population, yet Oregon's two thousand blacks became targets of the state's powerful Ku Klux Klan movement during the 1920s.

Among early Asian residents of the Pacific Northwest, the Chinese were by far the most numerous. They began arriving as individuals or in groups shortly after 1860, and although they could be found in numerous occupations, mining and railroad construction attracted the greatest numbers. In 1870 more than half of Idaho's 6,579 miners were Chinese. The region's Chinese reflected many different backgrounds, but to most whites they remained only objects of prejudice, violence, and various special taxes and property-holding restrictions.

Because Chinese miners were willing to work claims with great patience and accept a small return for their efforts, whites universally regarded their presence in the diggings as a sure sign that a mining region had passed its peak. The belief that Chinese had accumulated great quantities of gold through their frugality led to one of the most vicious massacres in Pacific Northwest history. In that incident, a gang of "cowboys" shot or hacked to

24. A Chinese vegetable peddler in Idaho City. Courtesy Idaho State Historical Society: 78–203.6.

death thirty-one Chinese miners. The site was north of Hells Canyon, the
year was 1887, and robbery was the probable motive. Prior to their slaying,
the victims were tortured in an apparent attempt to learn where they had
hidden a supposed cache of gold. Only the death count in the slaughter of
approximately fifty Chinese miners by Paiute Indians in 1866 exceeded this
toll.

On the railroads, trouble arose when white workers feared that the
importation of a potentially unlimited supply of cheap labor threatened

---

"NO CHINAMEN NEED APPLY"

The following editorial appeared in a Wallace, Idaho, newspaper during the height of the region's anti-Chinese agitation:

John Chinaman got into the California mines, into many other mines, but he must not think of attempting a visit into those of northern Idaho. If he insists on coming, however, let him bring a roast hog, plenty of fire crackers and colored paper, and all the essentials of a first class Chinese funeral. He need not bother to bring the corpse. It will be in readiness. Ta! Ta! John!—*Coeur d'Alene Sun*, March 22, 1884.

---

their jobs. When hard times hit the Pacific Northwest in the mid-1880s, unemployed white workers participated in several crusades to drive the Chinese from the region. The agitation led to anti-Chinese violence in Tacoma and Seattle, martial law, and the dispatching of federal troops to quell the disorder. In Pierce City, Idaho, in 1885, vigilantes lynched five Chinese who they believed were responsible for the murder of a white merchant.

The region's Chinese population declined slightly during the 1890s, while numbers of Japanese residents climbed dramatically. Seattle's Japanese population increased from 125 in 1890 to 3,000 in 1900. The exit of Chinese from the railroad, lumber, and canning industries opened a door for Japanese immigrants, typically young males who arrived without families. Some became successful truck gardeners, and other prosperous merchants in the region's larger cities. Even so, they experienced much the same racial animosity as the Chinese.

In addition to violence directed against Chinese, an anti-Hindu (East Indian) riot erupted in Bellingham and an anti-Japanese riot occurred in Vancouver, British Columbia, in 1907. Those were only the major outbursts. Until after the Second World War, hostility to Asians remained a prominent feature of Pacific Northwest life. At one time it was common for restaurants to post signs reassuring white customers that they employed no Chinese help.

THE ANTI-MORMON CRUSADE

Coexisting with racial prejudice in the Pacific Northwest was a virulent strain of religious intolerance in Idaho, where Mormons formed a larger percentage of the population than in any state or territory outside Utah. Beginning in the community of Franklin in 1860, members of the Church of Jesus Christ of Latter-day Saints (commonly called Mormons) steadily in-

25. The attempt to drive the Chinese out of Seattle
in 1886 resulted in a riot and a declaration of
martial law. Courtesy Museum of History and
Industry, Seattle: 3136.

creased in number until by 1877 Idaho had thirty-one distinct Mormon
settlements and, by 1890, about twenty-five thousand Mormon residents.
Mormons constituted about one-quarter of Idaho's total population at that
time and perhaps one-half of all its churchgoers. It was a religious division
unique in American history.

As they grew in population and influence in southeastern Idaho, Mormons were caught up in the sectional political rivalries that wracked the
territory. Their growing numbers gave Mormons power at the polls, especially when they tended to vote as a bloc for Democratic candidates, nearly

Hurl'd headlong flaming from th' ethereal sky,
With hideous ruin and combustion, down
To bottomless perdition. —*Paradise Lost.*

26. This vicious anti-Mormon cartoon appeared in full
color in the *West Shore,* a Portland booster publication.
Dating from the late 1880s, it depicts Idaho as an
avenging angel casting Mormonism into a fiery pit.
Courtesy University of Washington Libraries:
UW Neg. 6321.

Denomination	Washington	Idaho	Oregon	Utah
Roman Catholic				
Presbyterian				
Methodist				
Baptist				
Disciples				
Lutheran				
Congregational				
Episcopal				
Latter-Day Saints				
Adventist				
Eastern Orthodox				
United				
Friends				
Evangelical				
All others				

Number of Communicants (percent) by Denomination (1910)

Each symbol represents approximately 5 percent.

Because of rounding, totals may equal more than 100 percent.

Zimmerly

always the victorious side in Idaho before the 1880s. Because of the voting pattern, losers charged that Mormons took their orders from Salt Lake City and had no real interest in Idaho matters. Above all, however, it was their belief that males had the right to marry more than one wife, a practice referred to as polygamy, that made Mormons convenient targets for hostile non-Mormons (or Gentiles in the Mormon vocabulary). In fact, probably no more than 3 percent of Idaho's Mormons actually engaged in plural marriage.

More than anyone else, it was Fred T. Dubois who shaped the vague anti-Mormon resentments into a powerful political movement. After attending Yale College, Dubois moved to Idaho where he eventually became a United States marshal. When Congress passed the Edmunds Act in 1882, which barred polygamists from voting, holding office, or serving as jurors in cases involving plural marriage, it handed Dubois a powerful weapon to use against Mormons. Interested in more than simply harassing polygamists, Marshal Dubois sought to undermine the Idaho Democratic party by associating it with Mormons and then to elevate himself to a prominent position among territorial Republicans.

Dubois was successful in his quest: anti-Mormons in the legislature created the Idaho Test Oath, a stringent measure that could be used to force a person to testify under oath whether he belonged to the Mormon church or believed in its doctrines. A person did not have to be a practicing polygamist but only belong to an organization that sanctioned polygamy in order to be disenfranchised. After the Test Oath Act became law in 1885, Mormons fought it all the way to the United States Supreme Court and lost.

As Republicans grew in power, Dubois rode the wave of anti-Mormon sentiment to Capitol Hill, where as territorial delegate he worked to get Idaho admitted as a state. Framers added provisions of the Test Oath Act to the Idaho constitution, and voters overwhelmingly ratified it.

In September 1890 the church's president urged all Latter-day Saints to comply with civil laws regarding marriage, but this did not prevent Idaho's first legislature from barring Mormons from the polls. The 1893 legislature removed most of the anti-Mormon restrictions. As for Dubois, he became one of Idaho's United States senators before taking himself and the anti-Mormon cause into the Democratic party in 1900, thereby enlivening Idaho politics during the early years of the twentieth century. By that time the state legislature had restored the franchise to Mormons, some of whom voted against their old tormentor; others, in an ironic twist, became his political associates.

Some Idahoans wanted to disenfranchise Mormons because they continued to sanction plural marriage in heaven, but the state's judiciary ruled that so long as Mormons complied with civil law, Idaho could not extend its jurisdiction into the hereafter. In 1982 voters removed the anti-Mormon test oath from Idaho's constitution.

THE FIGHT FOR FEMALE SUFFRAGE

At the time of the Civil War, the population of the Pacific Northwest, like that of most frontier regions, was decidedly male. In Washington Territory males outnumbered females nine to one, a ratio that prompted Governor William Pickering to have three hundred single women transported from Boston to provide wives for his male constituents. Asa Mercer followed in Pickering's footsteps and brought another boatload of women to Seattle.

Despite the attention they received as prospective brides, Northwest women experienced various forms of discrimination, none more hotly contested than their ineligibility to vote. The region's suffrage crusade dates from 1871, when the prominent national activist Susan B. Anthony toured the Pacific Northwest in the company of Portland's Abigail Scott Duniway. The indefatigable Duniway continued the crusade for several more decades and justly deserves to be remembered as the mother of female suffrage in the Pacific Northwest. In addition to caring for a semi-invalid husband, raising six children, and publishing one of the region's leading reform papers, the *New Northwest* (1871–87), she crisscrossed the region numerous times to lecture on women's rights.

Duniway and her allies enjoyed some successes, as in 1878 when the Oregon legislature passed a law giving married women the right to own, sell, or will property and to keep their wages, and in 1881 when Washington passed a similar law. Two years later the territorial legislature extended the vote to women. One Washington pioneer, Phoebe Goodell Judson, recalled, "I took my turn on petit and grand jury, served on election boards, walked in perfect harmony to the polls by the side of my staunch Democratic husband, and voted the Republican ticket—not feeling any more out of my sphere than when assisting my husband to develop the resources of our country."[2]

But Judson, Duniway, and their sisters were doomed to disappointment

2. Phoebe Goodell Judson, *A Pioneer's Search for an Ideal Home* (1925; reprint, Lincoln: University of Nebraska Press, 1984), 277.

27. Abigail Scott Duniway (1834–1915), tireless
advocate of women's rights. Courtesy Oregon
Historical Society: 47215.

and years of frustration when Washington's territorial supreme court voided female suffrage in 1887 on a technicality. The legislature restored it a few months later, but in the bizarre Nevada Bloomer case of 1888, named for a saloonkeeper's wife who was the principal figure in a challenge mounted by liquor interests, the territorial supreme court again overturned the measure. During the next decade, Washington voters twice defeated female suffrage measures. Still the crusaders persisted, firm in their conviction that once women had the vote, economic and other rights could be obtained.

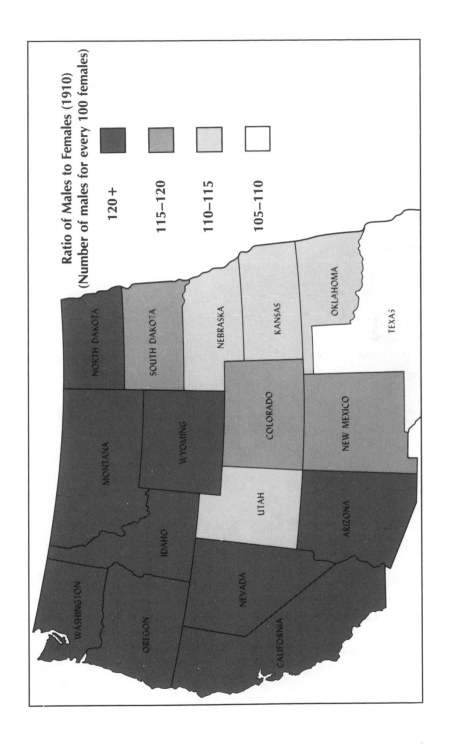

Ratio of Males to Females (1910)
(Number of males for every 100 females)

120 +

115–120

110–115

105–110

A breakthrough came in 1896 when, after a quiet and inexpensive campaign managed mostly by local women, Idaho overwhelmingly approved a constitutional amendment making it the first Pacific Northwest state to enfranchise women.[3] All but Custer County voted for the amendment. Ironically, the lone dissenter was the county Abigail Duniway had called home for several years. Her mocking and ridicule apparently had a tendency to alienate people of both genders. Three women won seats in the Idaho House of Representatives in 1898 and a token number of other offices. As they soon discovered, the right to vote did not mean that women gained real political power.

Fourteen years passed before Washington followed Idaho's lead: Emma Smith DeVoe, a friend of Duniway's, headed a campaign that won women the franchise in 1910 by a 2-to-1 margin. Duniway herself lived long enough to see Oregon's all-male electorate narrowly approve woman suffrage in 1912.

A combination of several fears explains why voting rights for women involved such a long struggle. Liquor interests were afraid that women would vote as a bloc to outlaw saloons and alcoholic beverages. In fact, some suffragists claimed credit for laws that made gambling illegal and closed saloons on Sunday. Democrats feared that women tended to vote Republican. Some over chivalrous males thought it best to protect women from the rough-and-tumble crowds that hung around polls on election day. Finally, some women feared that engaging in the practice of voting would reduce their feminine charms. In Duniway's case, she also faced a formidable foe in her own brother, Harvey Scott, the influential publisher of the Portland *Oregonian*.

SOCIAL RELATIONS IN PERSPECTIVE

In many ways the holes in the Northwest's social fabric reflected national trends. Religious and racial strife were facts of life from Boston to Birmingham, intergroup harmony seemingly reaching a low point in the United States during the 1890s and improving only slowly until the 1950s and 1960s.

From the perspective of the late twentieth century, the region's social fabric appears considerably stronger than it did in the 1870s and 1880s.

---

3. The Idaho territorial legislature in 1871 fell one vote short of providing for female suffrage.

Intergroup relations have changed for the better. Racial and religious equality is now a matter of law, although it is sometimes ignored in practice, and the region's various racial and ethnic minorities have made significant strides in becoming an integral part of Northwest society.

But various problems persist, and old prejudices occasionally take new and subtle forms. Idaho's governor between 1977 and 1987 was John V. Evans, the first Mormon to be elected as the state's chief executive.[4] At first glance, it would appear that anti-Mormon prejudice no longer agitated Idaho political life. But look again. When Evans ran for governor on the Democratic ticket in 1978, his Republican opponent was also a Mormon, and Mormonism became the chief, if unspoken, issue of the campaign. Terms like "Mormon conspiracy" appeared in the press. Because his opponent was more clearly identified with the Mormon church, Evans benefited from conservative and Republican voters who crossed over to vote Democratic. Latent anti-Mormonism remained alive in Idaho.

Anti-Indian prejudice reared its head in Washington in 1984 in the guise of Initiative 456 that sought to diminish Indian fishing rights. Although the measure was denounced as racist, voters narrowly approved it. Some would argue that Initiative 456 signified that the Pacific Northwest was growing more conservative and less tolerant of diversity after half a century of moving in the other direction.

4. Another Mormon, Arnold Williams, moved up to that office in 1945, having first been elected lieutenant governor on the Democratic ticket. He was defeated for reelection in 1946.

Part Three

From Frontier to Urban-Industrial Society

Profile: Henry Villard and the Last Spike

*

In this country, at this day, railroads are not a mere convenience to local population, but a vast machinery for the building up of empires.—Governor Marshall F. Moore to the Legislative Assembly of Washington Territory, December 9, 1862

*

At remote Gold Creek in Montana Territory, several hundred guests gathered to celebrate the completion of a railroad joining the Great Lakes and Puget Sound. The date was September 8, 1883. Fourteen years earlier at Promontory, Utah, the driving of a symbolic gold spike had joined Central Pacific and Union Pacific tracks to form America's first transcontinental railroad. The Northern Pacific Railroad through Montana completed a second transcontinental line. Henry Villard, a handsome, genial man in his midfifties, presided over the celebration.

As president of the Northern Pacific, Villard believed that his company's triumph over nature and economic adversity merited international attention. He invited to the last spike ceremony several hundred politicians, bankers, railroad officials, investors, and journalists, many from Great Britain and Germany, European countries that had given Villard substantial financial support.

To begin their journey, Villard's guests from the East Coast and Europe traveled to Saint Paul, a city that celebrated the last spike in a manner that future generations reserved for astronauts and Olympic champions. A parade nearly twenty miles long and including approximately twenty thou-

28. Henry Villard (1835–1900). Courtesy Oregon Historical Society: 55645.

sand marchers moved through the city's lavishly decorated streets. Not to
be outclassed by its neighbor and rival, Minneapolis staged a parade that
entertained an estimated hundred thousand onlookers. From Minnesota
the guests headed west across the prairies in four well-provisioned special
trains. A fifth train left Portland carrying dignitaries from the Pacific Coast;
cities and towns along the way scheduled additional festivities.

The last spike celebration took place approximately sixty miles west of
Helena, near the confluence of the Clark Fork River and Gold Creek. The
promoters erected a sign that read "Lake Superior 1,198 miles / Puget Sound
847 miles." A newly built wooden pavilion decorated with pine boughs,

bunting, and the flags of Germany, Great Britain, and the United States stood nearby. It was capable of seating nearly a thousand people.

Wherever railroad tracks went, the old West confronted the new, but seldom so dramatically as at Gold Creek. There, a band of Crow Indian participants encountered the financial barons of three nations. For one moment the old West of Indians, trappers, and pioneers stood face to face with the new West of high finance, nationwide markets, and rapid advances in communication and transportation.

At 3 P.M., Villard signaled for the ceremony to begin, and a brass band opened with the "Star-Spangled Banner" and other popular selections. Villard then summarized the history of the Northern Pacific. The day's featured speaker, the former secretary of state William Evarts, next addressed

29. A council of Crow Indians at the last spike ceremony near Garrison, Montana, on September 8, 1883. The opening of the first direct rail line from Puget Sound to the East contributed to a decade of spectacular growth for Washington. Courtesy Montana Historical Society: Photo by F. Jay Haynes, H-996.

the guests. A local paper observed that his oration was "impressive" but its weightier passages "bored to death" the Montana portion of his audience. Numerous other dignitaries extolled the glory and importance of the Northern Pacific's achievement.

After the speechmaking, everyone adjourned to the right-of-way to watch rival construction teams lay the last twelve hundred feet of track. The final spike and sledgehammer were specially wired so as to telegraph each blow to company officials waiting in Portland, Saint Paul, and New York. Their receivers recorded a last click at 5:18 P.M., signaling that America's second transcontinental railroad was at last a reality. Following a lavish banquet, Villard's guests continued to the West Coast, where still more celebrations and welcomes awaited them.

The final spike festivities proved a great promotional success for the Northern Pacific and signified the dawn of a new era for Pacific Northwesterners. The newness lay not in the railroad itself—local lines had existed in the region since the late 1850s—but in the direct and convenient connection it provided to the East.

The new link was several decades in the making. Because of America's expanding trade with China during the 1840s, the New York merchant Asa Whitney proposed a transcontinental railroad. Congress remained unmoved, but like earlier dreams of a Northwest Passage or an easy portage across the Rockies, his idea won enthusiastic backers. More than any other person, Whitney added serious discussion of a transcontinental railroad to the public agenda.

But who should pay for the massive project? The West was a debtor region; it contained few residents with capital sufficient to build local railroads much less national ones. The region was unlikely to attract the necessary funds from hard-headed eastern financiers. Unlike the situation in the East where railroad lines connected preexisting population centers and markets, western lines had to extend across hundreds and even thousands of miles of rugged and lightly populated country. They would have to generate passenger and freight revenue by running from nowhere in particular to nowhere at all. In other words, the railroads of the West would have to create new towns and markets and foster settlement of countless miles of farmland by promising investors a share of future wealth, a task that sobered even the most optimistic westerner. In the West, moreover, the labor needed for construction was high priced and difficult to obtain. Clearly, only the federal government had the resources to support a transcontinental railroad.

The imaginative Whitney petitioned Congress to grant him a sixty-mile-

30. The first train from Saint Paul to Portland officially
opened a railway line from the Pacific Northwest to
the upper Midwest. Courtesy Montana Historical
Society: Photo by F. Jay Haynes, H-999.

wide strip of land along the right-of-way of a proposed railway line from the
Great Lakes to the lower Columbia River. He would sell the land—an area
larger than the state of Illinois—to finance construction. Congress refused,
but Whitney's northern transcontinental scheme elicited proposals from
other regions, each with its special plan and route for reaching the Pacific.

In the early 1850s, Congress finally authorized the United States Army
to conduct five transcontinental railway surveys to find a feasible route to
the Pacific. The northern survey, under the direction of Isaac I. Stevens,
worked its way west from Saint Paul, while his subordinate, Lieutenant
George B. McClellan, explored the Cascade Range for suitable passes. The
government published the surveys between 1856 and 1861, but only in
1862—after the Civil War broke the regional deadlock over the best route—
did Congress authorize loans and grants of land to subsidize construction of
a railway along a central route. Sixty-one separate railroads received federal
land grants totaling 131,350,534 acres before Congress terminated the program in 1871.

Congress chartered the Northern Pacific Railroad in 1864. The staggering cost of the Civil War prevented it from providing a cash subsidy for each mile of track laid, but it authorized instead the largest land grant ever offered to an American railroad, a sixty million–acre swath of land six times the size of New England. On a map the Northern Pacific grant resembled an elongated checkerboard of alternating one-mile squares of government and railroad land extending from Lake Superior to the Pacific Ocean. It varied in width from forty miles in Minnesota and Oregon to eighty miles in the territories. The government deeded the odd sections to the railroad upon completion of each twenty-five miles of line.

This land grant, it must be noted, came with certain strings attached; ultimately the Northern Pacific forfeited some of the land through non-compliance with the terms of the grant. It actually received a total of a little more than thirty-nine million acres, an area twice as great as any other railroad received. The grant obligated it to provide reduced rates on federal shipments such as mail until 1946. Even so, the railroad's successor, Burlington Northern Incorporated, is today one of the largest nongovernment landholders in the United States.

As generous as the original Northern Pacific land grant was, the lack of a cash subsidy created severe financial difficulties and hampered construction. The company further labored under the twin burdens of having no sizable population centers to serve and the popular belief that the north country was too cold to permit successful railroading and settlement. One person who did come to believe in the Northern Pacific project was the noted Civil War financier Jay Cooke, who joined wholeheartedly in the venture after learning everything he could about the subject. His hired promoters so insistently proclaimed that the Northern Pacific country possessed a mild climate and other agreeable features that the region came to be popularly caricatured as "Jay Cooke's Banana Belt." With Cooke's prestigious Philadelphia firm acting as financial agent, money at last flowed in.

Groundbreaking took place just west of Duluth in 1870, and two years later the line had opened for business as far west as the Red River valley separating Minnesota and Dakota Territory. But not long after the tracks reached Bismarck, Cooke's firm failed, precipitating the panic of 1873. During the hard times that lasted most of the decade, construction halted and the Northern Pacific sank into bankruptcy.

Surely many Pacific Northwesterners must have wondered if they would live long enough to see the Northern Pacific completed. At the time of its financial collapse, the railroad consisted of two poorly built lines separated by more than 1,500 miles of mountain and prairie: the eastern section extended 450 miles from Lake Superior to the Missouri River, the western section a little over 100 miles from Tacoma to Kalama, a village on the north bank of the Columbia River. From that point, passengers and freight were ferried upriver to Portland.

When prosperity returned toward the end of the 1870s, the reorganized Northern Pacific line under the leadership of its president, Frederick Billings, again pushed construction forward. But not until Henry Villard gained control of the company in 1881 did the line at last realize its transcontinental destiny. Given the Northern Pacific's twenty-year ordeal, Villard had a right to celebrate its completion.

Like the early history of his railroad, Villard's life was a chronicle of triumphs and bitter disappointments. Born in Bavaria in 1835 as Ferdinand Heinrich Gustav Hilgard, he immigrated to the United States eighteen years later. Finding work as a newspaper reporter, he covered the Lincoln-Douglas debates, the 1860 presidential election, and the Civil War. Villard married Fannie Garrison, the daughter of the well-known abolitionist William Lloyd Garrison.

The ambitious young journalist also found time to study law and railroad promotion and finance. When he returned to Europe in the early 1870s to restore his fragile health, a group of worried Germans who had invested in American railroads selected him as their overseas agent, a move that soon made him a rich man. By the end of the decade, Villard had formed the Oregon Railway and Navigation Company and extended its tracks along the south bank of the Columbia River from Portland to a junction with the Northern Pacific near present-day Pasco, Washington. Bringing rail service to the expanding agricultural districts of the interior Northwest proved exceedingly profitable, but Villard still sought both a reliable connection to the East and a way to prevent a Puget Sound community from rivaling Portland. In an act of incredible financial daring, he raised $8 million to enable his company to buy the Northern Pacific in the famous "Blind Pool" in 1881. On the strength of his reputation alone, investors put their money into a project about which they knew nothing.

When Northern Pacific rails finally met at Gold Creek, Villard controlled a vast transportation empire and stood at the peak of his career. A few months later, cost overruns and other money crises caused by his haste to finish the line tested the limits of his financial genius. During the next decade Villard experienced a dizzying series of reverses. Forced to resign as head of the Northern Pacific in 1884, he regained a seat on the company's

145

31. A festive arch at First and Salmon streets welcomed Henry Villard and his special guests to Portland, September 11, 1883. Courtesy Oregon Historical Society: 26280.

board of directors three years later and served as its chairman from 1889 to 1893 when the railroad went bankrupt during the depression of the 1890s. The one-time railroad baron died in 1900, though not without leaving his signature across the Northwest. It was a signature written not just in iron and steel rails but also in the form of books, laboratory equipment, and other aid he gave the University of Oregon and the University of Washington during their years of financial struggle.

This, in short, was the meaning of Villard's final spike at Gold Creek: a journey that once required three to five months now took only five or six days. For investors and homeseekers from distant regions and for residents of the Pacific Northwest, an era of isolation had ended. Newcomers traveling by rail poured into the region—especially into Washington—at a rate unimaginable only a decade earlier. Cities and farms transformed the landscape, and large-scale business enterprises and organized labor attained a prominence and power not possessed before.

Thus, in September 1883, when his financial downfall lay yet in the future, a major builder of the new Northwest felt entitled to savor the good times, banquets, parades, bunting, flags, and accolades of his peers. Still, there were a few discordant notes, mainly from the unfortunate villages that Villard's twin ribbons of steel bypassed and thereby excluded from the new mainstream of Northwest life.

After Gold Creek, several more transcontinental lines were completed to the Pacific Coast, each extending numerous branches into the Northwest's mining, timber, and agricultural regions. No decade would rival the 1880s for the miles of track laid across the region. If the boundary-setting, government-creating decade of the 1840s represented the most important transition in the region's history, then the railroad-building decade of the 1880s surely followed a close second.

CHAPTER 8

Metropolitan Corridors: Transportation and the New Northwest

*

Give us a railroad! Though it be a rawhide one with open passenger cars and a sheet iron boiler; anything on wheels drawn by an iron horse! But give us a railroad.—Francis Cook, *Territory of Washington*, quoting the Walla Walla *Watchman* (1880)

*

Indians, fur traders, and missionaries had much in common in matters of transportation: their three basic modes of travel were by foot, water, and horse. To those the pioneer settlers added carts and wagons drawn by a variety of animals, but all such forms of transportation remained essentially private. Common carriers—enterprises specializing wholly in transporting goods and passengers with services available to any user—arrived in the Pacific Northwest only in the mid-1840s and did not become large-scale operations until the mining booms of the 1860s stimulated such enterprises. Thereafter, common carriers employing a variety of conveyances, from packtrains, stagecoaches, freight wagons, steamboats, and sailing ships to railroad freight and passenger trains, tied the region together and integrated it with the larger world. Without the construction of a railway network, it would be impossible to account for the rapid commercial and urban growth that the Northwest experienced after the mid-1880s.

EARLY TRAVEL BY WATER AND LAND

Inland rivers and valleys together with the Pacific Ocean and the many tidal estuaries along the coast formed the earliest and easiest avenues of communication and transportation. Because travel by water had its limits, a generation of fur traders and explorers, drawing in many cases upon knowledge supplied by local Indians, mapped out and blazed supplemental trails and roads. Overland travelers and government surveyors elaborated on this information, and railroad and highway builders later chose to follow some of the same routes. One such example is the old Oregon Trail across southern Idaho and through the Columbia gorge now traversed by the Union Pacific Railroad and Interstate 84.

Trails and crude territorial and military roads, often amounting to little more than footpaths, threaded their way across the Pacific Northwest before the coming of the railroads. One of those was the Mullan Road, perhaps second only to the Oregon Trail as a route of historical significance. That military highway, intended as an alternate to the Oregon Trail, owed its origin to the railroad-surveying project headed by Isaac I. Stevens, who designated Lieutenant John Mullan and thirteen men to gather data on winter weather in the Rocky Mountains. In 1854, after Congress appropriated $30,000 to survey a military road from Fort Benton, at the upper limit of steamer navigation on the Missouri River, to Fort Walla Walla, Mullan was appointed to head the project. Construction did not begin until 1859, after Congress had appropriated another $100,000 and Indian warfare on the Columbia plateau ceased. The 624-mile-long route opened in August 1862, but even before its completion, an army unit covered the distance in fifty-seven days.

Compared to twentieth-century highways, the Mullan Road was primitive: its grades were steep and in some places impassable in wet weather. Although it was billed as a wagon road, in the rugged Bitterroot and Coeur d'Alene mountains, it frequently amounted to little more than a pack trail. The quieting of Indian-white conflict in eastern Washington diminished its value as a military route, but it remained strategically important during the Civil War and helped to facilitate commerce to the gold camps of the northern Rocky Mountains. Immigrant parties occasionally used it on their way west to open new agricultural lands in the Palouse country.

One settlement on the Mullan Road that profited from the region's expanding transportation network was Walla Walla, a major supply center in the 1860s. Packtrains traveled from Walla Walla to camps on the Clearwater and Boise rivers, even as far north as the diggings in British Columbia's Kootenay region. Packers generally used mules and horses (an experiment with camels proved unsuccessful). Wagons sometimes replaced packtrains during the dry summer months.

Steamboats plying Pacific Northwest waters formed an integral part of the region's expanding transportation network. The *Beaver*, a diminutive paddle boat constructed in England for the Hudson's Bay Company and delivered to John McLoughlin at Fort Vancouver in 1836, was the first steamboat in the Northwest. Among the *Beaver*'s many tasks was supplying Russian Alaska. After more than fifty years of service, the steamer ran aground in British Columbia and sank.

The side-wheeler *Columbia*, which commenced regular service between Astoria and Portland in 1850, was the first steamship to ply the Columbia as a common carrier. Half a dozen steamships soon joined her on interior waters, and their number greatly increased after the gold discoveries of the 1860s.

Transportation up the Columbia and Willamette rivers from Portland was no simple matter. The falls at Oregon City required passengers and freight traveling to and from Eugene City and other upper Willamette landings to portage at that point. Even more formidable obstacles interrupted navigation on the Columbia. The construction of a wooden, mule-powered tramway at the Cascades during the late 1850s provided a short, easy portage for passengers and freight. Farther upriver, near Dalles City (now The Dalles), a longer portage line replaced a crude wagon road in 1863. The tracks of the first true railroad in the Pacific Northwest climbed eleven miles past the rapids to slack water above Celilo Falls. Steamboat service to the interior Northwest above Celilo commenced in 1858 with the stern-wheeler *Colonel Wright*.

THE RISE OF COMMON CARRIERS

Because isolation was the fate of immigrant settlers, inauguration of regular mail, passenger, and freight service, however crude and inefficient, was welcomed as a sign of liberation and progress. Probably the first common carrier in the old Oregon country was an ox-powered stage that began twice-weekly operation between Oregon City and the Tualatin plain in 1846. It promised to operate "rain or no rain—mud or no mud—load or no load—but not without pay." Other primitive stagecoach lines soon followed. By 1857 a Concord coach was able to complete the fifty-mile run from Portland to Salem in only one day.

The California Stage Company, one of the largest organizations of its kind in the United States, established direct and regular service between Portland and Sacramento in 1860. The seven hundred–mile journey required six days. Convenient connections linked Sacramento to the growing metropolis of San Francisco and to Saint Louis. The same stage company

32. The steamboat *Spokane* on the Snake River near
Lewiston, Idaho, in the early twentieth century.
Courtesy Idaho Historical Society: 78–203.6.

hauled passengers and mail between Oregon and California until completion of a railway line in 1887. Several other outfits offered express and light
package service, most notably Wells, Fargo and Company of San Francisco,
which established a far-flung network of stagecoach and freight lines in the
1860s and 1870s to serve mining regions in the interior Northwest.

A common feature in American business history has been for competing
local companies to fail or be merged into large-scale, often monopolistic,
enterprises. In the Northwest, that happened in the stagecoach business
when Ben Holladay created a transportation monopoly. A Kentuckian
whose drive and ruthlessness won him the titles of Stagecoach King and
Napoleon of the West, Holladay gained control of a small stagecoach outfit
in 1862. With the aid of federal mail contracts, he extended its lines from
Salt Lake City to the booming mining camps and supply towns of Boise
City, Walla Walla, and Virginia City, Montana. Ultimately, the Holladay
network connected the Missouri River port of Atchison, Kansas, to the
steamboat landing at The Dalles. This arrangement eliminated the need for
northwesterners to travel to the East by way of California.

Faced with financial reverses as a result of Indian attacks and other problems, Holladay sold his stagecoach empire to Wells, Fargo in 1866, but this was not the last the Pacific Northwest would hear from him. He invested in a company operating ships along the coast from Alaska to Mexico and used that as a means to gain ownership of railroad and steamship properties in Oregon. In the Willamette Valley he organized the Oregon and California Railroad, issuing millions of dollars' worth of bonds that were purchased by English and German investors—people who knew little about Holladay or the railroad.

Holladay's railway lines had pushed south as far as Roseburg by 1873, but hard times in the mid-1870s forced him to yield control of his empire to Henry Villard, the American representative of a group of German bondholders. Holladay retired from the transportation business and lived in Portland until his death in 1887.

Few businessmen exemplified better than Ben Holladay the ruthless, uninhibited spirit of the freewheeling capitalism of the nineteenth century. A self-made man, he entertained lavishly, spent money freely, and competed vigorously. Holladay's specialty was the ruthless elimination of competition: he was even reputed to have staged "Indian" attacks in an effort to drive rival stage companies out of business. To some he embodied the vulgar new materialism that was debasing American life; to others, he was a typical product of the Wild West.

When Villard gained control of the Oregon and California Railroad and other Holladay properties in 1876, he expanded upon and perfected his predecessor's dreams of empire. Using Holladay's rail and river monopoly in the Willamette Valley as his financial base, Villard gained a similar position in the Columbia Valley when he acquired the Oregon Steam Navigation Company for $5 million in 1879.

A group of local capitalists who organized the Oregon Steam Navigation Company in 1860 dominated traffic on the Columbia River and reaped a fortune during the inland gold rush. Although the company became an object of hatred to many northwesterners, its founders became wealthy. One of them, Simeon G. Reed, went on to invest in various enterprises, including mines in northern Idaho and livestock breeding, and thereby vastly enlarged his wealth. His widow willed $3 million toward the founding of Reed College, which opened in Portland in 1911.

When Villard acquired the Oregon Steam Navigation Company, he reorganized it as the Oregon Railway and Navigation Company. As its new name indicated, the firm operated steamboats and extended a network of railway lines from Portland to tap the agricultural riches of the Walla Walla

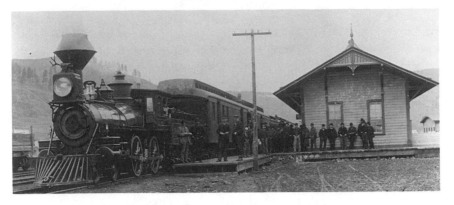

33. A train of the Oregon Railway and Navigation
Company photographed in La Grande, Oregon (erroneously labeled Starbuck by the photographer). It
was one of hundreds of small Northwest communities
linked to metropolitan centers by steel rails. Courtesy
Oregon Historical Society: 1596B.

Valley and other interior points. Like its predecessor, the Oregon Railway
and Navigation Company proved exceedingly profitable.

Of all the transportation advances that Pacific Northwesterners witnessed in the nineteenth century, the railroad was the most revolutionary,
although it did not completely displace steamboats and stagecoaches. Until
the advent of motorized vehicles in the early twentieth century, stages
continued to supplement rail service in several remote areas. The completion of the Cascades canal in 1896 and The Dalles–Celilo canal in 1915
opened the main body of the Columbia to through navigation, and yet river
transportation remained in the shadow of the railroads until the federal
government completed a series of dams and locks on the Columbia and
Snake rivers in the 1960s and 1970s. After that, railroads actually found
themselves at a rate disadvantage with barge lines for grain traffic from the
interior Northwest as far east as Montana, where grain went by truck to
Snake River ports.

RAILROAD BUILDING: LOCAL AND TRANSCONTINENTAL

The Pacific Northwest's earliest railroads served local needs, such as portaging passengers and freight around the falls of the Columbia or moving
wheat from the breadbasket of the Walla Walla Valley to a steamboat landing at Wallula on the Columbia River. Workmen in 1859 laid 4.5 miles of
wooden track between the site of what is now Bonneville Dam and Cascade

Locks, Oregon. Over its tracks rumbled trains of four or five cars pulled by horses and mules. A few months later a bearing surface of sheet iron was affixed to the wooden tracks, and the Oregon Pony, the first steam locomotive built on the Pacific Coast, began portaging passengers and freight.

The Walla Walla and Columbia River Railroad, a thirty-two-mile-long narrow gauge line that Dr. Dorsey S. Baker completed in 1875, illustrates how a pioneer entrepreneur could marshal local resources to build a short, low-cost railway. To keep expenses low, the Walla Walla businessman used regular T-shaped rails only on the curves; he substituted wooden rails topped with lengths of strap iron on the straight sections. This home-grown enterprise was variously called Dr. Baker's Road, the strap iron road, and the rawhide road, the latter a derisive name arising from a confused and erroneous notion that the cost-conscious Baker utilized strap leather instead of iron. One retelling of that myth in a national journal even claimed that during a particularly hard winter, wolves desperate for food ate the rawhide and temporarily severed Walla Walla's link to the outside world. The truth is that Baker's monopoly made such staggering profits that he was able to sell it for a handsome gain to the Oregon Steam Navigation Company in 1878. By becoming part of Villard's expanding empire, Dr. Baker's railroad and the portage lines along the Columbia formed a link in a railroad network extending east from Portland.

During the 1880s, tracklaying went forward throughout the region at a furious pace. When Villard's overextended holding company collapsed in 1884 and the Northern Pacific and Oregon Railway and Navigation Company fell into separate hands, the two companies raced to build a latticework of competing and often unprofitable lines across the agricultural lands of the Palouse.

Having lost direct access to Portland when its ally turned competitor, the Northern Pacific extended its own main line from the Columbia River up the Yakima Valley and over the Cascade mountains to Tacoma. After boring through the mountains under Stampede Pass in what was at that time the second-longest tunnel in the United States, the line opened in 1887; the Northern Pacific thus offered service to Tacoma, Seattle, and Portland entirely over its own rails. As Portland backers feared, the Stampede Pass line funneled a substantial portion of interior grain to Puget Sound ports.

The Union Pacific, a partner in building the first transcontinental railroad, emerged as the Northern Pacific's major competitor when it took steps to tap the resources of the Pacific Northwest. With that goal in mind, a subsidiary company, the Oregon Short Line, completed a railroad across southern Idaho in 1884. True to its name, the Oregon Short Line provided a shortcut between the Union Pacific main line in Wyoming and Huntington, Oregon, where it met the tracks of the Oregon Railway and Navigation Company, now part of the Union Pacific.

Despite the wealth of the Oregon Railway and Navigation Company, the sprawling Union Pacific system formed at best a rickety, overextended financial structure that collapsed during the hard times of the 1890s. Only after the financier Edward H. Harriman acquired and reorganized the company in 1897 did it become what it remains today, one of the most financially secure railroads in the United States.

Through rail service from the Pacific Northwest to California commenced in late 1887 following a final spike ceremony at Ashland, Oregon. Charles Crocker, the head of the Southern Pacific, reminded observers at the Ashland ceremony that the line now linked Portland and New Orleans to create the longest railway system in the world. For years the Southern Pacific was also the largest nongovernment employer west of the Mississippi River and, as a result of the sizable land grant acquired through the Oregon and California Railroad, became one of America's largest private landholders.

In late 1885 the Canadian Pacific Railway completed a line between Montreal and Vancouver; a connection to Seattle opened in 1891. Two years later the Great Northern Railway quietly finished a line from Seattle to Saint Paul. Last spike ceremonies by that time no longer had any publicity value. In June 1893, the same month the Great Northern completed its transcontinental line, a financial panic convulsed Wall Street and precipitated the worst depression in American history prior to the hard times of the 1930s.

Although local and regional lines continued to be built until the First World War and at least some construction continued until the early 1930s, the depression of 1893–97 brought to a close the greatest era of railroad building in Pacific Northwest history. The last to join the ranks of the northern transcontinentals was the Chicago, Milwaukee, and St. Paul Railway, which extended its track from the Midwest to Puget Sound in 1909. That line should never have been built, and the railroad's subsequent financial troubles highlighted major changes that overtook American transportation during the second decade of the twentieth century.

The Milwaukee Road, as it became popularly known, was a prosperous carrier before it decided to tap the commerce of the Pacific Northwest. Some financial analysts questioned the wisdom of that decision, and later

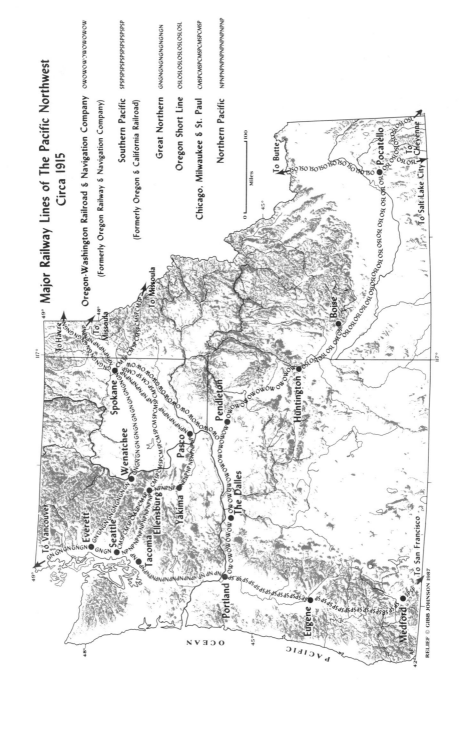

Major Railway Lines of The Pacific Northwest
Circa 1915

Oregon-Washington Railroad & Navigation Company OWOWOWOWOWOW
(Formerly Oregon Railway & Navigation Company)

Southern Pacific SPSPSPSPSPSPSPSPSPSP
(Formerly Oregon & California Railroad)

Great Northern GNGNGNGNGNGN

Oregon Short Line OSLOSLOSLOSLOSLOSL

Chicago, Milwaukee & St. Paul CMSPCMSPCMSPCMSPCMSP

Northern Pacific NPNPNPNPNPNPNPNP

0   100
Miles

RELIEF © GIBB JOHNSON 1987

events made them wise prophets. The completion of the Panama Canal in 1914 took a far larger bite from the transcontinental freight business than railroads expected. By 1928 the canal carried 20 percent of the lumber marketed in the United States and almost half the production of the Pacific Northwest.

Automobile and truck competition that first grew worrisome during the 1920s was similarly unanticipated when the Milwaukee Road built its Pacific extension. Moreover, between 1916 and 1920 the railroad took the bold step of electrifying much of its line from central Montana to Puget Sound. That technological marvel, representing the world's most extensive railroad electrification project at that time, excited the imaginations of jaded railroad travelers, science fiction writers, and regional promoters. The latter group especially appreciated how well the innovative railroad advertised the Northwest's abundance of "white coal," or hydroelectric power.

In the end, the hoped-for savings from electrification never offset the enormous cost of installation and thus contributed to the railroad's growing financial woes. The Milwaukee Road entered receivership in 1925, the first of three bouts of bankruptcy, and in 1981 it abandoned service west of Montana.

Of the entrepreneurs associated with the Northwest's great era of railway building, no one better merited the title of Empire Builder than James J. Hill, a businessman with diverse interests in the Pacific Northwest. The Canadian-born Hill began his business career modestly enough as a shipping clerk in Saint Paul, Minnesota. While he was still in his twenties, he started his own warehouse and express business. Shortly before turning forty, he acquired a decrepit railway line, the St. Paul and Pacific, in 1878. From that modest acorn grew a mighty oak, the Great Northern, financially the strongest of all the northern transcontinentals.

Unlike the Northern Pacific and Union Pacific, the Great Northern worked its way west almost entirely on a pay-as-you-go basis, constructing branch lines and encouraging agricultural settlement rather than depending on government land grants. So soundly was the Great Northern financed that it weathered the depression of the 1890s while scores of other lines, including the Northern Pacific, went bankrupt. Hill outmaneuvered Edward Harriman of the Union Pacific in 1901 in a battle for control of the Northern Pacific and also acquired the Chicago, Burlington, and Quincy to gain entrance to Chicago.

When the "Hill Lines" attempted to consolidate under the control of a holding company—the Northern Securities Company—the United States

34. The railroad baron James J. Hill (1838–1916)
is flanked by two powerful New York bankers,
George F. Baker and Charles Steele, during a visit
to Portland in May 1910. Courtesy James Jerome Hill
Reference Library.

Supreme Court blocked the move in 1904. But that setback did not stop Hill from expanding his empire in other ways by purchasing or building new lines to link Spokane and Portland and battling Harriman for access to central Oregon. "Give me enough Swedes and whiskey and I'll build a railroad to Hell," Hill is reputed to have said. The Empire Builder died in 1916, but the tracks of the Great Northern railroad pushed on to reach northern California in 1931.

A latter-day monument to Hill is the Burlington Northern Railroad, formed in 1970 from the trunk lines that seventy years earlier he had unsuccessfully attempted to combine under the Northern Securities banner. Since 1971, Amtrak has operated a daily passenger train between Chicago and Seattle called the Empire Builder, a name inherited from the Great Northern. In the early years of Amtrak operation, a portrait of James J. Hill occupied its accustomed place in the dining car.

THE RAILROAD-MADE NORTHWEST

Pacific Northwesterners had a love-hate relationship with the railroad companies. They welcomed new lines to their communities, believing that rail connections guaranteed permanence, growth, and prosperity; they sulked when railroads passed them by. Would-be cities on Puget Sound fought bitterly with one another in the early 1870s to be designated the terminus of the Northern Pacific. The new town of Tacoma won the prize, but its rival, Seattle, refused to concede, although the Northern Pacific initially relegated it to the end of a branch line. The future of Seattle looked considerably brighter after Hill selected the city as the Pacific terminus for his Great Northern.

After the fall of 1883 and the completion of a through line to the East, the coming of rails to a Pacific Northwest community meant major changes. Their routes functioning as metropolitan corridors, railroads linked the towns and villages of America's hinterland to Wall Street and Capitol Hill. Railroads not only opened the door to a nationwide market for local products—especially for bulky items like wheat and timber—but also increased competition for local merchants and redefined spatial relationships. If prices on main street were too high, citizens of once isolated communities like Klamath Falls and Coeur d'Alene needed only to thumb through catalogs and order merchandise from distant supply houses like Montgomery Ward or Sears Roebuck in Chicago and have it shipped west by rail. Travel on business or to visit friends and relatives became easy, and if one went first class in one of the ornate sleeping cars, the journey might actually be pleasurable.

But this new freedom had its price. Sometimes the price was relatively insignificant, as when railroads adopted standard time zones in 1883 and individual communities chose to abandon the multitude of local standards formerly used. For travelers it meant arranging their lives according to a railroad timetable.

Sometimes the price was much greater. Except in Pacific Coast ports, westerners were much more dependent upon railroads than most people living east of the Mississippi. After all, many western communities were children of the steel rail, and the timber, mineral, and agricultural industries of the interior Northwest looked to rail transportation for survival. Railroads made commercial agriculture the lifeblood of the Palouse, but they did not always respond to farmers' needs: in the early 1890s when farmers were unable to secure enough boxcars to haul their unusually heavy harvest of grain to market, they protested loudly. Farmers across the Pacific Northwest learned similar lessons in dependence.

When the Northern Pacific extended its main line across central Washington and the Cascade mountains in the mid-1880s, it gave the citizens of Yakima City a lesson in railroad power. By locating its station four miles away on its own land rather than in Yakima City, through which it had to pass, the company forced all but the most stubborn settlers of the original town to relocate in North Yakima. The new community officially shortened its name to Yakima in early 1918. Not surprisingly, antirailroad sentiment was the basis for several early political protest movements in the Yakima Valley.

A railroad could also bless or blight a community through freight rates. In an era lacking effective government regulation of economic matters, the only restraints on railroad rates were competition and the willingness of customers to pay. Citizens of Spokane battled that harsh truth for years. They complained that the railroads charged more to ship goods from Chicago to Spokane than to Seattle, four hundred miles farther west.

Spokane residents sought the lower or "terminal" rates for years. When the Interstate Commerce Commission issued an order in Spokane's favor in 1911, its citizens celebrated in the streets with bells, whistles, horns, and dancing. But their joy was premature, because the railroads appealed to the United States Commerce Court, and a lengthy legal contest followed. Not until 1914 did Spokane win its rate fight. And yet, ironically, in much of eastern Washington and northern Idaho, the rate structure had favored Spokane over other locales and helped it become a major supply center.

Railroad stations once functioned as centers of community life, civic showplaces, and portals to all other destinations along the metropolitan corridor. As late as 1919, when commercial radio had yet to make its debut, the best way to follow World Series action—other than to attend the game—was at the depot, where a kindly telegrapher might post each inning's score as it came in on the wire.

Railroads fostered tourism and promoted national parks: the Northern

RAILROADS AND WESTERN SETTLEMENT

Railroads avidly promoted settlement of their huge tracts of western land through sales campaigns both in North America and in Europe. Their advertisements appeared in thousands of newspapers, and they distributed tens of thousands of elaborate, often multicolored promotional brochures in English, German, Norwegian, and other languages. The Northern Pacific published its own promotional magazine, and its timetables carefully explained to travelers how to acquire a homestead in the new Northwest. Railroads regularly ran homeseekers' specials and hauled immigrant families and their belongings at reduced rates.

Agents met immigrants at dockside in New York and other East Coast ports and helped them travel west to settle on lands the company had reserved for certain nationalities. That arrangement is one reason why Germans, Scandinavians, and Russians tended to cluster in distinct rural settlements scattered from the Dakotas to Washington.

The selling price of the railroad land generally ranged from $1.25 to $20.00 an acre, depending on its perceived value, but with frequent discounts given for cash. The companies also instituted a variety of low down-payment plans to speed settlement and generated much-needed traffic.

Despite their apparent beneficence, railroads were often the targets of complaint. In eastern Washington, the slow rate at which the Northern Pacific proceeded with the managing of its land grant caused early settlers to fear that they might be evicted or forced to pay exorbitant fees to gain legal title to their holdings.

Pacific became synonymous with Yellowstone (created in 1872), and the Great Northern with Glacier (created in 1910). During the mid-1930s, the Union Pacific built a new resort complex called Sun Valley in the Sawtooth Range of southern Idaho that was a progenitor of other winter sports facilities in the West.

Given the fact that railroads were by far America's biggest business, whatever they did had an impact on citizens' lives in the new West. During their heyday from the 1870s until the late 1920s, railroads could not remain outside the public arena even had they wanted to. Their many activities furnished the basis for praise and condemnation, community prosperity and ruin. Their vast landholdings placed them second only to the federal government as agencies of settlement and development.

From the railway age to the present time, no private enterprise—not even the oil companies in the automobile age—occupied a position of similar power and influence. Thus, the story of the Pacific Northwest's railway era is inextricably linked to that of its urban growth, large-scale immigration, and political reform movements.

CHAPTER 9

The Stumps of Enterprise:
A Natural Resource-Based
Economy

*

It transpires that many Easterners still think of our West more as a holiday
hunting ground or an incubator for frenzied fiction than as an honest-to-
God part of our agricultural and industrial nation.—*New West* (1919)

*

Tree stumps symbolized prosperity to nineteenth-century Pacific Northwesterners, because felling trees was often associated with activities that
connoted growth and progress. From the forests, builders hacked townsites
where blackened stumps often still smoldered in the center of newly graded
streets; massive stumps once stood at the very doors of Tacoma's best
hotels; and enterprising settlers occasionally fashioned snug homes from
hollow stumps. Not without reason was early Portland nicknamed Stump-
town. The rail baron James J. Hill once quipped to a group of Northwest
businessmen that he had seen only four stumps on Puget Sound without a
town name attached.

In the early twentieth century, when the lumber industry was the Pacific
Northwest's largest employer and economic mainstay, few people questioned whether acres of stumps were ugly or wasteful. Harvesting the
region's "limitless" forests was popularly equated only with money and
jobs, prosperity and growth. During the "cut and run" era, it mattered little
if loggers saved time by sawing trees fifteen feet above ground and left
stumps containing thousands of board feet of perfectly good lumber. Beginning with the maritime fur trade, a key feature of the regional economy was
dependence on harvesting or extracting nature's wealth. As a result, the

162

history of the Pacific Northwest includes many examples of economic instability and the plunder of natural and human resources.

During the first four decades of the nineteenth century, the region's economic life centered on the trade in skins and furs. Then came an era of commercial agriculture, tidewater sawmills, fish canning, and periodic mining booms. The region's rapid growth during the final two decades of the nineteenth century rested upon an economic foundation that can be summarized in a few monosyllables: wood, fish, grain, and ore. To those basic commodities could be added cattle, sheep, fruit, and coal.

In the early 1880s—the formative decade of the region's modern economic history—much of the Pacific Northwest's future wealth could be described only as potential or undiscovered. At that time the forests blanketing western portions of Oregon and Washington and the Idaho panhandle, apart from the trees at tidewater where lumber could be easily transported to market by sea, had little economic value. Major coalfields in the Cascades and the great mineral bonanza of Idaho's Coeur d'Alene region remained yet undiscovered, and the agricultural potential of the semiarid interior was not yet apparent. It would take the transforming power of irrigation and a growing network of railway lines to make the sage-covered lands of the Yakima Valley yield an abundance of fruit and those of southern Idaho grow the state's famed potatoes.

FISHERIES

Commerce in skins and furs undoubtedly ranks as the oldest market activity in the Pacific Northwest, but what ranks second? Forestry? Agriculture? Fisheries? It could be any of those. Each was associated in some way with the Hudson's Bay Company, which, if not always a pioneer, was the first significant developer of the region's agriculture, timber, and marine resources. As early as the 1820s, remote company posts on the Columbia River sold fish to London buyers.

For many years the most important product of the region's fisheries was salmon. Five varieties of salmon were caught along the entire Pacific watershed, especially in Puget Sound and the lower Columbia River. Salmon are anadromous; that is, they spawn in fresh water and spend most of their adult life in the ocean, ranging over thousands of miles. After approximately five years they return to spawn, sometimes in remote tributaries of the Columbia River a thousand miles or more from the sea, although in recent years the building of dams has narrowed the fish's inland range.

Over the years, the region's commercial fisheries were by no means limited to salmon. Money was to be made in oysters, clams, shrimp, halibut, and dozens of other edible forms of marine life, not to mention production of fish oil, fertilizer, and algae. Salmon, however, ranked first in commercial value, and the image of millions of them returning upstream, driven by some mysterious instinct to leap rapids and low waterfalls, caused the fish to became as closely identified with the wild Northwest as cod was with New England.

The modern salmon industry of the Pacific Coast originated when Hapgood, Hume, and Company established a small cannery on the Sacramento River in 1864. Two years later the Hume brothers opened a cannery on the lower Columbia River, and that first year they produced 6,000 cases, each holding 48 one-pound cans of Chinook salmon, for a total value of $64,000. Profits were spectacular because canned salmon was popular in the East, Great Britain, and other areas as a cheap, nourishing working-class food. From that modest beginning, more than fifty canneries were built along the banks of the Columbia River and its tributaries by 1883, and numerous others dotted the banks of coastal rivers of Oregon and Puget Sound. Astoria, located near the mouth of the Columbia River, became a center of canning operations. The Columbia River salmon catch peaked in 1895 with 635,000 cases, but by that time the Puget Sound's cannery output was still larger. Cannery operations on the sound dated from 1877 and peaked in 1913 with 2.5 million cases. Alaska's salmon-canning industry, which had a later beginning, eventually eclipsed that of both Oregon and Washington.

Fishermen were predominantly Scandinavians and Finns, who logged or farmed in the off-season. Many cannery workers were Chinese. Canning was at first a slow, messy business with individual tins requiring careful soldering by hand. Beginning in 1903, however, a revolutionary machine called the Iron Chink dramatically thinned the ranks of cannery workers. By means of rotating knives and brushes, this machine automatically decapitated and cleaned fish at the rate of one per second. Another change occurred at the turn of the century, when numerous small canneries formed cooperatives such as the Columbia River Packers Association to market their products more efficiently and to stabilize profits.

Cutthroat competition and unsound practices, like stringing traps and nets across river mouths so that few adult fish survived to spawn, characterized commercial fishing almost from the beginning. At times such an armada of fishing craft jammed the lower Columbia that it seemed a person could walk across the river on their decks.

35. Unloading one of the huge salmon catches common on Puget Sound in the 1880s and 1890s. Courtesy Museum of History and Industry, Seattle: 10593.

Early on, cannery operators on the Columbia River expressed concern about yearly fluctuations in salmon runs. The Washington legislature declared a closed season in 1877; Oregon responded the following year with two weak conservation measures, one regulating the size of openings in gill nets to allow smaller fish to escape, the other prohibiting fishing during certain hours of the week. Neither Oregon nor Washington vigorously enforced early conservation measures. Over the decades a bewildering accretion of laws and regulations—such as those outlawing traps, explosives, and drugs—attempted to protect commercial fishermen from themselves. Quite simply, they possessed technology too efficient to insure their industry's long-term survival.

Hydroelectric dams created another set of problems. Grand Coulee Dam, which has no fish ladders, barred salmon from eleven hundred linear miles of streams in Washington, Idaho, and British Columbia when it was completed in 1941. Each additional dam on the Columbia and Snake rivers added nitrogen to water below the spillways. When absorbed into the bloodstream of fish, nitrogen creates a fatal condition known as the bends. At times 95 percent of the smolts or young salmon died during their hazard-filled trip to the sea, primarily as a result of the bends or being chewed up by turbines in the dams.

The Northwest Power Act of 1980 proposed to restore fish populations damaged by hydroelectric development. Whether it can actually do so by artificial propagation remains to be seen. The region's first hatchery was established on the Clackamas River near Portland in 1877. But even with numerous additional hatcheries during the twentieth century, anadromous fish still face many life threats, including the lack of genetic diversity that makes salmon vulnerable to diseases that occasionally kill millions of them while still in the hatchery. Some experts maintain that hatchery-raised salmon lack the superior taste and survival skills of wild salmon.

AGRICULTURE

Agriculture in the Pacific Northwest was clearly different from that practiced in the Midwest and border states where the region's first Euro-American settlers originated. The image of pioneers clearing wilderness to create a self-sufficient family farm is common in American history. But that is not an accurate portrait of events in the Pacific Northwest, where both commercial and subsistence agriculture existed simultaneously almost from the beginning. Even before pioneer families of the Willamette Valley first raised grain and livestock to meet their personal needs, Hudson's Bay Company farms supplied food to employees as well as to settlers in Russian Alaska.

The Oregon country produced more than 160,000 bushels of wheat in 1846. The provisional government declared wheat legal tender and pegged its value at one dollar per bushel. During the California gold rush, the price of Willamette Valley wheat soared to six dollars per bushel, and more than fifty ships entered the Columbia seeking cargoes of grain. Mining booms closer to home during the 1850s and 1860s further stimulated the growth of commercial agriculture.

Wheat and oats, cattle and sheep became the chief commercial products of farm and ranch, but conspicuously missing were the extensive fields of corn and the large herds of swine so typical of agriculture in the Mississippi and Ohio valleys. Corn, that great staple of American agriculture for two centuries, did not thrive in the Willamette Valley: the weather west of the Cascades was too dry during the summer growing season and the nights were too cool. The problem perplexed many an early settler.

Moreover, instead of a continuous expanse of farmland like that stretching across the Midwest from eastern Ohio to central Nebraska, agricultural regions of the Pacific Northwest resembled islands separated from one another by forests, mountains, and vast prairies of sagebrush and native grasses. The Willamette Valley, which received enough moisture to make farming relatively easy for emigrants from the Midwest, was the first of those islands to be settled. Twenty years later, in the early 1860s, the technique of dryland farming to conserve soil moisture transformed the semiarid Walla Walla Valley into an agricultural cornucopia. Its farmers raised substantial quantities of grain and cattle to feed the mining population of Idaho.

Another island of agriculture emerged on the well-watered land east of Puget Sound, which became famed for dairying and truck gardens. Farming techniques perfected in the Walla Walla Valley enabled fields of wheat to spread to other parts of the inland Northwest, relentlessly replacing native grasses on the uplands of eastern Oregon and the rolling hills of the Palouse to create the main breadbasket of the Northwest.

Last to be put to the plow was semiarid land that needed extensive irrigation to yield crops: the Snake River plain of southern Idaho around the turn of the century and the Columbia basin of central Washington beginning in the 1950s. As a result of irrigation, wheat and potato production boomed in southern Idaho, and orchards blossomed in numerous locations once considered too dry for grain or fruit. Irrigation first played a significant role in Northwest agriculture during the two decades after 1890.

Engaged in what was almost an agricultural sideshow were the region's stump farmers, a hearty but inevitably impoverished lot who had enough energy and optimism to spend countless hours blasting and pulling out stumps in an attempt to convert infertile patches of logged-off land into pastures and fields. Unscrupulous promoters lured many an unsuspecting person to that backbreaking way of life. The movement attracted the most attention during the first quarter of the twentieth century.

No agricultural commodity bulked larger in the Northwest economy than wheat. By 1910 it represented 44.5 percent of the value of all of Washington crops, and Whitman County was declared the richest county per capita in the United States. Wheat was raised mainly in Washington's southeastern quarter, which as early as 1889 accounted for 93 percent of the state's total. Idaho and Oregon also grew wheat, but their production never equaled that of Washington.

The development of an extensive network of railroads during the 1880s made it relatively easy to ship carloads of wheat from the inland Northwest

36. Asahel Curtis photographed this combination
thresher near Rosalia, Washington, in October 1912.
Courtesy Washington State Historical Society, Tacoma.

to the ports of Seattle and Portland. From that point, ships hauled the grain
to markets as distant as Great Britain. Before the great depression of the
1930s, most Northwest grain moved from farm to market in burlap sacks,
rather than in bulk as it does today. For that reason, long, low warehouses
rather than tall elevators were a common sight in the grain regions until
after 1910.

Grain growers used horses or mules—sometimes as many as fifty animals to a team—to plow, cultivate, seed, and harvest. Gasoline-powered
tractors and combines increased in number after 1914 until, by the mid-
1930s, mules and horses had largely disappeared from the harvest scene.
The amount of labor required to harvest the crops likewise changed. During
the years 1910–14, it required 106 man-hours to produce a hundred bushels
of wheat; by 1950 the same amount of wheat required only 28 man-hours.
Today a harvest crew consisting of a combine driver and one or two truck
drivers can do the work that required thirty or more men during the days of
the stationary steam-powered thresher. As a result, the army of casual
laborers once common in grain-producing areas has disappeared.

The soft white winter wheat that predominates in the Pacific Northwest is best suited for cake and pastry flour. By the mid-twentieth century its main market was Asia, where it was used mainly for noodles. In the mid-1970s, Japan imported 85 percent of Northwest wheat.

The agricultural product that ranks second only to grain in its contribution to the Northwest economy is livestock. The region's cattle industry originated from stock raised at several Hudson's Bay Company posts and at mission stations or from animals driven to the Pacific Northwest over the Oregon Trail or from California and Texas. Following the Civil War, cattle raising emerged as a large-scale enterprise on the open ranges of the interior. From there beef was supplied on the hoof to Idaho mining communities. Umatilla County, Oregon, and neighboring Walla Walla County, Washington, emerged as the leading livestock producers in the Pacific Northwest during the 1870s.

Capital from California and Nevada enabled several of the region's cattle kings to achieve prominence during the heyday of the open range. One of

37. The Japanese American photographer Frank Matsura recorded these ranchers swimming their cattle across the Okanogan River in north-central Washington. Until the coming of the railroads, herds were driven across the Cascade Range to Seattle stockyards. Courtesy Historical Photograph Collection, Washington State University Libraries: 81–059.

the most notable was Peter French of southeastern Oregon. Early in the 1880s he organized the French-Glenn Livestock Company, an empire that controlled a hundred thousand acres of land. Like his counterparts in Texas, French raised thousands of head of cattle and hired cowboys to manage them. A dominating personality who feuded with the homesteaders encroaching on his range, French died in 1897 when a settler gunned him down.

Railroads and the introduction of stock cars and refrigerated cars during the last years of the nineteenth century opened up markets as distant as Chicago for Northwest beef, but the new mode of transportation also brought an army of homesteaders to acquire prime grazing land for their farms. Their insistence that cattlemen confine their herds to privately owned and fenced-in land, together with a series of harsh winters that decimated the herds during the 1880s, hastened the end of the open range.

Sheep arrived in the Pacific Northwest by a variety of means, notably through the agricultural activities of the Hudson's Bay Company. Marcus Whitman imported sheep from Hawaii to his mission station and taught Indians how to herd them. From California, herders drove several thousand sheep north to the Willamette Valley, more came over the Oregon Trail, and some prized specimens arrived by boat from as far away as England, Australia, and New Zealand. Sheep thrived best on the open ranges of the interior, although not without resistance from cattlemen, who often competed for grazing land.

A celebrated case of conflict between sheep and cattle raisers occurred in southern Idaho in 1896, when "Diamondfield" Jack Davis was arrested for the murder of two sheepherders. Davis, the employee of a large cattle company, was found guilty on the basis of largely circumstantial evidence and sentenced to hang. The case aroused intense feeling among the cattlemen, who proclaimed his innocence, and the sheepmen, who favored conviction. Davis was later pardoned.

The economic value of sheep lay in their lambs, mutton, and wool, the latter finding its way to the region's mills after 1857. In that year the first textile mill west of the Mississippi opened in Salem. Five more woolen mills were in operation in the Willamette Valley by 1866. By the turn of the century, Pendleton had become one of the leading wool-processing centers in the United States. Today the town's name is synonymous with the quality clothing and blankets produced by the Pendleton Woolen Mills, a company that dates from 1894, although most of its plants are now located in places other than Pendleton. During the past century, Idaho frequently ranked as the nation's leading producer of lambs and sheep.

The region's first orchard was located at Fort Vancouver. Twenty years later, in 1847, Henderson Luelling established a nursery in Milwaukie near Portland. He and his brother carried eight hundred seedlings and a few grafted trees over the Oregon Trail in boxes fitted inside their covered wagons. By the early 1850s, enterprising Oregonians sold fruit to California miners. In one year alone in the early 1860s, 3.5 million pounds of Oregon apples reached San Francisco. After completion of a northern transcontinental railroad and the development of refrigerated cars, Northwest fruit traveled to eastern markets. During the next two decades, orchards became an important source of supplemental income to farmers in several parts of the region.

Large-scale commercial orchards became common between 1905 and 1915. Oregon's Hood River and Rogue River valleys and the irrigated lands of Washington's Yakima, Wenatchee, and Okanogan valleys emerged as major producers of apples, pears, prunes, and cherries. In 1908, during a phenomenon known as apple fever, Washington planted at least one million apple trees. By 1917 the state stood first in the nation in apple production.

During the boom years it seemed easier to develop new and better varieties of fruit than to market them or control the growers' tendency to overproduce. The result was a business that oscillated between good times and bad. During the apple glut of the 1920s, Northwest orchardists ripped out millions of fruit trees. In an effort to improve their marketing, orchardists formed cooperative organizations such as the Hood River Apple Growers Union, which developed a brand name, Diamond Brand, for its products.

The region's beet sugar industry is another story of boom-and-bust. Begun by Mormon pioneers in Utah, it became a big business in the early twentieth century when the Northwest's first beet sugar factory opened near Idaho Falls in 1903. This plant subsequently became part of the Utah-Idaho Sugar Company. When soft drink manufacturers increased their use of corn sweeteners during the 1970s, they dealt the beet sugar industry a severe blow.

MINING

The development of commercial agriculture in the Pacific Northwest owed much to mining booms that created the first sizable local and regional markets for the products of farm and ranch. The great era of western mineral bonanzas lasted fifty years—from the discovery of gold in California in 1848 to the Klondike rush of 1898. As an important economic activity in the Pacific Northwest, mining dates from the early 1850s, when prospectors discovered gold in several southern Oregon locales (notably

Jacksonville) and in north-central Washington near Fort Colville. A major find occurred on the Fraser River in 1858 and briefly rivaled the bonanza in California. The great number of Americans streaming across the international boundary so worried James Douglas, governor of Vancouver Island, that he preemptorily extended British authority to the mainland and thereby set the stage for the creation of British Columbia. The Fraser River rush was the first of many mining booms that lured Americans north of the international boundary to seek their fortunes.

More gold was discovered in eastern Oregon, Idaho, and Montana during the 1860s, but then Idaho suffered a disappointing lull that lasted more than a decade. Word of an important new find in 1884 caused a stampede to the Coeur d'Alene region of north Idaho, where miners unearthed one of the greatest mineral bonanzas in the Pacific Northwest. First to be discovered in the remote creek beds was gold, and many of its seekers were farmers from the nearby Palouse country. Prospectors soon found an even more important source of wealth in silver, the production of which increased almost 800 percent in Idaho during the 1880s. Idaho became one of America's leading silver-producing states. But Coeur d'Alene silver, unlike the gold discovered earlier, was not to be recovered by farmers who worked claims after the harvest.

That change occurred because mining in the Coeur d'Alenes rapidly became complex and expensive. At first the gold could be recovered relatively easily through a variety of placer-mining techniques. A prospector could remove the metal from gravel deposits in creek beds using such simple tools as a shovel, pick, and pan, or a rocker or sluice box constructed from wood near at hand. But other forms of placer mining required water cannons (monitors) or large dredges, equipment much too expensive for individual miners. Lode or hard-rock mining, which involved tunneling into the earth and hauling out gold-bearing rock by the ton to refine a few ounces of the precious yellow metal, compounded the problems of complex technology and high cost. Silver, unlike gold, never occurred naturally in pure form and thus could be recovered only through lode mining and expensive refining methods.

As a result of large-scale industrial mining, the Coeur d'Alene region quickly became the domain of giant mining enterprises whose hired miners held a status not unlike that of contemporary factory hands in the East. The miners were dependent upon employers for wages and lived in isolated communities that bore a remarkable resemblance to the drab, grimy industrial villages of Pennsylvania and eastern Ohio.

38. Hydraulic mining on Prichard Creek in the Coeur
d'Alene region of Idaho in the 1880s. Courtesy University of Idaho Library, # 8–X302, Barnard-Stockbridge
Collection.

All three Northwest states produced copper but never in the quantity
discovered under Butte, Montana, in the 1880s. As Butte evolved into one of
the greatest mining camps on earth, it exerted a major influence on industrial relations in the Coeur d'Alenes. Marcus Daly, an Irish immigrant,
purchased what he thought was a silver mine in 1878 for $30,000, the
Anaconda subsequently developed into one of the largest and most valuable
copper mines in the world, supplying a metal for which demand grew with
the dawn of the electric age. The recovery of copper, like silver, involved
lode mining, expensive reduction works, and a large force of hired miners
and other hands. And if anything, industrial mining gave Butte an even
grimmer physical appearance than that of the Coeur d'Alene towns. A
frequent by-product of large-scale silver and copper mining was the industrial violence that made Butte and the Coeur d'Alene region bywords for
labor disputes and bloodshed.

Besides metals and a variety of industrial minerals like sand, salt, gravel,

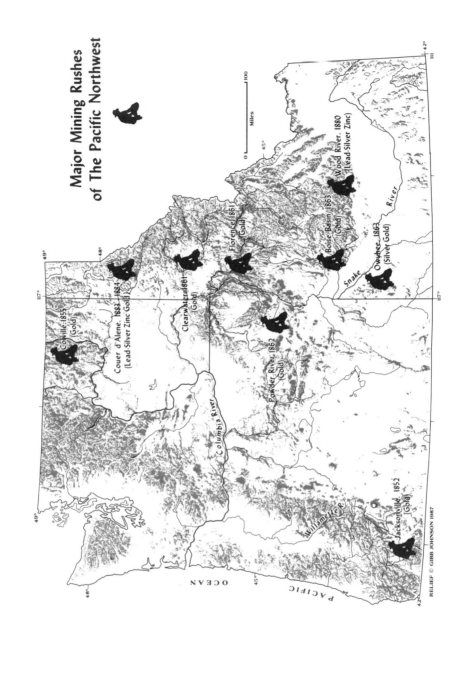

Major Mining Rushes
of The Pacific Northwest

Colville 1855
(Gold)

Couer d'Alene, 1883-1884
(Lead-Silver Zinc Gold)

Clearwater 1861
(Gold)

Florence 1861
(Gold)

Powder River 1862
(Gold)

Wood River, 1880
(Lead-Silver Zinc)

Boise Basin 1863
(Gold)

Owyhee 1863
(Silver Gold)

Jacksonville
1852
(Gold)

Columbia River

Willamette R.

Snake River

PACIFIC OCEAN

Miles

0   100

RELIEF © GIBB JOHNSON 1987

and phosphate, the Pacific Northwest contained deposits of coal. Modest-scale mines opened on Oregon's Coos Bay in 1853, and the coal sold profitably in California. During the 1870s and 1880s, much larger mines opened in the Washington Cascades. Sizable operations located in the foothills east of Seattle and Tacoma and west of Ellensburg employed several hundred men and supplied coal for railroads and home heating in markets as distant as San Francisco. Washington coal mines remained important until shortly after the First World War when they, and their Coos Bay and Vancouver Island counterparts, found it impossible to compete successfully with California oil. Oil, in fact, remains one important mineral not found in commercial quantities in the Pacific Northwest, although some geologists remain hopeful of finding deposits off the Oregon coast or under the basalt of the Columbia plateau.

FOREST PRODUCTS

An estimated seventy million acres of commercial forest land once blanketed the Pacific Northwest. Douglas fir, spruce, hemlock, and cedar were the predominant species west of the Cascade Range; ponderosa pine was dominant on the eastern slopes, and western white pine in the panhandle of Idaho. No economic activity is today more closely identified in the popular mind with the Pacific Northwest than logging and sawmilling, and for good reason. In 1910, when Washington was the nation's number one lumber-producing state, 63 percent of its wageworkers depended upon the forest products industry for jobs. That number remained well above 50 percent for many years.

Harvesting the vast timber wealth of the Pacific Northwest originally resembled mining more than agriculture. Here was a natural resource only to be exploited, with little thought given to conservation or sustained yields. First to consider the commercial possibilities of Northwest timber was the multifaceted Hudson's Bay Company, which erected the region's initial sawmill in 1827 near Fort Vancouver. After expanding its operations, the mill shipped lumber as far as the Hawaiian Islands. Many early facilities were crude and hand operated, but an increasing number were powered by water or steam. As early as 1850 a steam-driven mill operated in Portland, and by the following year Oregon City had five mills, all driven by water.

In 1853, F. C. Talbot and his partner, Andrew Jackson Pope, two young Maine natives who had gone to California during the gold rush and entered the timber business there, selected a site on Puget Sound to build a large steam-powered sawmill. Called Port Gamble, the development physically

39. "Cigar rafts" were a common way to transport logs
from the lower Columbia River to sawmills as far
south as San Diego, California. Courtesy Oregon
Historical Society: 79635.

resembled a New England mill village and was the first of several company towns to dot the shores of Puget Sound. Pope and Talbot chose the site because miles of virgin timber stretched back from the shoreline, and a natural deepwater anchorage protected ships from Pacific storms. By year's end, additional entrepreneurs had followed Pope and Talbot's lead, and during the next several years, Port Blakely, Port Ludlow, and other company towns kept busy meeting the lumber needs of San Francisco, Hawaii, and Asia. At one time the Puget Sound lumber fleet numbered approximately 150 vessels.

Until the early 1880s logging was largely confined to the water's edge, where the "cargo mills" of Puget Sound, Grays Harbor, the lower Columbia River, and Coos Bay served far-flung markets. The orientation of the industry was toward San Francisco, the largest consumer of timber products on the West Coast and home to several businessmen who reaped fortunes from cheap and easily acquired timberlands of the Pacific Northwest. The completion of the Northern Pacific line offered access to markets east of the Rocky Mountains, but the key to success remained railroad rates low enough to allow Pacific Northwest lumber to compete successfully with lumber from the Great Lakes and the South. That did not happen until after the turn of the century. Until then, the railroad boom of the 1880s and early 1890s created a local market for ties, bridge timbers, and building materials for stations and other trackside structures.

Loggers moving to the Pacific Northwest encountered problems unknown in the forests of the Great Lakes states. The uneven terrain and gargantuan size of Northwest trees—Douglas firs sometimes stood more than three hundred feet tall, and western red cedar occasionally grew fifteen feet in diameter—made logs difficult to transport to the mills, especially through the mud and snow of winter. One technique was to construct a corduroy roadway of logs partially sunk into the earth, grease them, and use oxen to skid timber across them to the mills at tidewater. When cheap drinking establishments appeared alongside the mills, the expression "skid road" acquired a dual meaning, the more enduring of which was corrupted into today's "skid row." Another technique for getting logs to the mill was to float them down the mountainsides in long water-filled troughs called flumes. A third method was to float logs down a river, sometimes with the aid of splash dams that temporarily raised the water level on remote tributaries.

The development of special narrow-gauge logging railroads in the 1880s opened up hitherto inaccessible stands of trees at a time when timber near tidewater was becoming depleted. Eventually, thousands of miles of such lines snaked through the woods; virtually every county in Oregon had at least one logging railroad by 1910. The development of heavy-duty trucks made logging railroads rarities by the end of the Second World War.

The railroad was only one of many technological innovations to change the nature of the timber industry. Until the 1880s, trees were felled with axes and cut or "bucked" into standard lengths with crosscut saws commonly called Swede fiddles or misery whips. When loggers in the California redwoods discovered that they could use saws to fell trees, the new technique spread quickly up the coast in the 1880s. The two-man crosscut saw became the logger's principal tool. Next came the steam donkey—a stationary steam engine invented by John Dolbeer in 1881 to yard logs to a railroad siding or to a waterway.

High-lead logging dates from the years 1905–10 and further speeded operations during the next forty years. A high-climber worked some two

40. A spar tree fully rigged with cables for yarding, the process of collecting logs at a central location. A steam donkey is positioned at the lower left of the photograph. Courtesy Oregon Historical Society: 5131.

hundred feet above ground to prepare a spar tree by chopping off its top and attaching the heavy pulleys and cables used to haul logs clear of stumps and debris to a landing. Like so many innovations, the high-lead technique increased the opportunity for mishap and helped make logging one of the most dangerous occupations in the United States.

Innovation also changed the nature of sawmilling, where circular saws gave way to band saws after 1876. Such saws decreased waste and increased by ten times the amount of lumber a mill could cut in a day. The new technology—especially the steam donkeys and logging railway—was expensive, however, and gave a competitive edge to individuals and corporations already having accumulated enough money to buy and operate it. Small firms (commonly called gyppo outfits after the 1930s) were increasingly forced to operate in the shadow of industrial giants.

The great age of Pacific Northwest timber production dawned at the turn of the century, when timbermen from the Great Lakes states looked west to replace their dwindling sources of supply. A harbinger of change occurred in

1888: a group of Minnesota businessmen purchased eighty thousand acres of Pacific Northwest timberland and founded the St. Paul and Tacoma Lumber Company. The firm opened the region's largest sawmill in Tacoma to produce for local needs, the cargo trade, and markets in the East. Directors of the company expected to receive the cheap railroad rates necessary for Puget Sound timber to compete successfully in markets east of the Rocky Mountains. But their dreams were not fully realized for more than a decade, when another Minnesota timber baron turned his attention to the forests of the far Northwest.

He was Frederick Weyerhaeuser, a businessman who reaped a fortune from the forests of Wisconsin and Minnesota during the post–Civil War era and who came to dominate the Pacific Northwest timber industry after 1900. Weyerhaeuser's Summit Avenue neighbor in Saint Paul was the railroad magnate James J. Hill, who badly needed capital for a financial transaction involving one of his railroads. Accordingly, Hill offered Weyerhaeuser and associates ninety thousand acres of the Northern Pacific Railroad land grant—mostly Douglas fir forest—for six dollars an acre. It was one of the largest private land transfers in American history.

Although the land Weyerhaeuser acquired from Hill in 1900 later seemed like a colossal bargain, many of the timberman's friends initially regarded it as an exceedingly speculative purchase. Could Northwest lumber compete successfully with lumber from the South? Perhaps not in 1900, but Weyerhaeuser was looking to the future, and because they trusted his judgment, many lesser capitalists soon joined the "great rush" to buy Pacific Northwest timberland. Sawmills went up by the hundreds. In eastern Washington and northern Idaho alone, more than three hundred sawmills were producing lumber by 1909. Lake Coeur d'Alene resembled an enormous millpond as log booms lined its shore. Construction of a giant mill in 1905 gave rise to the company town of Potlatch and typified the trend to bigness overtaking the industry. A construction boom in the Dakotas and the massive rebuilding after the San Francisco earthquake and fire of 1906 stimulated production of Pacific Northwest timber. During that year, mills ran extra shifts to meet the demand in California.

Weyerhaeuser's involvement in the Northwest timber industry took many forms because of the decentralized nature of his financial empire, one that once totaled more than ninety affiliated companies. The Weyerhaeuser family had substantial investments in nine Idaho timber firms, including Boise Payette (now Boise Cascade) and Potlatch, and in this way was instrumental in fostering the timber business in the western white pine forests of the state's panhandle. Prior to Weyerhaeuser involvement, the forests of this rugged and difficult country had little commercial value.

In the early twentieth century, Weyerhaeuser and its affiliated companies owned 26 percent of all timberlands in Washington and nearly 20 percent of those in Oregon. The Weyerhaeuser Timber Company constructed the world's largest sawmill in Everett, Washington, in 1914.

Between 1898 and 1914, Oregon and Idaho tripled their timber production. Shortly before the San Francisco earthquake and fire, Washington became America's leading lumber-producing state, a title it retained for all but one year from 1905 to 1938 when Oregon surpassed it. Oregon trailed Washington for so many years because its stands of timber were less accessible than those that crowded the shores of Puget Sound. From the beginning, Washington's timber industry also included larger, more heavily capitalized units than those in Oregon or Idaho.

Ruinous competition, overproduction, market chaos, and dependence on railroad rates to compete in distant markets plagued the lumber business. Firms often had to continue operations regardless of the price of lumber simply to cover fixed charges like timberland taxes and investments in equipment. The resulting glut inevitably forced down prices and wages and brought on militant labor activity. Operators formed the West Coast Lumbermen's Association in 1911 to establish industry-wide standards and marketing practices, but the problem of chronic instability endured.

Fire, too, menaced the industry. Several thousand fires blackened 3.3 million acres in four Northwest states in 1910 alone. Idaho with 744 blazes suffered 1.7 million scorched acres and the destruction of several communities including Wallace. Smoke from Idaho and Montana drifted as far east as Boston, and President William Howard Taft sent troops to help man the fire lines. The Tillamook burn in Oregon in 1933 charred more than 300,000 acres of Douglas fir. After 1940, a campaign of public education designed to keep Washington and other timber-producing states green supplemented state and federal fire prevention measures.

Two technological innovations helped mitigate the industry's financial instability. One was the discovery in 1909 of the sulphate or Kraft process to transform commercially worthless wood like western hemlock into newsprint. For many lumbermen it was like finding a whole new forest. The Northwest's paper industry dates from the construction of a mill at Oregon City in 1866 that used rags and straw, but it did not become significant until the erection of several sulphate- and sulphite-process pulp and paper mills in the 1920s. In time the Pacific Northwest became a leading producer of pulp and paper in the United States. A second innovation was plywood, developed in 1904 at a box and barrel factory near Portland, but that industry did not become commercially important until the mid-1920s. The development of plywood made it possible to recover millions of board feet of wood, once thought lost, from the great Tillamook burn.

A BOOM-AND-BUST ECONOMY

From early times, the fisheries, farms, ranches, mines, and mills of the far Northwest produced much more than the region's small population could consume. International markets thus played a vital role in the region's economy and were the primary cause of its instability. As early as 1868, a British ship left Portland with a cargo of Northwest wheat for the London market. Ten years later, eighty-one ships transported Northwest wheat to markets in Europe, Asia, and Australia. Both the Great Northern and Northern Pacific railroads operated steamship lines that linked the Pacific Northwest to Asian markets. The region was likewise dependent on distant markets within the United States. San Francisco, Saint Paul, and other financial centers supplied much of the capital necessary to develop Northwest resources.

Individual states, most notably Idaho, represented extreme cases of economic dependency. In 1900, 93 percent of Idaho employees engaged in stock raising produced for markets beyond the state. That figure was 97 percent in the gold and silver industry, 90 percent in the lead and zinc industry, and 67 percent in lumber and logging. By contrast, only 9.9 percent of Idaho employees engaged in general and crop agriculture produced for markets outside the state.

The Pacific Northwest, in short, was vulnerable to fluctuations in the national and international economy. At times the region's economy careened along like a roller coaster, as it alternated between phases of boom-and-bust. In no industry did the ride seem wilder than in lumber. Competition was keen—not only among Northwest firms, but also between companies in the Northwest and those in other regions, most notably the South. Because of the high cost of rail transportation, only the very best Northwest lumber could compete with Southern lumber in the Midwest market.

It was not easy for the Pacific Northwest to overcome its role as a producer of raw materials or semifinished items like dimensional lumber. Wage earners engaged in manufacturing constituted only 4.2 percent of Oregon's population in 1900. The figures for Washington and Idaho were 6.6

41. The Oriental Limited of the Great Northern Railway passes Smith Cove while the steamships *Minnesota* and *Dakota* lie at dock in 1905. The world's largest cargo carriers at the time, the two ships were part of James J. Hill's dream of funneling commerce with the Orient through Seattle and along his Great Northern Railroad. Courtesy University of Washington Libraries: Neg. UW 6577.

and 0.9 percent. Not until the United States entered the First World War in 1917 did manufacturing other than of wood products become a significant component of the region's economy.

Prior to the growth of the shipbuilding industry during the First World War, the region's largest manufacturing establishments were those that milled wheat into flour and wood into dimensional lumber. Until the Second World War, flour milling ranked second to lumber among all manufacturing industries in the Pacific Northwest. Smaller establishments canned fish, wove woolen fabric, or produced a variety of specialized wood products such as shingles, doors, molding, matches, and furniture. Other companies produced some of the tools used in the region's extractive industries. Foundries, woodworking shops, tanneries, meat-packers, bakeries, and breweries were among the important small-scale manufacturers.

Overoptimistic businessmen erected an iron works seven miles south of Portland in 1866 and a year later shipped fifty tons of iron to San Francisco. The plant was abandoned in 1894 because of the uncertain market and the low quality of local iron ore and coal. Peter Kirk, an experienced ironmaster from England, and a group of eastern investors attempted to build a steel mill near Seattle in the early 1890s, but the venture failed even before the mill was completed. Kirk's project lacked raw materials and a suitable market. It was the last attempt to develop an iron and steel industry on the West Coast until the Second World War.

Even with the growth of large-scale manufacturing outside the forest products industry after 1917, the Pacific Northwest was unable to escape the boom-and-bust cycles. Several times during the twentieth century, residents had to learn anew the unpleasant facts of economic life in a hinterland.

CHAPTER 10

A People on the Move: Immigration, Urbanization, Reclamation

*

It is the most enterprising and unsettled Americans that have come
West. . . . —James Bryce, *American Commonwealth* (1888)

*

During the thirteen years from 1880 to 1893, the Pacific Northwest experienced a rate of growth seldom equaled in other regions of the United States.
A person who visited Seattle in 1880 and returned in 1893 would barely
recognize the place. The straggling village of wooden structures and dirt
streets had blossomed into a metropolis of brick and stone, its thorough-
fares bustling with trade and commerce. There were substantial business
blocks, pretentious residences, churches, schools, a university, and social
organizations symbolizing economic achievement and cultural refinement,
electric lights, gasworks, and factories and plants manufacturing everything from soda water and cigars to furniture and stump pullers. An expanding network of streetcar lines encouraged the growth of new neighborhoods
at the city's edge.

The region experienced temporary setbacks, as when a short but severe
depression sparked social turmoil in the mid-1880s or when fires ravaged
Seattle, Spokane, and Ellensburg in 1889. A fire in June of that year reduced
to rubble more than thirty blocks of downtown Seattle; the damage totaled
as much as $20 million. Certainly not all statistics registered increases. The
commercial value of the output of Oregon's fish canneries fell 57 percent
between 1880 and 1889 and cost two thousand workers their jobs, but a
huge increase in the value of the output of Washington fish canneries offset

GROWTH DURING THE 1880S
(SELECTED STATISTICS)

Population:	*1880*	*1890*	*Percentage Increase*
Idaho	32,610	84,385	158.8
Oregon	174,768	313,767	79.5
Washington	75,116	349,390	365.1
Miles of Railroad (single track):			
Idaho	206	945	358.7
Oregon	347	1,433	313.0
Washington	212	1,775	737.3
TOTAL	765	4,153	442.9
True Value of Real and Personal Property	$245,000,000	$1,558,991,511	536.3
Capital in Manufacturing	$10,191,768	$77,732,470	662.7
Average No. Acres in Farms	5,951,931	12,391,344	108.2
Agricultural Production:			
Bushels of wheat	9,941,921	26,760,959	169.2
Pounds of wool	7,234,796	13,658,945	88.8

that loss. Certain statistics considered to be yardsticks of growth climbed impressively during succeeding decades, but so many statistics registered gains during the 1880s that Pacific Northwesterners perceived the decade as a time of unprecedented growth and of fundamental changes in a number of social and economic relationships.

Some of these changes are not easily quantified. Thousands of newcomers who arrived after the completion of the Northern Pacific in 1883 left an especially enduring impression upon the character of Washington Territory. Their numbers undermined the power and influence of the pioneer generation and gave Puget Sound and Washington an unsettled, sometimes rambunctious political character. Because a much lower percentage of newcomers settled in Oregon, they were easily absorbed into existing society; the established communities of pioneer families in Portland and Salem thus maintained their dominance in a conservative state. Moreover, Oregon remained essentially a state of home-owned enterprises during the 1880s, while Washington and Idaho grew increasingly dependent upon outside capital to develop their natural resources.

Who were the new arrivals and why did they come? Until the completion of a northern transcontinental railroad, the Pacific Northwest remained isolated from America's main population centers. Getting to the Northwest required a long and arduous journey. Additional impediments to settlement were the slow pace of federal land surveys and conflict with the Indians. Finally, there was the problem of ignorance of the region's natural resources. An Olympia editor complained in 1857, "Our territory is not yet fairly known." Twenty years later, however, every community with faith in its future seemed to have acquired a promoter.

Chief architects of the immigration boom of the 1880s were railroad and steamship companies, chambers of commerce, local immigration boards, and private associations. State and territorial governments seemed content to let those agencies shoulder primary responsibility for advertising the region's resources. Promoters issued millions of pamphlets in a variety of languages. The Oregon Immigration Commission, aided by the railroad baron Henry Villard, issued five different pamphlets in German and one each in Swedish, Norwegian, and Danish.

Regardless of the language, promotional publications conveyed the message that the Pacific Northwest was a land of boundless resources and get-rich-quick opportunities. The coal deposits of Washington, they typically boasted, were the "largest in the United States," the soil of the Willamette Valley was literally inexhaustible, and crop failures were virtually unknown. Another pamphlet claimed that it would "scarcely be possible to exaggerate the extent and value of the forests of the Pacific Northwest." Promoters portrayed the region as a health seekers' paradise, filled with hot springs and mineral baths, the nights "cool and conducive to sound slumber." To this paradise, they urged any person with drive and determination to migrate.

Newcomers arrived mainly from other parts of the United States, notably the Middle West. Even so, in 1900 Washington included a higher percentage of foreign-born residents than did the United States as a whole. In that year, 22 percent of Washington's population was foreign born, 16 percent of Oregon's, and 15 percent of Idaho's; the average for the United States was 14 percent. Even more revealing, 47 percent of Washington's residents had at least one foreign-born parent; the national average was 34 percent.

42. Low down payments, a timeless come-on used to
sell building lots in early Spokane. Courtesy Eastern
Washington State Historical Society: F-98.

Among the region's foreign born, immigrants from Scandinavia (Norway, Sweden, Iceland, and Denmark), Great Britain, Canada, and Germany were by far the most numerous. Those were the so-called old immigrants. The "new immigrants" from southern and eastern Europe did not arrive in significant numbers until the opening decade of the twentieth century. The character of Asian immigration changed as the number of Chinese decreased relative to the number of Japanese people. Seattle's Japanese population increased from 125 in 1890 to 6,127 in 1910. Portland's population in 1900 included 7,841 Chinese, some 9 percent of the total; the number of Japanese climbed from 20 in 1890 to 1,461 in 1910.

Some immigrant groups arrived as families, and some largely comprised single males. An unbalanced ratio between genders was typical of many early racial, ethnic, and religious groups. Washington's Chinese and Japanese residents in 1900 numbered 8,982 men and 264 women. Portland's Jewish community, which dates from the late 1850s, counted among its first arrivals a preponderance of young single men, nearly all of them German born or of German parentage.

RACE AND ETHNICITY, 1880–1910

	1880	*1890*	*1900*	*1910*
Blacks	865	2,989	3,912	8,201
Native Americans	6,239	20,375	19,216	19,575
Chinese	16,004	14,807	15,493	10,931
Japanese	3	385	9,409	17,710
Irish	6,883	14,607	13,135	16,957
English	6,143	18,660	20,087	32,411
German	7,982	29,813	33,145	52,395
Scandinavian	4,651	32,192	40,882	98,933

Note: The Indian population in 1880 includes only people not living on reservations.

It was widely believed that many newcomers were Scandinavians. Indeed, Scandinavians began arriving on Puget Sound in large numbers during the 1880s—often after having first settled in Minnesota or Wisconsin. More Swedes and Norwegians settled in Washington in proportion to the already resident population than in any other state. Scandinavians constituted 25 percent of Washington's foreign-born population by 1910, but Norwegians and Swedes never accounted for more than 7 or 8 percent of the state's total population, and the Danish population remained much smaller than that.

Patterns of immigration and settlement were not random. Puget Sound tended to attract Swedes and Norwegians because its climate, topography, and job opportunities reminded them of home. Most Greeks who migrated to Idaho clustered in Pocatello, where they formed a predominantly male subcommunity employed by the Oregon Short Line. Letters from first arrivals helped attract fellow nationals to a particular location, as did ties of family and neighborhood. The foreign-language press played a similar role. At one time, Swedish, Norwegian, Italian, Japanese, and German newspapers were published in Seattle; a Finnish paper was published in Astoria, and a German in Portland. Chinese- and Japanese-language papers in the Northwest date from the 1890s.

For similar reasons, immigrants gravitated to certain occupations and industries: Swedes to lumber and logging, Norwegians and Finns to fishing, Danes to dairying, Irish to construction and mining, Italians to agriculture, Greeks to railroad labor. The Japanese found employment in any one of several manual occupations—including railroad construction, logging and

43. The Northern Pacific Railroad advertised for Scandinavian laborers to help build its line across the Cascade mountains in the late 1880s. Courtesy Great Northern Railway Company Records, Minnesota Historical Society: 54215.

lumbering, fishing, and farming—which typically served them as way stations to entrepreneurship.

Portland's pioneer Jewish community was drawn to merchandising. As early as 1866, Jews achieved prominence in the city's retail trade and emerged as a significant influence in community life. Among the most noteworthy of the city's Jewish merchants was Bernard Goldsmith, a jeweler and wholesale merchant who arrived in Portland in 1861, having already become a wealthy man in California. Eight years later Goldsmith was elected to the first of two terms as mayor. The story was much the same in Seattle, a destination of Jewish immigrants from Germany, Poland, and Russia between 1880 and 1914. Members of this Ashkenazic group made up the bulk of Seattle's four thousand Jews in 1910. Since the early twentieth century Seattle also recorded the third-largest concentration of Sephardic (Spanish) Jews in the United States.

A number of distinctive ethnic communities appeared in the Pacific Northwest. Large numbers of Basques, for example, who had emigrated from the Iberian Peninsula to California and Nevada, came north to southern Idaho and the Yakima Valley between 1890 and the mid-1920s. Contrary to popular belief, not all Basques were sheepherders. Many congregated in Boise, which became the nation's leading Basque center, and from there ventured into mining or hired themselves out to construct irrigation canals and dams. As was the case in any community where members of one nationality collected, the Basque community developed its own hotels and boardinghouses. It established a mutual aid society in 1908 to assist people out of work, sick, or temporarily in need of money. There was also a Basque Roman Catholic church.

In all such communities, ethnic groups shared their language, foods, and customs, and in that way they found shelter from the nativist prejudice all too common at the time. Among Northwest Jews, the B'nai B'rith fostered intergroup aid. Modeled after fraternal organizations like the Free and Accepted Masons and International Order of Odd Fellows and established first in Portland in 1866, the B'nai B'rith provided a sense of fraternity and filled a need in a society that even denied Jews insurance coverage.

Not all such enclaves were located in large cities. In eastern Washington, German farmers established small settlements in the 1880s and soon attracted numerous compatriots. Italians formed a prosperous agricultural community in the Walla Walla Valley that in later years became famous for its produce, especially sweet onions. Though distinct ethnic enclaves tended to disappear as children and grandchildren were assimilated into the

44. A Basque sheepherders' band. Courtesy Idaho State
Historical Society: 70–42.154.

larger community, in Seattle and other cities, international districts remain viable.

URBANIZATION

The population of the Pacific Northwest increased by 165 percent during the decade of the 1880s, but it is significant that by far the largest part of this increase occurred in urban areas, and most notably in Portland, Seattle, Tacoma, and Spokane. In 1890, those four communities were the only ones in the region having more than eight thousand inhabitants. By 1910 these four cities included nearly one-third of the entire population of Oregon, Washington, and Idaho.

The noted English writer Rudyard Kipling visited the Pacific Northwest during the extraordinary urban growth of the 1880s and found Tacoma "staggering under a boom of the boomiest." He passed down "ungraded streets that ended abruptly in a fifteen-foot drop and a nest of brambles; along pavements that beginning in pine-plank ended in the living tree." Kipling observed a massive brick and stone foundation awaiting the erection of an opera house and, everywhere, the blackened stumps of trees. "The real-estate agents were selling house-lots on unmade streets miles away for thousands of dollars." On Tacoma's muddy streets "men were babbling about money, town lots, and again money."

URBAN GROWTH, 1880–1920

(RESIDENTS IN COMMUNITIES OF 2,500 OR MORE)

	1880	*1890*	*1900*	*1910*	*1920*
Number					
Boise	1,899	2,311	5,957	17,358	21,393
Portland	17,577	46,385	90,426	207,214	258,288
Seattle	3,553	42,837	80,871	237,174	315,312
Spokane	350	19,922	36,848	104,402	104,437
Tacoma	1,098	36,006	37,714	83,743	96,965
Walla Walla	3,588	4,709	10,049	19,364	15,503
Percent					
Idaho	0	0	6.2	21.5	27.6
Oregon	14.9	27.7	32.1	45.6	49.8
Washington	9.3	35.6	40.7	53.1	54.8

Kipling's traveling companion from California observed, "They are all mad here, all mad. A man nearly pulled a gun on me because I didn't agree with him that Tacoma was going to whip San Francisco on the strength of carrots and potatoes. I asked him to tell me what the town produced, and I couldn't get anything out of him except those two darned vegetables." Kipling's response was to take a steamer to British Columbia "to draw breath."[1] Another English visitor during the late 1880s, James Bryce, found Seattle and Tacoma feverish to create instant civilizations.

Every city on the Pacific Coast aspired to become the metropolis of the West. The more aggressive ones skirmished with real and imagined rivals, using weapons that ranged from climate and crime statistics to a barrage of promotional pamphlets. Urban rivalries were deadly serious contests fueled by money, optimism, and the conviction that only growth insured permanence, stability, and profit. At stake were real estate values, railroad and steamship connections, and community pride.

Tacoma's population at the beginning of the decade stood at 1,098, and at the time of Kipling's 1889 visit approached 36,000, an increase of more than 3,000 percent. At the start of the decade, Walla Walla still ranked as the

1. Rudyard Kipling, *From Sea to Sea and Other Sketches*, 2 vols. in 1 (Garden City, New York: Doubleday, Page, 1925), 2:90–93.

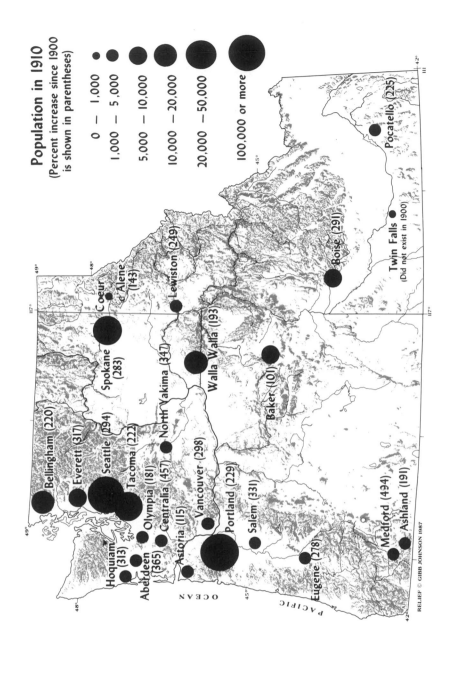

Population in 1910
(Percent increase since 1900 is shown in parentheses)

0 — 1,000
1,000 — 5,000
5,000 — 10,000
10,000 — 20,000
20,000 — 50,000
100,000 or more

Bellingham (220)
Everett (317)
Seattle (294)
Tacoma (222)
Hoquiam (313)
Aberdeen (365)
Olympia (181)
Centralia (457)
Astoria (115)
Vancouver (298)
Portland (229)
Salem (331)
Eugene (278)
Medford (494)
Ashland (191)
Spokane (283)
Coeur d'Alene (143)
North Yakima (347)
Lewiston (249)
Walla Walla (193)
Baker (101)
Boise (291)
Twin Falls
(Did not exist in 1900)
Pocatello (225)

PACIFIC OCEAN

RELIEF © GIBB JOHNSON 1987

territory's most populous town, but by 1890 that title belonged to Seattle, which had grown by an impressive 1,000 percent to more than 42,000 residents. Still more spectacular was Spokane's 6,000 percent increase. Portland's 164 percent increase seemed almost leisurely by comparison.

THE BIG FOUR CITIES PLUS BOISE

Portland was the city that gravity built. It enjoyed the natural advantage of a location that enabled it to dominate the commerce of both the Willamette and Columbia rivers. Situated on the west bank of the Willamette twelve miles upriver from its junction with the Columbia, Portland dates from 1843. In its early years it had several rivals, the most formidable being Oregon City and its growing complex of mills at the falls of the Willamette. But Portland possessed a superior deepwater anchorage, an advantage that proved decisive after 1848 in securing trade between the Willamette Valley and California's goldfields. Its wharves were piled with cargoes of lumber, wheat, fruit, and other farm products leaving the Pacific Northwest for distant markets.

Portland recorded a population of eight hundred in 1850 and was incorporated the following year. Several other milestones marked the community's progress toward metropolitan status. Ladd and Tilton became the Northwest's first bank in 1859 and a financial bulwark of the Oregon country. Five years later, William S. Ladd and Henry W. Corbett opened a telegraph line to California, and on March 5, 1864, the *Oregonian* printed a special edition of news from the East that was only twenty hours old.

The growing trade with the booming gold camps of the upper Columbia region brought Portland prosperity. During the Clearwater rush of 1862, more than ten thousand people traveled to and from the mines in Portland-based riverboats; that number grew to thirty-six thousand in 1864. Freight on the river increased also. New wharves had to be built to handle the traffic. Portland's role as hub of a steamboat monopoly and, later, of Henry Villard's railroad empire further enhanced the city's status. Gold and wheat had made Portland rich and smug by the late 1870s, a place untroubled by booms or depressions, unhurried, and not a little complacent in its role as the region's premier metropolis.

But Portland was not a city wholly devoted to material pursuits. In the 1860s it could boast of several churches, a library, a music store, and several newspapers. After a fire in 1873 leveled thirty blocks, substantial brick and stone structures replaced its original wooden buildings. Cities of the Pacific

Northwest had a mindless way of imitating their eastern counterparts by platting a monotonous grid of streets without regard for aesthetics or terrain. Despite this, Portland became a city noted for its physical dignity and charm, as well as its God-fearing respectability.

As the egalitarianism of frontier days gave way to a more structured society, Portland developed an aristocracy dominated by the Ladds, Corbetts, Failings, and other first families. Yet even in that self-proclaimed enclave of New England on the Willamette, society's villas, chateaus, and castles were forced to coexist with the 30 houses of prostitution and 110 saloons recorded in the 1880 census. A bridge spanned the Willamette River by 1890, and electric streetcars clanged down city streets that reached away from both banks of the river. Three years later, one of the first electric interurban lines in the United States connected Portland to neighboring Oregon City. Electric railways contributed to the growth of numerous satellite communities in Portland's orbit and thus initiated what a later generation would label suburbia and urban sprawl.

Tacoma, which during the 1870s seemed likely to emerge as Portland's main rival, had its beginnings in 1852 around a small sawmill built on the south shore of Commencement Bay at the southern end of Puget Sound. The original settlement became Old Tacoma when in 1873 the Northern Pacific selected a site three miles east for its terminus and platted a new Tacoma on the lowlands. The town grew rapidly as factories and wharves fringed the shore and building commenced on the tideflats. Dozens of steam- and sailing ships carried wheat, coal, and lumber from Tacoma's docks to distant markets.

The epithet City of Destiny seemed entirely appropriate when in 1888 Tacoma became the site of the world's largest lumber mill. A host of other sawmills and wood products factories soon followed, but the great depression of the 1890s hit Tacoma especially hard and shattered its dream. By 1900 the city's fate was clearly not to become the dominant metropolis on Puget Sound, though it might legitimately claim to be the lumber capital of America. Destiny, so it seemed, favored Tacoma's archrival to the north.

The growth of Seattle lagged dramatically behind that of Portland and remained barely ahead of Tacoma's until the 1890s. The first settlement inside the present urban boundary of Seattle was at Alki Point in 1851, but this proved such a poor location that settlers moved across Elliott Bay the following year to the foot of what is now Yesler Way. In 1853 the first steam-powered sawmill on Puget Sound formed the nucleus around which modern Seattle took shape.

From the waterfront Seattle gradually marched up steep slopes to the east. Early residents preferred to build their homes on ridges and hilltops that afforded pleasing vistas of the Olympic Mountains to the west and Lake Washington and the Cascades to the east. In time railroads filled the almost unused tideflats with their tracks and terminals; spur tracks to each wharf brought freight cars alongside cargo ships.

In its quest for urban greatness, Seattle faced a formidable obstacle because the Northern Pacific favored Tacoma. For a time the railroad relegated Seattle to a branch line known locally as the orphan road. Seattle's will to succeed was so strong that contemporaries labeled its special type of frontier boosterism the Seattle Spirit. The city's promotional efforts paid a handsome dividend in the form of the Great Northern Railway that James J. Hill completed from Saint Paul in 1893. From Seattle, Hill extended his reach across the Pacific by acquiring a steamship line.

When news of the fabulous Klondike bonanza reached Seattle in mid-

45. First Avenue and Yesler Way, the heart of Seattle in
1911. Courtesy Washington State Historical Society,
Tacoma: Photo by Asahel Curtis, # 21757.

	Columbia River	Puget Sound
FLOUR EXPORTS **(IN BARRELS)**		
1889–1890	523,412	16,755
1899–1900	1,093,648	983,840
1900–1901	1,005,420	1,073,200
1909–1910	454,173	1,529,370

1897, the city successfully promoted itself as the chief gateway to Alaska. A special Klondike edition of the *Post-Intelligencer* reached the country's seven thousand postmasters, six hundred public libraries, and four thousand mayors. The Great Northern distributed another ten thousand copies, and the Northern Pacific six thousand. This public relations feat not only aided Seattle's growth but linked Seattle and Alaska in the public mind for decades to come.

Between 1898 and 1910 Seattle enjoyed its greatest growth, becoming a cosmopolitan metropolis during that short span of time. Just after the turn of the century, Seattle embarked upon one of the most ambitious civil engineering programs in American history, one that literally moved mountains to reshape the downtown area and gave a new dimension to the Seattle Spirit.

During the course of three decades, sixty regrade projects sluiced some fifty million tons of earth into Elliott Bay and adjacent mud flats. The most remarkable of those projects was the Denny Regrade. Begun in 1898 and completed in 1930, it removed a hill that blocked the northward expansion of the city's business district, creating thirty-seven blocks of level building land and shaping a new harbor in the bay. Seattle's numerous railroad connections and a tireless campaign of self-promotion helped it to far outdistance Tacoma in population by 1900 and to overtake Portland for first place in the 1910 census.

Unlike Portland and the cities of Puget Sound, Spokane lacked the natural advantages of a port. Except for the falls of the Spokane River, it possessed no discernible assets prior to the coming of railroads. Dating from the building of a small sawmill at the falls in 1871, Spokane grew only slowly until the boom of the 1880s. When the community incorporated in 1881, the year the Northern Pacific reached town, its thousand residents could hardly have imagined that within ten years their pastoral village would evolve into a regional railroad hub, with lines radiating south to tap the agricultural riches of the Palouse and east to Idaho's mines and forests. Additional railway lines built by the local entrepreneur D. C. Corbin linked Spokane to the mining wealth of southern British Columbia, and as a result, the town was in closer touch with Canadian affairs than most other American cities were. By the turn of the century, Spokane clearly dominated economic and social life in the large area of eastern Washington and northern Idaho that the city's promoters called the Inland Empire.

Boise was clearly not in the same league as the big four cities of Oregon and Washington; nonetheless, it has ranked as the most populous community in Idaho since 1880. Boise resembled Spokane more than the cities of the coast for obvious reasons: both were landlocked, both profited from nearby discoveries of precious minerals, and both became hubs of agricultural empires.

Boise was platted in 1863 following the discovery of gold in nearby mountains. That year, the United States Army erected Fort Boise. When the town was selected territorial capital in 1864, Boise's population was 1,658, which included an influx of pro-Confederate refugees from Missouri.

Mining activity declined in the late 1860s, but Boise gained a look of permanence as trees grew from the sagebrush plains and substantial buildings replaced rough cabins. It became a city of families, unlike the typical mining camp, and profited from the growth of agriculture. In 1870, for example, when there were only 414 farms in all of Idaho Territory, 65 percent of them were located in the Boise area. The population of Boise increased to 2,311 by 1890, and that number would more than double during the final decade of the nineteenth century as a result of a boom in irrigated farmland in the Boise Valley. Although bypassed by the Oregon Short Line and relegated to the end of a spur track from 1887 until the mid-1920s, when the Union Pacific routed a line through the city, Boise suffered no worse transportation handicaps than other places in Idaho.

By 1910 the Pacific Northwest's major metropolitan centers had already assumed the roles they were to play for the remainder of the twentieth century, and the same was true for a myriad of the small, often single-industry towns that served as lumber, farm, mine, or railroad centers. Astoria became synonymous with fishing and canning; Everett, Aberdeen, and Klamath Falls with forest products; Hood River with fruit; Colfax, Pomeroy, and Ritzville with wheat; Shaniko with sheep; and Wallace with metal mining.

Mining towns were highly susceptible to boom-and-bust cycles. Idaho

46. Looking east down Boise's Main Street, ca. 1915.
The Idanha Hotel is the turreted building in the center
of the photograph. Courtesy Idaho State Historical
Society: 73–11.3.

City boasted six thousand residents in 1864 and outranked Portland for a year or two as the region's largest population center. Idaho City had only three hundred residents in 1980, but that fact alone made it one of the more fortunate of former mining communities. Not all ghost towns were connected with mining. Shaniko and Hardman, located in central Oregon, declined as a result of changes in transporting sheep to market. In one-industry company towns like Potlatch, the closure of the local sawmill made survival a matter of prolonged struggle. In the case of Valsetz, Oregon, the closing of the mill meant sudden death for the Boise Cascade community: the company literally bulldozed it into oblivion in the early 1980s.

THE LURE OF THE LAND: RECLAMATION

Even as the region's cities experienced rapid and seemingly uncontrolled population growth, another stream of population headed for the farmlands of the Northwest. The region's urban growth prior to the First World War did

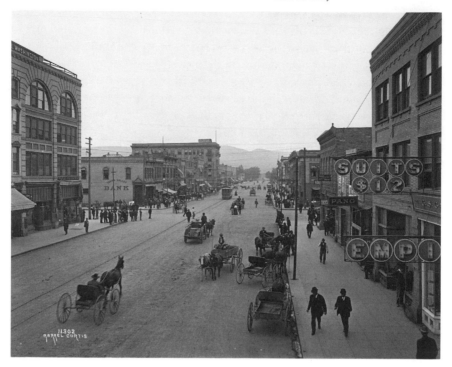

47. Downtown Yakima in October 1908. Courtesy
Washington State Historical Society, Tacoma: Photo by
Asahel Curtis, # 11302.

not come at the expense of rural depopulation. Especially in the early
twentieth century, when irrigation opened thousands of acres of land to
settlement, cities and towns served as spearheads for agricultural development of the surrounding countryside.

Large-scale settlement of irrigated lands marked the final phase of a
process that began when emigrants first plodded along the trail to Oregon.
The 1850 census listed 1,164 farms in the Oregon country, almost all of
them located in the Willamette Valley. The Donation Land Claim Act of
1850 conveyed virtually all the farmland in the valley to settlers during the
next half decade.

Congress passed several additional measures ostensibly designed to encourage settlement of federal land, but the laws were clumsily written and
poorly suited to the western environment. The Homestead Act of 1862
offered 160-acre plots to settlers, but it extended no credit to buy the
equipment necessary to start farming, provided no water, and offered no

services. In fact, the fertile and well-watered Willamette Valley was one of the few areas of the region where 160-acre plots approximated the optimum size for farms, but settlers had already claimed its lands under the Donation Land Law. Elsewhere, especially in the semiarid country of the interior, the traditional 160-acre homestead made little sense. Fewer than twenty thousand claims were filed in Oregon and Washington during the 1860s and 1870s under the provisions of the Homestead Act.

The Desert Land Act of 1877 granted 640 acres to a person willing to irrigate it for three years. But the irrigation requirement proved prohibitively expensive for individual farmers, especially when so much of the Northwest's interior was remote from rivers and lakes. The Timber and Stone Act of 1878 resulted in timber barons—not farmers—acquiring substantial holdings. Timbermen paid sailors, hoboes, and even their own employees to stake claims that eventually enlarged the company's domain. One Washington firm acquired a total of 100,000 acres in this way. Many would-be agrarians, in short, found it far more difficult to acquire suitable federal land than they expected. By the turn of the century, people who still dreamed of acquiring a farm from Uncle Sam placed their faith in the power of irrigation to transform the region's countless parched acres into desert gardens.

The Whitmans and Spaldings pioneered the use of irrigation to raise crops at their missions. Mormons in Utah solved many thorny problems involving water rights and engineering and exported their expertise to pioneer settlements in southern Idaho.

Early methods of irrigation varied greatly, from simply diverting water onto an open field to building extensive networks of ditches and canals. Inevitably, too, irrigation involved a certain amount of trial and error, of engineering guesswork that might leave a ditch unable to meet the water needs of people living along its banks. By such means irrigation projects went forward, if not always successfully. Construction proceeded slowly in the 1860s and 1870s, picked up speed in the 1880s, and accelerated dramatically throughout the region during the 1890s.

As irrigation in the Pacific Northwest matured, it passed through four somewhat overlapping stages: individual irrigators, corporate enterprise, government-aided private enterprise, and large-scale federal reclamation. Following in the steps of farmers who built simple ditches either individually or cooperatively to serve local and limited needs came private canal companies offering to irrigate substantially larger areas. Some companies were headquartered as far away as New York. All too often, however, private

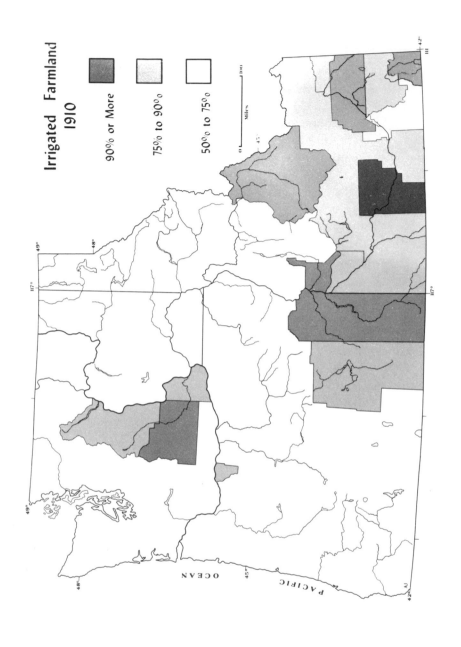

Irrigated Farmland
1910

90% or More

75% to 90%

50% to 75%

funds alone proved inadequate to do a proper job. Congress passed the Carey Act in 1894 to encourage state and private cooperation, and eight years later it created the Reclamation Service, offering western agrarians what amounted to a generous federal welfare program.

By the turn of the century, Idaho ranked first in irrigated land, Oregon second, and Washington a distant third. The Carey Act gave Idaho a major boost. This measure encouraged reclamation by giving each western state a million acres of land if it found a way to irrigate them, either with private or public funds. A national showcase for the Carey Act was Idaho, where three-fifths of all lands irrigated under its provisions were located. The Twin Falls project served as an example of what the Carey Act might accomplish. The largest private irrigation project in America gave birth to the community of Twin Falls, an infant agricultural boomtown by 1905. As impressive as such achievements were, the total amount of western land irrigated under the Carey Act equaled only two average-size agricultural

48. Twin Falls, Idaho, was barely a year old when this photograph was taken in 1905. Courtesy Idaho State Historical Society: P73–2.24.

counties in Illinois. The state of Washington, in fact, irrigated nothing under that law.

The Carey Act was designed to keep federal participation to a minimum. That policy changed with passage of the Newlands Act of 1902, which created the United States Reclamation Service (Bureau of Reclamation after 1923) to supervise a number of dam and canal projects. The Minidoka project, which received its first water in 1909, was one of two large reclamation projects allotted to Idaho, and it made possible not only the reclamation of thousands of acres of farmland but also the building of a host of new agricultural communities. The completion of the 349-foot-high Arrowrock Dam in 1915—the world's tallest until 1932—gave the Boise Valley a surplus of water for the first time and permitted the creation of 1,167 new irrigated farms comprising 67,454 acres.

Large-scale irrigation on the Snake River plain (the location of roughly two-thirds of Idaho's irrigated land) helped push agriculture past mining and timber as the state's chief economic asset. Today, other irrigated lands of the Pacific Northwest include the Yakima, Wenatchee, and Okanogan valleys, the Columbia basin project in central Washington, and scattered areas of eastern Oregon.

Reclamation was never simply a matter of economics and engineering, just as irrigation canals were never merely sources of water. Canals and their life-giving water created a special kind of oasis community that combined the complexity and dependency of urban life with a rural environment. Such communities were often described as gardens of Eden, but they were also highly vulnerable. One promotional slogan claimed that "the clouds may fail to bring rain, but the canal never fails," yet reality was not so simple. The well-being of dwellers on reclaimed lands depended on federal money, power, bureaucracy, the technological expertise of the few, and occasionally the caprice of nature. Such was reclamation's dark underside.

An irrigator might spend countless hours uprooting and burning sagebrush to transform arid land into fields of potatoes and sugar beets, only to have a drought reduce the amount of water available and cause crops to wither. Unscrupulous or inexpert operators who failed to deliver the amount of water they promised occasionally victimized irrigators. During the 1920s the total amount of irrigated farmland in Washington actually declined by thirty thousand acres. Some people simply walked away from their parched crops and desiccated hopes; many irrigators in southern Idaho

49. One of many abandoned farms in Washington's Columbia basin in the 1920s. Successful farming in the
area would await the water provided by the Columbia
Basin Project begun in the late 1930s. Courtesy Washington State Historical Society, Tacoma: Photo by
Asahel Curtis, # 40523.

channeled their anger into the Progressive party that sprang up in the early
1920s.

Framers of the Carey and Newlands acts expected that thousands of new
160-acre farms would be carved from the sage. Because the Newlands Act
made it easy for a United States citizen to acquire irrigated land, it was
hailed as a triumph of democracy. But in most areas of the West, it was
common for irrigation projects to favor very large operators. During a time
of low farm prices in the mid-1920s, it was estimated that settlers on the
Minidoka project needed $500 in capital to succeed. Because few had that
much money, over 40 percent of Minidoka's farmers ended up as the tenants
of wealthy landowners.

Irrigation districts were eventually supposed to repay the cost of reclamation; few ever did. The Newlands Act thus functioned all too often as a grandiose welfare program that proclaimed the virtues of family-sized farms while it made millionaires out of some western agrarians who managed to amass large holdings. A final irony lies in the word *reclamation,* which implied that land was being returned to its original state of productivity, and contained no hint that some was best left as the first settlers found it.

CHAPTER II

The Omnibus States and a Growing Regional Self-confidence

X

And so the Northwesterner, looking never behind, has anchored his confidence in the unmatched resources of his country and in the surety of reaching in trade the millions of Asia and the new population of Alaska.
—Ray Stannard Baker, "The Great Northwest," *Century* (1903)

✳

During the thirty-four years between the completion of the Northern Pacific in 1883 and American entry into the First World War, the Pacific Northwest moved inexorably into a postfrontier world. That transition was not always smooth or peaceable.

During those years a generation of men and women who had come to Oregon in covered wagons and sailing ships passed from the scene. They had been committed to building a new society in the wilderness; those who followed were also builders—of cities, railroad lines, irrigation works, and even of state constitutions in the case of Washington and Idaho. But circumstances forced the second generation to be adjusters and consolidators as well. They had to adjust inherited laws and patterns of thought to fit complex new realities unimaginable to their parents—the postfrontier world of urbanization, organized labor, nationwide transportation and communication networks, and expanded governmental responsibilities for the welfare of its citizens.

Economic depression and social dislocation in the mid-1880s and again from 1893 to 1897 punctuated the transition years. But after prosperity returned in the late 1890s, the Pacific Northwest exuded a newfound air of confidence, one that took visible form in two world's fairs, new skylines for cities, and prosperous-looking farms in once arid regions.

THE POLITICS OF PAROCHIALISM

Despite momentous issues raised by the great population influx of the 1880s, state and territorial legislatures conducted business as usual. Democratic and Republican politicians jockeyed for positions of power, occasionally joined in looting the public domain or the treasury, and promised voters to keep taxes low. Legislators seldom raised their sights above the pursuit of narrow, partisan, and material ends.

The prevailing philosophy of government was laissez faire, noninterference in economic matters. That mindset, together with bribes and other favors that railroads distributed to legislators, enabled corporations to dodge meaningful regulation. Businessmen like Ben Holladay, who bribed the Oregon legislature to obtain a land grant for his Oregon and California Railroad, served as role models encouraging public chicanery. The corrupt activities of Oregon's Senator John Hipple Mitchell underscored Mark Twain's quip that the United States had no distinctively native American criminal class except Congress. Mitchell's opponents accused him of declaring, "Whatever is Ben Holladay's politics is my politics, and whatever Ben Holladay wants, I want."

Neither Republicans nor Democrats completely dominated Northwest politics during that era. Oregon Republicans carried every presidential election between 1872 and 1908, but the Democrats provided a spirited opposition. The two parties traded the governor's chair five times between 1859 and 1895. After 1880, however, the Republicans retained control of the Oregon House of Representatives until 1935 and the state senate until 1957.

Idaho and Washington were not eligible to vote for a president until 1892, and territorial officeholders were appointed by presidents who, except for Grover Cleveland, were all Republicans. Republicans held a solid advantage over Democrats in Washington legislative elections, but Democrats held the edge in Idaho until Republicans succeeded in disenfranchising the Mormons in the mid-1880s.

Reformers seldom intruded into the political process before the 1890s. One of those infrequent insurgencies occurred in 1874 when Oregon voters elected independents to the state legislature, which subsequently passed laws regulating railroad freight rates and fares.

50. Senate Chamber, Old State Capitol Building, Boise,
1909. Courtesy Idaho State Historical Society: 2052–B.

THE OMNIBUS STATES PLUS IDAHO

A favorite topic of public discussion in Idaho and Washington during those years was statehood. Residents chafed at what they perceived to be a condition of vassalage—taxation without representation, no voice in the selection of territorial administrators, no settled public policy, and absentee governors who abused their veto power.

In 1889 thirty years had elapsed since Oregon achieved statehood. No new state had been admitted since Colorado in 1876, although Washington, Idaho, and several other territories considered themselves sufficiently ready.

The road to statehood for Washington had several potential pitfalls. Some residents fretted that the anti-Chinese agitation of the mid-1880s hurt their efforts because it gave Congress the impression that Washington was too immature for statehood. Others feared that when the territory enfranchised women it set a bad precedent, for no state had done so.

In the case of Idaho, it is a wonder that the territory survived intact until statehood. No less than four sessions of its legislature petitioned Congress

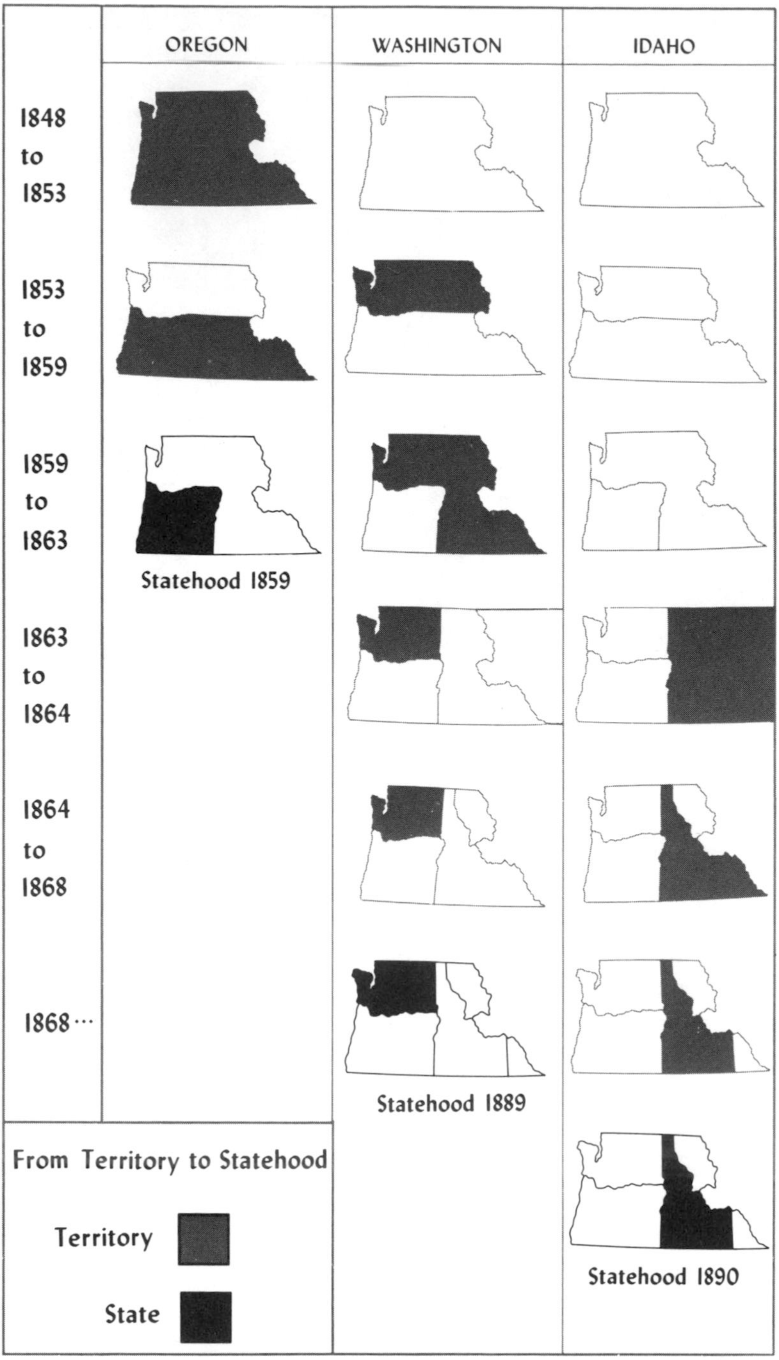

	OREGON	WASHINGTON	IDAHO
1848 to 1853			
1853 to 1859			
1859 to 1863	Statehood 1859		
1863 to 1864			
1864 to 1868			
1868 ···		Statehood 1889	
			Statehood 1890

From Territory to Statehood

Territory

State

to annex the panhandle either to Washington or to Montana. Northern Idaho participated in a constitutional convention in Walla Walla in 1878, and the area was included in Washington's statehood plans for more than a decade. Dismemberment seemed imminent in the mid-1880s when Senator William M. Stewart of Nevada suggested that Congress attach northern Idaho to Washington and give the remainder to Nevada—a state with serious economic problems because of the moribund condition of its mining industry.

Both houses of Congress approved the plan in 1887, but Grover Cleveland killed the bill with a pocket veto because of protests by Idaho's territorial governor, Edward A. Stevenson. Losing the panhandle was one thing, but the possibility of being swallowed up by a "rotten borough" like Nevada was apparently quite another. To placate the angry and frustrated northerners, the legislature voted in 1889 to locate Idaho's proposed university in the panhandle town of Moscow.

In the end, statehood for Idaho and Washington was delayed not so much by local matters as by a political impasse on Capitol Hill. Congress ignored petitions for statehood from the territories of the Northwest because the Democrats, who at various times controlled either the Senate or House, did not want to admit states that were likely to vote Republican. The logjam was not broken until Republicans captured the White House and both houses of Congress in 1888. In the lame-duck session of 1889, outgoing Democrats dropped their delaying tactics, apparently hoping to reap some last-minute favor for supporting statehood.

President Cleveland signed the omnibus bill and thus set in motion the admission process for Washington, Montana, and the two Dakotas. The measure, commonly known as an enabling act, required prospective states to pledge themselves to a republican form of government, racial equality in matters of civil rights, religious toleration, assumption of federal debts, and maintenance of public schools free from sectarian control.

The omnibus bill conspicuously slighted Idaho and Wyoming, although powerful senators urged both to prepare for statehood anyway. As Oregon had done earlier, so Idaho in 1889 proceeded without formal congressional approval to hold a special convention and draft a constitution. In that way, Idaho came to be classified with the omnibus states.

CONSTITUTIONAL CONVENTIONS

The framers of Washington's constitution who assembled in Olympia on July 4, 1889, represented a cross section of society. They included, among others, thirteen farmers, six merchants, six physicians, five bankers, twenty-one lawyers, one fisherman, three teachers, a preacher, a mining engineer, and two loggers. There were forty-three Republicans, twenty-nine Democrats, and three independents.

The Olympia gathering was not the territory's first exercise in constitution making. A reform-minded group of fifteen delegates had drafted a constitution in Walla Walla in 1878, but that effort failed to secure congressional approval. This time would be different.

Also meeting on July 4, 1889, were the seventy men who had gathered in Boise to write a state constitution for Idaho. They had come in response to a unilateral proclamation issued by Governor Stevenson (and reaffirmed by his successor, George L. Shoup) and had been selected by counties on a nonpartisan basis. In actuality, Republicans held a slight edge. The occupations represented in the group were similar to those in the Olympia gathering. Everything about the Idaho convention represented an act of faith: the Boise citizens who underwrote its expenses hoped to be reimbursed by the first state legislature.

State constitutions have a way of encapsulating the spirit and concerns of an era. Just as Oregon's constitution mirrored the hopes and fears of a pre–Civil War generation grappling with matters of race and slavery, so the constitutions that Washington and Idaho adopted thirty years later addressed the concerns of the first generation of Pacific Northwesterners to grapple with life in an increasingly complex urban and industrial America. In both Olympia and Boise, convention delegates who idealized the simple world of their pioneer forebears grappled with the unsettling new problems of how states should deal with corporate power, industrial violence, and dismemberment and death in the workplace.

As the older states had done earlier, both Idaho and Washington framed their constitutions from a variety of documents already at hand. Washington borrowed from the constitutions of Oregon and California, the abortive Walla Walla constitution of 1878, and a model constitution proposed by W. Lair Hill, former editor of the Portland *Oregonian* and a specialist in constitutional law.

The Idaho and Washington documents were also modeled after the Constitution of the United States and included similar guarantees of individual liberty. Both provided for bicameral legislatures. They defined the structure and scope of government. They also addressed concerns unique to each age and place: tidelands in Washington; water rights, livestock, and the Mormon franchise in Idaho.

Civil rights proved to be problematic. Washington affirmed the state's duty to provide education for all children within its borders "without distinction or preference on account of race, color, caste, or sex." Yet its constitution denied Chinese the right to hold real property or mining claims. Idaho's fundamental law denied aliens the privilege of working for the state or any municipality, and it disqualified from voting all bigamists, polygamists, Chinese or persons of Mongolian descent, and Indians who were not taxed or who had not severed their tribal relations. Despite a provision proclaiming freedom of religion, the Idaho Constitution also denied Mormons the right to vote.

In matters of administration, the number of state executive officers elected by voters varied from seven in Idaho to eleven in Washington. Washington's constitution gave its governor an item veto to apply to all measures; in Idaho the item veto applied to appropriations only.

As often happened at state constitutional conventions, delegates strayed from the task of enunciating broad and fundamental principles of government. Instead, they provided uninspired codes of laws that addressed matters better left to future lawmakers. Idaho's constitution set a ceiling on state salaries, a measure that made little sense in the face of inflation in later years. Reflecting a strong agrarian bias, convention writers in both states added precise and detailed controls of corporate enterprise, especially of railroads. In the end, Washington's constitution consisted of 25 articles subdivided into 245 sections, totaling approximately 30,000 words. That was seven times longer than the federal Constitution.

THE HOPES AND FEARS OF A GENERATION

Each section of the new state constitutions had some history behind it, but perhaps none was more curious than the background to Article I, Section 24 of the Washington Constitution: "The right of the individual citizen to bear arms in defense of himself, or the State, shall not be impaired, but nothing in this section shall be construed as authorizing individuals or corporations to organize, maintain, or employ an armed body of men." The first part of that section derived from the Bill of Rights, but the words that prohibited private armies addressed a problem of special concern to Washingtonians. On several occasions during the 1880s, employers had hired armies of private detectives to break strikes and eliminate unions in the isolated coal camps of the Cascade mountains.

An early draft of the constitution prohibited all private detective agencies from operating within the state. Although a majority of the delegates balked at supporting such a sweeping condemnation, they finally accepted a watered-down measure that prohibited private armies. Because subsequent legislatures hesitated to implement the measure, however, labor-management disputes continued to convulse the coal camps during the early 1890s. One consequence was the rise of populism, the most successful third-party movement in the state's history.

The Washington constitution makers also rejected a measure that would have provided for safety inspection of mines and given miners an eight-hour workday. Some delegates undoubtedly opposed the eight-hour-day concept as a matter of principle, while others likely believed that such specific matters should be left to future legislatures. In their rejection of this measure, the delegates evidently were determined to avoid framing a code of laws, a distinction they clearly failed to make in other sections. In the Idaho convention, a delegate seeking to include similar protections for labor in that state alluded to the prevailing agrarian bias in both conventions when he declared, "A great many who will vote against anything for the laboring classes will certainly support anything for the benefit of horses and cattle."

The debate over female suffrage offers another example of how constitution making mirrored the concerns of a generation. Although women had been unable to vote for delegates to the Washington constitutional convention, suffrage advocates made their presence felt. Their petitions flooded the gathering. But the assembly feared that a female suffrage provision jeopardized the constitution's chances of being ratified by the all-male electorate.

One delegate stated that he personally favored woman suffrage but, when acting in a representative capacity, had to vote against it. He preferred to leave the entire question to future legislatures. George Turner, a delegate who as a member of the territorial supreme court had played a major role in denying women the right to vote, made a lengthy speech urging that the people of the state rather than the legislature determine the question. The delegates finally added woman suffrage to a list of special issues for voters to consider separate from ratification of the new constitution.

Supporters also raised the issue of female suffrage in Boise, where Abigail Scott Duniway, an Idaho rancher at the time, made an appeal to the delegates. Idaho did not grant women the vote until six years after statehood.

STATEHOOD ACHIEVED

In a special election on October 2, 1889, Washington approved its state constitution by a vote of 40,152 to 11,879. At the same time, the female suffrage amendment lost by 35,527 to 16,613. The defeat meant that Washington women could vote in school elections (Article VI, Section 2), but—like Indians not taxed, males under twenty-one, people who did not meet the residency requirements, and all "idiots, insane persons, and persons convicted of infamous crime"—they were not enfranchised to vote in other elections. Voters also rejected a prohibition amendment by 31,487 to 19,546. In the contest for state capital, Olympia beat its chief rivals Ellensburg and North Yakima. And in the same election, Republicans swept to victory, capturing all of the state's executive offices, all but one of the thirty-five senate seats, and seventy of the seventy-nine house seats.

On November 11, 1889, President Benjamin Harrison proclaimed Washington a state. Seven days later, Elisha P. Ferry, a former territorial governor (1872–80), was inaugurated as chief executive. The first state legislature selected Republicans from opposite sides of the Cascades to serve as United States senators: John B. Allen of Walla Walla and Watson C. Squire of Seattle.

Idaho's constitution was submitted to the voters on November 5, 1889, who ratified it by 12,398 to 1,775. Congress narrowly approved the document despite its anti-Mormon provision and Idaho's lack of an enabling act. Idaho became the nation's forty-third state on July 3, 1890. George L. Shoup, who served as the last territorial governor, was elected the new state's first chief executive.

As a result of intricate maneuvering dictated by state sectionalism, Idaho's first legislative session had the dubious distinction of needing to select *four* United States senators during its brief term (three of whom were actually seated). In yet another concession to sectionalism, the constitution confirmed that Boise would keep the capitol and Moscow the state university, and it required the Idaho Supreme Court to hold sessions in various parts of the state in order to diminish geographic obstacles to litigation.

Wyoming joined the union one week after Idaho. For the first time in the nation's history, a line of states stretched from coast to coast. During no previous twelve-month period had Congress added so many new states. For each of them the commencement exercise was now over, and a new era had begun. In Idaho and Washington, as in Oregon earlier, the first months and years of statehood were devoted to perfecting the machinery of administration and creating or adjusting state institutions to meet a host of new circumstances.

Constitutions provided few guidelines on administrative matters, and thus as a result of piecemeal legislation, each state eventually possessed a bureaucracy composed of an overlapping welter of commissions, committees, bureaus, offices, agencies, and examining boards. As the system became increasingly cumbersome, people demanded reform.

Almost every legislature did some tinkering, yet over the years lawmakers established still more boards and commissions to study ways to improve state government. Idaho attempted to streamline the work of thirty-three boards, bureaus, and commissions and to consolidate eighty-seven state agencies into nine departments in 1919. Washington pursued a similar course in 1921, and Oregon did likewise in 1949. Administrative reorganization inevitably proved to be a complex and not always satisfying feat.

EXPRESSIONS OF REGIONAL SELF-CONFIDENCE

During the first decade of the twentieth century, Portland and Seattle each hosted a world's fair. Portland's Lewis and Clark Exposition of 1905 drew about three million visitors, and Seattle's Alaska-Yukon-Pacific Exposition of 1909 almost four million. At each fair a variety of popular entertainment enlivened the midway (the Trail in Portland and the Paystreak in Seattle), but the events also served to commemorate historic occasions and to boost the region. Portland's extravaganza commemorated one hundred years of regional growth since the Lewis and Clark expedition; the Seattle fair highlighted the accomplishments of the decade following the famous Klondike gold rush and helped to shape the new campus of the University of Washington. Promoters designed the fairs to attract the attention of the eastern United States and Europe, and both were harbingers of the mass culture that would include movies, radio, and eventually television.

Each extravaganza represented a coming-of-age party for a city and a region, a time to reflect on the past and wax eloquent about the future. It became common for residents to speak of the Lewis and Clark Exposition as the dividing line between the old and new Oregon, while the Alaska-Yukon-Pacific Exposition fixed in the popular mind a special connection between Seattle and Alaska.

Ray Stannard Baker, a prominent national journalist, observed in 1903 that in the Pacific Northwest "everything seems to have happened within the last ten years." And in so many ways it had. After enduring the worst depression in American history during the years 1893–97, the region at last seemed to have hit its stride. Between 1897 and 1912, the Pacific Northwest experienced its largest population growth prior to the Second World War and enjoyed one of the most prosperous periods in its history.

Every major city soon possessed a new skyline. Stimulated by the Lewis

51. The Court of Honor at Seattle's Alaska-Yukon-Pacific Exposition in 1909. The fountain remains a landmark on the University of Washington campus. Courtesy University of Washington Libraries: Neg. UW 1473.

and Clark Exposition, the city of Portland embarked on a building boom that gave it a vertical dimension. In Boise, completion of the Idanha Hotel in 1901, an elegant French chateau structure six stories high, initiated a building trend that created the appearance of a modern metropolis. Every city pushed out to the suburbs and beyond.

Urban planning with an emphasis on the "city beautiful" was another sign of modernity. The nation's foremost landscape architects, the Olmsted Brothers of Massachusetts, provided both Seattle and Spokane with plans for city parks and graceful boulevards. The Olmsteds likewise drafted Portland's first city plan in 1903. The Greater Portland plan of 1911 envisioned a Paris on the Pacific. Like the ambitious Bogue plan announced the same year for Seattle, it offered boulevards, a civic center, and harbor improvements as antidotes to the disorderly growth of the past. Whatever their functional aspects, the Seattle and Portland plans emphasized civic beauty,

52. Lake Washington Boulevard in Seattle, October
1914, with Mount Rainier in the background. The scenic drive showcased the talents of the landscape archi-
tect John C. Olmsted. Courtesy Washington State
Historical Society, Tacoma: Photo by Asahel Curtis,
31258a.

but both became entangled in local politics, and only fragments of each plan
were ever implemented.

Reflecting a concern similar to that of the city planners, the Oregon
engineer Samuel C. Lancaster designed the new Columbia River Highway, a
route that was to be beautiful as well as functional. When Oregon opened
the first section to traffic in 1915, the highway's spectacular engineering
and aesthetic appeal attracted world attention. The first major paved highway in the Pacific Northwest also made automobile travel possible from
Portland through the Columbia gorge to eastern Oregon.

New industries, like beet sugar in Idaho, first developed in the 1890s by
the Mormons of Utah, spurred economic growth in the Snake River country. With the erection of Idaho's first large beet sugar factory near Idaho Falls
in 1903, the region gained a new cash crop. Boosters pointed with pride to
the growing number of acres under irrigation—the number in Idaho dou-

bled from 1.2 million in 1900 to 2.2 million in 1910, to the completion of the world's tallest dam on the Boise River in 1915, and to a growing amount of hydroelectric power. Some regional boosters claimed that the Pacific Northwest possessed one-third of the hydroelectric power likely to be generated in the United States. Spokane boosters predicted that "white coal" and the city's extensive railroad connections would make it a great national manufacturing center. Developers of even greater vision talked of the prosperity that growing trans-Pacific commerce would bring to the Pacific Northwest.

That was not entirely wishful thinking, because a variety of statistical indicators offered reason to view the future with confidence. During the decade from 1900 to 1910, the population of Oregon increased by two-thirds, and that of Idaho and of Washington more than doubled. A total of 2.1 million people lived in the Pacific Northwest in 1910. The region's manufacturing output and payrolls doubled between 1900 and 1914, the year the Panama Canal opened, and gave regional boosters an additional reason to think that an era of growth was only beginning.

By the eve of World War I, the people of the Pacific Northwest had many reasons to be proud of their region. Boosters could point to numerous schools and libraries, literary, debating, and music societies, professional organizations, and intellectual and artistic achievements as evidence that the region had succeeded in removing many rough edges from a society shaped by its recent frontier past and its natural resource–based present. The appearance in 1905 of the first professional history of the region—*A History of the Pacific Northwest* by a University of Oregon professor, Joseph Schafer—represented an expression of maturing regional self-confidence every bit as significant as the formation of some new association to market the region's fruit or timber or a new statistic recording a growing market for Northwest wheat in Asia.

But regional self-confidence proved a fragile thing, and all it took to shatter the euphoric mood was the economic downturn that began in 1912 and grew progressively worse during the next two years. It became apparent that the Pacific Northwest's prospects had been overstated and that it had not escaped the stranglehold of an extractive economy. With the loss of confidence, festering social and economic problems of years past assumed a more menacing appearance, and the wartime years from 1914 to 1921 were neither happy nor settled.

CHAPTER 12

Removing the Rough Edges:
Society, Education, and Culture

*

Other sections of the United States can mention their literature as a body,
with respect. . . . The Northwest—Oregon, Washington, Idaho, Montana—
has produced a vast quantity of bilge, so vast, indeed, that the few books
which are entitled to respect are totally lost in the general and seemingly
interminable avalanche of tripe.—James Stevens and H. L. Davis,
Status Rerum (1927)

*

Euro-American settlement of the Pacific Northwest involved far more than
the frenzied pursuit of material gain, although at times it did seem that the
work of surveying boundaries, platting towns, grading streets, staking mining claims, felling trees, cultivating fields, and promoting railway lines took
priority over all else. But accompanying those basic economic activities
was the important work of removing the rough edges from pioneer society.
Many Pacific northwesterners desired schools, churches, clubs, and a sense
of order and cleanliness to give their upstart communities a settled air and
to dispel the notion lurking, they feared, in eastern minds that life in the
Northwest was crude and wholly materialistic. As recently established as
the region's urban settlements were in the 1870s and 1880s, their culturally
minded residents eagerly sought to organize music, literary, and art societies.

Schools were a special source of community pride, and Oregon, Washington, and Idaho funded public, nonsectarian educational institutions
from pioneer days. Together with private and church schools, they contributed to the low rate of illiteracy long a feature of Pacific Northwest life.

Libraries and other forms of adult education were established at an early date. The Hudson's Bay Company once supplied its posts with reading material from England, and by the 1880s it was common for fraternal organizations and union halls to maintain reading rooms stocked with newspapers, magazines, and books. The free public libraries that appeared during the 1880s and 1890s were aptly described as the "people's university."

Newspapers, theaters, lyceums, and churches functioned as popular sources of adult education. Especially during the 1880s and 1890s, reform clubs proliferated to debate temperance, government ownership, and other controversial ideas. A growing array of women's clubs contributed to the social, literary, and moral uplift of frontier settlements—often through the establishment of a public library. The transformation of a frontier society was not lost on promoters, who lured a new generation of settlers to the Northwest by advertising its cultural and social amenities alongside its economic opportunities.

SOCIETY WITH A CAPITAL *S*

The last thing many a northwestern urbanite wanted was to be viewed as an uncouth country bumpkin by easterners. To avoid that humiliation, the wealthy acquired social pretensions that often became more eastern than those of the East itself, especially in Portland, the Northwest's first metropolis and home of its oldest moneyed elite. Large fortunes had already been amassed through a variety of pioneer enterprises by the 1880s, and the city's nouveau riche yielded nothing to their counterparts in Boston or New York in the ostentatious display of wealth. Their residences were overornamented monuments to conspicuous consumption, palatial showplaces that sometimes encompassed entire city blocks. Proper deportment and fashionable attire imported from Paris were serious matters, and socializing often took the form of elegant costume balls and formal dinners impeccably served. No other city in the region ever fully duplicated Portland's ability to appear far more prim and proper than its short history might warrant.

Despite the attention given to civility and decorum, the region's rough-hewn pioneer heritage was by no means forgotten. Especially in Oregon, where an association of early settlers evolved into the state's historical society in 1898, the "cult" of the pioneer ancestor became nothing less than a regional version of the Daughters of the American Revolution. With an unmistakably elitist bias, early-day historical societies placed far more emphasis on society with a capital *S* and genealogical research than on history. At times their aim seemed to be preservation of the records and memories of the pioneers and their descendants for the purpose of distinguishing them from lesser northwesterners—those who arrived during a later era or who lived in one of the region's less imposing neighborhoods or in its many relatively unsophisticated rural districts.

Even within Portland, however, there existed an infamous and embarrassing section that reminded people of the city's nearness to the resources frontier, a section that had everything an itinerant logger or miner might spend his money on—shooting galleries, penny arcades, fortune-tellers, herb doctors, and saloons like Erickson's, which occupied a full block, had a bar six hundred feet long, and was equipped to serve one thousand drinking men at a time. An orchestra of female musicians gowned in pink performed on a platform protected by a brass rail charged with enough electricity to short-circuit any tipsy love-struck male.

That rambunctious young Northwest attracted much attention: it was the stuff of cheap blood-and-thunder novels and a sustainer of the illusion that America's frontier regions were seedbeds of democracy and egalitarianism. Yet, in every Northwest community that survived to maturity, economic and social stratification appeared early, and residents found themselves striving to reconcile the supposed openness of pioneer society with the formation of elitist organizations modeled after those in the East.

SCHOOL DAYS

Builders of a new civilization in the Northwest valued education. Missionaries of various denominations considered education an integral part of their religious program, and at their stations they established schools for Indians and non-Indians alike. Even after the creation of publicly funded school systems, parochial and private grammar schools remained common in important towns in Oregon and Washington at least until the turn of the century. Nonetheless, tax-supported school systems arose in every western territory because not all early settlers were satisfied with the alternatives.

The type of public educational system that evolved in Oregon and Washington was patterned after that of New England. The Oregon School Law of 1849 emphasized free education and locally controlled school districts, a permanent school fund, certification of teachers in an effort to impose professional standards, and religious freedom of teachers and pupils. But when the constitution of 1859 embodied the free public school principle, critics charged that the state was too sparsely settled to fund a quality alternative to parochial and private schools. Therefore, it was not until 1872

53. Turn-of-the-century "kid wagons" brought students
to the public school in Garfield, Washington. Courtesy
Historical Photograph Collection, Washington State
University Libraries: 70–0073.

that a functioning public elementary school program was actually in place. Since that time, the only substantive change has been to make elementary education compulsory.

The growth of public elementary schools was equally slow in Washington Territory. The Organic Act of 1853 provided that two sections of each township be reserved to fund the schools. A year later the territorial legislature authorized local public schools, but the territory's small and scattered population retarded their growth for nearly twenty years. Washington took an important step forward in 1895 with enactment of the so-called Barefoot School Boy Law that initiated the principle of state support for local school districts. That law allowed the state to levy a tax sufficient to provide for the education of each child of school age.

In Idaho, public schools generally antedated church schools (except for mission schools) and thus did not have to contend with the clerical hostility that remained part of the educational debate in Oregon until the close of the nineteenth century. Mormons opened Idaho's first non-Indian school in

223

Franklin in the fall of 1860. From 1864, when the legislature established a public school system for the territory, until the 1880s, the typical Idaho school was a one-room structure in a mining camp, and the term rarely lasted longer than three months. The public school in Boise was housed in an old brick building so crowded that students attended only half-day sessions. Though poorly funded and physically inadequate, schools functioned as centers of community life.

While most Pacific Northwesterners eventually accepted the idea of tax-supported elementary schools—and, in fact, Washingtonians at one time led every other state in per capita spending for education—the idea of public high schools was slow to win popular support. Especially in Oregon, their establishment was attacked repeatedly by influential people like Harvey Scott, the editor of the Portland *Oregonian* and a firm believer that high schools would serve only as havens for "drones," a luxury certain to undermine self-reliance and individualism. Other Oregonians agreed that the public need not be taxed to provide anything beyond elementary-level studies in reading, writing, spelling, arithmetic, history, and geography. School districts contested the issue on a district-by-district basis until the Oregon legislature created a statewide system of high school education in 1901. High schools in Washington date from Dayton in 1880 and Seattle in 1883. There were six high schools in Washington by 1889–90.

The region's colleges and universities were never subject to the same debate as its high schools, although the first tax-supported institutions of higher education amounted to more symbol than substance. Several of them traced their roots to private or denominational academies, which in the case of Oregon antedated all public colleges and universities. Willamette University in Salem traces its history to the founding of the Oregon Institute in 1842, giving it claim to the title of the oldest college or university in the Pacific Northwest, and Pacific University in Forest Grove dates from 1849. The Willamette Valley was in fact a veritable nursery of small church-related colleges.

The region's first college or university funded by public money was the University of Washington, which opened in Seattle in 1861 and was made possible when Congress seven years earlier gave Washington and Oregon two townships each to support higher education. In its first year, thirty pupils enrolled in the primary department, thirteen in the grammar school, seven in the preparatory department, and one in the college freshman class. All "departments" were taught by a faculty of one, Asa Shinn Mercer, who also served as acting president. The university operated only a few months each year and, before statehood, received at best meager funding.

Attempts to establish the University of Oregon encountered considerable opposition from those who felt that the Willamette Valley's several denominational academies and colleges provided the state adequate facilities for higher education. For several years after the university opened in Eugene in 1876, the critics seemed justified. Only seven students graduated in 1881 and only four in 1885.

The University of Idaho dates from 1889, although it did not formally open its doors until 1892. Teaching commenced in Moscow in the unfinished and unfurnished wing of a building that stood in the midst of a plowed field. The first president supervised a faculty of one, who had no books or apparatus of any kind and not a single student on the college level. Some 30 of the 133 students in attendance at the lower levels that first year could barely write their names, and only 6 were of college caliber, a reflection perhaps of the fact that only three accredited high schools existed in Idaho.

The curricula of Northwest colleges and universities were patterned after those of East Coast institutions. They emphasized Greek and Latin classics and the natural sciences. Toward the latter half of the nineteenth century, they included classes in the liberal arts, and in some schools it became possible to substitute French and English for classical languages. Even more dramatic changes occurred on the campuses of the region's three land-grant universities.

A land-grant institution, according to the provisions of the Morrill Act of 1862, received some federal support in exchange for providing military training to its male students and maintaining a curriculum that emphasized "practical" training in agriculture, home economics, and engineering. The region's three land-grant institutions are Washington State University, founded in 1890 in Pullman; Oregon State University in Corvallis, which evolved in 1886 from a Methodist institute into Oregon State Agricultural College; and the University of Idaho. Each state also operated normal schools or teachers' colleges, generally in small towns.

The region's private and public colleges and universities bore many resemblances. All passed through what could be labeled a heroic phase of development, a time of low enrollments and meager and uncertain funding, a time that required extraordinary dedication of faculty and administrators. Whitman College, which by the mid-1980s possessed a multimillion-dollar endowment, nearly closed during the 1890s for lack of money and owes its survival to the herculean labors of Stephen B. L. Penrose, who served as president from 1894 to 1934.

On all campuses, public and private, the morals and deportment of

54. Land-grant universities emphasized "practical"
learning. These University of Idaho students were
learning techniques of mine rescue. Courtesy University of Idaho Library: 1–223–1.

students and faculty were once a matter of close administrative concern and
scrutiny. Students at the University of Washington in 1863 were forbidden
to attend saloons, theaters, and balls and were required to assemble at the
university's chapel on Sunday afternoons "to study the Scriptures as a Bible
Class."

In those strenuous years of college and university education, instructors
were expected to teach a variety of disciplines. The head of the Departments of Physical Science and Natural History at the University of Washington alone taught classes in physics, chemistry, physiology, botany, zool-
ogy, biology, mineralogy, and geology.

ADULT EDUCATION IN PIONEER SOCIETY

In an age informed and entertained by television, radio, and the movies, it is
difficult to understand the importance of newspapers and periodicals as
social and educational vehicles in pioneer societies. It was a poor community, indeed, that could not boast of at least one newspaper, and over the

years the number of newspapers in the region certainly totaled in the thousands. Before radio achieved prominence in the late 1920s, no form of adult education was more influential than the press. Anyone with a modest amount of cash or a patron, a modicum of education and technical know-how, and a passion to say something could start a newspaper.

The region's first newspaper was the *Oregon Spectator*, a biweekly venture that began publication in Oregon City in 1846. Settlers who organized the Oregon Lyceum to promote science, temperance, morality, and the general intelligence were among its sponsors. The first newspaper in the region north of the Columbia River was the *Columbian*, launched in Olympia in 1852. Ten years later the rush of miners into the Clearwater region provided subscribers for Idaho's first newspaper, the *Golden Age* of Lewiston. The oldest Idaho newspaper still published is the *Idaho Statesman* of Boise, which dates from 1864.

A pioneer newspaper was an intensely partisan and personal operation,

55. The University of Oregon sophomore women's
basketball team, 1894–95. Courtesy University of
Oregon Archives.

227

AN EXAMPLE OF THE OREGON STYLE OF JOURNALISM

"The publisher of the *Union*, one R. M. Smith, is known to be a murderer, a thief, a bigamist, a pimp, and with the knowledge of these facts the public will know what credit to attach to statements that appear in the paper he controls. The fellow is incapable of writing a sentence of good English, and to make up for his deficiency he has in his employ a notorious shyster and dead beat, named Ross, who is his equal in infamy, and is a ready tool to do his dirty work."—Walla Walla *Statesman*, August 28, 1875.

---

vastly different from the bland standardized fare typical of today's corporate-dominated press. Editors advocated controversial and unpopular causes and published embarrassing news about individual citizens' manners and morals, items almost certainly libelous today. They attacked rival editors with all the invective at their command. Politics was a major concern in the fifties and sixties, and passions ran high as Democratic papers traded verbal blows with Whigs and later Republicans. These verbal excesses came to be known as the Oregon Style of journalism.

Personal threats from irate readers, some of whom were not satisfied merely with words, occasionally quickened the life of an editor. During the Civil War, Southern sympathizers in Lewiston took such violent exception to the views expressed by the Republican editor of the *Golden Age* that on several occasions they riddled with bullets the Union flag flying above his office. Readers expected a newspaper editor above all else to function as a community booster who promoted local attractions and damned all rivals. The worst thing an editor could do was to transfer his press and allegiance to a rival community.

In addition to community-oriented newspapers, the Pacific Northwest nurtured a host of specialty publications. Some were voices of literary criticism or church news; a good many others were protest journals promoting various causes. One of several oddities was a spiritualist publication that alternated each month under the titles the *World's Advance-Thought* and the *Universal Republic*. Each issue contained a "Soul-Communion Time-Table" that fixed a specific day and a time for residents of the leading cities of the world to hold collective soul-communion to invoke "the blessings of universal peace and higher spiritual light." The region's first literary journal, the *Oregon Literary Vidette*, began publication in 1879. A year earlier the region's first labor paper, the *Labor Gazette*, appeared in Portland. During the depression years of the 1890s, dozens of short-lived newspapers championed the cause of labor, populism, socialism, anarchism, spiritualism, and a host of other "isms and osophies." Although most publications were in English, the Pacific Northwest press included a lively foreign-language contingent.

The mortality rate among pioneer papers was extremely high. Operating on high hopes and a shoestring budget, few survived longer than a year or two. Yet, from the several thousand newspapers and periodicals published in the Pacific Northwest, a few outstanding editors and papers emerged.

The most influential voice in Oregon for nearly forty years belonged to Harvey W. Scott, editor of the Portland *Oregonian*. When he joined the paper in 1865, fifteen years after its founding, the *Oregonian* was an inconspicuous publication. Scott eventually acquired a part interest in it and well before his death in 1910 made it into the leading journal in the Pacific Northwest. As one of the region's first college graduates, Scott had a compulsion to educate his readers. His editorial columns preached the conservative doctrine of nineteenth-century individualism and untrammeled frontier opportunity. It was the kind of paper that Oregonians embraced or hated but could not ignore. Few men wielded more power in late-nineteenth-century Oregon than the remarkable editor who molded public opinion for many years.

The Spokane *Spokesman-Review* was the leading paper in the interior region of eastern Washington and northern Idaho. It originated as the weekly *Review* in 1883 when Spokane was a mere hamlet. Aided by the Coeur d'Alene mineral bonanza later that year, the paper evolved and grew until, by the turn of the century, it attained a circulation of more than forty thousand and covered a vast territory that stretched from Oregon to British Columbia and from the Cascades to the Rockies. Its Yale-educated publisher, William Hutchinson Cowles, was a young journalist who left the Chicago *Tribune* to come west in 1891; he became sole owner of the paper in 1894. Cowles gave its pages a progressive, reform-minded tone until the 1920s, when he steered it in an ever more conservative direction. The *Spokesman-Review* in the mid-1980s had become the flagship of the Cowles family media empire that includes two Spokane newspapers, a television station, two radio stations, and extensive real estate interests.

Seattle was home to numerous newspaper ventures, including the *Union-Record*, which from 1918 to 1928 was one of the few daily labor journals published in the United States. By the turn of the century, two general interest papers had emerged from a crowded field: the *Post-Intelligencer* and the *Times*, the latter a sensation-seeking journal edited and published by the bombastic Colonel Alden J. Blethen, who acquired it in 1896.

Another popular vehicle for adult education was the Chautauqua, a cultural uplift movement that originated in upstate New York and was named for the lake on which it was headquartered. The typical Chautauqua resembled a frontier camp meeting crossed with a college lecture. It drew together both urban and rural folk. For several years after 1889, the annual Chautauqua was a popular event on Washington's Vashon Island and after 1895 in Gladstone Park near Portland, where the third-largest encampment in the United States was held. Six thousand people came to the 78-acre park in 1896 to hear William Jennings Bryan speak on the "Prince of Peace."

CULTURE HIGH AND LOW

Popular culture came in many forms. One of its most controversial pur-veyors was the opera house, a name applied to a variety of forums that offered public entertainment. Some opera houses were home to productions staged by itinerant Shakespeare companies, while others featured balalaika players, dancing dogs, and an assortment of lewd offerings. Most notorious of the latter type were the box houses, so called because the balcony was partitioned off into curtained boxes from which the patrons and their guests could view the show without being seen themselves. In such establish-ments vaudeville entertainment—a type of diversion consisting of spe-cialty acts—functioned merely as an adjunct to the sale of liquor and sex.

In some box houses the female entertainers performed on the stage until midnight, then visited patrons in the boxes while another company pre-sented further melodrama on stage. During the 1890s the forces of morality declared war on the box houses, and in Tacoma they passed a law excluding women from variety theaters. The Washington legislature in 1905 outlawed the employment of women in places where intoxicating drinks were sold.

Vaudeville shows that had been "cleaned up" for family entertainment were offered occasionally in regular theaters by the same troupes who performed in the saloons and box houses. John F. Cordray, who came to the West Coast in 1888, was the first person to operate a vaudeville theater successfully without the attraction of liquor. Neither did his theaters toler-ate profane or boisterous language or rowdy characters.

John Considine, a box house operator in Seattle, started the first legiti-mate, popular-priced vaudeville chain in the world. At one time he and a partner operated twenty-one houses in the Pacific Northwest. Nonetheless, the advent of radio and talking motion pictures in the 1920s doomed vaudeville. Considine's rival was Alexander Pantages, a Greek immigrant who parlayed the unpretentious movie theater he opened in Seattle in 1902 into a multimillion-dollar chain of playhouses, one of the largest in the United States.

Like the stage productions that once toured the Pacific Northwest with forgettable names like "Three Weeks of Marriage" and "The Deuce Is in Him," a good many of the region's early novels and poems possessed few enduring qualities apart from their historic value. Repeating a pattern common in older regions, the early literature of the Pacific Northwest evolved from explorers' books of travel, diaries, and letters, to histories and polemical tracts by missionaries and pioneer settlers, and finally to novels, poetry, and other products of the imagination. Most works in the latter category fell into the local color genre in which authors employed elegantly descriptive yet trite language to tell an emotionally unsophisticated story in a regional setting. Because their theme was invariably the environment and the human response to it, authors filled their works with babbling brooks, murmuring rivers, whispering pines, and other hackneyed tributes to the region's stunning natural setting, but they seldom incorporated genuine elements of folk life and art.

Among the exceptions were Joaquin Miller and Charles Erskine Scott Wood. Though not natives of the region, they were the only early Northwest literary figures to achieve an enduring national reputation. Miller, born in Indiana as Cincinnatus Hiner Miller, had his first book of poetry published in Oregon in 1868. Entitled *Specimines*, it attracted little attention in the state. Only after the colorful Miller left the Pacific Northwest did his writing capture the fancy of English and American literary society.

Few Pacific northwesterners possessed more complex personalities or lived more diverse lives than Charles Erskine Scott Wood, who like Miller was something of a frontier original. Wood was born in Pennsylvania in 1852 and died in 1944; an officer who participated in the campaign against Chief Joseph, he was also a Portland lawyer who later became a prolific writer of short stories, books, and poems, a painter, humanitarian, and anarchist. His most popular work was *Heavenly Discourse* (1927); his most important was *Poet in the Desert*, which first appeared in 1915. In it Wood juxtaposed human cruelty and nature's beneficence as experienced in the eastern Oregon desert, and he did it without slipping into the romanticization of nature so typical of early Northwest writing.

The earliest novel written and published in the Pacific Northwest was

Margaret Jewett Bailey's thinly disguised autobiography, *The Grains; or, Passages in the Life of Ruth Rover* (1854). The book is at times flawed with the sentimentalism of the era, but it is of historical value for its unique and incisive perspective on the frontier era. The best selling of pre-1900 Northwest novels was Frederick Homer Balch's *Bridge of the Gods* (1890), a saccharine period piece about Indian life that went through twenty-nine editions between 1890 and 1935; and it is still in print. Like other early works of Northwest fiction, it was far more imitative than innovative.

As was then typical in the rest of the United States, most early novelists in the Northwest were women.[1] The suffragist Abigail Scott Duniway wrote several volumes of fiction, the most notable being *Captain Gray's Company* (1859), the tale of a mother and two children who leave home to make the long trip to Oregon. It includes several autobiographical sections but possesses little literary merit. Also in the matriarchal literary tradition were Ella R. Higginson, poet and short story writer, and Eva Emery Dye, who wrote a series of novels glamorizing the pioneer tradition. Her best-known work was *McLoughlin and Old Oregon* (1900).

Mary Hallock Foote (1847–1938) was the first writer to use Idaho as a setting, though she was often critical of what she observed. She came to the West with her husband, a civil engineer, and resided in Idaho from 1883 to 1893. Beginning with *The Chosen Valley* (1892), Foote wrote and illustrated a series of autobiographical novels and short stories about the mining and irrigation frontiers, most of them superficial and romantic. Her *Coeur d'Alene* (1894) viciously criticized the striking miners; it was filled with heroes and villains but no real understanding of the conflict.

It was the decidedly parochial character of the first seventy-five years of Pacific Northwest fiction and poetry that caused James Stevens and Harold Lenoir Davis to issue their 1927 manifesto, *Status Rerum*,[2] blasting so much of it as bilge. *Status Rerum* represented a youthful outburst against the literary establishment for works that failed to reflect accurately the historical and social milieu of the region. Stevens, who wrote *Paul Bunyan* (1925), and Davis, who won the Pulitzer Prize for his novel *Honey in the Horn* (1935), were two of the region's best writers. The honors that later came to Davis for *Honey in the Horn*, which one critic described as a story

1. Also in this category was Frances Fuller Victor, a gifted historian who ghostwrote the volumes on Oregon and the Pacific Northwest Coast for Hubert Howe Bancroft's western history series.

2. It was aptly subtitled *A Manifesto upon the Present Condition of Northwestern Literature: Containing Several Near Libelous Utterances upon Persons in the Public Eye.*

of the homestead era in Oregon that "deflowers the sweeter legend of the heroic pioneers, seeing them as average humans and none too civilized in speech and customs,"[3] were evidence of the significant changes that awaited Northwest literature after it escaped its early romantic infatuation with the region's natural setting. *Status Rerum* thus stands as a watershed in Northwest literary development.

Reasons for the character of early Northwest literature are several. The Montana historian and journalist Joseph Kinsey Howard observed at a Northwest writers' conference in 1946 that it was difficult for pioneers to devote much time to literary pursuits until the house was built, the harvest was in, and the fire laid. Other explanations centered on the region's physical and intellectual distance from the literary circles of Boston and New York or on its small population, which restricted the sale of works of genuine merit. In other words, the early literary output of the Pacific Northwest reflected its status as a cultural hinterland. Despite the limitations cited in the 1946 conference, Northwest literature reflected a region's determined effort to remove its rough edges.

3. *Oregon: End of the Trail*, WPA Guide (Portland: Binfords and Mort, 1940), 114.

Part Four

Progress and Its Discontents

Profile: The World of
May Arkwright Hutton

Some of the atrocities practiced on the prisoners in this improvised prison at Kellogg, Idaho, by old "General Bulldozium," Governor "Stepanfetchit" and his man "Friday," at the instigation of the Standard Oil Company and the silver and lead barons of the Coeur d'Alenes, are scarcely fit for polite ears. Read them, you curled darlings of wealth, you trifling puppets of society.—May Arkwright Hutton, *The Coeur D'Alenes; or, A Tale of the Modern Inquisition in Idaho* (1900)

Talk of gold and a sense of adventure brought May Arkwright to northern Idaho. Like thousands of others in 1883, the twenty-three-year-old from Ohio was lured to the mining country by advertisements proclaiming: "Nuggets weighing $50, $100, $200 of free gold for the picking up; it fairly glistens." But May had barely reached the Coeur d'Alenes before the transition from placer to lode mining gave the region an industrial character, with most miners now working for wages. The legitimate moneymaking opportunities open to women in such an economy were at best limited.

For the plain-faced and heavy-set May Arkwright, hardship was nothing new. Born out of wedlock and abandoned by her father, she spent her youth caring for an aged and blind grandfather. She became an accomplished cook by the age of ten. In the Coeur d'Alenes May earned a meager living feeding hungry miners at her boardinghouse. A diligent worker and a supporter of union labor, she got along well in the rough mining camp society of Kellogg and Wardner. Her good food and love of life won the hearts of the miners, and of a railroader, Levi W. "Al" Hutton, whom she married in 1887.

Coeur d'Alene Mining Region, (Silver Valley) Idaho, 1910

Idaho

Silver Valley

N

Montana
Idaho

Murray

Prichard Creek

Eagle Creek

Eagle

Beaver Creek

Delta

Coeur d' Alene R.

North Fork

Hercules Mine

Burke

Gem
Tiger-Poorman Mine

Frisco Mine

Mullan

Wallace

Coeur d' Alene River

Osburn

Big Creek

South Fork

Kellogg

Wardner

Pine Creek

Kingston

Mission

Coeur d'Alene River

0   3
    miles

Rice

May Arkwright Hutton had an inquisitive mind. She spent her spare time reading political tracts that fired her passion for justice and inspired her to fight for organized labor and female suffrage. In her unpolished and flamboyant way, she championed the underdog. In 1899 that meant getting her husband out of the hated "bull pen," the primitive stockade filled with men imprisoned in the latest mining war that convulsed the Coeur d'Alene region.

Two major episodes of industrial violence wracked the new state of Idaho during the decade of the 1890s, one in 1892 and another in 1899. Mineowners battled on one side; unionized miners, on the other. First in the town of Wardner in 1887, and then in Gem, Burke, and Mullan, hard-rock miners had secretly formed unions in response to their need for economic protection and fraternity. Unions provided camaraderie, hospital care for the sick or injured, and money for a decent burial. Union halls typically had an assembly room large enough to handle a crowd of two hundred or more and served as centers of community life—places where workers could gather for dances, picnics, public lectures, and boxing matches.

But miners' unions were more than fraternal lodges and community centers; they were also organizations fighting for decent wages and hours, for safety regulations to minimize the dangers of a cave-in or poisonous air, and for an end to company stores and boardinghouses, two vivid reminders of the mineowners' paternalism and power. In a larger sense, the miners' unions fought for the right to exist at a time when management regarded them as threats to its nearly absolute control of the workplace.

At about the same time as the miners organized, the most powerful mineowners in the Coeur d'Alenes formed a protective association. A variety of problems beset the owners, chiefly the falling price of silver and rising railroad rates, but their new association soon emerged as a vehicle to checkmate union labor. Mineowners employed a variety of effective weapons: they cut wages, and when workers struck, they hired spies and armed guards, fired union members, and substituted nonunion or scab labor imported from outside the region.

In late 1891 the owners hired a Pinkerton detective, Charles A. Siringo, to spy on union meetings. He succeeded beyond his employers' wildest dreams. Adopting the alias C. Leon Allison, Siringo took a job at the Gem Mine, joined the local miners' union, and proved to be one of its most earnest members. His fellow workers soon elected him recording secretary, a position that for seven months gained him access to the union's innermost secrets. At night under cover of darkness, he regularly walked the three miles from Gem to Wallace to mail his reports to the mineowners.

56. Charles A. Siringo, "the Cowboy Detective." Courtesy Idaho State Historical Society: 80–125.1.

When the mineowners discharged union members in midwinter and replaced them with scabs protected by armed guards, Siringo's spying proved vital. On several occasions his advance warnings enabled the owners to thwart union plans to stop scabs from entering the region. Suspicious union members finally unmasked Siringo, who eluded an angry mob when he sawed a hole in the floor of his rooming house and crawled under the board sidewalk to a nearby creek and freedom. But his treachery angered miners and triggered their violent retaliation against the owners.

The culminating act in the tense six-month drama began in the town of Gem on July 11, 1892, with the exchange of gunshots between union members and guards barricaded in the Frisco Mine's ore-processing mill. The fight spread to the Gem Mine. Sporadic shots continued for hours, then suddenly a roar shook the valley. Dynamiters had launched a bundle of explosives down a pipe that carried water into the Frisco mill. The blast demolished the structure, and falling timbers killed one worker and injured several others. The guards and scabs promptly surrendered, as did those at other mines and mills farther down the canyon. Miners disarmed the scabs and marched them to trains to ship them out of the valley. In the wake of the violence, six men were dead (three on each side), and more than a dozen were injured. But unrest had not ended.

At the Bunker Hill and Sullivan complex near Wardner, six hundred armed men seized a $250,000 concentrator and threatened to destroy it if the company—the most influential in the region—did not discharge its scabs. The manager agreed, and soon all the strikebreakers had left the Coeur d'Alenes. Someone tacked a broom onto the last boxcar to signify a clean sweep.

With the scabs gone, union miners celebrated their victory. But their jubilation was premature. Because of the violence, Governor Norman Willey declared martial law. State and federal troops soon arrived to put down the insurrection and protect scab workers. Union men, who had hoped never to see the strikebreakers again, were "crestfallen and sullen."

Charles Siringo, who had observed the violence from a concealed viewpoint in the hills, guided the soldiers as they rounded up hundreds of people. One witness predicted that "in two days the Coeur d'Alenes will be a vast military prison for the miners' union." That prophecy came true when authorities collected three hundred men in a vast dragnet—and not just union workers, but justices of the peace, lawyers, merchants, saloonkeepers—anyone sympathetic to the union and some who were not.

Troops herded the prisoners into the two bull pens at Wallace and Ward-

57. The United States Infantry arrived in Wallace,
Idaho, to suppress the industrial violence of mid-1892.
Courtesy University of Idaho Library: # 8–X483,
Barnard-Stockbridge Collection.

ner, where many of them were confined for nearly two months awaiting a hearing. At first most of the men considered their arrest a joke; they laughed and sang and enjoyed a supper prepared by the ladies. But as the weeks passed, they complained loudly, and tempers grew short. On one occasion when Siringo went into the prison yard to identify a certain person, the anger of the captives flared into a near riot. Only the cocked pistol Siringo held in his hand and the armed soldiers prevented bloodshed. Sanitary conditions became unbearable in the summer heat, and even those outside the Wallace stockade complained of "the most noxious odors" pervading the town.

In nearby Spokane, laboring people rallied in a show of support for the imprisoned miners. Nearly a thousand people met in the city's Haymarket Square in late July to hear speeches and music and to give donations for the prisoners. "The representatives of organized labor in Spokane have gone crazy," complained the Spokane *Review*, which supported the mineowners.

The state finally transported twenty-five union leaders to Boise for trial.

Siringo was there to testify, and one of his targets was Ed Boyce, a muscular young Irish immigrant and an officer of the Wardner Miners' Union. Boyce was subsequently sentenced to spend six more months in prison. During his stint in jail, he and his fellow union members laid plans for a bigger and more effective organization, the Western Federation of Miners, a union that soon included not only Coeur d'Alene miners but also workers in Montana, British Columbia, and other mining districts in the West.

In the short run, though, the future looked bleak for organized miners. Their union had proved no match for the combined might of the owners and the military. The scabs and armed guards were soon back on the job as if nothing had happened. Boyce returned home to find himself blacklisted, unable to obtain work in a major mine. But his imprisonment ultimately proved a blessing in disguise: to many people he was a hero, and north Idaho voters sent him back to Boise in 1894—this time as a state senator. And two years later fellow miners elected him president of the Western Federation of Miners.

As head of the new union, Boyce was a fire-breathing militant. He injected life into the shaky organization, expanded its influence throughout the West, and urged it down the road to socialism. His experiences in the bull pen, the Boise prison, and even the Idaho legislature made him cynical about power and politics and the miners' chances of ever obtaining justice. "Every union," he advised, "should have a rifle club." In the war between the classes, Boyce was determined to win next time.

Next time arrived in 1899. Unlike Boyce, May and Al Hutton had managed to avoid trouble in 1892, and they certainly did not go looking for it in 1899. Al's job as a railway engineer was normally uneventful: for ten hours a day he steamed up and down a Northern Pacific feeder line, setting out empty cars at one mine, picking up loaded ones at another. But a gun in his back interrupted Al's routine on Saturday, April 29, 1899.

"Get this thing going," ordered the miner who prodded him with the weapon. A second man covered the fireman. Behind the engine other men swarmed onto boxcars. Al eased his train slowly down the tracks that threaded the narrow canyon from Burke to Gem. "Stop at the Frisco powder house," his captor ordered. There Al's nonpaying passengers broke into the locked building and loaded almost two tons of explosives onto the little freight, transforming it into the "Dynamite Express," a train bound for history if not glory.

Along the way to Wallace and Wardner, Al paused to pick up more passengers as ordered. Soon almost a thousand riders—nearly half of them masked and armed with rifles—had crowded aboard. They were headed for

Wardner to teach the mighty Bunker Hill and Sullivan Company a lesson. Following the violence of 1892, the Western Federation of Miners had successfully persuaded most of the large mines in the Coeur d'Alenes to pay union-scale wages, but not the Bunker Hill and Sullivan. Its managers claimed that low profits had forced them to cut costs and to use only nonunion labor. Union members attempted to infiltrate the company's work force, but Bunker Hill and Sullivan invariably identified and discharged them. Tensions mounted until the day the miners commandeered Al Hutton's train.

When the Dynamite Express approached the Bunker Hill and Sullivan complex, the company guards fled along with the superintendent and manager—a wise move considering the odds. The workers burned the company's office and boardinghouse and placed three thousand pounds of dynamite around the concentrator's support pilings. At 2:26 P.M., seconds after the last stick was in place, someone, probably a miner, lit the fuse. Three explosions reduced the costly structure to matchsticks. Miners rejoiced and congratulated themselves on their victory in the "Second Battle of Bunker Hill," a reference to the revolutionary war battle. The deed done, the miners ordered Al Hutton to take them home. Next morning, most of them reported for work as usual. But one young miner prophesied correctly, "You can't steal railroad trains, dynamite mines, and burn villages without some reaction."

Telegraph lines sped news of the violence to Idaho's governor, Frank Steunenberg. A man who emphasized the common touch—he refused to wear a necktie to any state function—Steunenberg had once been a member of a printers' union. With the backing of labor he was elected governor in 1896 and again in 1898. But he could not condone what had happened in the Coeur d'Alenes. He promised to "punish and totally eradicate from this community a class of criminals who for years have been committing murders and other crimes in open violation of law."

Because the Idaho militia was then stationed in the Philippines in the aftermath of the Spanish-American War, Steunenberg wired for federal troops and declared the Coeur d'Alene region to be in a state of insurrection.[1] Leaders of the Western Federation of Miners hastily left the area, but most rank-and-file members calmly awaited their fate.

---

1. Martial law continued until the end of his term and no miner was allowed to work at any mine in the district without a state permit. A permit was denied to anyone unable to prove he had not participated in the Bunker Hill bombing.

PERMIT TO SEEK EMPLOYMENT.

No. 1363 ....*June* 8........ **1900.**

This is to certify that Jno F Hawkee ....,

a laborer .... *by occupation, is qualified under the proclamation issued by order of the Governor of Idaho, May 8th, 1899, to seek employment in any of the mines in Shoshone County and has permission by virtue hereof to do so. This card is to be deposited with the manager or superintendent of the mine where the person above named is employed, and must be held for purpose of periodical inspection pursuant to the terms of the aforesaid proclamation.*
Witness my hand this ..8... *day of* June .... *1900.*

DR. HUGH FRANCE.

By Geo J Edmiston *Deputy.*

58. A red-card work permit. A miner could obtain the card only after swearing to an anti-union pledge before Dr. Hugh France, county coroner and supporter of the mine operators. The state-backed permit system continued until January 1901, when Idaho's new governor, Frank Hunt, stopped the practice. Courtesy Idaho State Historical Society: 63–57.36.

Brigadier General H. C. Merriam and almost eight hundred blue-jacketed troops arrived by special train on May 3, and the general promptly ordered every miner herded into the bull pen—between six hundred and seven hundred people. One of the prisoners was Al Hutton. He protested his innocence, but his wife protested even more vigorously. She visited the pen daily, smuggling in food when possible. She was popular with the prisoners, but the soldiers resented her rough and abusive manner and became hostile and obscene. But after two weeks she finally got her husband released, apparently when she appealed to the fraternal spirit of his fellow Masons.

But May Hutton was not through with the bull pen or the authorities. With a pen dipped in rhetorical acid, she wrote a libelous novel entitled *The Coeur d'Alenes; or, A Tale of the Modern Inquisition in Idaho*. In it she referred to the Mine Owners' Protective Association as the Mushroom Mining Men's Association and to Frank Steunenberg as Governor Stepanfetchit. One of the heroes of her lurid tale was Ed Boyce, the militant president of the Western Federation of Miners and a friend of the Huttons.

Circumstances connected Boyce and the Huttons in several ways. After

59. The Hercules Mine, Burke, Idaho, 1901. May Arkwright Hutton is pictured on the tracks; Levi W. Hutton is at the far right. Courtesy University of Idaho
Library: # 8–X145, Barnard-Stockbridge Collection.

Al's release from the bull pen, the railroad refused to rehire him because a
coroner's jury had labeled him "a willing tool of the rioters." From then on
he devoted his working hours to a small, seemingly unproductive mine—
the Hercules—one in which he and May had invested their savings of a few
hundred dollars. Boyce acquired an interest in the same mine in 1901 when
he married Eleanor Day, a sister of the man who had sold the Huttons their
share of the property.

In many ways life in the Coeur d'Alenes in the 1890s was one big gamble:
workers gambled with their lives every day in the mines; investors gambled
with their dollars. For common folk, investing in a mine was a serious
matter but as chancy as playing a slot machine today. The pull of a handle or
the turn of a shovel might spell the difference between poverty and wealth.
If Lady Luck smiled, the payoff could be enormous, and in 1901 she smiled
on the Hercules. Shortly after Boyce married, the mine developed into one
of the great Coeur d'Alene bonanzas. The Huttons were rich; the Boyces
were rich.

The transformation of Ed Boyce was dramatic. He resigned as head of the Western Federation of Miners in 1902, reportedly because of ill health, and retired to Portland, where he lived another forty years. To give Boyce something to do, his wife and her family purchased the stately Portland Hotel, a genteel establishment in the heart of the city's financial district. Boyce managed it well, and for more than two decades members of the Portland business community favored its dining room, apparently unconcerned that its manager had once declared war on capitalists like them. The onetime militant had mellowed; gone was talk of violence and socialism. Improbable as it seemed, the former president of the Western Federation of Miners became president of the Oregon Hotel Association.

As for the Huttons, their small investment in the Hercules made them millionaires. They bought a big house in Wallace and entertained lavishly. In 1906 they moved to a mansion in Spokane and invested in real estate there. They had maids and a chauffeur-driven car, and May Hutton even tried to buy up and destroy all remaining copies of her embarrassingly amateurish novel. Yet despite all the changes in her life, she never lost her flamboyant style or her sympathy for the disadvantaged. She continued to campaign vigorously for woman suffrage and supported orphanages and day-care centers. In 1912 she became the first woman ever elected to the Democratic National Convention. Some people say May forgot her friends in organized labor after she became rich. That charge is false, because when she died in 1915, she left $5,000 to help build a labor temple in Spokane. Seventy years later, in 1985, along with William Boeing, Bing Crosby, and others, May Arkwright Hutton was named to the Washington State Hall of Fame.

One associate of the Huttons in the Hercules venture who failed to share in the great bonanza was Harry Orchard, a strange and violent man who wrote a bloody postscript to the Coeur d'Alene mining wars. It was Orchard who claimed to have touched off the blast that destroyed the Bunker Hill and Sullivan concentrator, but like many of his boasts, that assertion remains suspect. He apparently lost his share of the Hercules in 1898 or 1899 to settle a debt, although in a moralizing mood he later claimed that "women, gambling, and whisky got it all."

In late 1905 Orchard made headlines across America when he planted a bomb that killed Frank Steunenberg, the former governor, at his home in Caldwell. For that crime, the state convicted Orchard and sentenced him to spend the rest of his life in prison. He cheated the gallows only by confessing that the top leaders of the Western Federation of Miners had hired him to assassinate Steunenberg in revenge for his actions in the Coeur d'Alenes six years earlier. Boyce, of course, was no longer associated with the union, but Idaho officials quietly pursued William D. Haywood, its secretary-treasurer, and two others: Charles Moyer, the union's president, and George Pettibone, a blacklisted Coeur d'Alene miner now a hardware merchant. With the full support of the governors of the two states involved, Idaho lawmen kidnapped the three men in Denver and rushed them to Boise on a special train furnished by the Union Pacific Railroad. Idaho's high-handed extradition by abduction outraged organized labor and civil libertarians and thrust the case into the national spotlight.

The most sensational trial in Pacific Northwest history opened in Boise in 1907. It pitted Idaho's special prosecutor and newly elected United States senator William E. Borah against the famed Chicago attorney Clarence Darrow for the defense. In the end the jury acquitted all three defendants. Idaho law required a witness to corroborate Orchard's claim of a conspiracy, and the only person who might have been able to do so retracted a con-

60. (*Left to right*) George Pettibone, William D. Haywood, and Charles Moyer awaiting trial in 1907. Courtesy Idaho State Historical Society: 2004.

fession he claimed was coerced by a Pinkerton detective, James McParland. Many people found it difficult to believe Orchard's many sensational claims to bigamy, arson, assassination, and mass murder.

This profile of the world of May Arkwright Hutton is not simply a story of luck and misfortune in the Coeur d'Alenes or even a glimpse at the violent underside of mining. It is about one of the many disturbing changes that occurred in the Pacific Northwest during the decades from the 1880s to the 1930s, in this case, the rise of wagework and the attendant exploitation of labor.

During those years, existing laws and public policies often seemed incapable of addressing a growing array of social and economic ills that afflicted workers and the larger society. The juxtaposition of technological progress and grinding poverty and other forms of human misery perplexed the nation's leading thinkers and called forth new political movements and popular crusades. The paradox of progress and poverty together with a host of more specific injustices caused Pacific Northwesterners from various walks of life—agriculture, labor, and the professions—to participate in a series of crusades, some successful and others quixotic and doomed to failure. Collectively, however, they revealed the many stresses the region experienced during the rapid transition from frontier-agrarian to urban-industrial society.

CHAPTER 13

Evolution of the
Wageworkers' Frontier

*

The "blanket-stiff" now packs his bed
Along the trails of yesteryear—
What path is left for you to tread? . . .
Do you not know the West is dead?
—Ralph Chaplin,
"The West is Dead," *Wobbly* (1948)

*

The stereotypical picture of Oregon pioneers is of land-hungry farmers, but westbound ships and covered wagons also brought mechanics and artisans. Some of those new arrivals carried with them the seeds of trade unionism. Printers in Portland organized the Typographical Society in 1853, and locomotive engineers and longshoremen formed additional unions in the late 1860s. The few unions that predated 1880 were for the most part weak and tenuous, but after the completion of the Northern Pacific Railroad, labor's power increased noticeably. Oregon became the first state in the nation to legalize the Labor Day holiday in 1887; and for many years, the percentage of unionized nonagricultural workers was greater in Washington than in any other state. But the story of working people in the Pacific Northwest is more than the history of unions.

Work for wages is today the most common way Pacific Northwesterners earn a living. That was not true before 1880, when most people were self-employed. Early residents sustained themselves by farming or perhaps by running a small shop or store, but generally not by selling their labor for wages. Although wagework began as early as the era of fur companies, it did not become common until the construction boom of the 1880s. Building the region's railroads and cities, harvesting its timber and grain, and mining its coal and metals created a great demand for hired muscle. In many ways the rise of wagework in the Pacific Northwest mirrored national trends, yet within the region, the sometimes strained relationship between workers and their employers also reflected a frontier heritage. In fact, from the 1880s until the First World War, the Pacific Northwest could accurately be labeled a wageworkers' frontier.

Conflict between labor and management characterized the wageworkers' frontier, as it did industrialized areas of the East—but with the added volatility of frontier ideals of individualism and personal advancement clashing with the dependency inherent in working for wages. Because many unskilled or semiskilled workers headed west expecting to achieve personal success, they easily became disappointed and outraged by anything that prevented them from claiming the rewards promised by western opportunity. Time after time the clash between unrealistic expectations and harsh reality gave rise to radical crusades, militant unions, and violence. The existence of the wageworkers' frontier explains why the Pacific Northwest experienced a sometimes troubled transition from rural-agrarian to urban-industrial society. Because dramatic incidents like the Coeur d'Alene mining wars, bloody clashes in Everett and Centralia, and unconventional personalities like May Arkwright Hutton and William D. "Big Bill" Haywood enlivened the years from 1885 to 1919, popular writers have tended to romanticize the troubled time as colorful and exciting.

THE LABOR'S NORTHWEST

A key feature of early Pacific Northwest labor was a work force composed predominantly of young single males who depended upon the major extractive industries of the West for jobs. The world of those wageworkers exuded youthful vitality, although, in fact, it was quite vulnerable, forever at the mercy of market prices paid for its basic commodities. The population of the Pacific Northwest, a mere 1.5 percent of the national total in 1900, formed too small a market to absorb the region's outpouring of raw materials, and therefore major commercial producers had to depend on distant markets. The resultant boom-and-bust economy heightened workers' sense of dependency, encouraged their mobility, and added to their frustrations.

In some ways, settlements on the wageworkers' frontier resembled factory towns in Pennsylvania or Massachusetts, but with one exception—they were frontier-urban communities, and more important, they were western. This meant that workers in places like the mining towns of the Coeur d'Alenes or lumber towns of Grays Harbor lived in close proximity both in time and place to attitudes and ways of life rooted in the classic American West.

Apparently for many workers, the Pacific Northwest was not simply a fact of geography but a fantasy of mind inspired in part by the millions of promotional pamphlets issued by railroads, immigration bureaus, and real estate speculators. A typical example is a brochure that the Union Pacific Railroad distributed in 1889. Titled *The Wealth and Resources of Oregon and Washington*, it painted a bright future for unemployed workers who would move to either state and promised that "the opportunities for work are so extensive that the wage-earner has never been driven to seek relief or protection in the 'strike' nor the capitalist, to preserve or augment his power, ever resorted to the 'lock-out.'"

That assertion was totally false, as labor-management strife in the Cascade coalfields in the 1880s proved. But workers living in the eastern United States or in Europe would not know that. The pamphleteers were myth-makers, and effective ones, too, because workers planning to move to the Pacific Northwest or already there in the 1880s and 1890s occasionally repeated the belief that the region was a land of exceptional promise. This sense of regional advantage became a tool in the hands of labor organizers, who urged Northwest workers to unionize in order to prevent themselves from being reduced to the downtrodden status of eastern workers.

The physical dimension of the wageworkers' frontier changed as the Pacific Northwest became more urbanized. A map in 1900 would have shown railway lines crossing open spaces to link a series of dots representing mining and lumber camps, smelter and sawmill towns, ranches and orchards. Less easily depicted were the temporary communities of men who harvested grain, fruit, and vegetables or graded new railway lines and then dispersed only to re-collect on other jobs or to winter in the cheap hotels, soup kitchens, bars, socialist clubs, and hiring halls of the region's larger cities. On the map some dots clustered together to represent the mining camps of northern Idaho or British Columbia's Kootenays or the great ranches of the Palouse or the orchards of the Yakima Valley. The dots bore names like Butte, Wallace, Everett, and Medford, and the Burnside district in Portland and Pioneer Square in Seattle, two typical extensions of the wageworkers's frontier into urban centers. Every metropolis of the region had one such district.

PRIMARY GAINFUL OCCUPATIONS[a]

	1870	1880	1890	1900	1910	1920	1930
Miners[b]							
Idaho	5,579	4,708	5,200	4,089	2,971	1,898	981
Oregon	3,965	3,699	2,308	3,910	2,509	1,375	930
Washington	173	985	3,105	6,459	8,303	6,613	3,219
Loggers and Rafters							
Idaho	45	224	373	701	2,246	5,127	4,910
Oregon	232	642	2,555	2,681	6,189	10,394	15,392
Washington	642	998	5,947	8,290	21,949	24,424	24,931
Sawmill Workers							
Idaho	36	100	237	349	2,469	2,904	4,296
Oregon	145	865	1,962	2,449	8,432	11,482	16,480
Washington	c	684	3,734	5,936	23,171	25,133	26,990
Fishermen and Oystermen							
Idaho	0	6	13	11	15	12	26
Oregon	93	3,192	1,473	2,756	1,744	1,894	2,067
Washington	184	613	1,202	3,225	3,711	4,959	5,569
Agricultural Laborers							
Idaho	720	593	2,862	7,814	19,588	22,024	20,421
Oregon	3,126	6,598	10,605	17,316	27,136	23,815	26,769
Washington	742	3,304	8,224	17,455	34,658	28,991	34,374

[a]Federal census takers used the term "gainful occupations" to encompass all people earning a living from a particular trade or industry. Thus, for example, they made no distinction between fishermen who were owner-operators and those who worked for wages. The above figures represent approximations of the number of wageworkers.

[b]Before the 1900 census, compilers made no distinction between precious metals and coal mining; figures shown here represent both gold and silver miners and coal miners.

[c]The census lists no one in this category, an obvious error.

The size of the wageworkers' frontier was ever in a state of flux. It expanded as new agricultural lands and timber and mining camps opened, and it contracted when older camps were abandoned with the depletion of natural resources or, as infrequently happened, when one of the raw, socially unstable communities survived and matured. In 1870 the wageworkers' frontier consisted mainly of scattered fish canneries, tidewater sawmills, and woolen and flour mills; it would reach its greatest size after construction of the region's railway network in the 1880s and 1890s, then rapidly fade away following the First World War.

BINDLE STIFFS AND HOME GUARDS

The most noted aspect of the wageworkers' frontier was the mobility and apparent rootlessness of its work force. Certainly the act of moving to the Northwest meant the temporary loss of the stabilizing ties of the old neighborhood and perhaps also of family and church. Hence, because of the transient nature of their employment, some workers found it difficult to forge enduring social relations in the new setting. In all but the most skilled trades, occupational boundaries meant little as job seekers shifted back and forth from the docks or the woods to mining, construction, or harvesting. The boom-and-bust cycles of the region's extractive economy and the seasonal alternations between work and idleness placed a premium on physical mobility and a broad definition of personal job qualifications. Perhaps, too, a mobile life-style resulted from a worker's desire to grasp opportunities that were supposedly widespread but for some reason very elusive.

It would be a mistake to assume, however, that all Northwest workers had little skill and floated from job to job. During the 1880s the region became home to at least two categories of wageworkers. One was a stationary group sometimes known as home guards and composed mainly of skilled workers who married, raised families, and put down roots in the community. In another category was the migratory bindle stiff, so named because he carried his worldly possessions on his back in a blanket roll or bindle. Many such men seemed permanently anchored by temperament or lack of education or skill to the migratory way of life. There were also thousands of unskilled or semiskilled industrial workers who alternated from one category to the other as prosperity permitted or frequent unemployment demanded.

Coexistence between home guards and bindle stiffs gave a frontier character to work life even in metropolitan areas, where an unusual demographic pattern prevailed. The federal census of 1900 ranked cities with populations of twenty-five thousand or more by percentage of males. Butte, Montana, the self-proclaimed greatest mining camp on earth, ranked third in that category, with a population 59.64 percent male, a figure typical of mining settlements. Far more revealing was the city of Seattle, which ranked first in the United States with a population that was 63.87 percent

61. A group of harvest hands on a ranch probably
near Moro, Oregon. Courtesy Oregon Historical
Society: 6337.

male. By contrast, older settlements like San Francisco and industrial centers in the East recorded male populations of 50 percent or less.

As a rule, men on the wageworkers' frontier never labored alongside
women. Away from the job, a variety of situations prevailed. In the mining
camps, the ratio of males to females tended to normalize as miners got
married and raised families. But in logging camps, which essentially were
crude makeshift work sites in the woods, there were few females until
conditions changed after the First World War. The percentage of female and
child labor in the Northwest's nonagricultural work force remained signifi-
cantly lower than in the industrialized parts of the Northeast and South.

The Pacific Northwest remained also a stronghold of white labor. In
most locales, blacks were a rarity both on and off the job. One exception was
Roslyn, Washington, a coal-mining town in the Cascades seventy miles east
of Seattle, where blacks were about 10 percent of the twenty-eight hundred
inhabitants in 1900. That statistical anomaly dated from the 1880s and

255

62. Loggers stood on springboards as they cut trees
near Grays Harbor, Washington. The practice of cutting trees ten to fifteen feet above the ground was
wasteful but saved time. Courtesy Historical Photograph Collection, Washington State University
Libraries: Photo by Charles Pratsch, # 435.

1890s, when mineowners imported blacks from other regions to serve as strikebreakers in coal towns on both sides of the Cascades. Asians, particularly the Chinese, were the largest racial minority on the wageworkers' frontier.

THE RISE OF ORGANIZED LABOR

Organized labor never attracted more than a minority of wageworkers even in Washington, the most pro-union of the three Pacific Northwest states. At the same time, working-class organizations made their presence felt in a variety of ways; they sponsored dozens of protest journals and rallied support for reform legislation in state capitols, among other activities. The influence of organized labor was always most pronounced in western Washington and least effective in agrarian parts of southern Idaho and eastern portions of Washington and Oregon.

The distinguishing features of the wageworkers' frontier—notably the predominance of manual labor and a largely nonfactory work force—were reflected in the character of the Pacific Northwest's labor movement. The peculiar occupational composition of the local work force enabled industry-wide unions to overshadow specialized or craft unions in membership, influence, and public awareness. These conditions gave unions like the radical Industrial Workers of World (IWW) a prominence seldom attained in other parts of the United States. Confronting some of the roughest and most arbitrary working conditions in the nation, unions like the IWW exhibited a strain of militance that was seemingly a natural by-product of the struggle for existence. Even among more conservative unionists, a sense of westernness occasionally put them out of step with their eastern-oriented national leaders, creating friction that sometimes lessened union solidarity. The militant radicalism that encouraged workers to challenge the prerogatives and powers of management made violent clashes an ever present possibility.

Most residents of the Pacific Northwest grew concerned about labor's political influence, labor-related violence, and radicalism only after unions attracted widespread public attention during the 1880s. The first national labor organization to attract a mass following in the region was the Noble and Holy Order of the Knights of Labor, a union that originated in Philadelphia in 1869. An idealistic and reform-minded group, it emphasized the solidarity of all branches of honorable toil—both skilled and unskilled workers, including women and blacks (but excluding Asians, liquor dealers, lawyers, stockbrokers, and professional gamblers). Local assemblies of the

Knights combined the functions of a labor union, fraternal lodge, debate and educational society, and political reform group. They supported reading rooms, study groups, and guest lecturers to furnish adult education for workers. The Knights were early advocates of reforms like equal pay for men and women and elimination of child labor.

After the first local assemblies appeared in the Pacific Northwest in the early 1880s, the Knights grew rapidly. But their emphasis on labor solidarity revealed an ugly dimension when the Knights encouraged white workers to boycott businesses that hired Chinese labor. And when a sudden and severe depression followed the completion of the Northern Pacific and Canadian Pacific railroads in the mid-1880s, the Knights organized a crusade to expel the Chinese.

Acting without the approval of their national leaders, agitators for the Knights in the region recruited a large following on Puget Sound by skill-fully interweaving the issue of white unemployment with the region's enduring anti-Chinese prejudice. In all of the region's large cities and in several coal towns in the Cascades, agitators encouraged white labor to regard the Chinese as pawns of corporations that would deny Caucasians jobs and a living wage. The result was the first major outburst of labor-related violence in the Northwest.

The Knights of Labor in Tacoma together with the mayor and leading citizens orchestrated the expulsion of the city's seven hundred Chinese (about one-tenth of Tacoma's population) in November 1885. In much the same way, the Knights expelled Chinese labor from nearby coal towns. But in Seattle the following February, the white community divided on expulsion, and a conservative law-and-order group clashed in the streets with the Knights and their allies. When the confrontation left one worker dead and several injured, the territorial governor, Watson C. Squire, declared martial law. In Portland, where more Chinese lived than in all of Washington Territory, the city's powerful business establishment resisted the Knights, and the anti-Chinese crusade failed.

But the agitation and violence focused public attention on organized labor as never before. Here was a new force that frightened residents who idealized the supposed simplicity and self-sufficient individualism of pi-oneer days. Another consequence was the appearance of the first of several utopian colonies on Puget Sound. A group of Knights disenchanted by the street violence organized the Puget Sound Cooperative Colony near Port Angeles as an alternative to modern industrial society. Still other Knights turned to protest politics, organizing several short-lived third parties that supported the "Chinese Must Go" cause. They helped elect a reform mayor in Seattle in 1886 and a prolabor Democratic governor, Sylvester Pennoyer, in Oregon that same year. Pennoyer rewarded the Knights for their support when he persuaded legislators to make Labor Day a legal holiday.

The return of prosperity in the late 1880s diminished the Knights' appeal to the jobless. In addition, their reputation for radicalism and violence frightened away would-be members and divided the union's national and Northwest leaders. By the early 1890s, many skilled home guard workers had switched their allegiance to various craft unions affiliated with the newly formed (1886) American Federation of Labor.

But the Knights did not disappear at once. During the half decade following anti-Chinese violence on Puget Sound, the Knights led several worker protests in the Cascade coalfields. Their grievances centered on low wages and poor working conditions and led to violent confrontations with management in the late 1880s and early 1890s. Coal companies hired armies of detectives to battle the strikers, but those armies proved so odious that Washington's constitution of 1889 outlawed them. When state officials failed to enforce the ban and the hired guns returned to the coalfields, the Knights organized the Peoples (or Populist) party in 1891. The Knights were also prominent in Populist movements in Oregon and Idaho, and in Spokane and its tributary areas, they guided the labor movement until the early twentieth century.

Despite their decline and eventual disappearance, the Knights of Labor cannot be dismissed as inconsequential. They were the region's first major labor organization, and their involvement in anti-Chinese agitation and reform politics left an enduring and paradoxical legacy of race prejudice mixed with high-minded idealism. Those themes influenced the platforms of several subsequent reform organizations. For a full generation, the leaders of the region's union movement identified themselves by their acceptance or rejection of the Knights' basic policies. A legacy was the uneasy coexistence between reform-minded unionism that included nearly all workers and the cautious, craft-oriented unionism of the American Federation of Labor.

As time passed, skilled home guard workers reflected ever more strongly the conservatism of the American Federation of Labor and railway brotherhoods. The region's numerous transient and less skilled industrial workers pursued another tradition, one that animated the several militant and radical unions that arose on the wageworkers' frontier. But no clear line divided the two forms of organized labor, for even home guard workers sometimes

63. The Seattle Newsboys Union. Courtesy University
of Washington Libraries: Neg. UW 1473.

manifested attitudes shaped by their earlier experiences on the wageworkers' frontier, which for many had been a way station to a more stable style of
life. Some of those workers promoted industrial unionism within the
American Federation of Labor. That leaning was especially pronounced in
unions on Puget Sound before and during the First World War, and it irri-
tated the federation's conservative national leadership.

WOBBLIES

For a brief time in the late 1890s and early 1900s, unions affiliated with the
American Federation of Labor clearly predominated in the Northwest, and
they virtually abandoned the region's large pool of unskilled and semiskilled labor. But the ideal of labor solidarity did not die. The first group to
pick up the Knights' burden was the Western Federation of Miners. The
union that Ed Boyce and his fellow hard-rock miners organized in 1893
continued the tradition of industry-oriented, reform-minded unionism. It
also linked the Knights and the most famous of all Northwest labor organi-

260

zations, the Industrial Workers of the World (whose members were popularly referred to as the Wobblies), which western metal miners helped organize in Chicago in 1905.

The Wobblies represented the most alienated of Northwest laborers—migratory harvest hands, timberworkers, and similar categories of labor—a fact clearly stated in the IWW constitution: "The working class and the employing class have nothing in common." The Wobblies believed that all workers in each major industry should belong to the same union and that together the industrial unions should run society. The IWW gained widespread attention because of the militant radicalism expressed in colorful protest songs like "Dump the Bosses off Your Back" and unorthodox organizing tactics. Wageworkers who cared nothing for the Wobblies' syndicalist ideology might still join them to battle those who exploited labor.

Not long after the jury acquitted him in the 1907 Steunenberg assassina-

64. Women garment workers used their electric sewing
machines to make overalls and shirts in the Spokane
Dry Goods Factory around 1916. Courtesy Eastern
Washington State Historical Society: L85–79.133.

tion trial, William D. Haywood joined Wobblies seeking to organize workers in the Pacific Northwest. Free speech fights, which erupted in Missoula in 1909 and spread to Spokane, Vancouver, B.C., and about twenty-five other communities before culminating in the Everett massacre of 1916, aided the Wobbly mission.

The Spokane free speech fight popularized the new organizing tactic. At issue were dishonest employment agencies, or sharks, that took the workers' money and directed the job seeker to nonexistent employment. On occasion the agent split fees with foremen after a quick hiring and firing. When Spokane officials refused to redress their grievances, the Wobblies deliberately violated a city ordinance forbidding street-corner speaking. Some IWW members chained themselves to lampposts and read the Declaration of Independence. For five months city police jailed hundreds of Wobbly protesters, despite the fact that nearly every incoming train brought still more of the footloose rebels. Finally, the Wobblies overburdened Spokane's jail facilities and its treasury, and city officials revoked the licenses of nineteen employment agencies. The Washington legislature later passed a law regulating such establishments. Whatever its successes, the Spokane free speech fight gave Wobblies a notoriety they never had before. Their reputation for defiance aroused the deepest anxieties of many northwesterners and made Wobblies vulnerable to vigilantism and other forms of repressive action.

Although the Wobblies did not limit their activities to the Pacific Northwest, they were more at home in the region than elsewhere. At a time when nationally oriented trade unions concentrated their organizing efforts on skilled labor, the Wobblies emphasized the solidarity of all workers—men and women, whites and blacks, and even the Asians who were shunned by the Knights of Labor. The IWW kept membership dues low and ignored political action, which made little sense to workers who seldom remained in one locale long enough to qualify to vote. Moreover, the American political system made it difficult for third-party protest movements to win elections and to get their programs enacted. Wobblies also refused to sign contracts with employers, whom they regarded as mortal enemies. To businessmen, therefore, they appeared to be an utterly unreasonable and undisciplined work force. "Their policy is to demand more and work less until the industry is ruined," a lumber industry journal complained.

The unorthodox tactics of the IWW, its radicalism and contempt for authority, and its members' vulnerability to persecution as community outsiders led to several violent and celebrated clashes with employers and lawmen. Violence, more than any other characteristic, was popularly at-

65. The Industrial Workers of the World held a picnic
in Seattle in July 1919 to raise money for members
jailed during the First World War. Courtesy University
of Washington Libraries: Neg. UW 1534.

tributed to Wobblies. Zane Grey, the author of numerous western novels,
portrayed the Wobblies as pro-German saboteurs of eastern Washington's
wheat harvest during the First World War in *The Desert of Wheat* (1919). In
truth, Wobblies were more often the victims of violence than the perpetra-
tors of it. And it should be recalled that major episodes of labor-related
violence in the Northwest antedated the IWW by a full two decades. The
region's turbulent labor relations owed far more to the special circumstances of life on the wageworkers' frontier than to any single organization
or radical philosophy. Rather than initiate a new and violent era of labor-
management relations, the IWW merely elaborated on a tradition of militance and radicalism that already existed among Northwest wageworkers.

THE VIOLENT YEARS

Labor-related violence occurred most frequently during the decades that
began with anti-Chinese agitation in 1885 and ended with a notorious

shoot-out between Wobblies and American Legionnaires in Centralia, Washington, in 1919. During no other era did industrial and racial violence influence so many aspects of public life or raise so many troubling questions. A period of mass unemployment or an employer's arbitrary assertion of power usually set the stage for confrontation. When individuals and organizations voiced worker grievances and suggested a course of action— as the Knights of Labor did when they orchestrated removal of the Chinese on Puget Sound—violent clashes with employers or lawmen often took place.

The importance of such episodes does not rest only in the number of people killed or the value of property destroyed. By those measures, labor-related violence in the Pacific Northwest was not substantively worse than that which occurred in the industrialized states of the East. Rather, the impact of violence on public life made the episodes important. They spurred political protest movements or legislative attempts to redress worker grievances.

The labor-related violence of the 1880s and 1890s occurred during a time of profound economic change. Unemployed workers could expect no help from government, and no legal authority governed labor-management relations. Employers and workers groped their way along unfamiliar terrain toward the resolution of conflicts. Existing laws were usually the product of rural-agrarian thinking and did little to address the needs of industrial workers. To militant workers confronted by legislative inaction and powerful employers, it sometimes appeared that violence was the only alternative to subservience.

Lawmakers and other public officials began to address worker grievances and trim away the once nearly absolute power of employers mainly after 1900. A series of new laws provided for workmen's compensation, safer machinery and workplaces, and payment in money instead of scrip redeemable only at the company store. These measures helped some workers but did not completely eliminate incidents of labor-related violence involving groups (like the IWW) still confined to the fringes of society. It was the Wobblies who figured in the Everett massacre of November 1916, the bloodiest single episode of labor-related violence in Pacific Northwest history.

The oppressive tactics of Everett employers clashed with IWW stubbornness. The result was tragedy. A free speech fight began when Wobblies intervened in a strike initiated earlier by shingle weavers affiliated with the American Federation of Labor. In response, local deputies beat Wobblies and expelled them from town. Hoping to avoid the lawmen who patrolled the

MAJOR EPISODES OF LABOR-RELATED VIOLENCE, 1885–1919

	Lives Lost	Property Destroyed
Anti-Chinese agitation, 1885–86	4–6	Tacoma's Chinese quarter later burned
Idaho mining war, 1892	6	Idled ore concentrator destroyed in Gem
Idaho mining war, 1899	2	$250,000 Bunker Hill concentrator destroyed
Everett massacre, 1916	12	minimal
Centralia massacre, 1919	5	iww hall vandalized

highways and rail lines into Everett, more than two hundred Wobblies sailed north from Seattle on the steamship *Verona* on November 5, 1916. A large force of gun-toting deputies awaited them on the Everett dock. Shots rang out—from where was never proven—and when the firing stopped moments later, five Wobblies and two deputies lay dying. Several panicked Wobblies jumped overboard and apparently drowned; a total of fifty men on both sides were wounded. In the ensuing trial in Seattle of the first of seventy-four Wobblies charged with first-degree murder, the attorney George Vanderveer, the self-described "counsel for the damned," won an acquittal. Everett was the Wobblies' last major free speech fight.

As much as circumstances permitted, workers in the Pacific Northwest actively shaped their lives both on and off the job. More than most residents, they confronted the unpleasant reality that life in the urban-industrial Northwest was not the same as it had been in pioneer days. Worker responses varied across the region. Some took to the streets in strikes and protests; others organized unions and attended labor lectures; and still others created utopian colonies or participated in one of the several great political crusades that swept across America and the Pacific Northwest between 1890 and 1920. The wageworkers' frontier thus left its mark on the region's history.

CHAPTER 14

The Era of the Great Crusades

Oregon has more fundamental legislation than any other state in the Union excepting only Oklahoma, and Oklahoma is new. Oregon is not new; it is and it long has been corrupt, yet it has enacted laws which enable its people to govern themselves when they want to. How did this happen? How did this state of graft get all her tools for democracy? And, since it has them, why don't her people use them more? The answer to these questions lies buried deep in the character and in the story of W. S. U'Ren (accent the last syllable), the lawgiver.—Lincoln Steffens, "U'Ren, The Law-Giver," *American Magazine* (1908)

*

At no time was the crusading spirit more prominent in Pacific Northwest life than during the years between 1885 and 1920. Some crusades were little more than local spasms of moral indignation that rallied citizens to banish houses of prostitution or to attack corruption in city and county government. But others were national in scope and addressed a broad range of concerns that included woman suffrage, occupational safety, public health, alcohol consumption, and the maldistribution of wealth.

The frequency and variety of the crusades reflected a changing Northwest. They reflected the hopes and fears of two generations of northwesterners who experienced the disruptive transformation from rural-agrarian to urban-industrial ways of life. Social, political, and moral developments seemed to lag behind the era's impressive economic and technological achievements. Why, some wondered, should unparalleled technological progress and economic growth be accompanied by such a dramatic increase in poverty and other forms of human misery? A combination of qualities ranging from idealism and religious zeal to simple naïveté and fear of social upheaval motivated individual reformers.

Some of the more utopian minded believed that the relatively unspoiled Pacific Northwest was an excellent setting for a radical reconstitution of American society. As a consequence, the region, and especially western Washington, witnessed the rise of several communitarian ventures and an unusually militant strain of socialist politics. Both the radical political parties and the communes eventually failed, but the years of the great crusades left an impressive legacy of laws and practices that still influence the daily lives of Pacific Northwesterners.

THE POPULIST ERA

During the decade of the 1890s, the People's or Populist party attracted considerable attention. The Populists enjoyed greater support in the Pacific Northwest than any other third party in the region's history. Populism especially appealed to people who believed that during the post–Civil War decades a combination of evil forces had disinherited them: "The fruits of the toil of millions are boldly stolen to build up colossal fortunes for a few, unprecedented in the history of mankind; and the possessors of these, in turn, despise the republic and endanger liberty," thundered the party's famous Omaha platform of 1892. Populists in all three Pacific Northwest states advocated an assortment of reforms, among them, government ownership of railroad, telegraph, and telephone lines, laws to prevent abuses of corporate power and influence, a graduated income tax on the rich, and several inflationary measures designed to free debt-ridden farmers and small businessmen from the ruinous consequences of years of sustained deflation.

In the election of 1890, the Republican party scored many successes in all three states. But Idaho broke ranks in 1892, when 55 percent of the voters supported the Populist candidate General James B. Weaver in the state's first presidential election.[1] The new party subsequently emerged as an influential force in several counties and in the legislature. In 1896

---

1. As a result of fusion between Populists, silver Republicans, and dissident Democrats, Idaho gave the Democratic candidate and incumbent, President Grover Cleveland, only two votes.

Washington voters elected a Populist governor and a legislature dominated by reformers. Although Oregon Populists won few elections, the legacy of their most prominent spokesman, William S. U'Ren, overshadowed electoral victories in Washington and Idaho and remains a vital part of the region's issue- and personality-oriented political culture.

A religious mystic who cheerfully embraced several unorthodox notions, U'Ren fathered the "Oregon System" of direct legislation—the initiative, referendum, and recall—measures widely copied in Washington, Idaho, and other states. Although U'Ren's political career was limited to a single term in the Oregon legislature (1897–99), his activities as secretary of the People's Power League enabled him to wield great influence during the era of the reform crusades. American history texts still occasionally and incorrectly refer to him as the governor of Oregon. It was sometimes said that Oregon had two legislatures, one at the capitol and "one under W. S. U'Ren's hat."

The roots of Pacific Northwest populism are by no means easy to trace. The movement in Washington and Oregon originated in the troubled aftermath of anti-Chinese agitation, when proponents of removal redirected their cause from the streets to the ballot box. In the gubernatorial election of 1886, Oregon voters elected Sylvester Pennoyer, a Harvard-educated lawyer and Democrat who had skillfully harnessed anti-Chinese sentiment to propel his campaign. Pennoyer and other elected reformers rewarded their supporters with several modest prolabor measures. In Washington, an anti-Chinese party won control of Seattle's municipal government in mid-1886 and then proceeded to form a territory-wide organization. The return of prosperity before the fall elections destroyed the reform party at the polls, but the movement bequeathed its twenty-six-plank platform to the Populists of the 1890s.

When several Knights of Labor veterans of the anti-Chinese crusade joined with members of the Farmers' Alliance, a prominent agrarian reform group, to organize the People's party in Yakima in July 1891, they resurrected the 1886 platform virtually plank by plank. The tangled roots of populism in Oregon extended through several short-lived reform parties sponsored by prohibitionists, Knights of Labor, and the Farmers' Alliance; Governor Pennoyer converted to populism in the early 1890s.

The Knights of Labor and members of the Farmers' Alliance also joined forces in Idaho to organize the People's party there in mid-1892. Although the party's initial platform included an anti-Chinese plank to placate organized labor, Sinophobia was less important to Idaho populism than the

66. William S. U'Ren (1859–1949), indefatigable reformer and "father of the Oregon System of Direct Legislation." Courtesy Oregon State Historical Society: 4406.

turmoil in the state's vital silver-mining industry. From the first, Idaho
Populists advocated the free and unlimited coinage of silver by the federal
treasury, an inflationary measure supported by mineowners and workers
who believed that it would bolster their struggling industry. Agrarian

debtors prominent in newly developed parts of the West also supported the measure.

Opposing them were creditors, typically the eastern-based bankers and insurance executives who favored the gold standard and loathed the inflationary silver standard as a dishonest way to pay off debts. The battle of the standards was a very complex matter, but in Idaho it translated into the simple belief that what was good for the silver industry was good for Idaho. Those circumstances meant support for the Populist party and a prosilver wing of the Republican party. "Free silver" had become the most prominent plank in the Populist party's national platform by 1896 and commanded the widest support.

Although Idaho's Populist party originated in the southern half of the state, its emphasis on free silver quickly attracted a substantial following in the Coeur d'Alene mining district. Across the state line in Spokane—a city that depended heavily upon the output of Idaho metal mines for its economic health—and farther south in the grain belt of the Palouse region, it seemed that talk of free silver was on everyone's lips. In Whitman County, where nearly half of all farmers were in debt—the national average was 23 percent—the price of wheat had declined dramatically after 1890. Wheat that cost thirty-two cents a bushel to produce sold for twenty-three cents in 1894, and coming due were mortgages that had been contracted when grain prices were 50 to 75 percent higher. It is little wonder that the Palouse country contained many fanatic devotees of free silver and populism.

Populist parties in the Northwest exhibited state and regional peculiarities. Chief among those was the urban and labor orientation of their initial platforms. In the South and Midwest, the two great strongholds of populism, agrarians provided the primary impetus for the third-party movement. Of the Pacific Northwest states, only Idaho had a significant number of agrarians who converted to the party prior to the onset of hard times in 1893.

After half a decade of rapid growth, adversity "stole in like a thief" in mid-1893. The June financial panic that began on the East Coast severely shook the Northwest, and many of its financial institutions collapsed. Five banks failed in Spokane and fourteen in Tacoma. Across the United States, nearly five hundred banks and sixteen thousand businesses had failed by the end of 1893. Three of the nation's five transcontinental railroads went bankrupt.

Unemployment on a scale never experienced before compounded the nation's anguish. In a celebrated open letter to President Grover Cleveland, Oregon's Governor Pennoyer complained that two-thirds of the workers in his state were without jobs. Actually, no one was certain of the exact number of unemployed because neither the federal government nor many states kept such statistics. On Puget Sound, an unknown number of unemployed workers huddled together in driftwood shanties and subsisted on wild berries and clams. Some people claimed to have eaten so many clams that they could feel the tide rise and fall in their stomachs. But the great depression of the 1890s was hardly a subject for humor.

Even those who were fortunate enough to keep their jobs often saw their wages cut by 20 percent or more. Prices dropped, too, but that was little comfort to farmers. As the price of wheat fell to new lows, some Palouse agrarians allegedly committed suicide when faced with collection demands from implement dealers, who themselves often faced bankruptcy. Workingmen embittered by the loss of jobs or life savings in a failed bank and farmers and small businessmen who found it impossible to borrow needed money wanted more than ever to change the system that ruined them. Hard times had set the stage for insurgent politics.

Northwesterners were frightened not only by the unprecedented severity of the depression but also by two unusual upheavals that occurred in 1894: the Pullman strike, the first nationwide walkout by railroad workers, and the Coxey's army phenomenon, in which hundreds of unemployed workers from cities on the Pacific slope sought to make their way to Capitol Hill— occasionally by stealing a train—in a desperate effort to present Congress with a living petition for jobs. The Coxeyites commandeered freight trains in Oregon, Idaho, and Montana, and the United States Army retook them only after several dramatic chases.

Some people translated their anxieties into Populist votes; others shunned the party and blamed it for the excesses of the Coxeyites. Oregon rejected a bid by its two-term governor, Sylvester Pennoyer, to win a United States Senate seat as a Populist in 1894. Many Oregonians considered Pennoyer too sympathetic to Coxeyism when he refused to order state troops to recapture a train stolen near Portland. On the other hand, Washington voters sent twenty-three Populist legislators to Olympia in 1894 and all but eliminated the Democratic party in the state. Two years later, reform-minded Populists, Democrats, and silver Republicans held simultaneous conventions in Ellensburg, each party writing its own platform but dividing up state offices according to a prearranged formula. The tactic worked. Fusionists captured the state legislature and elected John R. Rogers, a former Knights of Labor member and reform journalist, to the governor's office.

In the 1896 presidential election, Washington and Idaho supported Wil-

67. John R. Rogers (1838–1901), Washington's Populist
governor from 1897 until 1901. Courtesy University of
Washington Libraries: Neg. UW 6347.

liam Jennings Bryan, the candidate of both the Democrat and Populist
parties and an advocate of free silver, while Oregon went narrowly for
William McKinley, the victorious Republican. In Idaho Bryan captured two-
thirds of the state's vote.

The 1896 campaign proved to be a poor predictor of the Populist party's
future. In the Oregon legislature of 1897, a handful of Populists held the
balance of power between Republicans and Democrats. Skillful maneuvering by William S. U'Ren and Jonathan Bourne, Jr., a wealthy and ambitious
silver Republican, prevented the legislature from organizing and thus catering to the corrupt political machine of the United States Senator John H.
Mitchell. The "Hold-up Session" proved a good argument for direct legislation; U'Ren and Bourne pressured subsequent legislatures to pass a voter
registration bill (1899) aimed at permanently eliminating political corruption, and they pushed through the initiative and referendum amendments
that Oregon voters approved in 1902. Armed with those two weapons and
prodded by U'Ren's People's Power League, Oregon voters enacted a host of
other reforms.

The Washington legislature of 1897 greatly disappointed the reformers. Although the insurgents had overwhelming numerical strength, members of the reform coalition did little except to battle one another. The legislature passed several specialized measures that organized labor supported, but it failed to secure a railway regulatory commission that farmers favored, and it referred the controversial issue of female suffrage to the voters (who turned it down). Olympia's entrenched railroad lobbies successfully took advantage of the reformers' disunity and confusion. When the session ended, the Populists had little to be proud of and found themselves fighting for survival.

Bickering between fusionists, who advocated compromise and a close working arrangement with major political parties, and a middle-of-the-road faction, which urged the Populist party to pursue its own interests, hastened the decline of populism in the Northwest. The return of prosperity in mid-1897, not long after word reached Seattle of a fabulous gold discovery in the Klondike, further damaged the movement. In the 1898 election, even Spokane went Republican after supporting the Populist cause for half a decade. In elections between 1900 and 1902, Northwest voters effectively buried what was left of the once promising Populist movement under a series of quiet but impressive Republican landslides.

In a flourish of political independence that has become a hallmark of Northwest politics during the twentieth century, Washington voters re-elected the popular John R. Rogers, a Populist turned Democrat, to a second term as governor in 1900. A few months later, Rogers died of pneumonia. Republicans did not lose another statewide race until 1912, and they remained the stronger of Washington's two major parties until the depression of the early 1930s. In much the same way Republicans maintained a dominant position in the Oregon legislature, although they occasionally alternated with reform-minded Democrats for control of the governor's office.

Idaho clung stubbornly to the free silver issue until turning overwhelmingly Republican in the 1902 election. Of the 120 contests for statewide offices held between 1902 and 1930, Republicans won all but 9. Only during the interval 1917–18 did Democrats control the legislature, and only two men succeeded in breaking the Republican hammerlock on the governor's office. They were James H. Hawley (1911–13) and Moses Alexander (1915–19), the nation's first elected Jewish state governor.

Although the Populist party disintegrated, it left an unfinished agenda and some uncommonly dedicated reformers. Some former Populists joined other reform movements. Ernest Lister, a labor leader and Populist officeholder in the administration of John R. Rogers, became a Democrat and

VOTING FOR PRESIDENT

(BY ELECTORAL VOTE)

Election	Idaho	Oregon	Washington
1892	P	1-P; 3-R	R
1896	D	R	D
1900	D	R	R
1904	R	R	R
1908	R	R	R
1912	D	D	PR
1916	D	R	D
1920	R	R	R
1924	R	R	R
1928	R	R	R
1932	D	D	D
1936	D	D	D
1940	D	D	D
1944	D	D	D
1948	D	D	D
1952	R	R	R
1956	R	R	R
1960	R	R	R
1964	D	D	D
1968	R	R	D
1972	R	R	R
1976	R	R	R
1980	R	R	R
1984	R	R	R
1988	R	D	D

(D) Democrat; (R) Republican; (P) Populist; (PR) Progressive

was elected governor of Washington in 1912 and again in 1916. At that time, Democrats demonstrated no strong commitment to change, but Lister proved receptive to the counsel of reformers.

Also picking up where Populists left off was the next generation of insurgents—men and women who were active in the Republican party's progressive wing or who gravitated to one of the region's radical movements. An alternative that increased in popularity after 1917 was nonpartisan politics. Guiding that movement was the Nonpartisan League, an insurgency that originated two years earlier in North Dakota and spread to the Pacific Northwest, where it rekindled the old Populist loathing for monopolies and the corrupt power brokers who often dominated Democratic and Republican politics.

Of all the great reform crusades, progressivism remains in many ways the hardest to categorize. Unlike populism, it attained prominence during a time of general prosperity, and it never took the form of a unified movement or became identified solely with a third party. Progressivism is best described as a commitment to the amelioration of a variety of social, economic, political, and moral ills by activists from considerably different backgrounds. The primary political vehicle for these activists was the reform wing of the Republican party, but they found support among some Democratic officeholders, too. Progressivism had its greatest impact in Oregon and Washington, and its least in Idaho.

Northwesterners who labeled themselves progressives included the indefatigable Oregon reformer William S. U'Ren and the former silverite Jonathan Bourne, Jr. Both became reform-minded Republicans, and Bourne became a United States senator (1907–13). Also prominent among Oregon progressives were the Democrats George E. Chamberlain, governor (1903–1909) and United States senator (1909–21), Oswald West, governor (1911–15), and Harry Lane, United States senator (1913–17).

Washington progressives included the leaders of labor and farmer groups like the Washington State Grange, the Farmers' Union, and the State Federation of Labor. Those individuals joined with urban middle-class reformers from the Direct Legislation League to create a Joint Legislative Committee. Beginning in 1907, that committee functioned for a decade as a pressure group marshaling both legislative and voter support for a variety of reform measures.

Washington's Joint Legislative Committee distinguished itself as one of the most influential of several reform committees that existed in the United States prior to the First World War. It contributed to the enactment of a direct primary law (1907), a model workmen's compensation program (1911), an eight-hour day for women (1911), and constitutional amendments providing for woman suffrage (1910) and direct legislation (1911). Following decades of agitation, Washington voters approved an initiative in 1914 that restricted the sale of alcoholic beverages, a measure in tune with

68. Washington women campaigned for the right to
vote in 1910. Courtesy University of Washington
Libraries: A. Curtis 19943.

the progressive belief that it was possible to improve society merely by
passing laws.

No progressive politician in the Pacific Northwest distinguished himself
in the fashion of Robert M. La Follette of Wisconsin, Hiram Johnson of
California, or George Norris of Nebraska. Idaho's William E. Borah, often
linked with those three names in the United States Senate, did not identify
with progressive causes at the state level. Washington progressives scored
their greatest victories during the administration of Marion Hay (1909–13),
a small-town merchant and Republican who became governor when his
predecessor, Samuel G. Cosgrove, died. But critics questioned Hay's personal commitment to reform because of his prodevelopment stand on the
state's natural resources. He also suffered from a drab personality and
lacked the political flair that characterized the nation's better-known progressive governors and senators.

Washington progressivism is most closely identified with Miles Poindexter, a lawyer and judge from Spokane. Working closely with local busi-

nessmen and reformers, he was elected to Congress in 1908, where he distinguished himself as an insurgent Republican. Poindexter ultimately broke with his party leader, President William Howard Taft, because he did not believe that Taft was fully committed to the conservation of natural resources. Poindexter handily won election to the Senate in 1910 and remained a Republican activist there until the First World War.

The high tide of Northwest progressivism occurred in 1912, when Idaho joined Oregon and Washington in adding initiative, referendum, and recall measures to its constitution. But during that year, several reformers in all three states embarked upon what they later realized was a disastrous detour into third-party politics. The Progressive or Bull Moose party originated when Theodore Roosevelt stormed out of the Republican National Convention when it renominated President Taft. Although Roosevelt's Progressive party platform appeared bold and innovative in some parts of the United States, in the Pacific Northwest its proposals for abolition of child labor and for woman suffrage had already become law.

Progressive party members were chiefly Protestant middle-class Republicans—often professionals in occupation but not party politics, who idolized Roosevelt. Most of them had little in common with Populists except that both refused to accept the status quo. Roosevelt carried Washington; Oregon and Idaho went for the Democrat Woodrow Wilson, the ultimate beneficiary of the Republican split. Apart from placing Wilson in the White House, the primary accomplishment of the Bull Moose insurgency of 1912 was to draw numerous reformers outside the Republican party into an ill-conceived protest vehicle that had no future. After Roosevelt's defeat and his subsequent return to Republican ranks, the seceders realized that in their third-party misadventure they had abandoned the Republican party to conservatives who would soon seek to undo past reforms.

The Washington legislature passed a handful of reforms in 1913, but by 1915 the political pendulum had swung far to the right, and conservative— even reactionary—Republicans controlled the body. They attempted to repeal or sabotage by amendment several progressive measures enacted in years past. Underscoring the conservatives' vengeance was their attack on Professor J. Allen Smith of the University of Washington, a middle-class reformer whose book *The Spirit of American Government* (1907) raised disturbing questions about undemocratic aspects of the United States Constitution. Unable to get at Smith directly, legislators introduced an amendment to a University of Washington appropriations bill proposing to abolish the political science department of which Smith was then the sole member.

In Idaho, where the rise of the Nonpartisan League frightened conservative Republicans, the legislature repealed the direct primary law in 1919.

Despite those efforts, an impressive body of reform legislation survived. During the Progressive era, all three Pacific Northwest states passed measures providing for direct legislation, workmen's compensation, abolition of child labor, and restriction of the manufacture and sale of alcoholic beverages. Women gained an eight-hour work day and the right to vote.

RADICAL ALTERNATIVES

Reformers have sometimes been likened to tree surgeons hacking away at ugly and misshapen growths while the tree continues to thrust out new shoots. As radicals, they preferred to uproot the whole diseased tree if necessary. Radical alternatives before the First World War took many forms, the most prominent being the Socialist Party of America and the Industrial Workers of the World.

The Socialist Party of America emerged in 1901 from several socialist splinter groups and the wreckage of the Populist movement. Some former middle-of-the-road Populists remained committed to reform and sought an alternative in the socialist movement. The new Socialist party and the socialist utopias on Puget Sound benefited from an infusion of the Populist spirit. The state of Washington eventually emerged as one of the movement's strongholds.

Washington was also an arena for conflict between moderate "gas and water" socialists and a revolutionary faction led by the physician Hermon Titus of Seattle. Members who sought little more than public ownership of utilities waged bitter fights with radicals like Titus, who called for worker ownership of the means of production and distribution.

Compared to the strength of the Democratic and Republican parties, Socialist electoral clout was seldom impressive even in Washington. But voters elected moderate socialists to several positions: city commissioner in Spokane, mayors in Pasco and Edmonds, and members of the Washington legislature. Eugene V. Debs, the party's best-known national figure and perennial candidate for president, received 12 percent of Washington's popular vote in 1912, setting a high-water mark for the region's socialist politics.

If socialism seldom influenced election results, it still had an impact on the region's labor and agricultural movements. C. B. Kegley, a Whitman County Populist who turned Socialist before becoming a Roosevelt Progres-

The Pacific Northwest has long been a favorite destination for political and religious utopian colonists. Wilhelm Keil viewed the region as a potential utopia when he led a party of Christian communists from Missouri to Willapa Bay on the Washington coast and then to the Willamette Valley in 1855, where they established the Aurora Colony.

During the years of the great crusades, utopians established several socialist communities and one anarchist commune on Puget Sound. Governor John R. Rogers encouraged social experiments and even joined one colony to participate in its insurance benefits. He also wrote a utopian novel called *Looking Forward; or, The Story of an American Farm* (1898). A Jewish utopia, New Odessa, appeared briefly in Oregon during the 1880s. In more recent times, "hippies" formed several rural and urban communes during the 1960s. That movement no doubt inspired Ernest Callenbach's 1975 novel, *Ecotopia*, the story of an environmental utopia located in northern California and the Pacific Northwest.

But no utopian experiment has attracted more attention in recent years than Rajneeshpuram, a sixty-four thousand–acre communal settlement established in rural Wasco County, Oregon, in 1981. At its height the Eastern-oriented religious cult attracted a population of seven thousand people, many of them affluent and highly educated professionals. When adherents took over the nearby village of Antelope (which they rechristened Rajneesh City) and bused in hundreds of potential voters from the slums of eastern cities in 1984 in an attempt to outvote longtime Wasco County residents, Oregonians became apprehensive. The $100 million experiment collapsed in 1985 following the arrest and deportation of its spiritual leader, Bhagwan Shree Rajneesh, who had entered the United States illegally from India. At one time the Bhagwan possessed ninety-five Rolls Royce automobiles as tokens of affection given to him by his orange-clad disciples.

sive and finally a supporter of the Nonpartisan League, is a good example. A respected leader, Kegley kept the Washington State Grange at the forefront of progressive reform between 1905 and 1917. The United States senator Homer T. Bone, a Democrat from Tacoma and staunch advocate of public power, was once a member of the Socialist party.

THE WAR TO END ALL WARS: 1917–1918

Above all else, progressivism was rooted in the idealistic notion that better living and working conditions would improve the human race. That belief fueled many progressive causes and even helped to inspire American participation in the First World War, a conflict that represented both the culmination of the crusading spirit and its perversion.

For nearly three years after the Great War erupted in Europe in August 1914, the United States tried to steer a neutral course between the Allies (Great Britain, France, and Russia) and the Central Powers (Germany, Austria-Hungary, Turkey, and Italy). Because Great Britain's fight was also that of the British Empire, war came to Canada in 1914. A few adventuresome Pacific Northwesterners went to British Columbia to enlist, but for most Americans the call to arms did not come until April 1917 when Congress formally declared war on the Central Powers. An idealistic President Woodrow Wilson promoted United States participation in the war as if it were a crusade, asking Americans to fight not for materialistic or territorial gain but "to end all wars" and "to make the world safe for democracy." Obviously, it did neither.

Democracy took a real beating on the home front. Members of Congress who voted against the declaration of war were vilified and publicly humiliated, as was Oregon's ailing Democratic senator Harry Lane. Others were soundly defeated at the polls, a fate suffered by the four-term Washington Republican congressman William La Follette when he failed to survive his party's primary in 1918.

Reformers were now denounced as "boat rockers." Radicals and nonconformists who identified with organizations like the Socialist party and the Industrial Workers of the World were singled out for special punishment. Emil Herman, the German-born secretary of the Socialist party in Washington, was arrested and sentenced to ten years in federal prison because someone discovered "disloyal" books and stickers in his office. Criminal syndicalism laws, first enacted in Idaho in 1917, made it illegal to advocate (as distinct from practice) crime, sabotage, or terrorism as a means to achieve industrial or political change.

Authorities also persecuted members of the Nonpartisan League, because its quasi-socialist program called for cooperative buying organizations and publicly owned power companies, railroads, and grain elevators. By resurrecting the Populist spirit, the league attracted the support of farmers who still nursed grievances against the monopolistic power of "big business." To enact their proposals, league members rejected the third-party alternative of the Populists and sought instead to use direct primaries to elect reformers under Republican and Democratic banners.

Conservative businessmen and politicians in all three Northwest states reacted to the Nonpartisan League with every weapon at their disposal, both fair and foul. With war turning many cherished values and traditions upside down, many a foul weapon not only became fair but also enjoyed the sanction of government. Federal and state agents shadowed league organizers and covertly pried into their private lives.

Vigilantism erupted on occasion. In Walla Walla in June 1918, when the annual convention of the Washington State Grange refused to repudiate the Nonpartisan League, vigilantes disrupted the gathering and forced nearly five hundred conventioneers to leave town. Many Grangers, ironically, had sons in the military and considered themselves good patriots. Their leaders wired President Wilson a formal protest, but the Justice Department concluded that nothing could be done to punish those who had harassed the grange in Walla Walla.

A favorite weapon used to discredit the Nonpartisan League was to identify it with the much-feared Wobblies, who were accused of being agents of Germany. When America entered the war, Wobblies were conducting perhaps their most successful strike in the Pacific Northwest lumber industry. Their protest—which included the classic on-the-job slowdown—cut production to 15 percent of normal and drove the industry to its wits' end before changed circumstances gave it a powerful new ally in Uncle Sam.

The number of strikes in the region's lumber industry soared from 44 in 1916 to 295 in 1917, severely hampering production for war. Because the lumber industry convinced the federal government that spruce, a light strong wood used in aircraft construction, was vital to the war effort, Uncle Sam was in no mood to tolerate a strike. The government's response to the Wobbly slowdown was a two-fisted attack: creation of a military organization, the Spruce Production Division headed by Colonel Brice P. Disque, which put twenty-seven thousand soldiers to work in the lumber camps; and a civilian organization, the Loyal Legion of Loggers and Lumbermen (4-L's), which was essentially an enormous company union. Formed during the summer of 1917, the Loyal Legion gained about one hundred thousand members who signed a patriotic pledge not to strike. Together those two organizations provided spruce and other lumber for the war effort. Membership in the Industrial Workers of the World declined precipitously not only because of the Spruce Production Division and the 4-L's but also because of federal raids and vigilante attacks on its meeting halls and leaders. Ironically, the presence of Uncle Sam's troops in the lumber camps mandated many improvements that Wobblies had long sought, such as the eight-hour day, shower facilities, and clean bunkhouses.

War brought change to the woods and to every main street in the Northwest. The region's newspapers carried headline stories of the struggle in

69. Troops from the Spruce Production Division near
Lake Crescent, Washington. Courtesy Washington
State Historical Society, Tacoma: Photo by Asahel
Curtis, # 38414.

France and urged citizens to conserve food and fuel and to buy war bonds.
Seemingly overnight, shipbuilding ranked second in size only to the lumber
industry. Seattle shipbuilders alone employed 35,000 workers, some of
them coming from as far away as Idaho and Montana. The Northwest's
forty-one boat- and shipyards delivered 141 wooden sailing ships and 156
steel vessels by June 1919. A young lumberman named William E. Boeing
founded a small company in Seattle in 1916 that became a major manufacturer of aircraft during the First World War. Of the many war-induced
changes, perhaps none was more profound than that of drafting men into
military service, a measure enacted in 1917 both in Canada and in the
United States. The United States Army also built Camp Lewis, seventeen
miles south of Tacoma that same year. It was the largest of sixteen military
cantonments constructed during the war. Approximately 130,000 Pacific
Northwesterners served in the armed forces.

Women from all parts of the Northwest joined the war effort: they provided a variety of knit goods, staged benefits and bazaars to raise money for the Red Cross, and promoted the conservation of vital supplies of meat, wheat flour, and sugar. Some took jobs in business and industry when the war temporarily eradicated lines of distinction between "men's work" and "women's work."

When the war ended on November 11, 1918, the world had changed radically since 1914. In war-weary Europe, the conflict toppled dynasties that had ruled Germany, Russia, and Austria-Hungary for centuries. Communist revolutionaries seized power in Russia—now the Soviet Union—in November 1917, and they led revolts in Germany and Hungary.

The Allied victory over Germany and the Central Powers brought Americans joy but not peace of mind. They now had another set of worries: four years of inadequate diets, carnage in the trenches, and stress opened the door to a new killer, Spanish influenza, that in late 1918 swept across Europe and North America with deadly results. The pandemic took a larger toll of Northwest lives than the war itself: five hundred thousand to seven

70. Women rivet heaters and passers, Puget Sound Naval Shipyard, Bremerton, May 1919. Courtesy National Archives: 86–GR11–F7.

71. Employees of a wholesale drug company in Seattle
don masks during the influenza pandemic of 1918–19.
Courtesy University of Washington Libraries:
Neg. UW 1538.

hundred thousand Americans died of influenza, whereas the combat toll was fifty thousand. Because of a ban on public gatherings, Thanksgiving festivities had to be cancelled in some parts of the region.

Still more unsettling was the belief that communism had spread to the United States, perhaps to Seattle, where in February 1919 a general strike by sixty thousand organized workers shut down the city for four days. Mayor Ole Hanson asserted that revolutionaries were responsible for the unprecedented work stoppage. After claiming to crush the strike—when in fact it expired of its own lack of clearly enunciated goals—he resigned and joined the lecture circuit, taking his message "Americanism versus Bolshevism" to the American people. Sometimes overlooked in all the excitement was the true cause of the Seattle general strike: wages that had failed to keep pace with the wartime inflation. Although Seattle's four-day "revolution" ended without bloodshed, and radicals did not control the strike, it cost organized labor popular support and contributed to the mounting national hysteria known as the great red scare.

The culminating event of the immediate postwar years occurred in Centralia, Washington, on November 11, 1919, where members of the newly formed American Legion staged a parade to celebrate the first anniversary of the end of the Great War. The parade route wound past the Wobbly hall, where some marchers broke ranks and charged toward the building. Shots rang out. Who fired first remains unknown, for both sides were armed, but in a confusing few seconds four Legionnaires fell to the ground, fatally wounded. That night vigilantes terrorized Wobbly prisoners held in the Centralia jail and seized Wesley Everest, a United States Army veteran, and hanged him from a nearby railroad bridge. After a celebrated trial, a court convicted eight Wobblies of second-degree murder and sentenced them to lengthy prison terms. The last of the jailed Wobblies was not released until 1939. No one was ever charged with the murder of Everest.

THE END OF THE GREAT CRUSADES

The crusading spirit spent itself during the war in several ways. The terrible slaughter on the battlefields of Europe disillusioned many progressives who believed that the human race was basically inclined to good conduct. In others, a martial spirit twisted the progressive faith into a caricature of its former self. One time progressives like Senator Miles Poindexter and Mayor Ole Hanson became reactionaries of the most rabid sort. An excess of patriotic fervor caused Poindexter to charge that the Seattle labor movement was a Communist conspiracy. In 1918 he introduced a bill to make strikes illegal. So drastically did the war change Poindexter that Washington voters dumped him in the 1922 election in favor of Clarence C. Dill of Spokane. Dill was the first Democrat elected to either house of Congress from Washington since it had become a state more than three decades earlier.[2]

In Washington the spirit of farmer-labor cooperation that had been so strong since the early days of the Populist movement exhausted itself in the 1920 election. That year a newly organized Farmer-Labor party ran better in Washington than in any state, in many races finishing well ahead of the Democrats, but not well enough to capture a single statewide election or congressional seat. The Nonpartisan League and the Idaho Progressive party of 1922 became major vehicles for expressing the discontent of farmers living on the Snake River plain. They grew angry when their crops died

2. Dill had earlier served in the House of Representatives, but he had been defeated for reelection largely as a result of his vote against American entry into the First World War. He was one of the few congressmen who voted against war to make a political comeback.

after irrigation projects repeatedly failed to deliver the water they had promised.

In the general election of 1922, Progressives beat Democratic candidates and captured control of several county governments in southern Idaho. But none of these producer protest movements endured, and what some hailed as the dawn of a new era was in reality the neo-Populist twilight of the great crusades. In Oregon in the early 1920s a perversion of the crusading spirit welled up in a brief but powerful spasm of Ku Klux Klan–directed hysteria that sought to outlaw private and parochial schools.

Prohibition, widely regarded as a key progressive reform, became the law of the nation in January 1920, so stated the Eighteenth Amendment to the Constitution and the Volstead Act. Proponents had long asserted that elimination of the saloon and alcoholic beverages would clean up politics and

72. The Columbia Saloon in Portland, Oregon. The era's many saloons were the favorite targets of temperance reformers who deplored the connection between alcohol, prostitution, and political corruption. Courtesy Oregon Historical Society: 11984.

bring much-needed sobriety and efficiency to the workplace, but like a good many reform measures, prohibition never achieved all that its supporters promised. Its fate—repeal by the Twenty-first Amendment in 1933—proved that no reform meant much unless grounded in popular support and backed by a long-term commitment to enforcement. The level of support for prohibition dropped during the 1920s, and its advocates realized only too late that the achilles heel of any reform law is the willingness of government officials to make it work. The prohibition experience serves, too, as a useful reminder that one person's reform may well be another's poison.

Whatever reservations an observer has about the reform crusades, the sheer variety of ameliorative measures dating from the years 1890 to 1920 remains impressive. Certainly, the lot of women, children, and industrial workers was substantially better in 1920 than it had been three decades earlier, and so, too, the general level of public health. During those years, the states of the Pacific Northwest democratized the political process and enlarged the electorate, mandated safer factories and mines, outlawed child labor, limited the hours of labor for women and other workers, created railroad and other regulatory commissions, and passed a variety of sanitary codes forbidding the sale of tainted milk and other foods. On more than one occasion—as with U'Ren's Oregon System or Washington's Workmen's Compensation Law—Pacific Northwesterners pioneered a course eventually followed by many other states.

CHAPTER 15

The Interwar Years, 1919-1941

Yet the program of the New Deal, with all its faulty management, represents the first conscious attempt of the government to utilize for all the people the vast, untapped resources of the frontier. Whatever else Mr. Roosevelt may have done to or for the country, that much he has accomplished in the Columbia River basin. Never again can the natural riches of the hinterlands be left as undeveloped as they were in the years before the New Deal.—Richard L. Neuberger, *Our Promised Land* (1938)

A variety of economic troubles cast long shadows across the lives of Pacific northwesterners during the interwar years. The high cost of living during the Great War elicited so many comments that newspapers resorted to the abbreviation HCL to save space in columns on inflation. The cost of living continued upward during the first several months of peace, until by 1920 it stood 70 percent higher than in 1913. Other leading economic indicators rose or fell in ways that portended troubled days ahead.

As the region's shipyards, sawmills, and mines scaled back war production, unemployment rose rapidly. In what was the largest cutback in the timber industry until that time, Oregon mills and camps laid off seven thousand men, while in Washington the number was fifteen thousand. Northwesterners soon worried less about the HCL than about labor unrest and agrarian dislocation, especially when the price of wheat dropped from nearly $2.06 a bushel in 1919 to $0.84 in 1921 and brought many farmers to the brink of ruin.

The abrupt turnabouts culminated in a brief but severe depression that jolted the United States in 1921, and although prosperity returned to enrich the lives of many urban dwellers, who fondly recalled the 1920s as the Jazz Age or the Prosperity Decade, the pall of hard times never really lifted from timber towns and agrarian areas. Most Northwest farmers remained mired in economic difficulties that originated during the boom years of the First World War, when government appeals for more food caused them to buy land on credit and expand their capacity to produce far beyond what a peacetime world could consume. The result was a dramatic postwar drop in farm income and land values, with debts and bankruptcies piling up alongside unsold stores of wheat and other commodities.

Hardest hit of the Pacific Northwest states was Idaho, where even in 1929 wheat brought only $1.30 a bushel. The state's all-important potato crop, which sold for $1.51 a bushel in 1919, sank to a low of $0.31 in 1922, and rose only gradually during the rest of the decade, nearly reaching the 1919 price in 1929 before plummeting to less than $0.25 a bushel in 1932. Because the farm crisis was both national and international in scope, Pacific northwesterners were quite helpless to do anything about it on the state level.

The Oregonian Charles L. McNary served in the United States Senate from 1917 until his death in 1944, and he was best known for his efforts in behalf of American farmers. The McNary-Haugen bill was formally introduced on Capitol Hill in 1924 and sparked one of the chief ideological debates of the 1920s. The emergency farm relief measure mandated that the federal government promote economic justice for farmers during hard times. Idaho's Senator William E. Borah supported a more radical form of farm relief, but with no more success than McNary, who never got his plan past a presidential veto.[1]

The prolonged agricultural depression accounted for the fact that Idaho was second only to Montana among western states in the number of residents who moved out during the 1920s. Idaho's chief export in the 1920s and 1930s was bright young men and women seeking jobs elsewhere.

After the stock market crash of October 1929, farmers were no longer alone in their misery, because in the wake of the Wall Street debacle, Americans experienced the worst depression in history. Hard times during

---

1. Borah opposed the McNary-Haugen plan because it taxed farmers in order to dispose of their surplus crops at competitive prices abroad; the Idaho senator favored direct federal relief to distressed agrarians.

the 1930s altered the course of Northwest politics, dramatically reversing the fortunes of the dominant Republican party and giving Franklin D. Roosevelt and the Democrats a sweeping victory in the 1932 elections. Federal, state, and local governments responded to the Great Depression with a variety of programs designed to provide relief or stimulate recovery, but prosperity remained stubbornly elusive until the eve of the Second World War.

CHANGE AND CONTINUITY

During the opening years of the twentieth century, the Pacific Northwest experienced rapid population growth, especially in its urban areas. The region's population climbed from approximately 1 million in 1900 to slightly more than 2.5 million in 1920, with an urban increase of 254 percent overshadowing a rural increase of 79 percent. Accounting for at least part of the urban growth were newcomers who moved to the Northwest from other regions and residents who relocated from farm to city within the region.

Both types of population movement continued through the interwar years, but urban growth was not uniform. Idaho urbanized at a much slower pace than either Oregon or Washington. Not until 1970 did the federal census record a majority of Idahoans living in urban areas—communities with populations of at least twenty-five hundred. Washingtonians, by contrast, crossed that divide in the census of 1910, and Oregonians in 1930, but only barely, for the next decennial censuses recorded them as having temporarily dropped to 48.8 percent urban.

The primary agents of urbanization and other significant social changes during the interwar years were technological innovations such as radio, talking motion pictures, and especially the automobile. The establishment of commercial radio stations in all three Northwest states in 1921 and 1922 quickly changed the nature of entertainment, further expanded the influence of the metropolis, and fueled the American passion to consume. The cosmetics industry set new records during the 1920s, and so, too, did the electrical industry, which powered a host of new consumer products ranging from refrigerators and vacuum cleaners to record players and hair curlers.

Of all the technological innovations, certainly none had a greater impact than the automobile. When they first appeared in the Pacific Northwest shortly before the turn of the century, automobiles were expensive and virtually inoperable in bad weather. Many observers regarded them as little more than rich men's toys. Then in a historic move in 1913, Henry Ford

CITIES WITH 10,000 OR MORE RESIDENTS					
	1910	*1920*	*1930*	*1940*	*1950*
Idaho	1	2	2	7	9
Oregon	2	4	6	7	11
Washington	7	10	15	14	20
U.S.	597	752	982	1077	1320

initiated assembly-line production of his Model-T automobile, dropping its price from $850 in 1909 to a relatively affordable $440 in 1915 (and even less for used models). Output leaped right off the production charts despite the fact that intercity roads in many areas consisted of little more than two muddy ruts across a field.

Oregon took a fundamental step to correct that deficiency in 1919 by

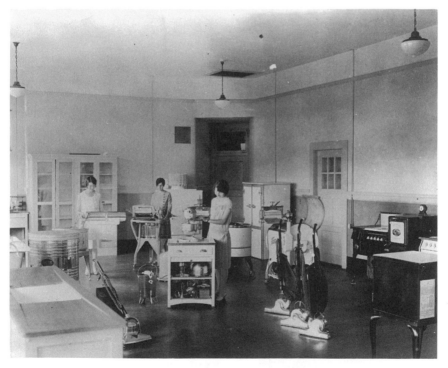

73. Preparing for a new age, students at Oregon State College in Corvallis take a short course in household electric equipment in 1930. Courtesy Oregon State University Archives, # 978.

74. Automobiles came to Liberty Lake, a resort near
Spokane, in increasing numbers in the 1920s. Courtesy
Eastern Washington State Historical Society: L85–248.

becoming the first American state to levy a tax on gasoline. With the
rallying cry "Lift Oregon out of the Mud," contractors soon blanketed the
state with hundreds of miles of good roads, many of them paved. Washington and Idaho followed the Oregon example by levying gasoline taxes in
1921 and 1923. During the interwar years the region's highway network
expanded at a rate never since equaled. During those two decades the
mileage of hard-surfaced all-weather roads increased in Idaho and Washington by nearly 300 percent and in Oregon by nearly 250 percent. The
Pacific Northwest contained a total of twelve thousand miles of roads in
1940.

The road-building boom of the 1920s stimulated the economy, provided
construction jobs, and made possible a host of new roadside businesses
catering especially to motorists. It encouraged school consolidations and
growth in the size and influence of regional trading centers at the expense of
smaller communities. During the 1920s the new intercity truck and bus
industries expanded rapidly with the growing network of all-weather roads.

PEOPLE PER MOTOR VEHICLE				
	1910	*1920*	*1930*	*1940*	*1950*
Idaho	700.5	8.5	3.8	3.2	2.2
Oregon	127.5	6.8	3.8	2.8	2.2
Washington	157.1	7.9	3.5	3.1	2.6
U.S.	197.2	11.5	4.6	4.1	3.1

Road building had a troubling impact on the once almighty railroad industry, which saw its nationwide network of track reach a peak in 1916 and passenger traffic decline sharply during the 1920s. A majority of commercial travelers, or salesmen, abandoned the passenger train for the automobile, and following them were many other categories of travelers. The railroad station once functioned as a community portal to the outside world, but the highway and the gas station increasingly assumed that role in the 1920s. It was not uncommon for railroad passenger stations less than two decades old to be boarded up or converted to other uses. Especially hard hit were the region's thousand miles of electric interurban lines, none of which had been in existence prior to 1893. Some, like the Puget Sound Electric that opened between Tacoma and Seattle in 1902, were entirely abandoned, while others, like the Oregon Electric linking Portland and Eugene, survived only by dropping passenger service and hauling freight.

One of America's pioneer bus operators was the Spokane, Portland, and Seattle Railway, which in 1924 began substituting buses for steam-powered trains linking Portland, Astoria, and Oregon's north coast. By the end of the decade, nearly every major railroad in the Pacific Northwest had done likewise on lightly patronized branch lines. Innovation was the keynote of early-day bus travel; some companies offered sleeper coaches between the Northwest and California, and some adopted a double-decked design especially suited for enjoying the scenery of the Pacific Northwest. The Greyhound Corporation, a holding company formed in the late 1920s, eventually acquired most of the bus lines of the Pacific Northwest.

Railroads also faced competition from the airline industry that originated in the 1920s. Few people then could have imagined that by the 1950s more people would travel by air than by rail. The first airlines were exceedingly small operations, often consisting of little more than one or two open cockpit planes that carried a passenger or two in addition to the mail. Until better aircraft and navigational aids became available in the late 1920s, none dared fly across the Cascades during winter months. One airline

75. Early casulties of the automobile age were the
region's electric interurban lines. Here a special train
on the Oregon Electric line meets a trolley in Albany.
The interurban trains linked Portland and Eugene from
1912 until 1933. Courtesy Oregon Historical Society:
1596B.

pioneer was the Boeing company of Seattle, which in 1926 inaugurated Boeing Air Transport, a progenitor of United Airlines. The Boeing company secured a federal contract to operate between San Francisco and Chicago carrying mail and two persons per plane. In 1933 Boeing built the model 247, an all-metal streamlined two-engine transport. Capable of carrying ten passengers plus a crew of three, it made possible coast-to-coast flight in twenty hours (with seven intermediate stops).

Railroads made no attempt to fight back in any meaningful way until the mid-1930s, when they introduced streamlined passenger trains that featured air-conditioned cars and clean-burning internal-combustion locomotives. The first of those in the Pacific Northwest (and one of the earliest in the United States) was the Union Pacific's innovative City of Portland, which after its introduction in 1935 reduced travel time between Chicago and the Rose City from fifty-eight to forty hours. But nothing short of fuel rationing and the speed limits of thirty-five miles per hour imposed during the Second World War could arrest the downward trend in railroad passenger travel, and then only temporarily.

Trucks, automobiles, all-weather highways, and gasoline-powered tractors and other implements noticeably altered the daily lives of farmers,
dramatically reducing their need for casual labor. Motor transportation
ended the isolation of the region's farms, ranches, and lumber camps and
eliminated what remained of the wageworkers' frontier after the First World
War. Many former harvest hands abandoned the life of the hobo, got married, and took their families with them to the job in their own automobiles.
In forest industries, too, the home guard logger driving to work in his own
car or truck replaced the bindle stiff. Like nothing else, owning a car—even
a used one—symbolized admission to the middle class. Organizers for the

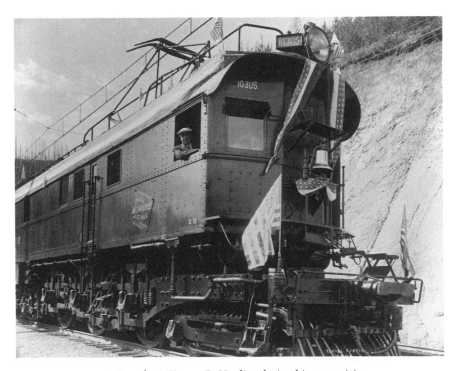

76. President Warren G. Harding during his 1923 visit
to the far Northwest took the throttle of an electric locomotive that pulled trains of the Milwaukee Road
over the Bitterroot Mountains of northern Idaho. From
1911 until 1961, the railroad's deluxe passenger trains
connected Puget Sound with Chicago and thereby advertised the Northwest's "white coal" or hydroelectric
power. Courtesy Washington State Historical Society,
Tacoma: Photo by Asahel Curtis, # 45362.

Industrial Workers of the World deplored the trend and complained that the automobile gave labor a false sense of upward mobility, but their complaint fell on deaf ears.

The impact of the automobile on Northwest life was little short of revolutionary—in the twentieth century perhaps only television had a similar impact—yet during the years immediately following World War I, the region's residents seemed more preoccupied with revolution of another sort, the Communist variety that began in Russia in 1917 and threatened to spread to eastern Europe and even to Portland and Seattle, or so some frightened people believed. That fear, coupled with the very real and disturbing changes brought by the First World War, contributed to a turbulent half decade of insurgent politics.

INSURGENTS AND CONSERVATIVES

The Republican party dominated politics in all three Pacific Northwest states during the 1920s. Republicans held every elected state and congressional office in Idaho. They also controlled Washington, where Roland H. Hartley, a mean-spirited antilabor timber baron from Everett, served as governor from 1924 to 1932 and gave the period a rancorous political tone. Democrats enjoyed only modest successes in Oregon and Washington.

Republicans won an impressive string of election victories and maintained overwhelming majorities in all three state legislatures, but too much emphasis on the party's apparent invincibility obscures important undercurrents of Northwest politics. In agrarian Idaho, which never fully tasted the fruits of prosperity during the 1920s, Republicans benefited at least in part from the Democrats' inability to resolve factional disputes over personalities and programs. Especially during the first half of the 1920s, a mood of insurgency complicated life for Northwest Republicans. On the left were the Nonpartisan League and the Progressive party, which frightened Idaho Republicans immediately after the war, and the Farmer-Labor party, which had the same effect on Washington Republicans. The main insurgency on the right was the Ku Klux Klan; it rose to power amidst the burning of crosses and public parades of new initiates in Oregon in the early 1920s.

Oregon, which included a large number of residents whose heritage was that of the Bible Belt, had a tradition of nativism. Together with the wartime mood of distrust and apprehension and the economic chaos caused by runaway inflation followed by a severe depression, it created the circumstances in which the Ku Klux Klan flourished. Discontent in the South after the Civil War gave rise to the original Klan, which faded away after a decade or two. A second Klan arose in 1915 and borrowed ritual and doctrine from its predecessor. But its targets now included not just the blacks singled out for persecution by the original Klan, but also Catholics, Jews, and immigrant groups.

The Klan entered Oregon from California in 1921 by capitalizing on the fears generated by the First World War. Spreading rapidly, it established branches in Portland and a number of outlying communities. By early 1922, its membership was estimated to be at fourteen thousand, with numerous sympathizers adding to its influence. Together with Freemasons, Klansmen spearheaded a drive to outlaw private and parochial schools, which they viewed as the primary obstacle in their drive for "Americanism" and national conformity. Such schools were operated by a number of groups, most notably the Roman Catholics. The Klan's weapon was an initiative that if passed by Oregon voters would require all children between the ages of eight and eighteen to attend public schools. The rallying cry of its sponsors was "One Flag! One School! One Language!" Opponents invoked the American tradition of free choice, but that apparently held little appeal in 1922. At the polls that fall, Oregon voters by a margin of eleven thousand votes made their state the first in America to mandate a monolithic school system.

Walter M. Pierce of Pendleton, a popular Democrat and uncompromising advocate of the public school measure, was elected by the largest vote given a gubernatorial candidate in Oregon up to that time. Though perhaps not a Klansman himself, he enjoyed the Klan's backing in the general election. The new speaker of the Oregon House of Representatives was a Klan-supported Republican with an interesting set of initials: Kaspar K. Kubli.

Opponents of the public school measure subsequently took their case to the federal court in Portland and obtained a temporary injunction, but supporters were confident that the new law would go into effect as scheduled in 1926. They launched a crusade in neighboring Washington, where the Klan had chapters in every major city. A measure identical to Oregon's "Compulsory Education" initiative appeared on the Washington ballot in 1924, but Washingtonians rejected it by sixty thousand votes. Much of the Americanism fervor had ebbed since 1922, and supporters of the initiative received a major setback in mid-1924 when the federal court in Portland declared the Oregon law unconstitutional. A year later, in the case of *Pierce v. Society of Sisters*, the United States Supreme Court dealt the Oregon measure a fatal blow. By that time the Klan was already a spent force.

Much about the Ku Klux Klan movement in the Pacific Northwest made it difficult to categorize. From one perspective it embodied the narrow-minded, illiberal spirit that swept across America with during World War I. It appeared to be conservative, even reactionary. But the Klan also embodied some of the region's old-time spirit of populism: angry and frightened citizens joining together to combat a host of, in this case, imagined enemies; Catholics, Jews, foreigners, and radicals substituting for Wall Street bankers and the gold standard of years gone by. In a perverse sort of way, the Klan insurgency tapped the crusading spirit of prewar decades.

The seemingly contradictory currents of Oregon politics during the 1920s were mirrored in the public life of the state's Klan-supported governor, Walter M. Pierce. As a politician, Pierce was never easy to classify: he possessed a populist streak that in 1919 caused him to cast the sole vote in the Oregon Senate against a harsh criminal syndicalism bill. Political opponents later charged that he was a radical, a secret member of the Nonpartisan League. Although defeated in his bid to be reelected governor in 1926, Pierce at the age of seventy-two made a comeback in 1932, when the Democratic tidal wave swept him into a seat in Congress. There he remained for ten years, a staunch backer of public power, farm relief, and other New Deal measures.

Oregon voters as a whole manifested similarly contradictory tendencies. Their legislators in 1923 passed the Alien Property Act, which in effect prohibited the state's growing number of Japanese residents from owning and leasing land. Corresponding measures had already been passed by California and Washington and upheld by federal courts. Yet Oregon voters in 1926 repealed the constitutional provision barring blacks from the state, and the following year they eliminated restrictions that discriminated against black and Chinese voters. In 1922 the Klan stirred up prejudice against Jews (who constituted approximately 1 percent of the state's population) in an unsuccessful effort to prevent Julius Meier from serving on a Portland commission studying whether to hold a special exposition. Eight years later, Meier—co-owner of Portland's Meier and Frank department store—ran for governor as an independent who championed the cause of public power and won with 55 percent of the vote.

Among insurgents of the 1920s, the cause of public power was especially popular. One of the idea's most determined supporters was Homer T. Bone of Washington. Bone jumped from party to party: he was a Socialist in 1912, was elected to the state legislature as a Farmer-Labor candidate in 1922, was a Progressive in 1924, a Republican in the late 1920s, and finally won election to the United States Senate in 1932 as a Democrat. But Bone never lost his devotion to public power. For the most part, however, public power remained an idea whose time did not come until Washington lawmakers approved Bone's public utility district bill in 1930, opening the door to statewide public power.

As for the Farmer-Labor insurgency, its time never did arrive. In the 1920 election, the Farmer-Labor party, which succeeded the Nonpartisan League in Washington, ran a respectable campaign. Robert Bridges, an old-time Populist and the Farmer-Labor candidate for governor, ran second to the victorious Republican, Louis Hart. But in the aftermath of the election, Farmer-Labor partisans bickered among themselves, and that infighting, together with growing prosperity in the state's urban areas, reduced the party to insignificance by the 1924 election.

Insurgency on the left took yet another twist when many one time Farmer-Laborites supported Robert M. La Follette, the Wisconsin senator who ran for president as a Progressive in 1924.[2] The La Follette campaign called for farm relief measures, public ownership of railroads and water-power, and legal recognition of collective bargaining.

The La Follette insurgency threw a genuine scare into the two major parties in Idaho, surpassing the Democrats in all but five of the state's forty-four counties and losing to the Republican Calvin Coolidge by only 15,000 votes out of the nearly 150,000 cast. La Follette also finished second in Oregon and Washington. In Washington he bested the hapless Democrats by nearly a 4-to-1 margin, yet the La Follette campaign represented the last hurrah of left-wing insurgency during the 1920s. In the last half of the decade, Republican dominance of Pacific Northwest politics went all but unchallenged. The only notable exceptions were Senator C. C. Dill and Congressman Sam B. Hill of Washington.

The region's Democratic party, especially in Idaho and Washington, remained in a woebegone condition, weak and generally ineffectual at the polls and badly divided as a result of personality conflicts and the inability of anyone to bring discipline to the motley assortment of disgruntled agrarians, trade unionists, onetime Populists, Nonpartisan Leaguers, and all-around political cranks who drifted into its ranks. With a history of defeat at the polls, the Democratic party could not afford to be too choosy.

2. In Oregon La Follette ran under the Independent banner.

BORAH OF IDAHO

Republicans dominated government not only in the Pacific Northwest during the 1920s but also in many of the states outside the South. The party elected three presidents—Harding, Coolidge, and Hoover—and controlled Congress. One of the most prominent Republicans both on Capitol Hill and abroad was Senator William Edgar Borah of Idaho. As chairman of the Senate Committee on Foreign Relations from 1924 to 1933 and an orator without peer, he played an influential role in national and international affairs, becoming better known abroad than any Northwest political figure before or since. In some countries he became the best-known living American. People of Idaho took an uncommon pride in Borah.

During the interwar years, few public figures more aptly exemplified the Northwest's tradition of political independence than the man who represented Idaho in the United States Senate from 1907 to 1940. Borah, who was born in Illinois in 1865 and moved to Idaho in 1890, remained a Republican all his life, yet the dictates of conscience always took precedence over party platforms or labels. Whatever his apparent inconsistencies and mistakes, Idaho voters remained loyal to Borah, and he to them. A man of amazing energy and drive, the senator returned to Boise every summer, rented a car, and drove around the state to visit his constituents, loggers and university presidents alike.

Shortly after his election in 1906, Borah gained national attention by serving as special prosecutor in the sensational trial of the union leader William D. Haywood and others for allegedly plotting the assassination of Governor Steunenberg. Despite his role in that trial and the probusiness inclination of his party, Borah was not antilabor. In the Senate he demonstrated his independence by representing the cause of labor and vigorously opposing corporate monopoly. During the First World War, he firmly supported civil liberties at a time when the Bill of Rights, if put to a popular vote, would almost certainly have lost. Borah supported Wilson's conduct of the war, and that was one reason why the Democratic president privately endorsed the Republican senator's bid for reelection in 1918. But a year later, Borah was involved in the successful fight against Senate ratification of the Treaty of Versailles and American participation in Wilson's beloved League of Nations.

The Idaho senator continued his independent ways during the 1920s by championing diplomatic recognition of the Soviet Union, an unpopular step that President Franklin D. Roosevelt took only in 1933. As chairman of

77. William Edgar Borah (1865–1940), the indepen-
dent-minded Republican senator from Idaho from 1907
to 1940. Courtesy Idaho State Historical Society:
D60–178.2.

the Senate Committee on Foreign Relations, Borah maintained the belief
that the United States must follow an independent course in world affairs.

In domestic politics, he worked for measures to aid farmers impoverished by low commodity prices and thus time and again put himself out of
step with Republican party officials on both the national and state levels.

He declined to support Herbert Hoover's reelection in 1932 because the president had opposed direct relief to the needy. With characteristic independence, Borah supported some of Roosevelt's New Deal reforms while adamantly opposing others. Throughout the 1930s he opposed American involvement in European wars.

Critics charged that Borah was in fact a "spearless leader," a do-nothing type of statesman who substituted oratory for solid accomplishments. Whatever the merit of that argument, Borah "represented a public asset through which Idahoans could be assured that the rest of the nation knew they existed." As senator he often functioned as Idaho's permanent ambassador to the outside world.[3]

Borah's status as an international celebrity brought more attention to the Pacific Northwest than the region would have received otherwise, and his lofty profile in the nation's capital helped Borah secure an ample share of New Deal money for Idaho. Such federal aid was especially welcomed during the years of the Great Depression.

DEPRESSION DAZE

The Great Depression dealt the Pacific Northwest's extractive industries a severe blow. About half of Idaho's population in 1930 depended directly upon agriculture for a living, about one-tenth relied on manufacturing—mostly timber—and a much smaller portion on mining. Agrarian Idaho had never shared the prosperity of the 1920s, but the disastrous economic decline of the early 1930s made the previous years seem almost prosperous by comparison. The average income of Idahoans plunged by 50 percent between 1929 and 1932. In Oregon the economic collapse brought 90 percent of the timber companies to the verge of bankruptcy, and at least half of the state's timberlands were tax delinquent. The Pacific Northwest as a whole experienced mortgage foreclosures, delinquent taxes, and sharply rising unemployment. A sense of desperation led to protest and in some cases to direct action and other forms of self-help by angry farmers and industrial workers.

Many of the region's jobless clustered under bridges and wherever else they could find shelter. One of the largest of their encampments was Seattle's Hooverville, a city of shacks fashioned from every conceivable sort of

3. From Robert James Maddox, *William E. Borah and American Foreign Policy* (Baton Rouge: Louisiana State University Press, 1969).

78. Seattle's Hooverville in 1937, a shantytown built
from scrap lumber, crates, and tarpaper. Courtesy University of Washington Libraries: Photo by James Lee,
Neg. Lee 20102.

material. It was home to hundreds of men, the Seattle authorities having
decreed that no women or children were permitted to live there. A good
many of the middle-aged laborers who predominated in this community
had once supplied the migratory muscle needed on the wageworkers' frontier.

Adding to the region's unemployment woes was the arrival of two hun-
dred thousand or more refugees from the Dust Bowl of the parched Great
Plains. "Drive out on any of the main highways of our State," observed
Idaho's Senator Borah, "and you will see cars, sometimes almost caravans,
fleeing from the devastations of the drought." These people were headed
West, as thousands had done before them, paralleling the route of the
Oregon Trail in search of a new life in the fabled promised land of the Pacific
Northwest. During 1936 alone, an estimated ten thousand farm families
fled the northern Great Plains for Washington, Oregon, Idaho, and western

79. Idaho advised indigents to avoid the state in
the 1930s. Courtesy Library of Congress:
USF34–655–40–D.

Montana. Were it not for the subsistence doles they received from state and federal authorities, many would have starved.

A NEW DEAL FOR THE NORTHWEST

A major beneficiary of the unrest of the early 1930s was the Democratic party. In the wake of the Great Depression, voters in all three Northwest states turned to the Democrats. When he ran for president in 1928, Herbert Hoover, a Republican, lost only one county in the three-state region, sparsely populated Fremont on the eastern edge of Idaho. Running for reelection four years later, Hoover, who in the popular mind bore primary responsibility for the hard times, lost all but two counties.[4] The abrupt swing to the Democratic party also benefited state and local candidates.

In the 1930 election, Idaho Democrats chose their first governor since

4. In 1932 Hoover carried Bear Lake County, Idaho, and Benton County, Oregon.

1917. He was C. Ben Ross, a reformer in the Populist tradition. Two years later they sent a liberal, James P. Pope, to the United States Senate and toppled the state's two veteran Republican congressmen, Burton French and Addison Smith, who between them had forty-six years of service on Capitol Hill. The sole Republican officeholder of any consequence was Borah, and he now remained aloof from the partisan struggle.

It was much the same story throughout the West. Of four states electing governors, all chose Democrats. Washington voters replaced Wesley L. Jones, a Republican senator since 1909, with the liberal Democrat Homer T. Bone. Capping the Democratic sweep of the West was the victory of Franklin D. Roosevelt, who promised Americans a New Deal. Exactly what that New Deal entailed, neither Roosevelt nor anyone else could say in 1932. This much was certain: after the president-elect took office in March 1933, each day brought dramatic new developments, beginning with his proclamation of a bank holiday to halt the general collapse of the nation's banking system.

Except during the First World War, the federal government had never been so involved in so many aspects of American life as during the era of Franklin D. Roosevelt and the New Deal. Pacific Northwesterners grew familiar with a host of new acronyms—CCC, PWA, WPA, AAA, NRA, and many

80. Forest-fire training at the Skagit Camp of the Civilian Conservation Corps, 1933. Courtesy Forest Service Collection, National Agricultural Library: 282778.

NEW DEAL OUTLAYS PER CAPITA, 1933–1939

(BY REGION AND STATE)

	Rank	Allocation in Dollars
Pacific	2	536
California	10	538
Oregon	12	536
Washington	13	528
Mountain	1	716
Arizona	4	791
Colorado	14	506
Idaho	5	744
Montana	2	986
Nevada	1	1,499
New Mexico	8	690
Utah	9	569
Wyoming	3	897

Source: Don C. Reading, "New Deal Activity and the State, 1933–1939," *Journal of Economic History* 33 (1973): 794–95.

others—each standing for a federal agency charged with implementing part of the president's program. The New Deal's imprint on the Pacific Northwest took many forms, some as awesome as the Grand Coulee Dam—frequently described as "the biggest thing on earth"—and others as mundane as new roads and trails through national forests, concrete sidewalks, picnic shelters, low income housing, wildlife refuges and ranges, highway bridges along the Oregon coast, and post office murals. The WPA constructed ten new courthouses in Idaho. Timberline Lodge, located at the six thousand-foot level on Oregon's Mount Hood, bore the handprint of New Deal CCC and WPA labor. Dedicated in 1937 by President Roosevelt, the 53-room lodge now ranks as one of the region's most popular tourist attractions.

A common thread running through many new federal programs was work for the unemployed. The Civilian Conservation Corps put young men to work on reforestation projects. In Idaho the CCC was probably the most popular New Deal agency: it employed eighteen thousand men and left a lasting impression on the state's landscape. Building the Bonneville and Grand Coulee dams on the Columbia River created thousands of new construction jobs. Projects undertaken by the Works Progress Administration were much smaller in scale and sometimes consisted of little more than leaf raking. But included in the WPA was the Federal Writers' Project, a novel program that put unemployed writers to work producing a series of state guidebooks. First to be completed was the *Idaho Guide* (1937) under the direction of the state's best-known novelist, Vardis Fisher. Though officials in Washington, D.C., were embarrassed that a small, unimportant state was first and tried to delay publication, the *Idaho Guide* blazed a trail for other states to follow.

Besides creating jobs, Bonneville and Grand Coulee dams were promoted as ways to control flooding and generate electricity. The Columbia River contained 40 percent of the nation's potential for hydroelectric generation. The United States Army Corps of Engineers supervised construction of Bonneville Dam forty miles east of Portland, begun in 1933 and placed in

81. The WPA offered a class in placer mining in
Spokane. The well-dressed students look as if they
could have been stockbrokers in more prosperous days.
Courtesy National Archives: 69-N-14467.

POWER FOR THE PEOPLE

The Pacific Northwest uses a prodigious amount of electricity. A seemingly limitless supply of cheap hydropower attracted heavy users like the region's aluminum industry, which after the first plant opened in 1940 supplied a material vital to aircraft builders. In more recent decades, household electric bills in Seattle have averaged one-sixth of those in New York City and helped to encourage residents to use four times as much electricity as New Yorkers. Largely as a result of the electric pumps and giant sprinklers that water crops on the Snake River plain, Idaho consumes far more electricity per capita than any other state.

Electric power in the Pacific Northwest dates from the early 1880s. The region's first hydroelectric dam was completed in Spokane in 1885 and supplied electricity to illuminate a part of the downtown area. Other early generating systems in Seattle, Portland, and smaller communities powered sawmills, printing presses, elevators, and streetcars. The first long-distance transmission of electricity in the world occurred in 1889, when a direct current line was strung from the Willamette Falls at Oregon City to Portland to provide power for streetlights.

Almost from the beginning, public- and investor-owned electric utilities had their proponents. McMinnville, Oregon, inaugurated the first municipally owned electric system in the Pacific Northwest in 1889. Within the next fifteen years, large publicly owned systems evolved in Tacoma and Seattle. Overseeing the rapid expansion of Seattle City Light was J. D. Ross, later to be the first administrator of the Bonneville Power Administration.

Most of the region's investor-owned electric companies—including Puget Sound Power and Light, Washington

service in 1938; the Bureau of Reclamation took charge of Grand Coulee Dam, begun in 1934 and placed in service in late 1941.

Grand Coulee, unlike Bonneville, was also conceived as part of a vast irrigation project. Its twelve massive pumps would lift water from Franklin D. Roosevelt Lake to transform thousands of acres of parched, sagebrush-covered land in central Washington into a garden that boosters hoped in time would support half a million people. The Columbia Basin Project first received water in 1951, and nearly forty years later it remains an evolving network of pumping plants, reservoirs, and canals. As of 1982 the project contained six thousand farms on 540,000 irrigated acres producing more than sixty different crops.

The Columbia River dam projects, like most New Deal projects, were not without their critics. An Indian chief told the Oregon journalist Richard Neuberger that the "white man's dams mean no more salmon." He was partly right, but the situation could have been far worse, because the original design for Bonneville Dam did not include fish ladders and thus would

Water Power, and Pacific Power and Light—were early acquired by giant holding companies headquartered in the Midwest and East. Absentee owners retained control until the 1940s, when the federal government broke up the holding companies.

The battle between public and private power intensified during the 1920s and 1930s as advocates of "people's power" confronted critics who warned of the dangers of socialism. Both Oregon and Washington passed legislation in the early 1930s to allow the formation of public utility districts (people's utility districts in Oregon). These measures permitted rural areas and small towns to acquire and operate their own electric systems.

Some rural electrification projects, primarily on Puget Sound, dated from the First World War, but many other rural areas did not receive electricity until the late 1930s and 1940s. When the New Deal's Rural Electrification Administration was established in

1936 to encourage the wiring of the countryside, 70 percent of the farms in Idaho were without electric power, 60 percent in Oregon, and 50 percent in Washington.

The issue of marketing hydroelectric power generated by the Bonneville and Grand Coulee dams first came before Congress in 1935. Senator James P. Pope of Idaho and Congressman Knute Hill of Washington, two public power Democrats, introduced legislation that would have created a comprehensive Columbia Valley Authority modeled after the Tennessee Valley Authority. It was the first of five unsuccessful attempts to pass such a measure. The Bonneville Power Administration (BPA) created in 1937 was originally seen only as a stopgap measure until the creation of the Columbia Valley Authority. The BPA is now more than fifty years old and exercises enormous influence as a federal agency that markets electric power throughout the West.

have blocked all salmon and steelhead from spawning farther upriver. Only a public outcry prevented that tragedy.

When Grand Coulee Dam was finished, it was as tall as a forty-six-story building and as wide as twelve city blocks. As the largest concrete structure on earth, it was often described as the Eighth Wonder of the World. Others called it a white elephant and wondered how the sparsely populated Pacific Northwest would ever use all the power it generated. The entry of the United States into World War II only months after the completion of Grand Coulee silenced the critics, for a host of war-related industries needed all the power that dams could generate.

CIRCUS POLITICS AND OTHER TRENDS

The political tide that buoyed up the political fortunes of Roosevelt and the New Deal also swept into office a number of new Democratic faces at the

82. In this photograph staged in 1934, an Oregon highway patrolman directs a job seeker to the Bonneville
Dam. Courtesy National Archives: 69-N-P-1004.

state and local level. In Washington, the electorate's swing to the Democratic party brought to prominence many of the reform-minded individuals
who had found the party a refuge during the lean years of Republican
domination. Joining them in the early 1930s was an assortment of idealists,
opportunists, and radicals. One commentator, remarking on Washington's
"Circus Politics," said: "A smart promoter could now put the entire state
under a tent, charge admission, and get it." Among the Democrats elected

to the legislature in 1932 were three candidates in trouble with the police for statutory offenses, and one of these was actually in jail for the rape of a twelve-year-old girl. The incoming lieutenant governor was Victor Meyers, a former speakeasy orchestra leader who had once run for mayor of Seattle dressed in the flowing robes of the Mahatma Gandhi and promising "a hostess on every street car." Despite his quirks, Meyers capably ran the state's volatile legislature and was subsequently elected to several terms as secretary of state.

Washington's Democratic governor was Clarence Martin, a conservative banker and wheat miller who espoused stringent economy in government, but within his party were dozens of reformers, each peddling his own specially bottled brand of political cure-all. The most influential of the left-wing pressure groups that operated within the Democratic party was the Washington Commonwealth Federation, an organization of liberals, socialists, and Communists formed in 1935. Claiming thirty thousand members across the state, it advanced a program advocating production for use, not for profit. This latest manifestation of the state's radical heritage prompted the Democratic national chairman James Farley allegedly to quip, "There are forty-seven states in the Union, and the Soviet of Washington."

Politics in neighboring Idaho and Oregon were sedate by comparison. Oregon voters chose General Charles H. Martin (1935–39) as governor. He was a conservative Democrat who opposed labor unions, public power, and the New Deal. The Oregon Commonwealth Federation was less radical than its counterpart in Washington, but it functioned to marshal support for New Deal measures in the state legislature and played a roll in defeating Martin's bid for reelection. In 1931 Idaho reinstated the direct primary (which was abandoned 12 years earlier), and Washington took the idea to its extreme by adopting the blanket primary in 1935, becoming the only state to give voters complete freedom to choose from among all candidates of all parties in primary elections.

ORGANIZED LABOR AND DAVE BECK

The 1930s were an especially stormy time of strikes and schism in the house of labor. In 1935 alone, fifty-one thousand Northwest workers went on strike and lost 1.6 million man-hours of work. The Washington National Guard intervened in strikes in Aberdeen and Tacoma. Trouble on the waterfront in 1934 closed West Coast ports for nearly four months, and a strike at the Seattle *Post-Intelligencer* in 1936 ended in recognition of the American Newspaper Guild.

The ranks of organized workers expanded rapidly as a result of federal prolabor legislation, but the nearly uncontrolled growth worsened friction between advocates of craft and industrial unions. When the American Federation of Labor expelled proponents of industrial unionism in 1937, they formed the Congress of Industrial Organizations (CIO) the following year. The labor rivalry was especially bitter in the Pacific Northwest, where the aggressive CIO in some ways embodied both the fiery militancy of the Industrial Workers of the World and the idealism of the Knights of Labor. The CIO's strength in the region lay in the timber and mining industries, in the fish canneries, and on the waterfront. The International Woodworkers of America, formed in 1937, battled for the CIO in the Northwest's woods and mills. The membership of the conservative, craft-oriented AFL was less concentrated, but under the leadership of Dave Beck, a fast-rising star in the Teamsters' Union, it vigorously opposed the CIO and labor radicalism.

Capitalizing upon the revolution in motor transport, Beck had moved rapidly through Teamster ranks—from organizing laundry drivers in Seattle to being elected national head of the union (1952–62). In the mid-1930s Beck was easily the Teamsters' most powerful regional leader and the dominant personality in Northwest labor. When the forces of Harry Bridges, an alleged Communist who headed the Longshoremen's Union of the CIO, attempted to "march inland" from the docks to organize the warehouses, Beck countered with club-swinging squads of hired thugs.

In time, both the strikes and labor's internecine warfare diminished, and Beck even came to be regarded as a respectable citizen of Washington; he served on numerous state boards and committees and was elected in 1946 to the Board of Regents of the University of Washington. Beck stood at the pinnacle of his career in 1962, when he was convicted of income tax evasion, lost his union post, and spent the next thirty months behind bars at the McNeil Island federal penitentiary.

THE INTERWAR YEARS IN PERSPECTIVE

Although the interwar years did not inaugurate the modern era of Pacific Northwest history, they did furnish numerous harbingers of the future. The New Deal institutionalized a vastly enlarged role for the federal government in the region. Planning on both state and regional levels became much more common, for New Deal conferences enabled administrators to explain and promote their programs. The Pacific Northwest Regional Planning Commission, a small group of private citizens, began in 1934 to hold annual meetings to study the best uses of the region's resources. But all of those new departures pale when compared to the impact of the Second World War, the event that more than any other inaugurated the modern era of the region's history.

Part Five

The Pacific Northwest Comes of Age

Profile: Tom McCall of Oregon

*

The developers said Tom McCall stunted our growth. Well, maybe he did, but we're growing anyway because where we live is so beautiful. Tom preserved the beauty.—quoted in William F. Asbury, "In the Mountains' Shadow," *Amtrak Express* (1984)

*

Thomas Lawson McCall was born in 1913 and died in 1983. Far more than most public officials before him, the controversial Oregon governor confronted the problems of a state and region coming-of-age. He did so with a gusto that made him legendary and his administration one of the best shows in the Pacific Northwest. His resourcefulness and farsightedness at a time when those qualities seemed sadly lacking in the administration of a fellow Republican, President Richard M. Nixon, gained McCall a national reputation and frequent mention as a possible presidential candidate in 1976.

New England–born and the grandson of a Massachusetts governor and congressman, McCall spent his childhood on the lingering edge of the frontier in central Oregon's Crooked River country near Prineville. On the family ranch he developed what became a lifelong respect for the environment. As a student at the University of Oregon, he furthered his ambition to become a sportswriter. During his Eugene years he met two of Oregon's future United States senators: Richard Neuberger, a gifted journalism student and campus liberal, and Wayne Morse, dean of the university's law school and later a fiery political maverick known to Oregonians as the tiger in the Senate. Although McCall did not realize it then, he would someday share the political spotlight with these two men.

Not long after he graduated in 1936 with a degree in journalism, McCall moved to Moscow, Idaho, where he eked out a living covering local news, mainly sporting events at the University of Idaho. As publicity chairman of the Latah County Wildlife Federation, he demonstrated a growing awareness of conservation issues. He also helped to form the Young Republican Club. The five years in Moscow and those that followed in Portland, where McCall worked as a reporter and radio newscaster, added to his political education. During the Second World War, he joined the navy and served in the South Pacific as a correspondent.

After the war, he returned to a broadcasting job in Portland and a growing involvement in Young Republican politics. A pivotal event in his career occurred in 1949 when Governor Douglas McKay, impressed by one of McCall's speeches, invited the young journalist to Salem to serve as his executive secretary. McCall's informal training for governor included two and one-half years with McKay and a term as secretary of state (1965–67), Oregon's second-highest elective office.

When not in government he continued to pursue a career in journalism. Working for KGW-TV in Portland, McCall produced a documentary called "Pollution in Paradise," which described the Willamette River as an "open sewer" clogged with the effluent of Oregon's four largest cities and several pulp and paper mills. The film won a national award as the outstanding documentary for 1962 and stimulated efforts to clean up the Willamette. By 1969, the river had clearly made a comeback. Soon its entire length was clean enough for swimming, boating, and fishing. More important, through the efforts of crusading journalists like McCall, a growing number of Pacific Northwesterners came to realize during the 1960s that pollution was not something that happened only to rivers and lakes east of the Rocky Mountains.

McCall was elected governor of Oregon in 1966, the year that another Republican, Ronald Reagan, was first elected governor of California. Although the two men were members of the same party, they represented its liberal and conservative wings. The blunt-spoken McCall later said of Reagan that he had no experience in government and had run on a simplistic platform composed mainly of conservative shibboleths. McCall's candor sometimes embarrassed associates and got him in trouble with party leaders, but his warm and friendly approach to people was a compensating trait. He was a large and handsome man, at six feet, five inches tall a standout in any crowd—and some would say with an oversized ego to match.

An increasingly important word in the vocabulary of Oregonians during the 1960s was *livability,* popularized by McCall's predecessor as governor, Mark O. Hatfield, a former professor of political science and dean at Willamette University. McCall soon gave the term added meaning by stressing the need for Oregon to acquire its beach land, and he made a dramatic commitment to clean up the Willamette by appointing himself interim chairman of the State Sanitary Authority. No Oregon governor before him had appointed himself to a state board or commission.

McCall propounded an eleventh commandment, "Thou shalt not Pollute," which he intended to enforce. Working closely with the 1967 legislature, he bragged that he and the lawmakers put together "the greatest bulk of environmental measures, the largest one-whack commitment of any state in history." Critics claimed that he happened along at the right time; nonetheless, by mid-1971 the governor had maneuvered more than one hundred environmental protection measures through the state legislature. The cornerstone, a comprehensive program to curb air and water pollution, established the Department of Environmental Quality in 1969. On a related front, in December 1969 McCall led a successful protest by Pacific northwesterners against shipment of thirteen thousand tons of army nerve gas from Okinawa to an ordnance depot near Pendleton, Oregon.

McCall served as governor during a particularly volatile time in American history, an era filled with violent protests against the war in Vietnam. On May 4, 1970, Ohio National Guardsmen shot fifteen students during a demonstration at Kent State University, killing four. A nationwide student strike followed, shutting down some twenty-five hundred colleges and universities. President Richard M. Nixon declared a state of emergency and invited the governors to the White House for a meeting to discuss the crisis. Oregon's chief executive declined, pointing out that he was needed at home, where every week many visitors stopped by his office to express their concern about America's faltering course.[1] In keeping with his campaign promise to make this a "citizens' administration," McCall conducted open house in his office for half an hour every day; during his first four months as governor, seventeen thousand constituents came to discuss their concerns.

Not long after Kent State, McCall received word that Oregon was to be the next battleground. That year the American Legion scheduled its national convention in Portland, and the Justice Department reported that fifty thousand young people calling themselves the People's Army Jamboree would come to town at the same time. Some of the group's members openly

1. McCall himself had been a supporter of the war in Vietnam.

83. Thomas Lawson McCall (1913–83), governor of
Oregon from 1967 to 1975. Courtesy Oregon Historical
Society: Cn 012693.

welcomed a riot. McCall arranged a free rock concert at McIver State Park
thirty-five miles southeast of Portland to defuse the threat. Called Vortex I,
the concert attracted thirty-five thousand people. Although some concert-
goers—much to the dismay of most Oregonians—engaged in nude bathing
and marijuana smoking, the crowd remained peaceful and friendly. Elsewhere in the United States that week, bombings killed one student and

injured four others at the University of Wisconsin, two died at an army arsenal in Virginia, and a bomb rocked American Legion offices in Seattle. In Portland the toll from the week's unrest was a broken window at Portland State University. McCall described Vortex I as "a great contribution to an understanding between the ages and generations."[2] Evidently a majority of Oregonians approved of McCall's performance, because later that year they reelected him governor with 56 percent of the vote. His Democratic opponent, Robert Straub, suffered an even greater defeat than he had when he ran against McCall four years earlier.

McCall never hesitated to plunge into controversial issues. During the struggle to save the Willamette from pollution, management shut down a Boise Cascade pulp and paper mill at Salem in the face of court action. The plant had been discharging 150,000 gallons of sulfite waste into the river daily. Fearful of losing their jobs, two hundred angry employees confronted McCall on the capitol steps.

"Hitler, Hitler," they chanted.

When explanations bellowed by the governor and his director of the Department of Environmental Quality got across—that workers were being used by their own management—one spokesman shouted back, "Okay, Governor, you lead us and we'll picket our own plant and management."

Eventually, industries and municipalities along the Willamette cleaned up their discharges, at the cost of many millions of dollars. The governor and others sought to implement the concept of a "greenway" or park extending from Portland to Eugene along the river's banks. But water pollution was not the only environmental problem confronting the Willamette Valley. Grass-seed farmers whose industry centered in the Salem-Eugene area, burned their fields each summer in order to produce a multimillion-dollar crop. In 1969 heavy smoke blanketed the freeway and poured into Eugene, creating an environmental crisis. The governor used his emergency police power to stop further burning temporarily and then undertook the difficult task of finding a long-range solution to the problem.

In 1971 McCall uttered his most famous remark to a Junior Chamber of Commerce convention in Portland: "We want you to visit our State of Excitement often," he said. "Come again and again. But, for heaven's sake, don't move here to live." The delegates listened in disbelief. They greeted the comment with a moment of silence followed by a burst of laughter. But

2. Unless otherwise noted, the quotations that follow in this chapter are from *Tom McCall: An Autobiography with Steve Neal* (Portland: Binfort & Mort, 1977).

McCall was serious; he was committed to livability. As he told a group of visiting businessmen from Los Angeles, "Oregon has not been an over-eager lap-dog to the economic master. Oregon has been wary of smokestacks and suspicious of rattle and bang. Oregon has not camped, cup in hand, at anyone's affluent doorstep. Oregon has wanted industry only when that industry was willing to want what Oregon is."

His statements provoked criticism. An angry California businessman who thought that McCall had originated the slogan Don't Californicate Oregon responded with a counterproposal, Don't Oregonize California. McCall noted, however, that some of his staunchest supporters in the controversy were Californians who had recently moved to Oregon. "They seem to resent bitterly the intrusion of another Californian."

A Eugene artist and greeting-card entrepreneur created a line of "Oregon Ungreeting Cards," one of which read: "Tom Lawson McCall, governor, on behalf of the citizens of the great state of Oregon, cordially invites you to visit. . . . Washington or California or Idaho or Nevada or Afghanistan." A popular bumper sticker read Oregon for Oregonians, and in the same vein a whimsical group, the James G. Blaine Society (named for a onetime presidential candidate from Maine), proposed building a freeway from California to Canada with no off-ramps.

In grappling with the problem of unchecked population sprawl, McCall was a modern pioneer. But he was bucking one of the oldest traditions in the American West, that of real estate promotion and an individual's assumed right to develop his own land, whether that meant carving pristine meadows into "mini-estates" or bulldozing wetlands to build a marina. That was the "Buffalo Hunter mentality," McCall complained, and he cited Lincoln City on the central Oregon coast as "a model of strip city grotesque." In his call for state land-use policy, new subdivision laws, and new standards for planning and zoning by cities and counties, he urged Oregonians to protect their present and future interests from "grasping wastrels of the land. We must respect another truism. Unlimited and unregulated growth leads inexorably to a lowered quality of life."

A major step toward realization of McCall's dream was the passage of Oregon senate bill 100 in 1973. That measure created the Land Conservation and Development Commission, which had the power to review land-use plans from Oregon's 278 localities and to accept or reject them on the basis of whether they complied with nineteen state land-use goals. Business and labor leaders who feared it would drive up the cost of land and make industries reluctant to locate in Oregon criticized the controversial measure.

Of all the reforms McCall sought during his ten years in elective state office, he took the greatest pride in the passage and implementation of the Oregon bottle bill, the first state measure enacted in the nation to outlaw pull-tab cans and nonreturnable bottles, sources of much highway litter. The new law required consumers to pay cash deposits on all beer and soft-drink containers. Before the legislature approved the bottle bill in 1971, McCall was subjected to the most intense opposition in his public life. For him the issue was larger than merely providing the money necessary to clean up litter along Oregon's streets and highways. It symbolized "the switch society has to make everywhere from profligacy to husbanding diminishing resources. It is a practical first bridge for this most wasteful of all countries to cross, in reducing a lifestyle bordering on opulence to a level of relative affluence." McCall credited the law with reducing the volume of litter by 47 percent during its second year of operation. The neighboring state of Washington, in contrast, has never been able to pass a similar litter measure, nor has it duplicated Oregon's tough standards for building nuclear power plants.

With characteristic directness McCall confronted a prolonged energy crisis that began in the spring of 1973. A severe water shortage that threatened the region's supply of hydroelectric power was followed by an Arab embargo on oil shipments to America. The Oregon governor directed thirty-two thousand state employees to minimize their use of office lights, hot water, and air conditioners, and to drive state cars sparingly. He issued an order banning all but the most essential outdoor display lighting, lowered the state's speed limit from seventy to fifty-five miles per hour, and caused a stir when he suggested that schools consider discontinuing night football. The gasoline shortage that fall created long lines at service stations, and there were reports of angry customers menacing station operators with tire irons. Working with dealers statewide, McCall implemented a voluntary plan in January 1974 to sell gasoline on alternate days to motorists with odd- or even-numbered license plates. The Oregon plan was soon adopted in other states as an alternative to ration coupons.

Criticizing gas-guzzling American cars as "Belchfire Eights" and "Gas Glutton Supremes," the governor switched to a German-made compact car. The attempt to set a good example soon conflicted with the uncomfortable reality of his more-than-six-foot frame, and he returned to a standard-size car. Even Tom McCall came to realize that he could not implement all of his good intentions.

McCall's unorthodox ways captured the attention of many Americans yearning for an alternative to the sleazy politics and wooden-headed policies of the Watergate era. He was the first Republican governor to call for President Nixon's resignation as a result of the deepening scandal. Discussions of a McCall campaign for president in 1976 appeared in several respected national publications, including *Time* and the Washington *Post*. McCall talked of a "Third Force" alternative to Democratic and Republican parties. Quite in the Pacific Northwest tradition of political independence, he emphasized to eastern Republicans that "for some time, I have enunciated the thesis that issues are more significant than party labels." William S. U'Ren could not have stated the essence of the Oregon System more succinctly. The exact nature of the Third Force eluded definition, as McCall himself acknowledged. "Its genesis," he explained, "was the Oregon Story with the story's emphasis on problem solving in a climate of openness and probity, reverence for nature, and sometimes daring innovation—free from conniving, coercion, and partisan gamesmanship." That was McCall's corollary to the good-government dream of U'Ren.

McCall left the governor's office in January 1975 but declined to run for president the following year, preferring to let Gerald Ford and Jimmy Carter contest that prize while he and his wife temporarily retired to campus life at Oregon State University. After a stint as professor of journalism, McCall produced five television and six radio commentaries a week in addition to a Sunday television show.

An abiding interest in the governor's office caused him to attempt a political comeback in 1978, but Victor Atiyeh defeated him in the Republican primary. Equally unsuccessful was McCall's long battle with cancer that began in 1972 while he was still governor.

Confronting the third of the initiative measures to overturn the land-use planning law, McCall acknowledged in 1982 that it would be his last fight: "You all know that I have terminal cancer, and I have a lot of it. But what many of you might not know is that stress induces its spread and induces its activity. Stress may even bring it on. Yet stress is the fuel of the activist. This activist loves Oregon more than he loves life. I know I can't have both very long, but the tradeoff is all right with me." McCall died three months later, but the land-use protections remained, as did other McCall-era innovations[3].

3. Neal R. Peirce and Jerry Hagstrom, *The Book of America: Inside 50 States Today* (New York: Warner Books, 1984), p. 826.

During his public life, McCall promoted civil rights and administrative and tax reforms. A commentator in the *New Yorker* observed in 1974 that Oregonians "have laws so progressive that, by comparison, many other states look doddering," and he attributed much of that progress to McCall's policies.[4] But Oregon's activist governor will probably be remembered longest for championing environmental causes. He was the region's first prominent public official to make a career out of reminding voters that the Northwest's age of environmental innocence was past. McCall's crusade highlighted the conflicting forces that are shaping the present and future Pacific Northwest.

With the state's unemployment rate topping 12 percent in 1982 and Oregon's corporate climate ranked a low thirty-sixth in the continental United States, Governor Victor Atiyeh sought to send a distinctly new message to the world: "Oregon is open for business." Whether Oregon—and the entire Pacific Northwest—can balance economic growth with McCall's vision of environmental quality remains to be seen. The ongoing dilemma was perhaps best expressed in a 1985 *Wall Street Journal* headline that read: "Eugene, Ore., May Be a Great Place to Live, But Not Without a Job."

4. E. J. Kahn, Jr., *New Yorker* (Feb. 25, 1974), 88–99 *passim.*

CHAPTER 16

The Second World War
and After

*

"What's going to happen," some ask, "when the fighting stops? Can the
Northwest go back to fish, fruit, and sawmills, or have these changes come
to stay?"—Frederick Simpich, "Wartime in the Pacific Northwest,"
National Geographic Magazine (1942).

*

The Second World War inaugurated the modern era of Pacific Northwest
history. Although no region of the United States escaped the impact of war,
few if any experienced more rapid and intense changes than the Pacific
Northwest. Wartime social and economic pressures scarcely left a corner
untouched.

Change was visible in the region's two main centers of war production—
Puget Sound and the Portland-Vancouver area—no less than in seemingly
remote and isolated places like Lake Pend Oreille, where in 1942 Uncle Sam
built Camp Farragut, the second-largest United States naval training center
and for a time the largest city in Idaho. Most improbable of all was the war's
dramatic impact on the village of Hanford in central Washington. On that
Columbia River site and in the surrounding expanse of sage and sand, the
federal government erected a multimillion-dollar complex in 1943 to produce plutonium for the world's first atomic bombs. The army removed
almost 1,500 residents from the 670-square-mile area, and in their place, it
assembled a force of nearly 45,000 workers to erect a top secret installation.
The atomic bomb that devastated Nagasaki, killing 73,884 people, was one

84. Sailors drill in snowshoes at the Farragut Naval Training Station during the Second World War. Courtesy Idaho State Historical Society: D60.171.0004.

of Hanford's products. Yet, until the war's end most Hanford workers did not know what the strange complex produced.

Located nearer the Pacific conflict than any other part of the lower forty-eight states, the Pacific Northwest with its several vital war industries feared invasion and air raids. Military and civilian volunteer units patrolled the coast looking for Japanese invaders, antisubmarine nets guarded Puget Sound, and Boeing Aircraft Company cleverly camouflaged the roof of its sprawling facilities to resemble a residential area.

The Second World War brought social dislocation, privation, and death. It also created unprecedented prosperity and a rare sense of common national purpose. At no time since then have Americans been so united in the conviction that they were fighting a "good war" to defeat unmitigated evil. Such a belief, reinforced in countless ways by patriotic exhortations and demonstrations, helped Pacific Northwesterners adjust to rationing, high prices, overcrowded streetcars, and news of destruction and death.

WINNING THE BATTLE FOR PRODUCTION

Even before the United States formally declared war on the Axis nations of Japan, Germany, and Italy in December 1941, the Pacific Northwest experienced the impact of increased production for defense and for aid to friendly nations already at war. The surprise Japanese attack at Pearl Harbor rapidly accelerated that trend. Industries large and small produced ships, barges, aircraft, lumber and various kinds of wood products, metals, food, machinery, clothing, munitions, and armaments. Seattle alone secured war contracts totaling $5.6 billion, ranking it among the nation's top three cities in per capita war orders.

The region's two best-known war industries were the Kaiser shipyards in the Portland-Vancouver area and the Boeing airplane company. Boeing had large assembly plants in Seattle and Renton and several smaller subassembly and parts factories located throughout the Pacific Northwest. Before war broke out in Europe in September 1939, it employed about four thousand people and produced military planes for the Army Air Corps and a limited number of commercial aircraft.

One of Boeing's models from the 1930s was the B-17 or Flying Fortress, which Britain's Royal Air Force purchased to strike at the Germans. By mid-1941 nearly ten thousand people worked for Boeing, a number that jumped to twenty thousand in September, and to thirty thousand when the United States officially entered the war a few months later. At the peak of B-17 production, Boeing's Seattle plant rolled out sixteen B-17s every twenty-four hours.

A larger and longer-range Boeing plane, the B-29 Super Fortress, became operational in 1943. On each of its assembly lines in Renton, Boeing was capable of building a B-29 bomber in five days. By mid-1945 six new planes rolled out of the plant each day, for a wartime total of 1,119 B-29s, in addition to nearly 4,000 B-17s produced in the Seattle plant. At its peak of production in 1944, Boeing employed nearly fifty thousand people in the Seattle area and amassed total sales of more than $600 million, an impressive sum considering that in 1939 the value of all Seattle manufacturing totaled only $70 million.

Vital to the success of the aircraft industry were the region's five new aluminum reduction plants—the first of which Alcoa opened near Vancouver in 1940—and Bonneville and Grand Coulee dams, which supplied the cheap power necessary to convert alumina (aluminum oxide) into ingots of aluminum. Congress provided the Bonneville Power Administration

85. The arsenal of democracy: producing B-17s at a
Boeing plant in Seattle. Courtesy Library of Congress:
LC-15760-LC US262–59739.

more than $2 billion to increase the generating capacity of the dams sixfold
between 1941 and 1945. Most of the electricity went to the aluminum
reduction plants.

In the production of aluminum goods, the Pacific Northwest supplied
little more than electricity and reduction facilities. Aluminum originated
in the tropics as bauxite ore, and after being refined in the Columbia Valley,
it was shipped across North America to be fabricated into semifinished
products. Another reminder of the region's continuing status as an economic colony was the fact that, of all the major components in a B-29,
Boeing itself fabricated only the spar chord (a support assembly in the wing).
Wing tips were manufactured in Cleveland, landing gear in Milwaukee,
engine housings in Detroit, and engines in a Dodge factory in Chicago.
Puget Sound businesses handled no more than 5 percent of Boeing's sub-
contracted work.

Even more spectacular than Boeing's accomplishments were those of the three Kaiser shipyards in the Portland-Vancouver area. With the aid of federal subsidies, the aggressive and blunt-spoken industrialist Henry J. Kaiser became the world's foremost shipbuilder. For a time nearly one hundred thousand people worked in the Kaiser yards, which displaced Pacific Telephone and Telegraph as Portland's biggest employer. Between mid-1941, when his first yard opened on the banks of the Willamette River, and August 1945, Kaiser constructed about fifty "baby flattop" aircraft carriers and several hundred Liberty ships. The shipyards used fast and simplified methods of welding and steel produced in Kaiser plants in Utah and California.

In mid-1942, a Kaiser yard could build a ship in seventy-two days, half the national average. By the war's end, one of Kaiser's Oregon yards launched a ship in a mere five days. The Kaiser facilities in Vancouver and Portland built more vessels than were constructed anywhere else in the United States and compiled a productivity record unmatched among shipyards.

Other shipyards in the Portland-Vancouver area employed from a few hundred to several thousand workers. Subassembly plants for ships and airplanes, and industries manufacturing wartime chemical, aluminum, steel, and other products were also located in Portland. Elsewhere, smaller plants like the Pacific Car and Foundry Company in Renton converted from making logging trucks to Sherman tanks. Eighty-eight ship- and boatyards in Washington—including the navy's big facility at Bremerton—employed a total of 150,000 workers in 1944.

FEATURES OF WARTIME LIFE

War industries and military installations wrought profound population changes in the Pacific Northwest. In the state of Washington were located more than fifty relatively large army and navy bases, with the greatest concentration of military personnel being in the Fort Lewis–Camp Murray–McChord Field area south of Tacoma. The population growth that accompanied the establishment of military bases nearly overwhelmed small communities like Ephrata, Soap Lake, Moses Lake, and Oak Harbor.

In Portland, where Kaiser shipyards employed nearly 70 percent of the city's labor force, job seekers arrived from ranches in Idaho and Montana— even from as far away as New York City—by special Kaiser trains. Five such trains left New York City on a single weekend in late 1942 carrying five thousand workers. Kaiser charged a fare of $75 to be deducted from subsequent paychecks.

330

The region's population shifts were phenomenal. Between 1940 and 1944, Seattle increased from 368,302 to approximately 530,000 people (650,000 in the greater metropolitan area); Tacoma from 109,408 to 140,000; and Bremerton from 15,134 to 48,000. Portland gained 160,000 new residents, a figure that did not include another 100,000 people in the industrial suburbs of Troutdale, Oregon City, Vanport, and Vancouver. Oregon's population growth during the 1940s nearly equaled its increase for the entire nineteenth century.

Although many war workers came from outside the Pacific Northwest, residents of the region made up the largest percentage of the work force. As a consequence, urban growth represented mainly a redistribution of population within the region. The exodus of people to the boom areas and into the armed forces resulted in stationary or declining populations in agricultural areas east of the Cascades. Except for Camp Farragut and a large naval ordnance plant in Pocatello, Idaho contributed mainly the traditional products of its mines, forests, and fields to the war effort. The state actually lost 15,000 residents between 1940 and 1945. During that same time, the states of Oregon and Washington gained 194,000 and 533,000 new residents respectively.

Seattle doubled its number of manufacturing employees between 1940 and 1942. Nearly half the people initially hired in its war plants were men under twenty-five. The rapid influx of young males without strong community ties was common to all the major cities of the region. Typically, they came from small towns or rural areas where, if previously employed, they had been working in one of the region's principal extractive industries—forestry, mining, and fishing. About 10 percent had formerly worked on farms. In addition to the lure of high pay offered by war industries, such jobs were exempt from the draft, at least in the early part of the war.

Married men among the newcomers faced the problem of finding suitable housing for their families or leaving them behind—as Kaiser advised his imported East Coast workers to do. In the late summer of 1941 when the large influx of new residents began, the vacancy rate for housing in Seattle, Tacoma, and Everett dropped to 1 or 2 percent, and rents rose accordingly. Nearly one-third of all Seattle dwellings renting for less than $50 a month suddenly commanded higher rents, a far greater proportion of increases than occurred in any other large city in the United States. That was one reason why inflation in Seattle exceeded that in any comparable city, climbing 74 percent from 1939 to 1947.

Wartime Seattle and Portland also confronted some of the nation's worst

331

housing problems. To alleviate the shortages, shortcuts were taken, few of them satisfactory. Many existing dwellings were hastily divided into apartments; trailer camps were established; obsolete and condemned houses were patched up; and chicken coops, sheds, lodge halls, empty service stations, and offices were converted into dwellings. Even tents were used. People lived in the back seats of cars or took turns sleeping around the clock in "hot beds." The result was overcrowded and substandard facilities—houses without adequate sanitary arrangements—that created considerable dissatisfaction among war workers. In an attempt to relieve the shortage, federally financed housing projects were hastily constructed, such as the Hudson House Dormitory in Vancouver, which accommodated six thousand men in single and double rooms.

The most spectacular effort to address the housing problem was a completely new working-class town built in a lowland area adjacent to the Columbia River just north of Portland. Called Kaiserville and then Vanport, it became one of the world's largest housing projects. In mid-1942, Henry J. Kaiser's son, Edgar, signed a contract with the United States Maritime Commission to build a six thousand–unit project. Five thousand construction workers (including two hundred women who pushed wheelbarrows and wielded shovels) literally slapped Vanport together. Units were built on wooden block foundations and had thin fiberboard walls. Vanport received its first tenants in December and increased almost overnight to thirty-five thousand residents, making it the second-largest community in Oregon.

Housing was only one of many wartime shortages. More physicians, dentists, and hospital facilities were desperately needed in communities experiencing exceptional growth. Many people feared that crowded conditions, substandard housing, inadequate and overloaded sewage and garbage disposal systems, vermin and rodents, and communicable diseases—especially syphilis and gonorrhea—menaced public health. Even so, health care throughout the Pacific Northwest was probably better than in many parts of wartime America, thanks in part to Henry J. Kaiser's establishment of the Northern Permanente Foundation to furnish medical and hospital care to his shipyard workers and their families.

An ordeal often as bad as finding housing or adequate medical care was getting to and from work. On some Seattle streets the traffic flow nearly doubled by late 1941, and when gasoline and tire rationing restricted automobile use in mid-1942, streetcars and buses labored under crushing passenger loads. Everyday shopping posed the challenge of standing in long check-out lines or doing without. The daily discomforts endured by shift workers may have been responsible for the unusually high absentee rates in places like Portland and Vancouver. The annual rate of labor turnover reached 150 percent in 1943. It became so great at Boeing that observers described the company as a "giant turnstile."

The shortage of labor created jobs for all seekers. The number of lines in the "help wanted" section of the *Seattle Times* jumped from 28,631 during the first nine months of 1940 to 225,515 during the same period in 1943. Employers paid good wages and competed with one another for workers. They used newspapers, billboards, radio, and movies to attract help: "Older Men and Women, We Have a Place for You . . ."; or "Contribute to Victory by Doing Your Share on the Home Front . . ."; or "New and Higher Wage Scale."

At the peak of wartime production, some 46 percent of Boeing's nearly fifty thousand employees were women. In the spring of 1942 approximately 80 percent of the local trainees for aircraft-manufacturing jobs were women, many of them wives of military personnel. At the Puget Sound Navy Yard, employment of women in production jobs increased from virtually none in 1941 to 21 percent of the yard's thirty thousand employees in mid-1943. In all the important industrial facilities of the Puget Sound area combined, women formed about one-fourth of the work force. Housewives without any work experience or educational qualifications beyond a few years in grade school earned $200 to $250 a month at Boeing, at the shipyards, or as bus drivers. Day-care centers for the first time became a significant feature of urban life. Although women performed many jobs traditionally done by men, they rarely received the same pay. Their entry into the work force, moreover, was regarded as a temporary wartime expedient by most men— and by many women, too.

Not every woman, of course, became Rosie the Riveter. Those who remained at home contributed to the war effort by raising victory gardens; preparing meals that took into account shortages of meat, sugar, vegetables, and other staples of the American diet; saving tin cans, shortening, and other items for salvage drives; and often raising a family while a husband was away at war.

Organized labor experienced a great influx of new members during the war, but life in the burgeoning union ranks was not harmonious. Industrial workers who had been recruited from rural regions and small towns often regarded unions with apathy or even antagonism and resented paying any dues. The addition of women and blacks to the industrial work force further disrupted several unions. Tensions arose when blacks in the aircraft and shipbuilding industries applied for union membership. At Boeing, the union

333

86. During the Second World War, women held a wide range of jobs in the timber industry. "Timberettes" employed by the Snoqualmie Falls Lumber Company pulled rough green lumber off a moving chain and did a job that many thought only husky men could handle. Courtesy Forest History Society.

refused to admit them and thus helped to shape company policy. Boeing never hired a significant number of blacks during the war. Kaiser opposed racial discrimination, but nearly all his employees were members of metal trades unions that had no desire to admit blacks to membership. The Boilermakers' Union segregated black shipyard workers into auxiliary unions and blocked them from holding skilled jobs. Blacks paid dues but had no vote in union matters, and when the war ended, they found that their classification as temporary members gained them no seniority in the scramble for jobs.

High wages in shipyards and factories created an unreal situation for many people who had weathered hard times during the 1930s. Yet even as the prevailing standard of living rose, consumer goods and services became increasingly high priced, rationed, or simply unavailable. During the war, meat, milk, and clothing were all in short supply; overcrowded passenger trains and the rationing of tires and gasoline discouraged vacation travel or even short pleasure trips. People coped in a variety of ways: Idaho fish and game officials used horses and other forms of nonmotorized transport; vacationers stayed close to home; cooks substituted honey for sugar in dessert recipes. Because of gasoline rationing in late 1942, Idaho's Sun Valley converted from a resort to a navy convalescent center.

People saved part of their newly acquired earnings and spent the rest on the goods and services that were available. As a consequence, retail sales boomed, and new department stores opened. Bulging savings accounts helped to fuel a sustained buying spree when the conflict ended.

RACE AND RELOCATION

The Second World War noticeably altered the region's racial composition. Between 1941 and 1945 the Pacific Northwest experienced a significant influx of blacks and the forced removal of the Japanese. When the war began, there were approximately seven thousand to eight thousand persons of Japanese ancestry living in the Seattle and Portland areas. Prevailing anti-Asian prejudice together with the surprise attack on Pearl Harbor created among Pacific Coast residents an almost hysterical fear of Japanese invasion. In the spring of 1942 all Japanese living in western portions of Oregon and Washington—approximately two-thirds of whom were American citizens—were preemptorily dispatched to inland camps by the Wartime Civil Control Administration.

Japanese Americans were not removed from the interior Northwest, and as a consequence, some relocated to Idaho to escape internment. What they could not escape was prejudice. In the fall of 1942, in what was labeled the Retreat from Moscow, the University of Idaho denied admission to six persons of Japanese descent born in the United States after having initially accepted them as transfers from the University of Washington. Local citizens created such a furor that two of the women were temporarily housed in jail under "protective custody."

Federal authorities sent Japanese Americans to inland camps like Minidoka on the Snake River plain in southern Idaho. Many hundreds were subsequently released to harvest the crops of the inland Northwest. Legal challenges to the relocation order, like that mounted by Gordon Hirabayashi, a University of Washington student who refused to leave Seattle, reached the United States Supreme Court. But in each case, the high court upheld the constitutionality of the removal order.

The property of the Japanese was held for them by the United States

87. "Camp Harmony" in Puyallup, Washington, where
Japanese Americans from the Puget Sound area were
temporarily housed in former horse stalls at the Washington State Fairgrounds. Courtesy University of
Washington Libraries: Neg. UW 1673.

Alien Property custodian and, in many cases, returned after the war. Some
belongings were vandalized, however, and in urban areas, former Japanese
dwellings and jobs went to newcomers, many of whom were black. The
black population living west of the Mississippi River totaled about 171,000
in 1940; it increased to approximately 620,000 by 1945. During that time
the black population of the Pacific Northwest probably doubled, while in
urban areas like Portland and Seattle, it increased even more. By early 1945,
7,000–8,000 blacks lived in Seattle where, a reporter noted, "the feeling
against them is high. In Portland, where there are 15,000 it is much higher."
The number of blacks in Portland actually climbed from 2,000 to 22,000,
then declined to 11,000 after the war.

Many blacks moved to the region to take industrial jobs. Of 7,541 non-
white workers in Portland on September 1, 1944, 7,250 were employed in
the shipyards. Other blacks arrived as army and navy personnel. Though the
black population in the region remained small compared to that in other

---

OREGON UNDER ATTACK

During the Second World War, Oregon was the only American state to be shelled by enemy naval craft, to be bombed by enemy aircraft, and to suffer civilian deaths as a result of enemy action. The latter incident occurred near Bly on May 5, 1945, when a Japanese balloon bomb killed six children on a church outing. During the final weeks of the war, Japan launched hundreds of incendiary balloon bombs from its home islands in a desperate effort to set American fields and forests afire.

---

parts of the United States—an estimated 14,000 in Washington in 1943—racial hostility caused some smaller communities to exclude blacks from nearly every form of public recreation. Discriminatory signs such as "We Cater to White Trade Only" appeared for the first time in Northwest cities. Army officials occasionally retaliated by placing such establishments off limits, but some residents found it difficult to understand why the army expected civilians to practice nonsegregation when the military segregated its own eating and recreation facilities. Scuffles between white and black industrial workers flared on occasion in Vancouver, Bremerton, Seattle, and other cities, and the question of admitting blacks to union membership remained controversial.

THE IMPACT OF WAR

Even while the war continued abroad, planning for postwar America began. "In Seattle everybody has a postwar plan," observed a correspondent for the *New Republic*. Pacific Northwesterners dreamed of a new day when the West Coast would escape the essentially colonial economy of the past. Washington's governor, Arthur Langlie, predicted in mid-1944 that "our colonial status as shippers of fruit, timber, and other raw materials will be overcome by facilities set up within our states to produce for vast new markets across the Pacific." Others spoke glibly of the region's expanding array of new manufacturing and service industries and a growing trade with the "unsaturated markets" of the Pacific basin that contained half the world's population. The timber industry envisioned a bright future supplying materials to rebuild the cities of Europe. Yet all but the most optimistic northwesterners couched their predictions in words like *should* and *must* that betrayed lingering doubts about whether old economic patterns could be broken.

The postwar economic situation in the Pacific Northwest simply did not inspire much confidence. "The unemployment that is going to hit the West Coast when the war ends will be disastrous—unless something is done about it," predicted a writer for *Fortune* in early 1945, and statistics soon underscored that gloomy assessment. After the region's index of business activity reached an all-time high in January-February 1945 (in contrast to the national peak in October-November 1943), it dropped sharply in May 1945 with the war's end in Europe. By August 1 employment in the Portland-Vancouver shipyards had already dropped to sixty-five thousand and would soon drop much farther; payrolls in Portland declined from a mid-1943 peak of $44 million to $18 million in early 1947. Many predicted that Boeing would retain only 10 to 15 percent of its wartime work force. The inevitable cutback in ship and aircraft building seemed certain to create massive unemployment that would place a heavy burden on employment services, public works, and relief agencies.

Moreover, many who had migrated temporarily for jobs or military service now wanted to establish permanent homes in the Pacific Northwest. This resulted in a lasting population increase. By 1947 the region's population had climbed an estimated 25 percent higher than it had been in 1940. Could enough peacetime jobs be found for all takers, and what, if anything, could be done to prevent massive unemployment and concomitant social unrest?

History served as a grim reminder of what happened during a troubled and unplanned conversion from war to peace. After the First World War, employment in Northwest shipyards dropped from thirty thousand workers to a few hundred. People who recalled Seattle's 1919 general strike feared that it would be difficult to avoid similar unrest after the Second World War.

In contrast to the Midwest or East, the Pacific Northwest had converted from peace to war production in a peculiar way: the war superimposed huge new industries on top of an existing extractive economy. There was no reason to believe that war industries would outlive the conflict or that the region's traditional natural resources–based industries could absorb more wage earners, or even maintain the record levels of wartime output.

Uncertainty also accompanied the postwar return of the Japanese. Residents of the White River and Puyallup valleys of western Washington, where the Japanese had once had extensive agricultural holdings, were vehemently opposed to their return. Among the most frequently stated reasons were that "the Japanese stabbed us in the back at Pearl Harbor"; that "one can never tell what a Jap is thinking"; or that "they want social

338

equality." Several organizations passed resolutions opposing the return of the Japanese. In time, of course, the Japanese did return, and despite the potential for violence, there was no serious trouble.

As it turned out, the Northwest's postwar economic adjustments also proceeded far more smoothly than experts dared to predict. Population growth coupled with a contracting job market failed to produce hard times and social unrest. Unemployment increased immediately after the war, but then it dropped dramatically in 1946. There were many reasons for that pattern: instead of immediately flooding the job market, a number of service men discharged in the Northwest exercised their option to attend college under the GI bill, a congressional package of veterans' benefits. Many female war workers, observed one contemporary, were "retiring to their homes." That made room, another added, for the fifteen thousand servicemen who returned to jobs in Spokane.

For others, wartime savings, termination pay, and unemployment compensation discouraged a desperate scramble for jobs. Moreover, savings accumulated during the war enabled a record number of people to purchase cars, new homes, and a comfortable middle-class life in the suburbs, thus buoying up the nation's construction and forest products industries. An inadequate number of houses built during the war coupled with the move to suburbia and an increase in the number of new families kept the Northwest's forest products industry producing at record levels for more than two decades after the war, though at the cost of reducing the region's timber supply. Logging and sawmilling regained their prewar status as Oregon's leading industry as early as 1946. Tourism boomed too. When gasoline rationing ended, tourists withdrew money from their bulging savings accounts, cashed in their war bonds and stamps, and took to the road in record numbers. The number of visitors to Mount Rainier in 1946 broke all previous records.

The souring of relations between the United States and the Soviet Union led to a cold war and then to conflict in Korea that prolonged indefinitely the life of many old war industries. As a result, the region's aircraft factories employed twice as many people immediately after the Second World War than in 1939—some nine thousand at Boeing—and the shipyards three times as many as before the war. "Air power is peace power," declared William M. Allen, president of Boeing in 1947, and during the cold war years of the late 1940s and 1950s, his company remained the region's largest manufacturer, meeting military and, later, civilian needs.

The Second World War brought dramatic change to the Pacific Northwest, but though some changes endured—perhaps forever in the case of Hanford's atomic waste storage tanks—others proved only temporary. Camp Farragut on Lake Pend Oreille closed permanently, and forests and fields reclaimed the land that later became an Idaho state park. Nature also reclaimed the swampland from which Vanport arose; on Memorial Day 1948 a Columbia River flood left 39 people dead and obliterated the declining settlement.

For all the lasting changes that the Second World War brought to the Pacific Northwest—including the enlargement of Boeing and the development of a regional aluminum industry—the economic well-being of the region remained closely tied to the fate of its forest, mining, fishing, and agricultural industries. Distance from markets, freight rates, and a small population base explain much of the region's enduring economic backwardness. Yet there were also a few Pacific Northwesterners who as early as the late 1940s believed that quality of life should not be sacrificed to rapid and unchecked economic growth. They did not want the City of Roses to become another Pittsburgh, and people who wondered what an industrial future would bring had only to observe how wartime manufacturing had fouled the waters of the Willamette River to know the answer. The war experience, in short, hastened a confrontation between Pacific Northwesterners and the economic, demographic, and environmental problems that increasingly beset their maturing region during succeeding decades.

CHAPTER 17

Recent Times, 1950-1985

*

Many Pugetopolitans are now worried about whether, in the process of industrialization, their paradise will be lost. "How can our state grow with grace?" asks Governor Evans. "We have been the beneficiaries of time and space, we have not suffered the silt and smoke of overindustrialization—yet. We have not succeeded in completely obliterating the beauty of our countryside or polluting our waters—yet. But time, which has been on our side, is rapidly running out."—*Time*, May 27, 1966

*

A motorist who drove from Pocatello to Portland and Seattle and then circled back to Spokane and the Coeur d'Alene mining region in 1950 and repeated that trip in 1985 would have sampled most of the important changes that occurred in the Pacific Northwest following the Second World War. Not all changes were as dramatic as those from the growth decade of the 1880s or from the two world wars, but they were significant. This two-chapter overview of recent Pacific Northwest history begins by reflecting on the changes such a traveler might have observed.

THE CHANGING FACE OF THE PACIFIC NORTHWEST

Between 1950 and 1985, two-lane U.S. 30, which once threaded its way west across the Snake River plain and along the south bank of the Columbia River, was supplanted by Interstate 84, a four-lane superhighway that was part of a forty-one thousand–mile national network authorized by Congress

341

in 1956. Before the oil shortage of 1973, a motorist could follow this route across Oregon at the legal speed limit of seventy miles per hour and hardly worry whether an automobile got ten miles or twenty miles to a gallon of gasoline. Few American-made cars got more than that, and as late as 1973 regular gasoline seldom cost more than thirty-five cents a gallon. The speed limit in 1985 was 55,[1] the cars were smaller and often foreign made, and the price of a gallon of gasoline hovered around a dollar.

Billboards that once lined portions of the old route were mostly gone by 1985, as the result of a federal highway beautification program initiated in the mid-1960s. But there were trade-offs, because travelers crossing tedious stretches of the Snake River plain missed the diversion offered by advertisers' wry comments.

The mighty and picturesque falls of the Columbia River at Celilo, east of the Dalles, were gone, too. The falls and a way of life for Indian tribes who fished there disappeared in 1957 beneath forty feet of slack water created by the Dalles Dam, one of nearly a dozen dams constructed on the Columbia and Snake rivers after 1950. The dams impounded water to generate much of the region's electricity and turn arid regions into farmland.

In the 1930s and 1940s dams were widely viewed as good and useful legacies bequeathed to future generations, but by the 1980s many Pacific Northwesterners condemned them because of declining fish runs and the inadequacy of their supposedly limitless supply of electricity. How ironic that the Portland General Electric Company chose to build a large coal-burning power plant near Boardman, Oregon, in the late 1970s, not too many miles from McNary Dam on the Columbia River; and that in 1976 the utility put into operation one of the nation's largest nuclear power plants. Situated on the bank of the Columbia approximately forty miles downstream from Portland, the $240 million Trojan Nuclear Plant represented a significant departure from the region's dependence upon hydropower.

Trojan was one of at least twenty nuclear power plants once projected for the Pacific Northwest. Its location and operation have been the subject of controversy and protest since the early 1970s, yet the facility generated nothing like the controversy that surrounded the nuclear power debacle of the Washington Public Power Supply System.

---

1. In 1987 the speed limit was increased to 65 on rural sections of interstate highways.

The WPPSS debacle is a sad tale of the technological euphoria of the 1960s gone awry. When sixteen public utility districts formed the Washington Public Power Supply System in 1957, it was distinctly a low-budget operation. It successfully built a hydroelectric plant at Packwood Lake in the Washington Cascades and a nuclear plant on the Hanford reservation. From there it plunged headlong into the construction of five nuclear plants and in the process became the largest issuer of tax-free municipal bonds in American history. Several of the region's major private utilities and nearly one hundred public utility districts guaranteed the bonds in exchange for future WPPSS electricity.

Originally estimated at slightly more than $4 billion, the price tag for the five plants ballooned to some $24 billion before WPPSS defaulted on the bonds for plants 4 and 5 in 1983. That was enough money in current dollars to build both the Alaska Pipeline and the Panama Canal. By the mid-1980s, two of the units had been abandoned, two had been mothballed at a cost of $21 million a year, and only one plant produced electricity—which was far more expensive than hydroelectric power. One of the mothballed plants was 75 percent completed when construction halted.

What went wrong? First, the projected demand for electricity in the Pacific Northwest actually fell slightly instead of doubling every decade as the experts had originally predicted. The Bonneville Power Administration estimated that the Pacific Northwest would need ten nuclear plants by the year 2000, and it used its considerable influence to back the bonds issued for three WPPSS facilities.

The financial and technological complexity of the projects apparently overwhelmed the WPPSS board of directors, a group that was best suited to run a local public utility district. Compounding their problems was the fact that the five plants were to be built according to three different designs by three different contractors and dozens of subcontractors, and no one seemed capable of taking charge. The result was managerial bumbling and labor greed on a monumental scale.

In some ways the nation's largest municipal bond default represented yet another chapter in the Northwest's lengthy saga of popular democracy. Public protests mounted as ratepayers came to realize that, whether or not the plants were ever built, they were legally obligated to holders of WPPSS bonds. This meant staggering increases in their monthly electric bills. The twenty-five thousand ratepayers of the Mason County Public Utility District, for example, discovered that they owed approximately $200,000 a month for the next thirty-five years. "We are not going to pay the bigwigs on Wall Street," a former mayor of Hoquiam told the Seattle *Post-Intelligencer* in 1981. And they didn't. When the Washington State Supreme Court sided with ratepayers, the losers were those who had purchased WPPSS bonds thinking they had made a safe investment. The legal outcome remains uncertain.

The sole operational power plant of WPPSS (pronounced "whoops") is not easy for casual travelers to spot: it is located on the sprawling Hanford reservation near Richland, Washington, a two-hour detour off the main highway from Pocatello to Portland. Of concern to ratepayers and investors are the four other WPPSS plants that remain unbuilt or in mothballs. The program's financial collapse in 1983 ranks as the largest municipal default in American history and will certainly remain the subject of lengthy litigation.

The motorist of 1950 and 1985, continuing down the Columbia River, would have passed a grandfather among Columbia dams: Bonneville. The completion of a series of dams on the lower Snake River in 1975 made it possible for towboats and barges passing through Bonneville's locks to continue upriver as far as Lewiston, Idaho. Over Bonneville's fish ladders pass numerous salmon and steelhead trout returning upstream to spawn, though their numbers were far smaller in 1985 than before the river was dammed.

At the height of the dam-building boom of the 1960s, federal outlays for development in eastern Washington topped $100 million, about 10 percent of the federal public works budget for an area with .4 percent of the nation's population, a tribute perhaps to the power of Washington's congressional delegation. Washington, unlike Oregon and Idaho, also received large military installations, such as the Trident submarine base at Bangor on the Olympic Peninsula. One Trident submarine carries enough nuclear warheads to vaporize 240 Soviet cities. The new base will ultimately house ten such submarines.

Not everything along the highway has changed. A traveler entering the Portland metropolitan area in 1985 would have seen a large pulp and paper mill across the river at Camas, Washington. That mill and its predecessors have operated there since the 1880s, and if the wind was blowing from a northerly direction, the motorist would have noticed a distinct odor. To some people it was the smell of rotten eggs; to others it was the smell of jobs. Travelers around the Northwest can still smell those effluents and similar ones at locations scattered from Lewiston to Bellingham to Coos Bay.

The region's pulp and paper industry expanded rapidly following World War II. It represented one way the forest products industry efficiently utilized the region's natural resources. Another tribute to efficiency was clear-cutting, a logging practice that left a bold and unsightly signature across the mountain landscape. Clear-cutting, like nuclear power, has its advocates, but critics have turned both technologies into topics of public debate.

Battles over the fate of the region's natural resources were frequent during the years 1950 to 1985, and while monumental ones like the Hells Canyon controversy were won by advocates of recreation and scenic preservation—not hydroelectric power—the struggle continued. In the mid-1980s a major fight erupted over the fate of the scenic Columbia River gorge.

Resistance to Oregon's environmentalists surfaced late in 1971 when industrial and union leaders formed a unique alliance called the Western Environmental Trade Association to fight the "environmental hysteria" they claimed was hurting the state's economy. Continued conflict over wilderness land raised vexing questions that go to the heart of the Pacific Northwest's identity as a region. So vital are these environmental issues to an understanding of the region's past and future that they form the concluding chapter of this book.

A traveler would also have noted dramatic changes in the region's urban landscape. Seattle's tallest building in 1950 was the twenty-six–story L. C. Smith Tower. By 1985, from a distance the city's skyline resembled a bar graph; now the most prominent profile belongs to the seventy-six–story Columbia Center, the tallest building west of Minneapolis and north of San Francisco.

Seattle hosted its second world's fair in 1962. Called Century 21, it not only provided Seattle a needed economic boost but also bequeathed it the Space Needle, a monorail, and a vastly enhanced civic center. Across the Cascades in Spokane, the 1974 world's fair brought even more dramatic changes by converting an unsightly thirty-eight hundred–acre complex of warehouses and railroad tracks into park and recreation facilities along the Spokane River and by revitalizing the city's center. The theme of the Spokane fair, "Progress without Pollution," was in tune with the region's growing environmental consciousness.

Architectural daring rather than size characterized Portland's new downtown buildings, and certainly no city in the Northwest rivaled Portland for architectural excitement. Boise, alas, for a time represented the other extreme. Its downtown renewal program removed many structures but seemed incapable of replacing them with anything other than parking lots. One critic likened Boise to a doughnut because of its disappearing downtown structures and booming suburbs. But during the 1980s Boise also made progress in renovating its historic buildings.

The single most dramatic physical change in the urban Northwest since 1950 was probably suburban sprawl. Some observers feared that a strip of

88. Night at Century 21. The 1962 world's fair bequeathed two of the modern symbols of Seattle: the monorail and the futuristic Space Needle. Courtesy University of Washington Libraries: Neg. UW 856.

suburban tract homes and shopping centers extending from Eugene to Portland would forever compromise the natural beauty of the Willamette Valley. Of equal concern was the rise of Pugetopolis, a composite city that may one day stretch north from Olympia to encompass Tacoma, Seattle, Bellevue, and Everett. Once "Boeing's bedroom," Bellevue is the capital of the region's computer software industry and possesses a skyline that mimics Seattle's on the opposite side of Lake Washington. A motorist traveling in 1985 from Puget Sound to the Idaho panhandle would within a day's drive have been able to contrast the economic vitality that transformed Bellevue with the stagnation in the Coeur d'Alene mining region, one part of the Northwest afflicted with massive unemployment and population decline.

ECONOMIC BOOM-AND-BUST CONTINUED

Economic changes in recent years created the two Pacific Northwests so obvious today, one centering on trans-Pacific commerce and high technology enterprises like Boeing and the electronics and computer software industries of Bellevue, Beaverton, and Boise, and the other Northwest, still dependent on traditional natural resources–based industries. For a time, both prospered, but a series of mine and mill closures in the late 1970s and early 1980s revealed how weak and erratic the region's economy really was.

During decades following the Second World War, the economic health of the Pacific Northwest remained closely linked to extractive industry, although manufacturing and service enterprises grew in importance. Boeing was the region's largest manufacturer and private employer; at its postwar peak in 1968, there were 101,500 people on its Washington payroll. Writing and manufacturing computer software increased in importance in the 1980s, Microsoft in Bellevue becoming a multimillion-dollar enterprise and a national leader in its field. Even so, the Pacific Northwest remained a long way from overtaking California and Massachusetts in high technology enterprise, and some wonder whether the region's chronically underfunded public universities can provide the brain power necessary to compete with "Silicon Valley," which draws upon nearby Stanford and the University of California at Berkeley.

While glamorous new "high tech" enterprises fostered the illusion of sustained growth and prosperity, a truly sobering day of reckoning jolted the region's old mainstay, the forest products industry. During the first two decades after World War II, the industry prospered as never before. Eugene, Springfield, and Coos Bay vied for the title of lumber capital of the world.

The number of people employed in the woods and mills and the production of lumber topped even the record years of World War II as a result of a building boom in the nation's suburbs.

As late as 1964, 30 percent of the lumber used on the East Coast came from the Pacific Northwest. Oregon remained the nation's leading timber-producing state for nearly five decades after 1937, but its output peaked in 1955 and was followed by a gradual decline that accelerated in the late 1970s and early 1980s when a variety of ills caused mills all over the Pacific Northwest to close.

Among the problems plaguing the industry were antiquated and inefficient mills, the revival of southern pine forests (which Pacific Northwesterners once dismissed as having the quality of weeds), competition from Canadian imports, a housing slump caused by high interest rates, and a shifting market. Producing for the Japanese market involved a fundamental change in the way the industry did business. Instead of sawed timber, the Japanese purchased shiploads of logs and cut lumber in their own mills. That arrangement cost Northwest jobs.

When the economic downturn of the early 1980s was viewed from a national perspective, it was a recession. But to residents of mill towns like Potlatch and Coos Bay, which were devastated by an unemployment rate that occasionally topped 25 percent, the downturn was nothing less than a great depression that persisted even when the national economy boomed in the mid-1980s. Some 60 percent of Oregon loggers lost their jobs: a total of forty-eight thousand lumber jobs disappeared in the Pacific Northwest. The shutdowns exacted a psychological and social toll measurable in an increase in family-related problems.

The Georgia-Pacific Company's decision to move its headquarters from Portland to Atlanta, Georgia, in 1982 typified the long-term changes that overtook the timber industry. The forest products giant believed that the future looked brighter in the timber belt of the South, where a warm and humid climate supposedly grew trees faster than the cool weather of the Pacific Northwest. Even when the industry revived—as it did in the late 1980s, innovative technology that included computers and lasers enabled modern sawmills to employ far fewer hands than they had only a decade earlier. Such changes forced many workers to make painful and permanent transitions in their life-style. Never again would it be possible to describe the Pacific Northwest as a Sawdust Empire.[2]

2. Howard M. Brier, *Sawdust Empire: Washington and Oregon* (New York: Alfred A. Knopf, 1958).

Mining was another of the region's extractive industries to face an uncertain future. The silver mines of northern Idaho boomed during the late 1970s, when Americans, frightened by an inflation rate that reached 18 percent, rushed to buy gold and silver as a hedge against further erosion of the dollar's buying power. But when the rate of inflation dropped during the 1980s, so did the price of silver. That slump coupled with rising labor costs caused several large companies to close their mines rather than operate them at a loss.

An era came to an end when the Bunker Hill Mine and Smelter halted operations in Kellogg in 1981. The shutdown of Idaho's second-largest employer idled two thousand workers. Five years earlier, Kellogg had been a bustling community of five thousand, hub of the fifty-mile-long silver valley where one-quarter of the twenty thousand residents worked in mining. By the mid-1980s Kellogg's population had fallen below three thousand, and fewer than four hundred people remained employed in the valley's mines. For many miners the era was a replay of the Great Depression of the 1930s. Even when silver prices rebounded, technological changes in the mining industry—like those in the lumber industry—permanently eliminated hundreds of jobs. To some, it seemed that if the silver valley had a future it was as a ski resort.

Agriculture, too, experienced change following the Second World War. The waters impounded by Grand Coulee Dam were raised by a complex system of pumps and siphons to irrigate a vast stretch of semiarid land in central Washington. The Columbia Basin Project transformed sagebrush plains into fields of sugar beets, potatoes, and dozens of other crops. An influx of settlers swelled the populations of towns like Moses Lake and Othello. But farmlands of the Columbia Basin Project proved no more immune to changing prices and tastes than those elsewhere. Sugar beet producers suffered a severe blow when soft-drink bottlers responded to rising sugar prices in the mid-1970s by switching to less expensive corn sweeteners. Orchardists planted thousands of acres to Red and Golden Delicious apples only to face severe losses and forced changes when public taste turned to new varieties, like the tart green Granny Smith. Washington production of this popular variety increased tenfold between 1975 and 1985.

For more than a century, wheat had been the mainstay of the region's export economy, yet in the mid-1980s huge piles of unsold grain dotted the landscape of eastern Washington. Exports of wheat to Asia were down 55 percent from those five years earlier. A global glut of wheat severely jolted the Northwest economy, and not just in rural areas. In Spokane, for example, twenty-five to thirty jobs out of every hundred were directly dependent

89. Columbia Basin Project: a couple dreams of making the desert bloom when the water arrives. Courtesy Oregon Historical Society: 79631.

on agriculture. Largely as a result of the malaise in timber, mining, and agriculture, Idaho in the mid-1980s experienced its largest net out-migration in fifteen years, as people looked elsewhere for jobs. From 1980 to 1985, Oregon experienced a total net migration of −1.7 percent, while Washington's rate was a minuscule 2.1 percent. That was a far cry from the previous decade when the population of all three states grew at rates that exceeded 20 percent.

There are those who think the economic health of the Pacific Northwest will be closely tied to an Asian export economy and the so-called clean industries of electronics, computer software, and tourism. The region has long sought to attract tourists by capitalizing on its natural beauty. Well before the turn of the century, railroads promoted tourism to places like Yellowstone Park in an effort to increase passenger traffic. For the same reason, the Union Pacific in the midst of the Great Depression created a winter resort at Sun Valley that featured the country's first ski lift and a 220-room lodge. The rival Milwaukee Road promoted skiing at Snoqualmie Pass in Washington, and the Great Northern did likewise in northern Idaho and northwestern Montana. All-weather highways made possible the development of numerous other ski areas.

Tourism is predicted to become Oregon's largest industry by the year 2000. It has already become Idaho's largest employer and third-ranked industry in number of dollars generated. Even tourism, however, came with strings attached. The Oregon coast, paralleled for most of its length by U.S. Highway 101, was a top tourist attraction, yet an unpicturesque string of pizza parlors, salt-water taffy stands, and rock hound shops detracted from the seashore's natural beauty. The proliferation of such unsightly businesses made some people wonder how benign tourism really was. Locals blamed the nine million to ten million tourists who came to Oregon every year, mainly from California, for crowded state parks, litter, and vandalism. Tourism, moreover, tended to generate mainly low-paying service jobs.

As for high tech's economic magic, the industry proved no more immune to swings of the business cycle than traditional resource-based industries. During the early 1970s and again in the early 1980s, Boeing experienced slowdowns that cost thousands of jobs and temporarily dimmed the economic outlook of Seattle and the Puget Sound region. As a result of massive layoffs at Boeing, Seattle experienced 13 percent unemployment in 1971, the worst in the United States. In 1970, the Portland area's biggest employer was Tektronix, which kept six thousand workers busy assembling oscilloscopes, but during the slump of the early 1980s it discharged many of its workers. In Idaho during one six-month period in 1985, major electronics companies laid off two thousand people.

EDUCATIONAL AND SOCIAL TRENDS

The growth of tourism reflected one way post–Second World War northwesterners spent their increased leisure time. Another recreational pursuit was television, development of which owed much to the Idaho inventor Philo T. Farnsworth, who in 1930 patented the picture tube electronics he leased to the Radio Corporation of America.

Instead of listening to popular radio programs like "Amos and Andy" or "The Jack Benny Show", families in the 1950s followed their old favorites on new small black-and-white television screens. Television was initially available only in the region's major cities. With the advent of cable television and home satellite receivers in the 1970s and 1980s, even the remotest village was plugged into the fare that television offered.

Television's impact on the region's newspapers was visible in the changes that occurred after the Second World War. Where once half a dozen papers competed in metropolitan areas, the trend was toward one newspaper—or a morning and evening paper controlled by the same company. Among the important survivors were the Portland *Oregonian*, Eugene *Register-Guard*, Boise *Statesman*, Spokane *Spokesman-Review*, the Seattle *Times* and *Post-Intelligencer*, and the Tacoma *News-Tribune*. Fine papers continue to be published in the region's smaller towns and cities, but many were acquired by regional or national chains. Sometimes the infusion of outside capital and talent improved a newspaper. But too often the emphasis was on advertising and profits, and the result was editorials so bland as to offend no one—especially the advertisers. The growth of newspaper chains dominated by city dailies, together with the outreach of television, increased the influence of the Northwest's largest metropolitan centers over its rural hinterlands.

Another form of education undergoing change was the region's public school system. In all three states, higher education evolved along similar lines during the decades following the Second World War. Starting in the fall of 1945, veterans aided by federal money swelled the region's college and university population. At the University of Washington, where civilian enrollment dropped from 10,000 to 7,000 during the war, the student population climbed to 16,650 by the fall of 1948. After the veterans graduated, many campuses experienced a slight decline in enrollments. That changed in the mid-1960s when the first members of what became known as the baby boom generation (people born between 1946 and 1971) arrived on campus. Enrollments burgeoned as a result of the "baby boomers" and because the unpopular Vietnam War encouraged young men to attend college in order to qualify for student draft deferments.

Despite campus unrest in the late 1960s, the decade may well be viewed as higher education's golden age. Across the region, colleges expanded into universities, and campuses came alive with the construction of new buildings, the inauguration of new departments and majors, and rapid faculty promotion. Several entirely new institutions were founded, especially in the category of two-year community colleges. During the twenty years after Washington created a state system of community colleges in 1967, the number of campuses increased from nineteen to twenty-seven, and enrollment climbed from 50,000 to 159,000.

Illustrative of the era's unprecedented expansion was the evolution of Boise State University: founded in 1932 as a private junior college, it developed into a four-year college in 1964, became a state-supported school in

1969, and achieved university status in 1974. Another metropolitan campus, Portland State University, originated as the Vanport Extension Center in 1946 and attained university status in 1969. Of the new public colleges and universities, none was more innovative—or controversial—than the Evergreen State College, which opened in Olympia in 1971. Eschewing a traditional curriculum, it placed great emphasis on individualized courses of study that seemed especially attuned to the "do your own thing" urges of the 1960s and 1970s. Yet by the mid-1980s, the school had acquired a national reputation for academic excellence.

The campus population leveled off in the mid-1970s, shortly before the region's economy slumped. As a result, the 1980s will be remembered as years of academic malaise, of recurrent funding crises and drastic retrenchment, of salaries that failed to keep pace with inflation, and of declining faculty morale. During the euphoric 1960s and early 1970s, it had been politically popular to create new campuses and institutions, but the consequence was diminished financial resources and diluted educational quality for all state schools during the hard times that followed. When the recession of the early 1980s cut state tax revenues and decreased funding for higher education, the Pacific Northwest's public universities eliminated personnel, programs, and in some cases entire departments.

Northwest elementary and secondary schools experienced a similar cycle. The postwar baby boom swelled school populations in the 1950s and 1960s, created crowded classrooms, and forced school boards to construct a number of new facilities, far more than could be fully utilized when the number of school-age children dropped in the late 1970s. The cost of public education continued to climb, even as parents and educators worried about declining standards and the graduation of high school students woefully unprepared in such basics as mathematics and science, English composition, public speaking, and history.

The baby boom was perhaps the most significant of several population changes to follow the Second World War. Census statistics reveal that Pacific Northwesterners continued to move from rural to urban areas and from urban to suburban areas. They also show that, while the human face of the Pacific Northwest remained overwhelmingly Caucasian and western European in origin, important demographic changes were taking place. In the mid-1980s, Washington had the region's largest non-Caucasian population, more than 10 percent of the state's total—the fastest-growing segment being Asians. This included a new population of refugees from Southeast Asia.

353

90. In an assertion of Native American sovereignty, the
Kutenai Indians of northern Idaho "declared war" on
the United States government in 1974 to gain money
and land. Courtesy *Idaho Statesman*.

Hispanic Americans form the region's largest minority. When the Second World War created a shortage of agricultural labor, the United States government imported workers directly from Mexico to the Pacific Northwest. At one time more than thirty-nine thousand Mexican males were employed in Oregon, Washington, and Idaho. Most lived in farm labor camps, subjected to various forms of exploitation and discrimination. Not allowed to bring their families, workers were thus encouraged to return to Mexico.

In the late 1940s a new wave of Hispanic labor arrived from the Southwest, one that included families lured to the Pacific Northwest by jobs. More migration from Mexico permanently changed the region's minority composition. People of Spanish origin numbered 222,478, or 2.9 percent of the region's total population by 1980. Predominantly Mexican in origin, male, and youthful, they made up at least 10 percent of the population in Yakima, Grant, Adams, and Franklin counties, Washington; Malheur County, Oregon; and Minidoka and Owyhee counties, Idaho. Though these were rural counties and though people of Mexican origin were often stereotyped as agricultural workers, an ever-increasing number of Hispanics found employment in white-collar jobs.

MORE ABOUT THE ARTS

During the years beginning in the late 1920s, but especially after the Second World War, the Pacific Northwest recorded some notable achievements in the arts. Encouraging Northwest writers was *Frontier*, a college literary journal launched in 1927 at the University of Montana by Harold G. Merriam to offer an outlet for regional writing. Together with *Status Rerum*, it goaded Northwest writers to rise above the region's reputation for literary mediocrity and to seek national prominence and critical acclaim. H. L. Davis's Pulitzer Prize–winning novel *Honey in the Horn* (1935) offered inspiration to Northwest novelists and poets.

Another writer of note was Vardis Fisher, whose thirty-six published books began with *Toilers of the Hills* (1928), a novel that vividly portrayed the trials of pioneers in the dry and lonesome sagebrush country of his native Idaho. Fisher, who held a Ph.D. from the University of Chicago, headed the New Deal project to produce a state guide to Idaho. He and his researchers collected so much material that he produced two companion volumes, *The Idaho Encyclopedia* (1938) and *Idaho Lore* (1939), which continue to reflect his skills as a writer.

Theodore Roethke, who arrived from the Midwest to teach at the University of Washington in 1947, stayed until his death in 1963. He produced brooding and introspective poetry that captured the spirit of the Northwest's environment without trivializing it as so many of the region's early poets and novelists had done. Roethke won the 1954 Pulitzer Prize in poetry and had an enormous influence on the region's writers. Richard Hugo, a native of the Pacific Northwest, took advantage of the GI bill to study creative writing with Roethke at the University of Washington and became his disciple. Hugo reflected on his experiences in the Pacific Northwest in several collections of poems that achieved national visibility.

No Northwest writer reached a larger audience than Ken Kesey, whose 1962 novel *One Flew over the Cuckoo's Nest*, a story of individualism versus authority set in an Oregon mental hospital, was made into a prize-winning film. Kesey's other well-known work, *Sometimes a Great Notion* (1964), which is set on the Oregon coast and details the struggle of an individualistic family of gyppo loggers defying bureaucratic organization and authority, was also made into a movie.

Ivan Doig, a professionally trained historian and novelist living in the Seattle area, won critical acclaim with his first book, *This House of Sky: Landscapes of a Western Mind* (1978), an autobiographical account of his youth in Montana. Among his subsequent works is *English Creek* (1984), the first of a trilogy of novels set in post-frontier Montana. The Oregonian Don Berry wrote two novels, *Trask* (1960) and *Moontrap* (1962), which offered sensitive treatment of a mountain man undergoing social transition.

A distinctive, coherent school of thought was more noticeable among the region's postwar visual artists than among its writers. The term Northwest School was first used in 1947 to describe a group of paintings shown in museums in the East. They included the abstract art of Morris Graves, Mark Tobey, Kenneth Callahan, Guy Anderson, and others who found inspiration in rain- and mist-obscured scenes of the Pacific Northwest. That movement attained its greatest prominence during the 1950s.

Not one of the Pacific Northwest states lavished public money on the arts. In the mid-1980s, Idaho's appropriation for the arts placed it dead last in the United States, behind even Puerto Rico, Guam, and American Samoa. When the national average was 85 cents per capita, Idaho spent 13 cents, Oregon 18 cents, and Washington 43 cents. If state spending for the arts is any reflection of public support, then Northwest artists gave the region far better than it deserved.

91. Ivan Doig (b. 1939), historian and award-winning
novelist. Courtesy Ivan Doig.

POLITICAL LIFE: PERSONALITIES AND ISSUES

During the years immediately following the Second World War, Republicans clearly dominated politics in Oregon. Richard Neuberger, one of the
persons most responsible for the rebirth of a viable Democratic party,
quipped in the early 1950s that there were so few Democrats in the Oregon

357

legislature that they could hold their caucus in a phone booth. That changed in 1954 when Neuberger won election to the United States Senate, the first Democrat to do so since 1914. In 1957 Democrats gained control of both houses of the Oregon legislature for the first time since 1878.

In Idaho, Democrats held one of the state's United States Senate seats during all but six years between 1945 and 1981 and the governor's office continuously after 1971, but Republicans clearly dominated public affairs. In Washington during most of the postwar years, Democrats controlled the United States Senate seats, but Republicans claimed the governor's office, particularly during the 1960s and 1970s.

The men and women who represented the Pacific Northwest in the halls of Congress and the statehouses were for the most part uncommonly able people. To put the Northwest's political good fortune in perspective, one need only think of the South's sizable crop of postwar racist demagogues or the Midwest's red-baiting senators, Joseph R. McCarthy of Wisconsin and his cohort William Jenner of Indiana. In the Northwest, only Herman Welker, an Idaho senator from 1951 to 1957, really fit that mold: his staunch support for McCarthy earned him the nickname Little Joe from Idaho.

To be sure, the Pacific Northwest was not immune to political scandal, corrupt public servants, officeholding nonentities, or embarrassments like the Idaho congressman George Hansen, whose zany behavior and stubborn defiance of public disclosure laws earned him the contempt of House colleagues, a felony conviction, and a term in prison. But more than balancing these were senators like Warren G. Magnuson and Henry M. "Scoop" Jackson of Washington, Frank Church of Idaho, and Wayne Morse, Mark Hatfield, and Robert Packwood of Oregon.

In a similar category was Congressman Thomas Foley, a moderate Democrat who represented Washington's Fifth District, a stronghold of conservatism that included both Spokane and Walla Walla. First elected in 1964, Foley won the respect of both his constituents and his colleagues, who chose him as House majority leader in 1987.

Oregon's Tom McCall was one of a trio of exceptionally competent chief executives that included Daniel J. Evans of Washington and Cecil Andrus of Idaho. The two Republicans and the Idaho Democrat got along like brothers. In a reminder that personality and issues commonly took precedence over party labels in Pacific Northwest politics, McCall endorsed Andrus for reelection at some personal risk in 1974, and Evans did likewise when Andrus ran for governor again in 1986. Both Democrats and Republicans could claim outstanding political leaders, while the maverick Morse was at various times a member of each party and an independent.

92. (*Left to right*) Thomas Foley (b. 1929), Henry M.
Jackson (1912–83), and Warren G. Magnuson (b. 1905),
three of the biggest names in Washington politics during the middle and late twentieth century. Courtesy:
University of Washington Archives.

During the years from the mid-1950s until 1980, when the Democrats
controlled the United States Senate, Magnuson and Jackson formed an
exceedingly powerful duo, gaining more seniority than any other senators
from the North and more, too, than most of their colleagues from the one-
party Democratic South. Both men headed major committees and became
noted for aiding their constituents, for looking after the interests of the
Pacific Northwest.

Both senators were New Deal liberals, but Jackson's support for a strong
national defense puzzled other liberals and earned him the reputation of
being "hawkish"—a derogatory term in the liberal vocabulary—of being
"the Senator from Boeing." The former Minnesota senator Eugene McCarthy once laughingly remarked, "You can't get enough security for Henry. If
he had his way the sky would be black with supersonic planes, preferably
Boeings, of course." Jackson's interests actually ranged far beyond national
defense from electric power to the environment. He helped to steer a

number of conservation bills through the Senate, most notably the Wilderness Act of 1964, the Redwoods National Park Act, the Natural Environmental Policy Act of 1969, and the North Cascades National Park Act.

Democrats and Republicans alike respected Jackson as a man of great integrity. At the polls he was unbeatable: he served in Congress from 1941 (the Senate from 1953) until his sudden death in 1983. In the 1970 election he crushed his Republican opponent with an amazing 83.9 percent of the vote. Magnuson served even longer, from 1937 (the Senate from 1944) until the Republican Slade Gorton defeated him in the 1980 election.

When Republicans gained control of the Senate in 1980 for the first time in twenty-five years, Oregon's Mark Hatfield and Robert Packwood assumed roles not unlike those Magnuson and Jackson had played. Joining them after Jackson's death in 1983 was another Republican, Daniel J. Evans, Washington's only three-term governor and a man rated as one of the nation's ten best governors in the twentieth century. From 1963 to 1977, Evans had proved a popular and able chief executive. An engineer by training, he was well suited to deal with matters of administrative reorganization, tax reform, and environmental and social issues. As governor, Evans was regarded as more liberal than many of his Democratic opponents, although during his early years in the Senate he surprised some constituents by sometimes siding with conservatives.

Frank Church was elected to the United States Senate from Idaho in 1956 at the age of 32. Like his idol William Borah, he eventually chaired the Senate's prestigious Committee on Foreign Relations and emerged as a major critic of America's interventionist foreign policy. His outspoken opposition to American participation in the Vietnam War, his support for phasing out American control over the Panama Canal, and an investigation of CIA misdeeds cost him votes in conservative Idaho. A liberal Democrat for twenty-four years in a state growing increasingly conservative, he was narrowly defeated for reelection in 1980 by Steven D. Symms, a Republican spokesman for right-wing causes.

A flamboyant style seemed one way to gain the attention of voters in geographically divided Idaho. Long before Ronald Reagan and other actors entered politics, Idaho had Glen H. Taylor, "the Singing Cowboy." A liberal Democrat, he served in the United States Senate from 1945 to 1951 and as the running mate of Henry Wallace on the 1948 Progressive ticket. Accompanying himself on the banjo, Taylor once gave an informal concert on the Capitol steps that attracted national attention. Though he was a staunch advocate of civil rights and a progressive internationalist, many people

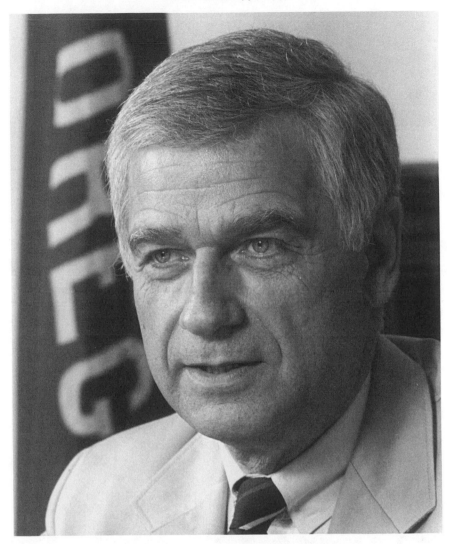

93. Mark O. Hatfield (b. 1922), governor of Oregon
from 1959 to 1967. He was first elected to the United
States Senate in 1966. Courtesy Mark O. Hatfield.

regarded him as nothing more than an opportunist who avidly sought
publicity.

Despite their obvious political differences, Senator Symms was as
skilled a publicist as Taylor. Symms turned up at an anti–gun control news
conference packing two revolvers. "They can call me a right-wing kook," he

94. Daniel J. Evans (b. 1925), governor of Washington
from 1965 to 1977 and United States Senator from
1983 until 1989. Courtesy Daniel J. Evans.

declared, "but I'm out there on the fringe with Ronald Reagan." He won
reelection in 1986, narrowly beating Governor John V. Evans.

From 1983 until 1987, for the first time in fifty years, Republicans held

95. Frank Church holds a portrait of William Edgar
Borah, his predecessor on the Senate Foreign Relations
Committee. Flanking him *left to right* are Senators J.
William Fulbright of Arkansas, Mike Mansfield of
Montana, and Wayne Morse of Oregon. Church (1924–
84) served in the Senate from 1957 to 1981. Courtesy
Boise State University Library, Frank Church Papers.

all six United States Senate seats from the Pacific Northwest. That changed
with the election of 1986 when Brock Adams, former transportation secretary under President Jimmy Carter, unseated Slade Gorton. Two other
Carter cabinet officers also emerged winners: another former transportation secretary, Neil Goldschmidt, was elected governor of Oregon; and
Cecil Andrus, Idaho governor from 1971 to 1977 and secretary of the interior under Carter, returned to the governor's office. Describing himself as a
problem solver, Andrus worked closely with the Republican legislature to
get major funding increases for Idaho education.

Conspicuously missing from the ranks of Northwest politicians has

96. Cecil D. Andrus (b. 1931), governor of Idaho from 1971 to 1977, and 1987–; and United States secretary of the interior, from 1977 to 1981. Courtesy Cecil Andrus.

97. Jeanne Givens (b. 1951), a Coeur d'Alene Indian, is
the first Native American woman elected to the Idaho
legislature (1984–88). Courtesy Jeanne Givens.

been a serious contender for president of the United States. Borah, Church, Jackson, and Morse threw their hats into the ring, but none survived the primaries.[3] Running for president from a remote state with 1 percent or less of the nation's population presented formidable obstacles. Besides, uncommon ability and intelligence were never qualities Americans typically sought in their presidents.

Among high-ranking elected officials in the Pacific Northwest since World War II have been several women. Five served in the House of Representatives—two each from Washington and Oregon and one from Idaho[4]—and one in the Senate. Following the death of Oregon's Senator Neuberger, a liberal Democrat, his wife, Maurine, completed his term and was elected to a full term of her own (1961–67). Another Democrat, Dixy Lee Ray, was elected governor of Washington in 1976. Ray, one of the first two women in the United States elected governor without benefit of a husband's coattails, had never held elective office before, but she benefited from the opportunities afforded newcomers by Washington's open primary system. Though the holder of a doctorate in marine biology from Stanford, Ray was outspoken in her criticism of measures favored by environmentalists, and she also earned the enmity of the press. After one term as governor, she lost a bid for renomination in the Democratic primary. Ray later admitted that she was more a Republican in attitude than a Democrat, something many had long suspected.

No single issue dominated Pacific Northwest politics during the three and one-half decades following the Second World War. Instead, a series of issues competed for public attention. Among those were administrative reorganization, highway construction, tax reform, prison reform, better schools and social services, and a host of environmental issues. Oregon voters on several occasions rejected a sales tax, and Washingtonians an income tax. The fact that Idaho had both income and sales taxes yet remained financially strapped should convince voters in Oregon and Washington that higher taxes alone will not fill a state's treasury.

For a time the cold war and fear of communism were a major issue,

3. Senator Charles McNary of Oregon ran for vice-president on the Republican ticket headed by Wendell Willkie in 1940.

4. These are Nan Wood Honeyman (D) representing northwestern Oregon from 1937 to 1939; Edith Green (D) representing northwestern Oregon from 1955 to 1975; Gracie Pfost (D) representing northern Idaho from 1953 to 1961; Julia Butler Hansen (D) representing southwestern Washington from 1960 to 1975; and Catherine May (R) representing southeastern Washington from 1959 to 1971.

especially in Washington, where conservative Republicans gained control of the state legislature in the 1946 election. The new red scare spilled out of the political arena and onto the campus of the University of Washington. There, three professors were fired following a 1948 investigation by an un-American activities committee under the direction of the state legislator Albert F. Canwell. Professors circulated an open letter criticizing the firing, but only 103 of a faculty of 700 signed it. The case was a model for the rest of American higher education during the McCarthy era.

One exceedingly compelling political issue has been the Pacific Northwest environment at risk. This subject offers a fitting way to conclude the study of a region where arts, politics, and economics seem so closely linked to the natural setting.

CHAPTER 18

An Environment at Risk

*

Below Wallace, the valley of the Coeur d'Alene R[iver] is like something out of Dante's "Inferno." In the days before measures were taken against stream pollution, the R[iver] overflowed every spring, carrying mine wastes into the bottoms & destroying all vegetation.—*The American Guide* (1949)

*

In the Pacific Northwest, as in few other parts of the United States, regional identity is almost wholly linked to natural setting. The Pacific Northwest without its mountains, its rugged coastline, its Puget Sound fogs, its vast interior of sagebrush, rimrock, and big sky is as unthinkable as New England without a Puritan heritage, the South without the Lost Cause, the Midwest without its agricultural cornucopia, or California without its gold rush mentality.

In the Pacific Northwest, however, nature long had to perform double duties. While on one hand she was revered as a source of aesthetic pleasure and outdoor recreation, on the other she was exploited and abused to provide profits and jobs. Until the twentieth century there was little tension between those two views of the environment. Nature had so lavished her favors on the region that few could conceive of her limits—or wanted to. Wilderness was something to be subdued, and water had a limitless capacity to absorb the effluents of industry. Even in the latter part of the twentieth century, the pioneer's belief in nature's abundance refused to die, despite considerable evidence of nature's limits.

To early settlers of the region, nature assumed heroic proportions. People used words like *endless, inexhaustible,* and *spectacular* to describe the land

368

and its resources. Trees like the Douglas fir, sometimes 12 feet in diameter at the base and more than 250 feet tall, were incomparably larger than anything pioneers had known in the East; the fertile topsoil of the Willamette Valley was thought to be dozens of feet deep; and year after year the rivers and tidal estuaries yielded their abundance of fish, clams, and other edibles. When the tide was out, the table was set, according to a pioneer saying. Perpetually snow-clad mountains like Hood, Rainier, and Baker awed and inspired their beholders, and their beauty together with a general lack of severe and destructive storms heightened the impression that nature especially favored the Pacific Northwest.

And so loggers felled the trees—letting daylight into the swamp they called it—with wasteful methods and a misplaced confidence that the region's forests were without end; farmers worried little about conserving the topsoil; fishermen assumed there would always be another big catch; and industries dumped wastes into the Willamette River and Puget Sound, certain that they could always dispose of more. A day of reckoning inevitably arrived, and with it the loss of jobs, diminished yields, and bankruptcies. In a region so heavily dependent upon the bounties of nature, abuse and exhaustion of natural resources raised searching questions about short-term economic readjustments and about the future of the region itself. Coming face to face with nature's limitations—a confrontation especially traumatic in the forest products industry in the late 1970s and early 1980s—produced unease and something of an identity crisis in a region where economic well-being had long been rooted in nature's largess. This brief examination of an environment at risk reveals a region standing at a major crossroads in its history.

A CHANGING LANDSCAPE

Humans have left their mark on the landscape since they first arrived in the Pacific Northwest. Indians occasionally set fire to the forest and thereby altered small sections of their surroundings. But the Indian impress was for the most part subtle and nearly invisible compared to the impact of whites—settlers and nonresident exploiters. Whites not only surveyed the land and laid out their farms and towns in more or less artificial geometric patterns, but they also hastened depletion of natural resources, a characteristic first observed in the maritime fur trade. But that first encounter with nature's limits meant little to a region blessed with so many other resources to exploit.

In the late 1870s commercial fishermen on the lower Columbia noticed diminished catches, and during that decade Oregon took its first halting steps toward conservation. Industry simply shifted its attention to the waters of Puget Sound and continued its profligate ways. The idea that Americans should conserve their abundant natural resources simply had little appeal until the early twentieth century, and even then it remained unpopular in the developing Northwest.

The federal government in the person of President Theodore Roosevelt made a major conservation move shortly after the turn of the twentieth century, when it greatly enlarged the nation's forest preserves. The first of those had been set aside under President Benjamin Harrison in 1891. Roosevelt dramatically increased the number of acres of forest land from 33 million to 150 million and added 23 new forests to the system, for a total of 157 national forests. But to many Pacific Northwest residents, the president's move appeared to be an ill-conceived attempt to atone for the nation's profligate past by controlling its remaining forest lands instead of continuing to sell or give them away to private owners. In a region with millions of acres of federal lands waiting to be exploited, the conservation ethic imposed by Uncle Sam seemed certain to lock up resources and stunt growth. A secondary consideration was states' rights: some Pacific Northwesterners believed that individual states, not the federal government, should manage public lands within their boundaries. Others, however, feared that individual states would only give away more land to private interests.

The battle between development and conservation—and later preservation—would be waged on many fronts during the twentieth century. A popular general concern for the environment is relatively recent, however. Before the 1970s, environmental concern tended to be restricted to protection of a single natural resource so as to preserve profits and livelihoods. Later, pollution came to be viewed as a threat to public health or recreational activities like swimming and sport fishing. Attention then focused on a particular lake or river. Only since the 1970s has a significant portion of the public viewed environmental matters philosophically or in terms of comprehensive biological systems and processes. Indicative of changing attitudes was the Washington legislature's creation of the Department of Ecology in 1970 and its passage a year later of the state's comprehensive Environmental Policy Act. Oregon's Department of Environmental Quality dates from 1969.

One of the earliest cases of environmental concern expressed as a need to protect jobs and profits occurred in the 1920s, when people realized that there were limits to Puget Sound's magnificent water resources, a concern raised first by the growing number of sulphite-process pulp mills along its shores. The problem was not so much the stench in the air as it was the pulp liquor that flowed untreated into Puget Sound. The waters of the sound had long absorbed the organic wastes of fish canneries without difficulty, although residents sometimes complained about the smell, but not even crabs and barnacles could survive in waters laden with pulp liquor.

The prospects of a paper mill in Shelton alarmed commercial oyster growers, who raised the shellfish in beds protected by networks of dikes. In June 1926 they appealed to the state supervisor of fisheries for protection from harmful effluents, but officials did nothing, for oyster growing was a small-scale enterprise with no great influence in Olympia. The yield of the beds declined, and the industry's fear of pollution—primarily a simple matter of economics—proved well founded.

The need to conserve a declining resource for economic reasons also prompted commercial salmon fishermen and cannery operators to address environmental issues. Here was an industry that at one time ranked second only to logging in importance. But the Northwest salmon pack peaked between 1910 and 1919 and declined afterwards. In an effort to halt the downward trend, commercial fishermen and an influential legion of sports fishermen in the 1920s joined forces against destructive practices on Puget Sound. Their primary concern was a proliferation of fish traps. These became illegal in Oregon in 1927 and in Washington five years later.

The law failed to address the fact that net-fishing boats powered by internal-combustion engines were simply too efficient to insure the industry's long-term survival. Craft of that type first appeared on Puget Sound shortly before the First World War, and their numbers increased after the Second World War. Technological advances such as the hydraulic-powered winches first employed in the mid-1950s to work a salmon seine net made them still more efficient. Fishing periods had to be shortened to avoid complete depletion of the fish, but short seasons made it difficult for commercial fishermen to earn a living, much less a profit. Clear-cutting along stream banks exposed spawning grounds to the sun's heat, warming the water and killing salmon fry, which are sensitive to variations in temperature. Removing the riparian vegetation also diminished the insect population, a source of food needed to sustain the fish population.

In their fight for survival, commercial fishermen eventually turned against their former allies, the sports fishermen, although both groups opposed the pulp mills that continued to dump whatever they liked into

Puget Sound. More than anything else, the mills became regional symbols of pollution. The movement that oystermen had initiated in a limited way during the 1920s was taken up by sport fishermen, and in 1945 a bill passed the Washington legislature establishing the state's first independent pollution control board. It was a landmark, but at first the board lacked enough power to be effective, and certainly not all the sound's pollution was caused by pulp and paper mills.

In the mid-1950s, concern about pollution and public health caused residents of the Seattle area to do something about the sewage dumped into Lake Washington. After a lengthy battle, proponents of a big pipeline linking communities around the lake to a treatment plant won a crucial bond vote. The METRO project represented one of the earliest commitments to fight pollution made by any major metropolitan area in the United States. Within a decade Lake Washington was nearly as clean as it once had been.

But Puget Sound remained an object of environmental concern. A federal government report indicated as early as 1951 that the sound was the sixth most polluted area in the United States. But attempts to control the discharge of pulp liquor by requiring the industry to use evaporating ponds raised community hackles in Port Angeles, Bellingham, and other communities that depended on the manufacture of pulp and paper and feared that pollution control measures would cause the mills to close.

Concern mounted in 1969 when a company announced that it planned to lay an oil pipeline under Puget Sound. The Northern Tier project was part of a scheme to transport Alaskan oil to the Midwest. Arriving by supertanker at Port Angeles on the Olympic Peninsula, oil would flow east from that point by pipeline. Opponents ranging from Indian tribes to the Sierra Club feared that if the underwater line ever sprang a leak, the resulting spill would create a monumental disaster, killing wildlife and perhaps permanently fouling one of the state's great natural attractions. Although Washington's Democratic governor, Dixy Lee Ray, favored the project, another and far more powerful Democrat, Senator Warren G. Magnuson, did not. He was responsible for federal legislation that effectively killed the project.

Even without the pipeline, Puget Sound faced a severe pollution problem. The Washington legislature in 1985 formulated a long-term clean-up plan and provided preliminary funding through a tobacco tax. The cleanup of Puget Sound could ultimately cost from $4 billion to $14 billion, more money than it took to build the Alaska pipeline.

The Oregon equivalent of the cleanup of Lake Washington centered on the Willamette River, where the battle cry was sounded by conservation

THE BOLDT DECISION

To non-Indian commercial fishermen, the Boldt decision of 1974 (*United States* v. *Washington*) compounded the problems besetting their declining industry. In a 254-page decision that drew heavily on the region's history and anthropology, the federal judge George Boldt ruled that treaty Indians of Puget Sound were entitled to half of all fish that passed, or normally would pass, by the "usual and accustomed grounds and stations" and that could be caught without endangering the runs.

Indians had long contended that treaties signed in 1854 and 1855 with Isaac I. Stevens guaranteed them the right to continue fishing at all their traditional locations regardless of state laws. To emphasize their concern, In-

dians staged "fish-ins" during the early 1970s. Those acts of civil disobedience were similar to the "freedom rides" that blacks staged in the South in the early 1960s, and both forms of protest occasionally resulted in violence.

To Indians, the Boldt decision represented vindication. To white fishermen, it meant that they were suddenly competing for half as many fish and that Indians now had the other half to themselves. Even after the United States Supreme Court upheld Boldt's decision in 1979, the issue remained a sensitive and potentially explosive blend of economics and race. Boldt was burned in effigy, vilified, accused of having an Indian mistress; he also received several death threats.

groups that described the river as a "stinking, slimy mess" and by Tom McCall's award-winning documentary "Pollution in Paradise." Even Idaho, which included within its boundaries more wilderness land than any other state outside Alaska, discovered major pollution problems. For decades the south fork of the Coeur d'Alene River transported a dangerous load of zinc, cadmium, and lead from numerous mine tailings to the muddy bottom of seemingly pristine Lake Coeur d'Alene.

The lead level in the Coeur d'Alene River delta in the mid-1980s ranged from one thousand to eight thousand parts per million; a normal range was fifteen to twenty parts per million background count. That was perhaps the highest lead level recorded in the United States. As early as 1932 an investigator recommended construction of settling ponds to deal with the problem, but not until 1968 when mining firms were subjected to heavy pressure from state and federal governments did they take that step.

No less dangerous was the smelter-polluted air that hung above Idaho's silver valley until the early 1980s. It resulted in the highest levels of sulphur dioxide gas recorded in the United States. As acid rain, the smelter effluents were responsible for denuding the surrounding hillsides. Schoolchildren in Kellogg, where the massive Bunker Hill smelter was located, recorded abnormally high levels of lead in their blood. Toxic residues so contaminated the silver valley that the Environmental Protection Agency placed it on a list of hazardous sites to be cleaned up by a federal program.

Mining, metal-processing, and pulp mill wastes from Montana increasingly fouled the waters of another northern Idaho river, the Clark Fork, which flows into Lake Pend Oreille. Cleanup will necessarily require cooperation between the two states or federal intervention.

Water and more recently air pollution were two of the Northwest's most talked about environmental problems because they most directly affected the region's largest urban centers, but problems with the land proved serious, too, though many residents remained unaware of them. To pioneers, no natural resource seemed more abundant than land. But how land could be abused and exhausted under the impact of agricultural technology could clearly be seen in the fertile Palouse country of eastern Washington and northern Idaho.

Before the rolling hills of the Palouse became synonymous with the highest wheat yields per acre in the United States, they formed a bunch-grass-covered rangeland favored by sheep and cattle raisers. Toward the latter part of the nineteenth century, new barbed wire fences marked the boundaries of an ever-increasing amount of land devoted to wheat. But with sodbusting came the new problems of the rapid spread of alien weeds and soil erosion.

When it rained, silt-laden water coursed down the steep hillsides and turned the once sparkling Palouse River into a sluggish, dirty stream; after 1910 dust storms became frequent. Despite the warnings of experts, as long as the fertile land produced good crops, farmers did little to stop the soil loss. The historian and agribusinessman Alexander C. McGregor estimated that one small conservation district in Whitman County annually lost the equivalent of a 148-mile-long train of gondola cars filled with silt. A scientist observed in 1973 that the worst soil erosion in the United States was in the Palouse country. There were no easy solutions, however, because alternative methods of farming such as minimum tillage only increased the need for herbicides to kill the weeds not removed by plowing and disking.

Land abuse was not just a matter of soil erosion but also of lack of vision and poor planning. At the time Washington's constitution was written in 1889, the public owned the state's tidelands. But the 1889–90 legislature authorized their sale to private individuals. When the practice was halted in 1971, some 60 percent of Washington's noncoastal tidelands were in private hands.

98. An abandoned farm fifteen miles south of Boardman, Oregon. Badly overgrazed land was subject to
wind erosion. Courtesy Oregon State University
Archives, P89:251.

Public planning designed to prevent private abuse of the land took a
different turn in Oregon. As early as 1899 Clatsop County declared its
beaches to be a public highway. Governor Oswald West declared that
Oregon beaches were public highways in 1911, and two years later the state
extended the right of public access to all its beaches. The enactment of
senate bill 100 in 1973 called for all cities and counties to adopt comprehensive planning to meet state standards known as Statewide Planning Goals.

Depletion of the region's timber supply, perhaps more than any other
resource, had a profound and unsettling impact on Pacific northwesterners.
Tall trees, loggers, and sawmills are so much a part of the region's identity
that it is hard to imagine a Pacific Northwest without them. The belief that
there would always be more trees to cut permeated the thinking of the
region's timber industry. The "cut and run" philosophy led to tremendous
waste, social dislocation, and community instability as one district after
another was logged off.

Disposing of the region's logged-off land was long a vexing question. If it was federal land, the answer was left to Uncle Sam. Logged-off land in private hands might be sold to stump farmers, who attempted to eke a meager living from its thin soil, or it might be simply abandoned to avoid tax liabilities. Another possibility was reforestation. The Weyerhaeuser Timber Company in 1941 initiated the development of tree farms. The dream was to reforest logged-off land so as to produce a sustained yield, but many smaller concerns did not have the financial strength or vision necessary to operate a successful reforestation program. After all, a company needed a source of income until new growth timber matured some thirty or forty years later. Sustained yield remained an elusive goal, especially when companies might turn their attention to maturing stands of second growth timber in the South.

WHAT OF THE FUTURE?

Livability is a quality often attributed to Pacific Northwest towns and cities. But whether cities of the next generation remain livable remains to be seen. Portland, which had taken great pride in its ranking as the nation's most livable city in 1975, slipped to eighth place in 1981 and to sixty-third place in 1985. Uncertainties clouded the future of the region's outdoor recreation facilities, too.

The Pacific Northwest's environment remains vulnerable on two fronts. One is thoughtless development and the other is pollution. Development is not simply a matter of filling in wetlands to create a golf course or a condominium complex. It also means the transformation of prime agricultural land into look-alike suburban housing tracts and other tasteless outgrowths of metropolitan America. And it means damming scenic canyons to control floods or produce electricity.

One of the monumental political battles in the Pacific Northwest since the Second World War has centered on damming up the Snake River's scenic Hells Canyon. The controversy began in 1950 and ultimately ended up in the United States Supreme Court. It pitted proponents of private power against backers of public power and both of them against preservation, an issue that arose in the mid-1960s and gradually won the day. Environmental concerns helped turn a local issue into a national one. The outcome was the 650,000-acre Hells Canyon National Recreation Area created in 1975 despite a last-minute effort by Congressmen George Hansen and Steve Symms of Idaho to turn the canyon over to private power companies. Nonetheless, Idaho Power completed a massive dam at the southern end of

NATIONAL PARKS IN THE PACIFIC NORTHWEST

	Location	Size in 1982 (Acres)	Date Created
Yellowstone	Wyoming/Montana/Idaho	2,219,823	1872
Mount Rainier	Washington	235,404	1899
Crater Lake	Oregon	160,290	1902
Glacier	Montana	1,013,595	1910
Olympic	Washington	914,579	1938
North Cascades	Washington	504,781	1968

the natural wonder in 1968, and developers still talk of building another north of the canyon.

A similar battle in the 1980s centered on a ninety-mile-long section of the Columbia River gorge between The Dalles and Portland. Opponents of a national scenic area feared that communities hemmed in by the preserve would become ghost towns; they preferred development to aesthetics. Late in 1986 President Ronald Reagan signed a bill creating the Columbia River Gorge Scenic Area, its 277,000 acres to be managed by the United States Forest Service.

Besides the Columbia Gorge Scenic Area, the Pacific Northwest today includes six national parks, national monuments like the Oregon Caves and Idaho's Craters of the Moon, national recreation areas like Hells Canyon on the Oregon-Idaho border and Oregon Dunes on the coast, more than 6.5 million acres of wilderness land, and numerous Forest Service campgrounds. After Mount Saint Helens National Volcanic Monument opened in 1983, it became an increasingly popular tourist attraction. Oregon led the way in creation of state parks, with Idaho a very distant third, although, ironically, Idaho created the region's first true state park in 1911 at Lake Chatcolet (now Heyburn State Park).[1]

Setting aside state and federal land as parks and recreation areas was often justified in economic terms—either the land was worthless, lacking minerals and timber, or the action was a way to generate tourist dollars. But what about wilderness lands? For many people, that question poses another, whether it is better to log or mine the backcountry for the sake of jobs

1. Washington obtained its first state park in 1915 and Oregon in 1920.

99. Crater Lake, Oregon's only national park, was
created by Congress in 1912. A party of prospectors
discovered the natural wonder in 1853. Courtesy
Oregon State Historical Society: 48833.

and profits or to preserve the region's remaining wilderness areas for their
own special qualities. Critics charge that locking up land is elitist and
economically indefensible. The Idaho congressman Larry Craig proposed in
the summer of 1986 to build a two-lane paved highway into the heart of the
2.2-million-acre Frank Church River of No Return Wilderness area so as to
make it more accessible to tourists. To lovers of wilderness the idea makes
as much sense as crushing Plymouth Rock and distributing the pieces to
the fifty states to make history more accessible to schoolchildren. Environmentalists respond that the nation needs wild country even if most people
only drive to the edge for a quick look.

The wilderness controversy has a lengthy history. America's first designated wild land areas were set aside in 1924. By the end of the 1950s, it
became obvious in the face of a housing boom that some of the Forest
Service's dwindling wild lands would have to be reserved. In the Wilderness
Act of 1964 Congress gave its protection to 9.1 million acres of forest land in

the West previously classified as wild or wilderness, and in so doing, it precipitated a lengthy debate on how much more land to include in those areas. Environmental groups and timber and mining interests locked horns for a protracted fight. As of 1985 the amount of congressionally designated wilderness land totaled 3,868,254 acres in Idaho, 1,214,208 acres in Oregon, and 1,502,050 acres in Washington.

The region's ongoing battles over pollution are not entirely removed from the controversy over wilderness lands. Some struggles have been won, but others, potentially more severe, remain to bedevil future generations of Pacific Northwesterners. These run the gamut from destructive oil spills on Puget Sound to chemical dumps leaching into the groundwater. Yet none of those problems will endure longer than that of improper disposal of nuclear waste at the Hanford reservation.

In May 1986, Hanford gained the dubious distinction of being selected one of three semifinalists to become the nation's sole dump site for high-level nuclear waste. Except for residents of nearby Richland, Kennewick, and Pasco who envisioned the possibility of new jobs, most Washingtonians were dismayed at the prospect of becoming the nation's nuclear garbage can. The state's Democratic governor and Republican attorney general joined hands to mount a court challenge to the federal decision.

Why the concern? Since the Second World War, Washingtonians had generally accepted Hanford's nuclear presence without protest or undue worry. In early 1986, however, some thirty-nine thousand pages of declassified federal documents disclosed that the Hanford reservation was anything but a good neighbor. The documents revealed that several thousand tons of pollutants—including radioactive arsenic, iodine, manganese and other heavy metals—had been dumped into the Columbia River during Hanford's first decade of operation. Over a forty-year period, billions of gallons of radioactive cooling water containing six hundred pounds of plutonium and hundreds of thousands of pounds of uranium had simply been dumped onto the soil. Those wastes, which were poured into septic tank–like cribs, ponds, and ditches, contained 3.2 million curies of radiation. Plutonium, one of humanity's most toxic substances, causes lung cancer if inhaled.

On several occasions beginning in the mid-1940s, substantial amounts of radioactive material were released into the atmosphere—340,000 curies of Iodine 131 gas in 1945 alone—thousands of times the 14 curies released by the Three Mile Island accident in Pennsylvania in 1979. The largest discharges were detected in Spokane, a hundred miles to the northeast. All

100. The age of environmental innocence: a picnic on
the Coeur d'Alene River during the lazy days of summer 1897. Courtesy University of Idaho Library:
8–X331, Barnard-Stockbridge Collection.

of this led some people to wonder whether these releases and the 160 percent increase in infant mortality recorded in three downwind counties in the 1940s, a time when the rest of Oregon and Washington recorded a decrease, were somehow related.[2] Finally, only weeks before the May 1986 announcement, a disaster at the Chernobyl nuclear power facility in the Soviet Union caused heavy loss of life and heightened global fears of the atom.

In the fall of 1986, even before the full extent of the Hanford mess was revealed, Washington voters approved referendum 40 by a lopsided 86 percent. The state hoped to send Congress the message that it did not want to be the nation's first high-level nuclear depository. Russell Jim, a tribal spokesman for the Yakima Nation, which borders the Hanford reservation,

2. In addition to radioactive discharges, during a two-year period in the mid-1980s, a plutonium plant at Hanford spewed some 20 tons of the carcinogen carbon tetrachloride into the air of eastern Washington.

said of the referendum, "This is the first time in history that the state of Washington and the Yakima Nation have ever been on the same side."

Late in 1987 Congress chose Nevada as the depository site. It would have been a terrible irony if the Pacific Northwest, a region long famed for its special environmental qualities, had become home to all the high-level nuclear waste generated in the East. Even so, as the region heads toward the year 2000, its environment remains at risk from a number of other threats, including the radioactive waste already stored at Hanford.

Epilogue: A Hinterland Still?

Is it still appropriate to describe the Pacific Northwest as an American hinterland? In what way does the region remain remote from the nation's centers of population and influence?

In his 1982 best seller, *Megatrends,* John Naisbitt classified Washington as one of America's five bellwether states. Along with California, Colorado, Connecticut, and Florida, it was a state "in which most social invention occurs in this country." Naisbitt noted that Washington was one of the first states to elect a woman governor in her own right and that Seattle was the first place in the nation to outlaw mandatory retirement laws. He might have added that in the 1970 election, Washington became the first state in which a majority of voters favored legalized abortion. Such trend-setting behavior hardly seems characteristic of a hinterland.

As the United States faces a future that is increasingly linked to Asia, the cities of Seattle, Tacoma, and Portland function as strategic gateways to the Pacific rim. Washington's international trade topped $33 billion in 1985, airplanes being the state's chief export, followed by grain, logs, aluminum, and fish. Japan alone accounted for 50 percent of Oregon's total trade dollars in the mid-1980s; Korea and Taiwan ranked a distant second and third. Some observers already speak of the old Pacific Northwest as Japan's new opportunity-rich Pacific North*east*.

Evidence of the region's loss of hinterland status abounds. An observer need spend only a few hours at the Seattle-Tacoma International Airport ("Seatac") to realize how the sprawling complex of runways and terminals functions as a hub for an air transportation network that links remote communities in the Pacific Northwest with New York and Washington, D.C., in a matter of hours. Even a casual reading of computer magazines reveals how great an impact the programmers of Bellevue and Redmond have on future generations of computer software. The University of Washington ranks first among the nation's public universities in the amount of federal research and development money received. Any farm or ranch with a satellite television receiver gains instant awareness of events around the world.

Yet, if it is no longer appropriate to describe the entire region as an American hinterland, it is undeniable that many parts the Pacific Northwest do retain hinterland characteristics. The juxtaposition of metropolitan trend-setter and hinterland is, in fact, the defining quality of life in the modern Northwest. The accessibility of the hinterland from metropolitan centers remains the *key* feature of what residents regard as a desirable lifestyle. It is appropriate that two of the nation's best-known manufacturers and marketers of outdoor wear —Eddie Bauer and REI—originated and are still headquartered in Seattle.

The juxtaposition of trend-setter and hinterland is apparent in a myriad of different ways across the Pacific Northwest. Even as I type these words in Moscow, Idaho, using the most up-to-date version of Microsoft Word, I glance south across a rolling landscape of wheat and barley that stretches as far as the horizon. From my hilltop office I see an occasional barn and storage bin, but mostly the country is empty. Although farm equipment is modern, some of the seasonal rhythms of ranch life in the Palouse country have scarcely changed during the past century.

Yet within eight miles of my home are two public universities conducting state-of-the-art research in many fields. In such a setting it hardly seems possible that only last fall a bear ambled into Moscow from the nearby mountains and had a good look around before being captured. Or that one day last summer a large hawk flew into my classroom to enliven a discussion of Pacific Northwest history. I recall, too, the nights spent camped with a class on the Lewis and Clark trail in the Bitterroot Mountains. At dusk when the stars first came out and only the profiles of the mountains were still visible, we saw almost exactly what Lewis and Clark saw nearly two hundred years ago. The closest telephone and gas station were fifty miles away.

When an anthropology professor from Washington State University proposed to use sophisticated equipment to search the mountains of southeastern Washington for a "sasquatch," a legendary Northwest creature also known as a bigfoot, that somehow managed to elude humans in that remote region, many people scoffed. Yet, whether the venture is credible or not, anyone who has tramped through remote canyons in the Blue Mountains, the Cascades, or the Olympics can understand the feeling that in some remote part of the region an unsolved mystery of nature may still await the persistent searcher. In this regard, it is worth recalling that the mountainous interior of the Olympic Peninsula was first entered by white explorers only in 1890, well after their counterparts had penetrated into the heart of Africa.

The juxtaposition between hinterland and trend-setter is observable when killer whales beach within sight of Seattle's tall buildings. It occurs when new vineyards rise from the sagebrush-covered hills of southeastern Washington. Wine is one of the Pacific Northwest's newest industries, and wineries are located in all three states. During the last ten years, the wineries of Washington have grown from a handful to sixty-seven, and vintners now brag that they produce more premium wine than any other state except California.

Obviously, some parts of the Pacific Northwest will long remain hinter-lands in the thinking of metropolitan Pacific Northwesterners, and of many easterners, too. For urban dwellers on Puget Sound, a trip to Pullman to attend a conference at Washington State University on the state's eastern edge is a venture into the hinterland. The entire state of Idaho remains a hinterland in the minds of many Americans, and an article of Idaho folklore is the person who when back East introduces himself as being from Idaho, and is met with the misinformed response, "Yes, but back here we pronounce it Ohio."

Not without reason does Idaho currently sell itself as the Great Getaway. The Frank Church River of No Return Wilderness area is the largest in the lower forty-eight states. Capitalizing on nature's abundance, Idaho lures tourists from the city to dude ranches, white-water rafting, and mountain trails. White-water rafting is now a multimillion-dollar business for outfitters and guides.

Yet even in Idaho, the hinterland is receding. Boise has more Fortune 500 companies than any other city of its size in America. High tech firms have located plants in Boise and Nampa. Farther east on the Snake River plain is the Idaho National Engineering Laboratory, which employs ten thousand people and provides 5 percent of Idaho's jobs. Dating from 1949, the laboratory produced the nation's first electricity from nuclear energy in 1951 and still trains hundreds of nuclear submarine crewmen every year. Its scientists engage in a number of research projects involving electric vehicles, lasers, and biotechnology. In the Idaho panhandle, Duane Hagadone spent $60 million to build a world-class resort on the shore of Lake Coeur d'Alene.

It is the continuing juxtaposition of hinterland and trend-setter that will likely shape the course of public debate into the twenty-first century. Legislatures and courts will probably have to resolve the conflict that is inevitable between metropolitan dwellers who regard the nonagricultural hinterland as a recreational escape and those people who wish to exploit it for its natural resources.

In the name of jobs will legislators and other public officials permit logging or mining of lands better set aside as a wilderness heritage for future generations of northwesterners more likely to spend their working lives in offices than in the fields, forests, or mines? It is worth noting that the Pacific Northwest already has more teachers than loggers, more professionals than commercial fishermen. A sense of the region's past will help the present generation to understand better the kind of Pacific Northwest that evolved in recent years when the modern metropolis intersected with a hinterland rich in beauty and natural resources.

The Pacific Northwest:
A Statistical Portrait

TABLE I: AREA

(IN SQUARE MILES)

	Land Only	Total	Rank among States
Idaho	82,677	83,557	13th
Oregon	96,184	96,981	10th
Washington	66,570	68,912	20th
Total		249,450	

Note: The Pacific Northwest constitutes 8.2 percent of the total area of the continental United States.

For Comparison:

	Land Only	Total	Rank among States
Alaska	569,600	589,757	1st
Texas	262,134	267,338	2d
California	156,361	158,693	3d
Montana	145,587	147,138	4th
Delaware	1,984	2,057	49th
Rhode Island	1,049	1,214	50th
British Columbia		365,950	
France		210,040	
Federal Republic of Germany		96,011	
Switzerland		15,941	

TABLE 2: COASTLINE AND SHORELINE

(IN MILES)

	Coastline	Shoreline
Oregon	296	1,410
Washington	157	3,026
For Comparison:		
California	840	3,427
Alaska	6,640	42,819
Atlantic and Gulf coasts (U.S.)	3,700	45,814

TABLE 3: RIVERS

	Average Discharge at Mouth (Cubic Feet per Second)	Length (Miles)	Drainage Area (Square Miles)
Columbia	262,000	1,243	258,000
Snake	50,000	1,038	109,000
Willamette	35,660	270	11,200
Pend Oreille	29,900	490	25,820
Deschutes	5,800	250	10,500
John Day	2,000	281	7,580
Fraser	128,000	850	89,900
For Comparison:			
Mississippi/Missouri	640,000	3,710	1,247,300
Amazon	7,000,000	4,000	2,722,000
Nile	100,000	4,145	1,107,227

TABLE 4: STATE POPULATIONS, 1980

	Number	*Rank among States*
Idaho	943,935[a]	41st
Oregon	2,633,105	30th
Washington	4,132,156	20th
Total	7.5 million[b]	
	For comparison:	
California	23,667,902	1st
Alaska	401,851	50th
U.S.	226,545,805	

[a]The population of Idaho was only slightly larger than that of Dallas, Texas, with 904,078 residents.
[b]The total population of the Pacific Northwest was approximately equal to that of the Los Angeles–Long Beach metropolitan area, with 7,477,503 residents.

TABLE 5: POPULATION DENSITY, 1980
(PER SQUARE MILE OF LAND AREA)

Idaho	11.5
Oregon	27.4
Washington	62.1
For Comparison:	
Alaska	0.7
New Jersey	986.2
California	151.4
U.S.	64.0

Note: If the Pacific Northwest were as densely populated as New Jersey, it would contain more residents than the entire United States currently does.

TABLE 6: POPULATION CHANGE, 1970–1980

	Percent	Rank among States
Idaho	+32.4	7th
Oregon	+25.9	11th
Washington	+21.0	13th
For Comparison:		
Nevada	+63.5	1st
New York	− 3.8	50th

TABLE 7: RESIDENT POPULATION IN METROPOLITAN AREAS, 1985

	Percent	Rank among States
Idaho	19.1	50th
Oregon	67.2	23d
Washington	80.9	13th
For Comparison:		
New Jersey	100.0	1st
California	95.7	2d
U.S.	76.5	

TABLE 8: POPULATION AGED 10 YEARS AND YOUNGER, 1980

	Percent	*Rank among States*
Idaho	18.7	2d
Oregon	14.7	31st
Washington	14.6	33d
	For Comparison:	
Utah	23.0	1st
Florida	12.2	50th
U.S.	14.6	

TABLE 9: SELECTED MINORITY POPULATIONS, 1980

	Black		*Hispanic*		*Native American*	
	number	*percent*	*number*	*percent*	*number*	*percent*
Idaho	2,716	0.3	36,615	3.9	10,418	1.1
Oregon	37,059	1.4	65,833	2.5	26,587	1.0
Washington	105,544	2.6	119,986	2.9	58,159	1.4
	For Comparison:					
California		7.6		19.2		0.8
Mississippi		35.2		1.0		0.2
New Mexico		1.9		36.5		8.1
U.S.		11.7		6.7		0.6

TABLE 10: RESIDENTS BORN OUTSIDE THE USA
(PERCENTAGE)

Idaho	2.3
Oregon	4.2
Washington	5.8

For Comparison:

California	14.8
Mississippi	0.9
U.S.	6.2

TABLE 11: PER CAPITA PERSONAL INCOME, 1985

	Dollars	*Rank among States*
Idaho	11,120	41st
Oregon	12,622	29th
Washington	13,876	16th

For Comparison:

Alaska	18,187	1st
Mississippi	9,187	50th

	High School		*College*	
	Percent of population	*Rank among States*	*Percent of population*	*Rank among States*
Idaho	72.8	12th	16.1	22d
Oregon	74.7	8th	17.2	18th
Washington	77.0	5th	18.8	11th
		For Comparison:		
Alaska	82.9	1st	22.4	2d
Arkansas	54.9	48th	9.7	50th
Kentucky	51.9	50th	11.0	48th
U.S.	66.3		16.3	

	Dollars	*Rank among States*
Idaho	2,509	48th
Oregon	4,123	12th
Washington	3,705	20th
	For Comparison:	
Alaska	8,349	1st
Mississippi	2,305	49th
Utah	2,297	50th
U.S.	3,723	

TABLE 14: MAJOR CRIMES, 1980
(PER 100,000 POPULATION)

	Rate	Rank among States
Murder and Negligent Manslaughter		
Idaho	3.1	42d
Oregon	5.1	35th
Washington	5.5	34th
	For Comparison:	
Nevada	20.0	1st
South Dakota	0.7	50th
Forcible Rape		
Idaho	22.4	39th
Oregon	41.5	13th
Washington	52.7	5th
	For Comparison:	
Nevada	67.2	1st
North Dakota	9.5	50th
Robbery		
Idaho	46.8	43d
Oregon	152.4	21st
Washington	135.1	24th
	For Comparison:	
Nevada	460.6	2d
New York	641.3	1st
North Dakota	7.7	50th

Suggestions for Further Reading

CHAPTER I: A SENSE OF PLACE

Athearn, Robert G. *The Mythic West in Twentieth-Century America.* Lawrence: University Press of Kansas, 1986.

Austin, Judith. "Desert, Sagebrush, and the Pacific Northwest." In *Regionalism and the Pacific Northwest,* edited by William G. Robbins, Robert J. Frank, and Richard E. Ross. Corvallis: Oregon State University Press, 1983.

Bingham, Edwin R., and Glen A. Love, eds. *Northwest Perspectives: Essays on the Culture of the Pacific Northwest.* Seattle: University of Washington Press, 1979.

Brown, Richard Maxwell. "Rainfall and History: Perspectives on the Pacific Northwest." In *Experiences in a Promised Land: Essays in Pacific Northwest History,* edited by G. Thomas Edwards and Carlos A. Schwantes. Seattle: University of Washington Press, 1986.

Cantwell, Robert. *The Hidden Northwest.* Philadelphia: J. B. Lippincott, 1972.

Clark, Norman H. *Washington: A Bicentennial History.* New York: W. W. Norton, 1976.

Dicken, Samuel N., and Emily F. Dicken. *Oregon Divided: A Regional Geography.* Portland: Oregon Historical Society, 1982.

Dodds, Gordon B. *The American Northwest: A History of Oregon and Washington.* Arlington Heights, Ill.: Forum Press, 1986.

———. *Oregon: A Bicentennial History.* New York: W. W. Norton, 1977.

Edwards, G. Thomas, and Carlos A. Schwantes, eds. *Experiences in a Prom-*

ised Land: Essays in Pacific Northwest History. Seattle: University of Washington Press, 1986.

Garreau, Joel. *The Nine Nations of North America.* Boston, Houghton Mifflin, 1981.

Gastil, Raymond D. *Cultural Regions of the United States.* Seattle: University of Washington Press, 1975.

Highsmith, Richard M., Jr., and A. Jon Kimerling. *Atlas of the Pacific Northwest.* 7th ed. Corvallis: Oregon State University Press, 1985.

Jensen, Merrill, ed. *Regionalism in America.* Madison: University of Wisconsin Press, 1965.

Limerick, Patricia Nelson. *The Legacy of Conquest: The Unbroken Past of the American West.* New York: W. W. Norton, 1987.

Loy, William G., Stuart Allan, and Clyde P. Patton. *Atlas of Oregon.* Eugene: University of Oregon, 1976.

Paul, Rodman. *The Far West and the Great Plains in Transition, 1859–1900.* New York: Harper and Row, 1988.

Peirce, Neal R. *The Mountain States of America: People, Politics, and Power in the Eight Rocky Mountain States.* New York: W. W. Norton, 1972.

———. *The Pacific States of America: People, Politics, and Power in the Five Pacific Basin States.* New York: W. W. Norton, 1972.

Peterson, F. Ross. *Idaho: A Bicentennial History.* New York: W. W. Norton, 1976.

Pomeroy, Earl. *The Pacific Slope: A History of California, Oregon, Washington, Idaho, Utah, and Nevada.* New York: Alfred A. Knopf, 1968.

Ramsey, Jarold. " 'New Era': Growing up East of the Cascades, 1937–1950." In *Regionalism and the Pacific Northwest,* edited by William G. Robbins, Robert J. Frank, and Richard E. Ross. Corvallis: Oregon State University Press, 1983.

Schwantes, Carlos, Katherine Morrissey, David Nicandri, and Susan Strasser, eds. *Washington: Images of a State's Heritage.* Spokane: Melior Publications, 1988.

Shane, Scott. *Discovering Mount St. Helens: A Guide to the National Volcanic Monument.* Seattle: University of Washington Press, 1985.

Warren, Sidncy. *Farthest Frontier: The Pacific Northwest.* 1949. Reprint. Port Washington, N.Y.: Kennikat Press, 1970.

Winks, Robin. "Regionalism in Comparative Perspective." In *Regionalism and the Pacific Northwest,* edited by William G. Robbins, Robert J.

Frank, and Richard E. Ross. Corvallis: Oregon State University Press, 1983.

The Compact Atlas of Idaho. Moscow: University of Idaho, 1983.

PROFILE: THE THIRD VOYAGE OF CAPTAIN JAMES COOK

Beaglehole, J. C. *The Life of Captain James Cook.* Stanford: Stanford University Press, 1974.

Conner, Daniel, and Lorraine Miller. *Master Mariner: Capt. James Cook and the Peoples of the Pacific.* Seattle: University of Washington Press, 1978.

Cook, James. *The Journals of Captain James Cook on His Voyages of Discovery.* 3 vols. Edited by J. C. Beaglehole. Cambridge: Hakluyt Society, 1955–69.

Fisher, Robin, and Hugh Johnson, eds. *Captain James Cook and His Times.* Seattle: University of Washington Press, 1979.

Goetzmann, William H. *New Lands, New Men: America and the Second Great Age of Discovery.* New York: Viking, 1986.

Gough, Barry M. *Distant Dominion: Britain and the Northwest Coast of North America.* Vancouver: University of British Columbia Press, 1980.

Hough, Richard. *The Last Voyage of Captain James Cook.* New York: William Morrow, 1979.

Pethick, Derek. *First Approaches to the Northwest Coast.* Vancouver: J. J. Douglas, 1976.

Villiers, Alan. *Captain James Cook.* New York: Charles Scribner's Sons, 1967.

Withey, Lynne. *Voyages of Discovery: Captain Cook and the Exploration of the Pacific.* New York: William Morrow, 1987.

CHAPTER 2: THE FIRST PACIFIC NORTHWESTERNERS

Cole, Douglas. *Captured Heritage: The Scramble for Northwest Coast Artifacts.* Seattle: University of Washington Press, 1985.

Drucker, Philip. *Indians of the Northwest Coast.* New York: McGraw-Hill, 1955.

Fagan, Brian M. *The Great Journey: The Peopling of Ancient America.* New York: Thames and Hudson, 1987.

Kirk, Ruth. *Tradition and Change on the Northwest Coast: The Makah,*

Nuu-chah-nulth, Southern Kwakiutl and Nuxalk. Seattle: University of Washington Press, 1986.

Kirk, Ruth, with Richard D. Daugherty. *Exploring Washington Archaeology*. Seattle: University of Washington Press, 1978.

McFeat, Tom, ed. *Indians of the North Pacific Coast*. Seattle: University of Washington Press, 1967.

Madsen, Brigham. *The Bannock of Idaho*. Caldwell: Caxton Press, 1958.

Miller, Christopher L. *Prophetic Worlds: Indians and Whites on the Columbia Plateau*. New Brunswick, N.J.: Rutgers University Press, 1985.

Ramsey, Jarold, ed. *Coyote Was Going There: Indian Literature of the Oregon Country*. Seattle: University of Washington Press, 1977.

Ruby, Robert H., and John A. Brown. *A Guide to the Indian Tribes of the Pacific Northwest*. Norman: University of Oklahoma Press, 1986.

Stern, Theodore. *The Klamath Tribe: A People and Their Reservation*. Seattle: University of Washington Press, 1966.

Walker, Deward E., Jr. *Indians of Idaho*. Moscow: University Press of Idaho, 1978.

―――. *Myths of Idaho Indians*. Moscow: University Press of Idaho, 1980.

Zucker, Jeff, Kay Hummel, and Bob Høgfoss. *Oregon Indians: Culture, History and Current Affairs; An Atlas and Introduction*. Portland: Oregon Historical Society, 1983.

CHAPTER 3: THE NORTH PACIFIC MARITIME FRONTIER

Anderson, Bern. *Surveyor of the Sea: The Life and Voyages of Captain George Vancouver*. Seattle: University of Washington Press, 1960.

Cook, Warren. *Flood Tide of Empire: Spain and the Pacific Northwest, 1543–1819*. New Haven: Yale University Press, 1973.

Doig, Ivan. *The Sea Runners*. New York: Atheneum, 1982. This novel is based on a true account of escape by canoe from New Archangel, Alaska, to Astoria, Oregon.

Engstrand, Iris H. W. *Spanish Scientists in the New World: The Eighteenth-Century Expeditions*. Seattle: University of Washington Press, 1981. Especially pp. 44–75 on the Malaspina expedition.

Fisher, Raymond H. *Bering's Voyages: Whither and Why*. Seattle: University of Washington Press, 1977.

Henry, John Frazier. *Early Maritime Artists of the Pacific Northwest Coast, 1741–1841*. Seattle: University of Washington Press, 1984.

Lower, J. Arthur. *Ocean of Destiny: A Concise History of the North Pacific, 1500–1978.* Vancouver: University of British Columbia Press, 1978.

Pethick, Derek. *First Approaches to the Northwest Coast.* Vancouver, B.C.: J. J. Douglas, 1976.

———. *The Nootka Connection: Europe and the Northwest Coast, 1790–1795.* Vancouver, B.C.: Douglas and McIntyre, 1980.

Tikhmenev, P. A. *A History of the Russian-American Company.* Translated and edited by Richard A. Pierce and Alton S. Donnelly. Seattle: University of Washington Press, 1978.

Vaughan, Thomas. *Soft Gold: The Fur Trade and Cultural Exchange on the Northwest Coast of America.* Portland: Oregon Historical Society, 1982.

Walker, Alexander. *An Account of a Voyage to the Northwest Coast of America in 1785 and 1786 by Alexander Walker.* Edited by Robin Fisher and J. M. Bumsted. Seattle: University of Washington Press, 1982.

CHAPTER 4: CONTINENTAL DREAMS AND FUR EMPIRES

Allen, John Logan. *Passage through the Garden: Lewis and Clark and the Image of the American Northwest.* Urbana: University of Illinois Press, 1975.

Billington, Ray Allen. *The Far Western Frontier, 1830–1860.* New York: Harper and Brothers, 1956.

DeVoto, Bernard, ed. *The Journals of Lewis and Clark.* Boston: Houghton Mifflin, 1953.

Galbraith, John S. *The Hudson's Bay Company as an Imperial Factor, 1821–1869.* Berkeley: University of California Press, 1957.

Goetzmann, William H. *Exploration and Empire: The Explorer and Scientist in the Winning of the American West.* New York: Alfred A. Knopf, 1966.

———. *New Lands, New Men: America and the Second Great Age of Discovery.* New York: Viking, 1986.

Hafen, LeRoy R., ed. *Mountain Men and Fur Traders of the West.* Reprinted from *Mountain Men and the Fur Trade of the West,* 10 vols., 1965–72. Lincoln: University of Nebraska Press, 1982.

Irving, Washington. *Astoria; or, Anecdotes of an Enterprise beyond the Rocky Mountains.* Edited by Richard Dilworth Rust. Boston: Twayne Publishing, 1976.

Jackson, Donald, ed. *Letters of the Lewis and Clark Expedition with Re-*

lated Documents, 1783–1854. 2d ed. Urbana: University of Illinois Press, 1978.

——. *Thomas Jefferson and the Stony Mountains: Exploring the West from Monticello*. Urbana: University of Illinois Press, 1981.

Merk, Frederick, ed. *Fur Trade and Empire: George Simpson's Journal*. rev. ed. Cambridge: Harvard University Press, 1968.

Moulton, Gary E., ed. *The Journals of the Lewis and Clark Expedition*. 5 vols. to date. Lincoln: University of Nebraska Press, 1983–.

Rich, E. E. *The History of the Hudson's Bay Company, 1670–1870*. 2 vols. London: Hudson's Bay Record Society, 1958–59.

Ronda, James P. *Lewis and Clark among the Indians*. Lincoln: University of Nebraska Press, 1984.

Ross, Alexander. *Adventures of the First Settlers on the Oregon or Columbia River, 1810–1813*. 1849. Reprint. Lincoln: University of Nebraska Press, 1986.

PROFILE: THE WHITMAN MASSACRE

Drury, Clifford M. *Marcus and Narcissa Whitman and the Opening of Old Oregon*. 2 vols. Glendale, Calif.: Arthur H. Clark, 1973.

Idaho Yesterdays 31 (Spring/Summer 1987): 2–116. This special issue is devoted entirely to the missionary era of Pacific Northwest history. Its thirteen essays cover various facets of the topic.

Ruby, Robert H., and John A. Brown. *The Cayuse Indians: Imperial Tribesmen of Old Oregon*. Norman: University of Oklahoma Press, 1972.

Thompson, Erwin N. *Shallow Grave at Waiilatpu: The Sagers' West*. Portland: Oregon Historical Society, 1973.

Whitman, Narcissa Prentiss. *My Journal, 1836*. Edited by Lawrence Dodd. Fairfield, Wash.: Ye Galleon Press, 1982.

CHAPTER 5: BOUND FOR THE PROMISED LAND

Bowen, William A. *The Willamette Valley: Migration and Settlement on the Oregon Frontier*. Seattle: University of Washington Press, 1978.

Clark, Malcolm, Jr. *Eden Seekers: The Settlement of Oregon, 1818–1862*. Boston: Houghton Mifflin, 1981.

Cloud, Barbara. "Oregon in the 1820s: The Congressional Perspective." *Western Historical Quarterly* 12 (1981): 145–64.

Dicken, Samuel N., and Emily F. Dicken. *The Making of Oregon: A Study in Historical Geography*. Portland: Oregon Historical Society, 1979.

Drury, Clifford M. *Nine Years with the Spokane Indians: The Diary, 1838– 1848, of Elkanah Walker*. Glendale, Calif.: Arthur H. Clark, 1976.

Faragher, John Mack. *Women and Men on the Overland Trail*. New Haven: Yale University Press, 1979.

Horner, Patricia V. "Mary Richardson Walker: The Shattered Dreams of a Missionary Woman." *Montana, the Magazine of Western History* 32 (Summer 1982): 20–31. This issue is devoted to nineteenth-century women on the frontier.

Johansen, Dorothy O. "A Working Hypothesis for the Study of Migrations." *Pacific Historical Review* 36 (1967): 1–12. This essay examines why westering emigrants selected either Oregon or California as destinations.

Loewenberg, Robert J. *Equality on the Oregon Frontier: Jason Lee and the Methodist Mission, 1834–43*. Seattle: University of Washington Press, 1976.

Nash, John J. "The Salmon River Mission of 1855." *Idaho Yesterdays* 11 (Spring 1967): 22–31.

Newsom, David. *The Western Observer, 1805–1882*. Portland: Oregon Historical Society, 1972.

Schoenberg, Wilfred P. *A Chronicle of Catholic History of the Pacific Northwest, 1743–1960*. Portland: Catholic Sentinel Printing, 1962.

Unruh, John D., Jr. *The Plains Across: The Overland Emigrants and the Trans-Mississippi West, 1840–1860*. Urbana: University of Illinois Press, 1979.

Warre, H. J. *Overland to Oregon in 1845: Impressions of a Journey across North America*. Edited by Madeline Major-Fregeau. Ottawa: Public Archives of Canada, 1976.

CHAPTER 6: REARRANGING THE POLITICAL LANDSCAPE

Barkan, Frances B., ed. *The Wilkes Expedition: Puget Sound and the Oregon Country*. Olympia: Washington State Capital Museum, 1987.

Bensell, Royal A. *All Quiet on the Yamhill: The Civil War in Oregon; The Journal of Corporal Royal A. Bensell, Company D, Fourth California Infantry*. Edited by Gunther Barth. Eugene: University of Oregon Books, 1959.

Clark, Malcolm, Jr. *Eden Seekers: The Settlement of Oregon, 1818–1862.* Boston: Houghton Mifflin, 1981.

Edwards, G. Thomas. "Holding the Far West for the Union: The Army in 1861." *Civil War History* 14 (1968): 307–24.

Graebner, Norman A. *Empire on the Pacific: A Study in American Continental Expansion.* New York: Ronald Press, 1955.

Hendrickson, James E. *Joe Lane of Oregon: Machine Politics and the Sectional Crisis, 1849–1861.* New Haven: Yale University Press, 1967.

Hilleary, William M. *A Webfoot Volunteer: The Diary of William M. Hilleary, 1864–1866.* Edited by Robert B. Nelson and Preston E. Onstad. Corvallis: Oregon State University Press, 1965. This is a firsthand account of military life in the Pacific Northwest during the Civil War.

Hussey, John A. *Champoeg: Place of Transition; A Disputed History.* Portland: Oregon Historical Society, 1967.

Johannsen, Robert W. *Frontier Politics and the Sectional Conflict: The Pacific Northwest on the Eve of the Civil War.* Seattle: University of Washington Press, 1955.

Limbaugh, Ronald H. *Rocky Mountain Carpetbaggers: Idaho's Territorial Governors, 1863–1890.* Moscow: University Press of Idaho, 1982.

Murray, Keith A. *The Pig War.* Tacoma: Washington State Historical Society, 1968.

Richards, Kent D. *Isaac I. Stevens: Young Man in a Hurry.* Provo: Brigham Young University Press, 1979.

Wells, Merle. "Walla Walla's Vision of a Greater Washington." *Idaho Yesterdays* 10 (Fall 1966): 20–32.

CHAPTER 7: HOLES IN THE SOCIAL FABRIC

Beckham, Stephen Dow. *Requiem for a People: The Rogue Indians and the Frontiersmen.* Norman: University of Oklahoma Press, 1971.

Beeton, Beverly, and G. Thomas Edwards, "Susan B. Anthony's Woman Suffrage Crusade in the American West." *Journal of the West* 21 (1982): 5–15.

Brown, Mark H. *The Flight of the Nez Perce.* New York: G. P. Putnam's Sons, 1967.

Burns, Robert Ignatius. *The Jesuits and the Indian Wars of the Northwest.* New Haven: Yale University Press, 1966.

Fisher, Robin. "Indian Warfare and Two Frontiers: A Comparison of British

Columbia and Washington Territory during the Early Years of Settlement." *Pacific Historical Review* 50 (1981): 31–51.

Halseth, James A., and Bruce A. Glasrud, eds. *The Northwest Mosaic: Minority Conflicts in Pacific Northwest History*. Boulder, Colo.: Pruett Publishing, 1977.

Josephy, Alvin M. *The Nez Perce Indians and the Opening of the Northwest*. New Haven: Yale University Press, 1965.

McLagan, Elizabeth. *A Peculiar Paradise: A History of Blacks in Oregon, 1788–1940*. Portland: Georgian Press, 1980.

Madsen, Brigham D. *The Shoshoni Frontier and the Bear River Massacre*. Salt Lake City: University of Utah Press, 1985.

Moynihan, Ruth Barnes. *Rebel for Rights: Abigail Scott Duniway*. New Haven: Yale University Press, 1983.

Murray, Keith A. *The Modocs and Their War*. Norman: University of Oklahoma Press, 1971.

Stern, Theodore. *The Klamath Tribe: A People and Their Reservation*. Seattle: University of Washington Press, 1965.

Stratton, David H. "The Snake River Massacre of Chinese Miners, 1887." In *A Taste of the West: Essays in Honor of Robert G. Athearn*, edited by Duane A. Smith. Boulder, Colo.: Pruett Publishing, 1983.

Trafzer, Clifford E., and Richard D. Scheuerman. *Renegade Tribe: The Palouse Indians and the Invasion of the Inland Pacific Northwest*. Pullman: Washington State University Press, 1986.

Wells, Merle W. *Anti-Mormonism in Idaho, 1872–92*. Provo: Brigham Young University Press, 1978.

Wynne, Robert Edward. *Reaction to the Chinese in the Pacific Northwest and British Columbia, 1850–1910*. New York: Arno Press, 1978.

PROFILE: HENRY VILLARD AND THE LAST SPIKE

Belknap, George N. *Henry Villard and the University of Oregon*. Eugene: University of Oregon, 1976.

Grinnell, George Bird. "Building the Northern Pacific." *Idaho Yesterdays* 16 (Winter 1972–73): 10–13. First-person account from 1882.

Hedges, James B. *Henry Villard and the Railways of the Northwest*. New Haven: Yale University Press, 1930.

Nolan, Edward W. " 'Not without Labor and Expense': The Villard–Northern Pacific Excursion, 1883." *Montana, the Magazine of Western History* 33 (Summer 1983): 2–11.

———. *Northern Pacific Views: The Railroad Photography of F. Jay Haynes, 1876–1905*. Helena: Montana Historical Society Press, 1983.

Seckinger, Katherine Villard, ed. "The Great Railroad Celebration, 1883: A Narrative by Francis Jackson Garrison." *Montana, the Magazine of Western History* 33 (Summer 1983): 12–23.

Smalley, Eugene V. *History of the Northern Pacific Railroad*. New York: G. P. Putnam's Sons, 1883.

CHAPTER 8: METROPOLITAN CORRIDORS

Athearn, Robert G. *Union Pacific Country*. Chicago: Rand McNally, 1971.

Bryan, Enoch A. *Orient Meets Occident: The Advent of the Railways of the Pacific Northwest*. Pullman, Wash.: Students Book Corp., 1936.

Due, John F., and Giles French. *Rails to the Mid-Columbia Wheatlands: The Columbia Southern and Great Southern Railroads and the Development of Sherman and Wasco Counties, Oregon*. Washington, D.C.: University Press of America, 1979.

Greever, William S. "A Comparison of Railroad Land-Grant Policies." *Agricultural History* 25 (1951): 83–90.

Hidy, Ralph W., Muriel E. Hidy, and Roy V. Scott, with Don L. Hofsommer, *The Great Northern Railway: A History*. Boston: Harvard Business School Press, 1988.

Hofsommer, Don L. *The Southern Pacific, 1901–1985*. College Station: Texas A and M University Press, 1986.

Jackson, W. Turrentine. *Wells Fargo and Co. in Idaho Territory*. Boise: Idaho State Historical Society, 1984.

Johansen, Dorothy. "The Oregon Steam Navigation Company: An Example of Capitalism on the Frontier." *Pacific Historical Review* 10 (1941): 179–88.

Jonasson, Jonas A. "They Rode the Train: Railroad Passenger Traffic and Regional Reaction." *Pacific Northwest Quarterly* 52 (1961): 41–49.

Jones, Larry R. "Staging to the South Boise Mines." *Idaho Yesterdays* 29 (Summer 1985): 19–25.

Kline, M. S. and G. A. Bayless, *Ferryboats: A Legend on Puget Sound*. Seattle: Bayless Books, 1983.

Lewty, Peter J. *To the Columbia Gateway: The Oregon Railway and the Northern Pacific, 1879–1884*. Pullman: Washington State University Press, 1987.

Martin, Albro. *James J. Hill and the Opening of the Northwest*. New York: Oxford University Press, 1976.

Mills, Randall V. *Stern-Wheelers up Columbia: A Century of Steamboating in the Oregon Country.* 1947. Reprint. Lincoln: University of Nebraska Press, 1977.

Pomeroy, Earl. *In Search of the Golden West: The Tourist in Western America.* New York: Alfred A. Knopf, 1957.

Runte, Alfred. *Trains of Discovery: Western Railroads and the National Parks.* Flagstaff: Northland Press, 1984.

Smart, Douglas. "Spokane's Battle for Freight Rates." *Pacific Northwest Quarterly* 45 (1954): 19–27.

Stilgoe, John R. *Metropolitan Corridor: Railroads and the American Scene.* New Haven: Yale University Press, 1983.

Weinstein, Robert A. *Tall Ships on Puget Sound: The Marine Photographs of Wilhelm Hester.* Seattle: University of Washington Press, 1978.

Willingham, William F. "Engineering the Cascades Canal and Locks, 1876–1896." *Oregon Historical Quarterly* 88 (1987): 229–57.

Winther, Oscar Osburn. *The Old Oregon Country: A History of Frontier Trade, Transportation, and Travel.* 1950. Reprint. Lincoln: University of Nebraska Press, 1969.

CHAPTER 9: THE STUMPS OF ENTERPRISE

Arrington, Leonard J. *Beet Sugar in the West: A History of the Utah-Idaho Sugar Company, 1891–1966.* Seattle: University of Washington Press, 1966.

Carstensen, Vernon. "Distant Markets: The Early Days," *Portage* (Autumn 1983): 4–9. This issue is devoted to international trade in Washington State.

Cohn, Edwin I., Jr. *Industry in the Pacific Northwest and the Location Theory.* New York: Crown Press, 1954.

Coman, Edwin T., Jr., and Helen M. Gibbs. *Time, Tide and Timber: A Century of Pope and Talbot.* Stanford: Stanford University Press, 1959.

Cox, Thomas R. *Mills and Markets: A History of the Pacific Coast Lumber Industry to 1900.* Seattle: University of Washington Press, 1974.

Dodds, Gordon B. *The Salmon King of Oregon: R. D. Hume and the Pacific Fisheries.* Chapel Hill: University of North Carolina Press, 1959.

Ficken, Robert E. *The Forested Land: A History of Lumbering in Western Washington.* Seattle: University of Washington Press, 1987.

Freeman, Otis W., and Howard H. Martin, eds. *The Pacific Northwest: An Overall Appreciation.* 2d ed. New York: John Wiley and Sons, 1954.

Gibson, James R. *Farming the Frontier: The Agricultural Opening of the*

Oregon Country, 1786–1846. Seattle, University of Washington Press, 1961.

Hidy, Ralph W., Frank Ernest Hill, and Allan Nevins. *Timber and Men: The Weyerhaeuser Story*. New York: Macmillan Publishing, 1963.

McGregor, Alexander Campbell. *Counting Sheep: From Open Range to Agribusiness on the Columbia Plateau*. Seattle: University of Washington Press, 1982.

Meinig, D. W. *The Great Columbia Plain: A Historical Geography, 1805–1910*. Seattle: University of Washington Press, 1968.

Morgan, Murray. *The Last Wilderness*. New York: Viking Press, 1955.

———. *The Mill on the Boot: The Story of the St. Paul and Tacoma Lumber Company*. Seattle: University of Washington Press, 1982.

Netboy, Anthony. *The Columbia River Salmon and Steelhead Trout: Their Fight for Survival*. Seattle: University of Washington Press, 1980.

Oliphant, J. Orin. *On the Cattle Ranges of the Oregon Country*. Seattle: University of Washington Press, 1968.

Robbins, William G. *American Forestry: A History of National, State, and Private Cooperation*. Lincoln: University of Nebraska Press, 1985.

———. "The Social Context of Forestry: The Pacific Northwest in the Twentieth Century." *Western Historical Quarterly* 16 (1985): 413–28.

Seufert, Francis. *Wheels of Fortune*. Edited by Thomas Vaughan. Portland: Oregon Historical Society, 1980. This is the story of the Seufert Brothers salmon packing company on the Columbia River.

Shepherd, James F. "The Development of Wheat Production in the Pacific Northwest." *Agricultural History* 49 (1975): 258–71.

Simpson, Peter K. *The Community of Cattlemen: Social History of the Cattle Industry in Southeastern Oregon, 1869–1912*. Moscow: University of Idaho Press, 1987.

Throckmorton, Arthur L. *Oregon Argonauts: Merchant Adventurers on the Western Frontier*. Portland: Oregon Historical Society, 1961.

Trimble, William J. *The Mining Advance into the Inland Empire*. Madison: University of Wisconsin, 1914.

CHAPTER 10: A PEOPLE ON THE MOVE

Abbott, Carl. *Portland: Planning, Politics, and Growth in a Twentieth-Century City*. Lincoln: University of Nebraska Press, 1983.

Brown, Arthur J. "The Promotion of Emigration to Washington, 1854–1909." *Pacific Northwest Quarterly* 36 (1945): 3–17.

Clark, Norman H. *Mill Town: A Social History of Everett, Washington, from Its Earliest Beginnings on the Shores of Puget Sound to the Tragic and Infamous Event Known as the Everett Massacre*. Seattle: University of Washington Press, 1970.

Corning, Howard McKinley. *Willamette Landings: Ghost Towns of the River*. Portland: Oregon Historical Society, 1973.

Dahlie, Jorgen. "Old World Paths in the New: Scandinavians Find a Familiar Home in Washington." *Pacific Northwest Quarterly* 61 (1970): 65–71.

Dunbar, Robert. *Forging New Rights in Western Waters*. Lincoln: University of Nebraska Press, 1983.

Edwards, G. Thomas. " 'The Early Morning of Yakima's Day of Greatness': The Yakima County Agricultural Boom of 1905–1911." *Pacific Northwest Quarterly* 73 (1982): 78–89.

Etulain, Richard W. "Basque Beginnings in the Pacific Northwest," *Idaho Yesterdays* 18 (Spring 1974): 26–32.

Fargo, Lucile F. *Spokane Story*. New York: Columbia University Press, 1950.

Idaho Yesterdays 30 (Spring/Summer 1986): 2–76. Irrigation in Idaho is discussed in depth in ten essays published in this special issue.

Lovin, Hugh. "How Not to Run a Carey Act Project: The Twin Falls–Salmon Falls Creek Tract, 1904–1922," *Idaho Yesterdays* 30 (Fall 1986): 9–15; 18–24.

MacColl, E. Kimbark. *The Shaping of a City: Business and Politics in Portland, Oregon, 1885 to 1915*. Portland: Georgian Press, 1976.

MacDonald, Norbert. *Distant Neighbors: A Comparative History of Seattle and Vancouver*. Lincoln: University of Nebraska Press, 1987.

Merriam, Paul G. "Urban Elite in the Far West: Portland, Oregon, 1870–1890." *Arizona and the West* 18 (1976): 41–52.

Morgan, Murray. *Puget's Sound: A Narrative of Early Tacoma and the Southern Sound*. Seattle: University of Washington Press, 1979.

———. *Skid Road: An Informal Portrait of Seattle*. Seattle: University of Washington Press, 1982.

Nesbit, Robert C. *"He Built Seattle": A Biography of Judge Thomas Burke*. Seattle: University of Washington Press, 1961.

Nicandri, David L. *Italians in Washington State: Emigration, 1853–1924*. [Tacoma]: Washington State American Revolution Bicentennial Commission, 1978. Other books in this series study Washington's Chinese, German, Gypsy, Indian, Scots, and Yugoslav populations.

Petersen, Keith C. *Potlatch, Idaho, and the Potlatch Lumber Company*. Pullman: Washington State University Press, 1987.

Quiett, Glenn Chesney. *They Built the West: An Epic of Rails and Cities*.

New York: D. Appleton-Century, 1934.

Reisner, Marc. *Cadillac Desert: The American West and Its Disappearing Water.* New York: Viking, 1986.

Reps, John W. *Panoramas of Promise: Pacific Northwest Cities and Towns on Nineteenth-Century Lithographs.* Pullman: Washington State University Press, 1984.

Robbins, William G. *Hard Times in Paradise: Coos Bay, Oregon.* Seattle: University of Washington Press, 1988.

Sale, Roger. *Seattle, Past to Present.* Seattle: University of Washington Press, 1976.

Scott, Mary Katsilometes. "The Greek Community in Pocatello, 1890– 1941." *Idaho Yesterdays* 28 (Fall 1984): 29–36.

Stimson, William. *A View of the Falls: An Illustrated History of Spokane.* Northridge, Calif.: Windsor Publications, 1985.

Toll, William. *The Making of an Ethnic Middle Class: Portland Jewry over Four Generations.* Albany: State University of New York Press, 1982.

Weinstein, Robert A. *Grays Harbor, 1885–1913.* New York: Viking Press, 1978.

Wells, Merle. *Boise: An Illustrated History.* Woodland Hills, Calif.: Windsor Publications, 1982.

Worster, Donald. *Rivers of Empire: Water, Aridity, and the Growth of the American West.* New York: Pantheon Books, 1985.

CHAPTER 11: THE OMNIBUS STATES AND A GROWING
REGIONAL SELF-CONFIDENCE

Abbott, Carl. *The Great Extravaganza: Portland and the Lewis and Clark Exposition.* Portland: Oregon Historical Society, 1981.

———. "Greater Portland: Experiments with Professional Planning, 1905– 1925." *Pacific Northwest Quarterly* 76 (1985): 12–21.

Beckett, Paul L. *From Wilderness to Enabling Act: The Evolution of a State of Washington.* Pullman: Washington State University Press, 1968.

Fahl, Ronald H. "S. C. Lancaster and the Columbia River Highway: Engineer as Conservationist." *Oregon Historical Quarterly* 74 (1973): 104–44.

Hart, I. W., ed. *Proceedings and Debates of the Constitutional Convention of Idaho, 1889.* Caldwell, Idaho: Caxton Printers, 1912.

Hicks, John D. *The Constitutions of the Northwest States.* Lincoln: University of Nebraska Studies, 23 (January-April 1923): 5–152.

Hynding, Alan. *The Public Life of Eugene Semple: Promoter and Politician of the Pacific Northwest*. Seattle: University of Washington Press, 1973.

Limbaugh, Ronald H. *Rocky Mountain Carpetbaggers: Idaho's Territorial Governors, 1863–1890*. Moscow: University Press of Idaho, 1982.

Mullen, W. Frank, John C. Pierce, Charles H. Sheldon, and Thor Swanson, eds. *The Government and Politics of Washington State*. Pullman: Washington State University Press, 1978.

Rosenow, Beverly Paulik, ed. *The Journal of the Washington State Constitutional Convention, 1889*. Seattle: Book Publishing, 1962.

Rydell, Robert. "Visions of Empire: International Expositions in Portland and Seattle, 1905–1909." *Pacific Historical Review* 52 (1983): 37–66.

Thompson, Dennis L. "Religion and the Idaho Constitution." *Pacific Northwest Quarterly* 58 (1967): 169–78.

Wells, Merle. "Idaho's Season of Political Distress: An Unusual Path to Statehood." *Montana, the Magazine of Western History* 37 (Autumn 1987): 58–67.

————. "Politics in the Panhandle: Opposition to the Admission of Washington and North Idaho, 1886–1888." *Pacific Northwest Quarterly* 46 (1955): 79–89.

CHAPTER 12: REMOVING THE ROUGH EDGES

Bailey, Margaret Jewett. *The Grains; or, Passages in the Life of Ruth Rover with Occasional Pictures of Oregon, Natural and Moral*. 1854. Reprint. Corvallis: Oregon State University Press, 1985.

Bingham, Edwin R., and Glen A. Love, eds. *Northwest Perspectives: Essays on the Culture of the Pacific Northwest*. Seattle: University of Washington Press, 1979.

Bingham, Edwin R. "Pacific Northwest Writing: Reaching for Identity." In *Regionalism and the Pacific Northwest*, edited by William G. Robbins, Robert J. Frank, and Richard E. Ross. Corvallis: Oregon State University Press, 1983.

Blair, Karen J. "The Seattle Ladies Musical Club, 1890–1930." In *Experiences in a Promised Land: Essays in Pacific Northwest History*, edited by G. Thomas Edwards and Carlos A. Schwantes. Seattle: University of Washington Press, 1986.

Etulain, Richard. "Novelists of the Northwest: Opportunities for Research." *Idaho Yesterdays* 17 (Summer 1973): 24–32. Includes bibliography.

Foote, Mary Hallock. *A Victorian Gentlewoman in the Far West: The Reminiscences of Mary Hallock Foote*. Edited by Rodman Paul. San

Marino: Huntington Library, 1972.

Gates, Charles M. *The First Century at the University of Washington, 1861–1961.* Seattle: University of Washington Press, 1961.

H. L. Davis Collected Essays and Short Stories Moscow: University of Idaho Press, [1986].

Henderson, Robert A. "Culture in Spokane: 1883–1900." *Idaho Yesterdays* 11 (Winter 1968): 14–19, 32.

Knight, Oliver. "The *Owyhee Avalanche:* The Frontier Newspaper as a Catalyst in Social Change." *Pacific Northwest Quarterly* 58 (1967): 74–81.

Nash, Lee. "Harvey Scott's 'Cure for Drones': An Oregon Alternative to Public High Schools." *Pacific Northwest Quarterly* 64 (1973): 70–79.

Simonson, Harold P. "Pacific Northwest Literature: Its Coming of Age." *Pacific Northwest Quarterly* 71 (1980): 146–151.

Stegner, Wallace. *Angle of Repose.* Garden City, N.Y.: Doubleday, 1971. A Pulitzer Prize–winning novel based on Mary Hallock Foote's career.

Strelow, Michael, ed. *An Anthology of Northwest Writing: 1900–1950.* Eugene: Northwest Review Books, 1979. This volume contains a copy of *Status Rerum,* of which Stevens and Davis printed only two hundred.

Warren, Sidney. *Farthest Frontier: The Pacific Northwest.* New York: Macmillan, 1949. Emphasizes high and low culture in the region.

Wyman, Mark. "Frontier Journalism." *Idaho Yesterdays* 17 (Spring 1973): 30–36.

PROFILE: THE WORLD OF MAY ARKWRIGHT HUTTON

Conlin, Joseph R. "The Haywood Case: An Enduring Riddle." *Pacific Northwest Quarterly* 59 (1968): 23–32.

Fahey, John. *The Days of the Hercules.* Moscow: University Press of Idaho, 1978.

———. "Ed Boyce and the Western Federation of Miners." *Idaho Yesterdays* 25 (Fall 1981): 18–30.

Fargo, Lucile F. *Spokane Story.* Minneapolis: Northwestern Press, 1957.

Hart, Patricia, and Ivar Nelson. *Mining Town: The Photographic Record of T. N. Barnard and Nellie Stockbridge from the Coeur d'Alenes.* Seattle: University of Washington Press, 1984.

Jensen, Vernon. *Heritage of Conflict: Labor Relations in the Nonferrous Metals Industry up to 1930.* Ithaca: Cornell University Press, 1950.

Kaiser, Benjamin. "May Arkwright Hutton." *Pacific Northwest Quarterly* 57 (1966): 49–56.

Livingston-Little, D. E. "The Bunker Hill and Sullivan: North Idaho's Mining Development from 1885 to 1900." *Idaho Yesterdays* 7 (Spring 1963): 34–43.

Montgomery, James W. *Liberated Woman: A Life of May Arkwright Hutton.* 1974. Reprint. Fairfield, Wash.: Ye Galleon Press, 1985. Includes a reprint of May Arkwright Hutton's, *The Coeur d'Alenes; or, A Tale of the Modern Inquisition in Idaho* (1900).

Smalley, Eugene V. "The Great Coeur D'Alene Stampede of 1884." *Idaho Yesterdays* 11 (Fall 1967): 2–10. A reprint of a first-hand account.

Smith, Robert Wayne. *The Coeur d'Alene Mining War of 1892: A Case Study of an Industrial Dispute.* 1961. Reprint. Gloucester, Mass.: Peter Smith, 1968.

CHAPTER 13: EVOLUTION OF THE WAGEWORKERS' FRONTIER

Broyles, Glen J. "The Spokane Free Speech Fight, 1909–1910: A Study in IWW Tactics." *Labor History* 19 (1978): 238–52.

Chaplin, Ralph. *Wobbly: The Rough-and-Tumble Story of an American Radical.* Chicago: University of Chicago Press, 1948.

Dembo, Jonathan. *Unions and Politics in Washington State 1885–1935.* New York: Garland Publishing, 1983.

Hawley, Lowell S., and Ralph Bushnell Potts. *Counsel for the Damned: A Biography of George Francis Vanderveer.* Philadelphia: J. B. Lippincott, 1953.

LeWarne, Charles Pierce. "The Aberdeen, Washington, Free Speech Fight of 1911–1912." *Pacific Northwest Quarterly* 66 (1975): 1–12.

Phipps, Stanley S. *From Bull Pen to Bargaining Table: The Tumultuous Struggle of the Coeur D'Alenes Miners for the Right to Organize, 1887–1942.* New York: Garland Publishing, 1988.

Prouty, Andrew Mason. *More Deadly than War! Pacific Coast Logging, 1827–1981.* New York: Garland Publishing, 1985. A detailed study of work and its hazards in the lumber industry.

Robbins, William G. "Labor in the Pacific Slope Timber Industry: A Twentieth-Century Perspective." *Journal of the West* 25 (April 1986): 8–13.

Schwantes, Carlos A. "The History of Pacific Northwest Labor History." *Idaho Yesterdays* 28 (Winter 1985): 23–35.

———. "Patterns of Radicalism on the Wageworkers' Frontier." *Idaho Yesterdays* 30 (Fall 1986): 25–30.

Stone, Harry W. "Beginning of Labor Movement in the Pacific Northwest." *Oregon Historical Quarterly* 47 (1946): 155–64.

Tyler, Robert L. *Rebels of the Woods: The I.W.W. in the Pacific Northwest.* Eugene: University of Oregon Books, 1967.

White, W. Thomas. "Railroad Labor Relations in the Great War and After, 1917–1921." *Journal of the West* 25 (April 1986): 36–43.

Williams, William J. "Bloody Sunday Revisited." *Pacific Northwest Quarterly* 71 (1980): 50–62. An eyewitness account of the Everett massacre.

CHAPTER 14: THE ERA OF THE GREAT CRUSADES

Allen, Howard. *Poindexter of Washington: A Study in Progressive Politics.* Carbondale: Southern Illinois University Press, 1981.

Boylan, Bernard L. "Camp Lewis: Promotion and Construction." *Pacific Northwest Quarterly* 58 (1967): 188–95.

Clark, Norman H. *The Dry Years: Prohibition and Social Change in Washington.* Seattle: University of Washington Press, 1965.

Copeland, Tom. "Wesley Everest, IWW Martyr." *Pacific Northwest Quarterly* 77 (1986): 122–29.

Friedheim, Robert L. *The Seattle General Strike.* Seattle: University of Washington Press, 1964.

Gaboury, William J. *Dissention in the Rockies: A History of Idaho Populism.* New York: Garland Publishing, 1988.

Graff, Leo W., Jr. *The Senatorial Career of Fred T. DuBois of Idaho, 1890–1907.* New York: Garland Publishing, 1988.

Griffiths, David B. "Far-Western Populist Thought: A Comparative Study of John R. Rogers and Davis H. Waite." *Pacific Northwest Quarterly* 60 (1969): 183–92.

Gunns, Albert F. *Civil Liberties in Crisis: The Pacific Northwest, 1917–1940.* New York: Garland, 1983.

LeWarne, Charles Pierce. *Utopias on Puget Sound, 1885–1915.* Seattle: University of Washington Press, 1975.

Lovin, Hugh T. "The Red Scare in Idaho, 1916–1918." *Idaho Yesterdays* 17 (Fall 1973): 2–13.

McClelland, John M., Jr. *Wobbly War: The Centralia Story.* Tacoma: Washington State Historical Society, 1987.

McClintock, Thomas C. "Seth Lewelling, William S. U'Ren and the Birth of the Oregon Progressive Movement." *Oregon Historical Quarterly* 68 (1967): 197–220.

Riddle, Thomas W. "Populism in the Palouse: Old Ideals and New Realities." *Pacific Northwest Quarterly* 65 (1974): 97–109.

Rockafellar, Nancy. " 'In Gauze We Trust': Public Health and Spanish Influenza on the Home Front, Seattle, 1918–1919." *Pacific Northwest Quarterly* 77 (1986): 104–13.

Ruckman, JoAnn. " 'Knit, Knit, and then Knit': The Women of Pocatello and the War Effort of 1917–1918." *Idaho Yesterdays* 26 (Spring 1982): 26–36.

Schwantes, Carlos A. *Radical Heritage: Labor, Socialism, and Reform in Washington and British Columbia, 1885–1917.* Seattle: University of Washington Press, 1979.

Sharbach, Sarah E. "A Woman Acting Alone: Louise Olivereau and the First World War." *Pacific Northwest Quarterly* 78 (1987): 32–40. The story of a Seattle woman's opposition to the First World War.

Sims, Robert C. "Idaho's Criminal Syndicalism Act: One State's Response to Radical Labor." *Labor History* 15 (1974): 511–29.

Tripp, Joseph F. "An Instance of Labor and Business Cooperation: Workmen's Compensation in Washington State (1911)." *Labor History* 17 (1976): 530–50.

Woodward, Robert C. "William S. U'Ren, A Progressive Era Personality." *Idaho Yesterdays* 4 (Summer 1960): 4–10.

Woolley, Ivan M. "The 1918 'Spanish Influenza' Pandemic in Oregon." *Oregon Historical Quarterly* 64 (1963): 246–58.

CHAPTER 15: THE INTERWAR YEARS, 1919–1941

Ames, William E., and Roger A. Simpson. *Unionism or Hearst: The Seattle Post-Intelligencer Strike of 1936.* Seattle: Pacific Northwest Labor History Association, 1978.

Arrington, Leonard J. "Idaho and the Great Depression." *Idaho Yesterdays* 13 (1969): 2–8.

Ashby, Leroy. *The Spearless Leader: Senator Borah and the Progressive Movement in the 1920s.* Urbana: University of Illinois Press, 1972.

Austin, Judith. "The CCC in Idaho." *Idaho Yesterdays* 27 (Fall 1983): 13–17.

Barrett, Gwynn, and Leonard Arrington. "The 1921 Depression: Its Impact on Idaho." *Idaho Yesterdays* 15 (Summer 1971): 10–15.

Burton, Robert E. *Democrats of Oregon: The Pattern of Minority Politics, 1900–1956.* Eugene: University of Oregon Books, 1970.

Dembo, Jonathan. "Dave Beck and the Transportation Revolution in the Pacific Northwest, 1917–41." In *Experiences in a Promised Land: Essays in Pacific Northwest History,* edited by G. Thomas Edwards and Carlos A. Schwantes. Seattle: University of Washington Press, 1986.

———. "The Pacific Northwest Lumber Industry during the Great Depression." *Journal of the West* 24 (October 1985): 51–62.

Freidel, Frank. "Franklin D. Roosevelt in the Northwest: Informal Glimpses." *Pacific Northwest Quarterly* 76 (1985): 122–31.

Lovin, Hugh. "The CIO and that 'Damnable Bickering' in the Pacific Northwest, 1937–1941." *Pacific Historian* 23 (1979): 66–79.

Lowitt, Richard. *The New Deal and the West.* Bloomington: Indiana University Press, 1984.

Johnson, Claudius O. *Borah of Idaho.* 1936. Reprint. Seattle: University of Washington Press, 1967.

McKinley, Charles. *Uncle Sam in the Pacific Northwest: Federal Management of Natural Resources in the Columbia River Valley.* Berkeley: University of California Press, 1952.

Malone, Michael P. *C. Ben Ross and the New Deal in Idaho.* Seattle: University of Washington Press, 1970.

Neal, Steve. *McNary of Oregon: A Political Biography.* Portland: Western Imprints, 1985.

Neuberger, Richard. *Our Promised Land.* New York: Macmillan, 1938.

Pierce, Walter M. *Oregon Cattleman/Governor, Congressman: Memoirs and Times of Walter M. Pierce.* Edited by Arthur H. Bone, Portland: Oregon Historical Society, 1981.

Taber, Ronald W. "Vardis Fisher and the 'Idaho Guide': Preserving the Culture for the New Deal." *Pacific Northwest Quarterly* 59 (1968): 68–76.

Tollefson, Gene. *BPA and the Struggle for Power at Cost.* Portland: Bonneville Power Administration, [1987].

Toy, Eckard V. "The Ku Klux Klan in Oregon." In *Experiences in a Promised Land: Essays in Pacific Northwest History,* edited by G. Thomas Edwards and Carlos A. Schwantes. Seattle: University of Washington Press, 1986.

PROFILE: TOM MCCALL OF OREGON

McCall, Tom. *Tom McCall: Maverick; An Autobiography with Steve Neal.* Portland: Binford and Mort, 1977.

Peirce, Neal R. *The Pacific States of America: People, Politics, and Power in the Five Pacific Basin States.* New York: W. W. Norton, 1972. Chapter on Oregon titled: "For God's Sake, Don't Move Here."

Peirce, Neal R., and Jerry Hagstrom. *The Book of America: Inside Fifty States Today.* New York: Warner Books, 1984. Chapter on Oregon titled: "Fearing Growth, Seeking Growth."

"Tom (Lawson) McCall." *Current Biography* (1974): 252–54.

CHAPTER 16: THE SECOND WORLD WAR AND AFTER

Abbott, Carl. "Planning for the Home Front in Seattle and Portland, 1940–45." In *The Martial Metropolis: U.S. Cities in War and Peace*, by Roger Lotchin, New York: Praeger, 1984.

———. "Portland in the Pacific War: Planning from 1940 to 1945." *Urbanism Past and Present* 6 (1981): 12–24.

Anderson, Karen. *Wartime Women: Sex Roles, Family Relations, and the Status of Women during World War II*. Westport, Conn.: Greenwood Press, 1981. Contains much useful information on wartime Seattle.

Daniels, Roger. *Concentration Camps USA: Japanese Americans and World War II*. New York: Holt, Rinehart and Winston, 1972.

Droker, Howard A. "Seattle Race Relations during the Second World War." *Pacific Northwest Quarterly* 67 (1976): 163–74.

Kerr, Clark. *Migration to the Seattle Labor Market Area, 1940–1942*. Seattle: University of Washington Press, 1942.

Mull, Robert. "Hanford's Desert Landmarks." *Landmarks: Magazine of Northwest History and Preservation* 4 (1985): 12–13.

Nash, Gerald. *The American West Transformed: The Impact of the Second World War*. Bloomington: Indiana University Press, 1985.

Ourada, Patricia K. "Reluctant Servants: Conscientious Objectors in Idaho during World War II." *Idaho Yesterdays* 31 (Winter 1988): 2–14.

Ritchie, Art, and William L. Davis, eds. *The Pacific Northwest Goes to War: State of Washington*. Seattle: Associated Editors, 1944.

Schmid, Calvin F. *Social Trends in Seattle*. Seattle: University of Washington Press, 1944. Especially useful is the discussion in Appendix C of World War II's impact on cities and towns of Washington.

Schwantes, Carlos A., ed. *The Pacific Northwest in World War II*. Manhattan, Kans.: Sunflower University Press, 1986. A compilation of seven essays on the Second World War in the Pacific Northwest and Alaska.

Simpich, Frederick, Sr. "Wartime in the Pacific Northwest." *National Geographic Magazine* 82 (1942): 421–64.

Taylor, Quintard. "The Great Migration: The Afro-American Communities of Seattle and Portland during the 1940s." *Arizona and the West* 23 (1981): 109–26.

Webber, Bert. *Retaliation: Japanese Attacks and Allied Countermeasures on the Pacific Coast in World War II*. Corvallis: Oregon State University Press, 1975.

Woodward, William, ed. *Military Influences on Washington History: Proceedings of a Conference*. Tacoma: Washington Army National Guard,

1984. A compilation of eighteen scholarly essays covering all facets of Washington's military history.

CHAPTER 17: RECENT TIMES, 1950–1985

Anderson, D. Victor. *Illusions of Power: A History of the Washington Public Power Supply System.* New York: Praeger, 1985.

Ashby, LeRoy. "Frank Church Goes to the Senate: The Idaho Election of 1956." *Pacific Northwest Quarterly* 78 (1987): 17–31.

Blank, Robert H. *Regional Diversity of Political Values: Idaho Political Culture.* Washington, D.C.: University Press of America, 1978.

Burton, Robert E. *Democrats of Oregon: The Pattern of Minority Politics, 1900–1956.* Eugene: University of Oregon Books, 1970.

Chasan, Daniel Jack. *The Fall of the House of* wppss. Seattle: Sasquatch Publishing, 1985.

Church, F. Forrester. *Father and Son: A Personal Biography of Senator Frank Church of Idaho by His Son.* Boston: Faber and Faber, 1985.

Cumming, William. *Sketchbook: A Memoir of the 1930s and the Northwest School.* Seattle: University of Washington Press, 1984. A memoir treatment of Morris Graves, Mark Tobey, Guy Anderson, Kenneth Callahan, and others.

Dwyer, William L. *The Goldmark Case: An American Libel Trial.* Seattle: University of Washington Press, 1984. A case of anti-Communist hysteria in Washington.

Gamboa, Erasmo. "Braceros in the Pacific Northwest: Laborers on the Domestic Front, 1942–1947." *Pacific Historical Review* 56 (1987): 378–98.

———. "Mexican Migration into Washington State: A History, 1940–1950." *Pacific Northwest Quarterly* 72 (1981): 121–31.

Metzler, Ken. *Confrontation: The Destruction of a College President.* Los Angeles: Nash Publishing, 1973. A story of 1960s campus protest at the University of Oregon.

Neuberger, Richard L. *Adventures in Politics: We Go to The Legislature.* New York: Oxford University Press, 1954.

[Norwood, Gus]. *Columbia River Power for the People: A History of the Policies of the Bonneville Power Administration.* Portland: Bonneville Power Administration, 1981.

Peterson, F. Ross. *Prophet without Honor: Glen Taylor and the Fight for American Liberalism.* Lexington: University of Kentucky Press, 1974.

Robbins, William G. "Lumber Production and Community Stability: A

View from the Pacific Northwest." *Journal of Forest History* 31 (1987): 187–96.

Sanders, Jane. *Cold War on the Campus: Academic Freedom at the University of Washington, 1946–64.* Seattle: University of Washington Press, 1979.

Slatta, Richard W., and Maxine P. Atkinson. "The 'Spanish Origin' Population of Oregon and Washington: A Demographic Profile, 1980." *Pacific Northwest Quarterly* 75 (1984): 108–16.

Smith, A. Robert. *The Tiger in the Senate: The Biography of Wayne Morse.* New York: Doubleday, 1962.

CHAPTER 18: AN ENVIRONMENT AT RISK

Ashworth, William. *Hells Canyon.* New York: Hawthorn Books, 1977. Legislative and political history of the Hells Canyon controversy.

Chasan, Daniel Jack. *The Water Link: A History of Puget Sound as a Resource.* Seattle: University of Washington, 1981.

Cohen, Fay G. *Treaties on Trial: The Continuing Controversy over Northwest Indian Fishing Rights.* Seattle: University of Washington Press, 1986.

Dodds, Gordon B. "The Fight to Close the Rogue." *Oregon Historical Quarterly* 60 (1959): 461–71. A study of the Rogue River fishing controversy.

Johnson, Ralph W. "Regulation of Commercial Salmon Fishermen: A Case of Confused Objectives." *Pacific Northwest Quarterly* 55 (1964): 141–56.

Loeb, Paul. *Nuclear Culture: Living and Working in the World's Largest Atomic Complex.* Philadelphia: New Society Publishers, 1986. An account of Richland, Washington, and the Hanford Nuclear Reservation.

Murray, Keith A. "The Trail Smelter Case: International Air Pollution in the Columbia Valley." *BC Studies* (Autumn 1972): 68–85.

Parman, Donald L. "Inconsistent Advocacy: The Erosion of Indian Fishing Rights in the Pacific Northwest, 1933–1956." *Pacific Historical Review* 53 (1984): 163–89.

Pyle, Robert Michael. *Wintergreen: Rambles in a Ravaged Land.* New York: Charles Scribner's Sons, 1986. Reflections on the environment of the Willapa Hills area of southwestern Washington.

Rabe, Fred, and David C. Flaherty. *The River of Green and Gold.* Moscow: Idaho Research Foundation, 1974. An environmental history of the Coeur d'Alene River.

Rakestraw, Lawrence. "Before McNary, the Northwestern Conservationist, 1889–1913." *Pacific Northwest Quarterly* 51 (1960): 49–56.

Runte, Alfred. "Burlington Northern and the Legacy of Mount Saint Helens." *Pacific Northwest Quarterly* 74 (1983): 116–23.

Scott, James W., Melly A. Revling, and Don Bales. *Washington Public Shore Guide: Marine Waters*. Seattle: University of Washington Press, 1986.

Shepherd, James F. "Soil Conservation in the Pacific Northwest Wheat-Producing Areas: Conservation in a Hilly Terrain." *Agricultural History* 59 (1985): 229–45.

White, Richard. *Land Use, Environment, and Social Change: The Shaping of Island County, Washington*. Seattle: University of Washington Press, 1980. This is a model environmental history.

EPILOGUE: A HINTERLAND STILL?

Robbins, William G., Robert J. Frank, and Richard E. Ross, eds. *Regionalism and the Pacific Northwest*. Corvallis: Oregon State University Press, 1983. This book contains perceptive essays on recent trends in Pacific Northwest regionalism by Richard Maxwell Brown, John M. McClelland, Jr., David Sarasohn, and Richard White.

Index